Causes of the Revelation of the Verses of the Quraan

Imam As-Suyuti

Soorah Al-Baqarah

A narration on the authority of Mujaahid that he said: Four Aayaat from the beginning of Soorah Al-Baqarah were revealed in connection with the believers (al-Mumineen), two in connection with the disbelievers (al-Kaafireen), and thirteen in connection with the hypocrites (al-Munaafiqeen). [Al-Firyaabi and Ibn Jareer]

Verse Number 6-7

6- As to those who disbelieve, it is the same to them whether you warn them or do not warn them; they will not believe. 7- Allaah has set a seal on their hearts (Qalb) and on their hearing, and on their eyes is a veil; and they will have a great torment.

A narration on the authority of Ibn 'Abbaas [Allaah be pleased with them] that those two Aayaat (6-7) were revealed in connection with the Yahood of Madeenah. According to the narration of Ar-Rabee' Ibn Anas, they were revealed in connection with fighting the Confederates (in the battle of Al-Ahzaab). [Ibn Jareer]

Verse Number 14

14- When they meet those who believe, they say: "We believe;" but when they become alone with their devils (that is the evil ones of their chiefs and masters), they say: "We are really with you (following your religion): we were only jesting."

A narration on the authority of Ibn 'Abbaas [Allaah be pleased with them] that he said: This Ayaah was revealed in connection with 'Abdullaah Ibn Ubayy and his companions. One day, they came out and were met by some of the Companions of the Prophet [peace and blessings of Allaah be upon him]. 'Abdullaah Ibn Ubayy said: "Consider how I will avert from you those fools". He went and took hold of the hand of Abu Bakr [may Allaah be pleased with him] and said to him: "Welcome to As-Siddiq, the chief of Banu Taym, the Shaykh of Islam and the second of two men after the Prophet [peace and blessings of Allaah be upon him] in the cave (of Thawr), who sacrificed his life and property for the sake of the Prophet [peace and blessings of Allaah be upon him]".

Then he took hold of the hand of 'Umar and said: "Welcome to the chief of Banu 'Adiyy Ibn Ka'b, Al-Faarooq (who distinguished truth from falsehood) and the strong in the religion of Allaah, who sacrificed his soul and wealth for the sake of the Prophet [peace and blessings of Allaah be upon him]".

Then he took hold of the hand of 'Ali [may Allaah be pleased with him] and said: "Welcome to the paternal and son-in-law of the Prophet [peace and blessings of Allaah be upon him], the chief of Banu Haashim after the death of the Prophet [peace and blessings of Allaah be upon him]". Then they all left.

'Abdullaah said to his companions: "How did you see my doing? If you see them do the same as I have done".

They praised him. The Muslims returned to the Prophet [peace and blessings of Allaah be upon him], and told him about that. On this occasion, this Quraanic Ayaah was revealed. [Al-Waahidi and Ath-Tha'labi: This narration is very weak]

Verse Number 19

19- Or (another similitude) is that of a rain-laden cloud from the sky: in it are zones of darkness, and thunder and lightning: they press their fingers in their ears to keep out the stunning thunderclap, the while they are in terror of death. But Allaah is ever round the disbelievers (al-Kaafireen)!

A narration on the authority of Ibn 'Abbaas, Ibn Mas'ood [Allaah be pleased with them] and others that they said: Two hypocrites (al-Munaafiqeen) from the people of Madeenah fled away from the Prophet [peace and blessings of Allaah be upon him] to the polytheists, and on the way they were afflicted with that rain mentioned by Allaah Almighty (the Most High) in the Ayaah which had strong thunder, thunderclaps and lightning: every time they were afflicted by thunderbolts they placed their fingers in their ears, out of fear lest those thunderbolts might damage their hearings and kill them. Whenever the lightning shone, they walked towards its light, and whenever it darkened, they would see nothing, thereupon they would returned to their place. They said to each other: "Would that in the morning we should come to Muhammad and put our hands in his". They went to him and embraced Islam, and placed their hands in his hand; and they were perfect in their faith.

Allaah Almighty (the Most High) set forth the example of those hypocrites (al-Munaafiqeen) for all hypocrites (al-Munaafiqeen) of Madeenah. It was the habit of the hypocrites (al-Munaafiqeen) that whenever they attended the gathering of the Prophet [peace and blessings of Allaah be upon him], they would place their fingers in their ears for fear of the words of the Prophet [peace and blessings of Allaah be upon him], lest something would be revealed in connection with them leading to their destruction, the same as did the two hypocrites (al-Munaafiqeen) mentioned above. [Ibn Jareer]

Verse Number 26

26- Verily, Allaah disdains not to set forth an example - that of a mosquito or what is smaller than it. Those who believe know that it is truth (which is firm and never changes across time) from their Lord (Rabb); but those who disbelieve say: "What does Allaah mean by this similitude?" By it He causes many to stray (that is the disbelievers (al-Kaafireen) because they reject it), and many He leads to the right path (that is the believers (al-Mumineen) who give trust to it); but He causes not to stray except the disobedient.

A narration on the authority of As-Suddi that when Allaah Almighty (the Most High) put forward those examples for the hypocrites (al-Munaafiqeen), that is that of the fire and that of the rain, the hypocrites (al-

Munaafiqeen) said: "Allaah is too high and great to set forth such examples". On that occasion, Allaah Almighty (the Most High) revealed this Quraanic Ayaah. [Ibn Jareer]

A narration on the authority of Qataadah that he said: When Allaah mentioned the flies and the spider (as examples for the false gods of the polytheists), the polytheists said: "What is the matter that flies and spider are mentioned in this Quraan?". On that occasion, Allaah revealed this Ayaah. [Ibn Jareer]

A narration on the authority of Al-Hasan that when Allaah revealed (what means): {O people, an example is presented, so listen to it. Indeed, those you invoke besides Allaah will never create (as much as) a fly, even if they gathered together for that purpose. And if the fly should steal away from them a (tiny) thing, they could not recover it from him. Weak are the pursuer and pursued}. [Al-Hajj, verse 73] The polytheists said: "That is not like the examples to be set forth". On that occasion, Allaah Almighty (the Most High) revealed this Quraanic Ayaah [26]. [Ibn Abu Haatim] However, the first narration seems to be the most authentic.

Verse Number 44

44- Do you enjoin right conduct on the people, and forget (to practice it) yourselves. And yet you study the Book? Will you not understand (That you do something bad so that you would retract from it)?

A narration on the authority of Ibn 'Abbaas [Allaah be pleased with them] that he said: It was the habit of the Yahood that anyone of them might say to his relative/in-law/foster brother/father/son or so from among the Muslims: "Keep firm on the religion (of Islam) on which you are and obey the command of this man (Muhammad)". But he himself would not do it. On that occasion, this Noble Ayaah was revealed. [Al-Waahidi and Ath-Tha'labi]

Verse Number 62

62- Those who believe (in the Prophets sent before Muhammad [peace and blessings of Allaah be upon him]), the Yahood, the Nasaara and the Sabians: any (among them) who (at the time of our Prophet Muhammad [peace and blessings of Allaah be upon him]) believes in Allaah and the Last Day, and works righteousness (in accordance with Muhammad's law and Sharee'ah), shall have their reward with their Lord (Rabb); on them shall be no fear, nor shall they grieve.

A narration on the authority of Mujaahid that he said: Salmaan [may Allaah be pleased with him] said: I asked the Prophet [peace and blessings of Allaah be upon him] about the people of a religion with whom I was, and made a mention of their prayer and worship. On that occasion, Allaah Almighty (the Most High) revealed this Quraanic Ayaah. [Ibn Abu Haatim]

A narration on the authority of Mujaahid that he said: When Salmaan [may Allaah be pleased with him] related to the Prophet [peace and blessings of Allaah be upon him], the story of his companions, he said: "They are in the Fire". Salmaan said: "I then grieved so much as if the earth darkened on me". On that occasion, Allaah Almighty (the Most High) revealed this Quraanic Ayaah. [Al-Waahidi]

The same is narrated on the authority of As-Suddi that he said: This Quraanic Ayaah was revealed in connection with the companions of Salmaan Al-Faarisi. [Ibn Jareer]

Verse Number 76

76- Behold! when they (the hypocrites (al-Munaafiqeen) among the Yahood) meet the believers (al-Mumineen), they say: "We believe (that Muhammad is the Prophet about whom the glad tidings were given in our Scriptures)": but when they meet each other in private, they say: "Shall you tell them what Allaah has revealed to you (about the attributes and qualities of the Prophet Muhammad and the glad tidings about him in the Torah), that they may engage you in argument about it before your Lord (Rabb) (in the hereafter)?" Do you not understand (their aim)?

A narration on the authority of Mujaahid that he said: On the day of Quraythah, the Prophet [peace and blessings of Allaah be upon him] stood near their fortresses and called out to them saying: "O brothers of apes! O brothers of pigs! O worshippers of Taaghoot!" They said: "Who has told Muhammad about that? This information has not come except from anyone of you (Yahood). Do you tell him of what Allaah revealed unto you so that he would use it as a proof against you?" On that occasion this Ayaah was revealed. [Ibn Jareer]

A narration on the authority of Ibn 'Abbaas [Allaah be pleased with them] that he said: Whenever the Yahood met the believers (al-Mumineen) they would say to them: "We believe that your companion (Muhammad) is the Messenger of Allaah, but he has been sent to you in particular". But whenever they become with one another, they would say: "Do you talk to the Arabs like this? You used to pray for victory over them with the help of this (Messenger) who then came from among them". On that occasion, Allaah revealed this Quraanic Ayaah. [Ibn Jareer]

A narration on the authority of As-Suddi that he said: It was revealed in connection with some Yahood who believed and then practiced hypocrisy. They used to tell the believers (al-Mumineen) from among the Arabs of what they talked. They said to one another: "Do you tell them of what Allaah revealed to you of the torment (in the hereafter for the disbelievers (al-Kaafireen)) so that they would say: 'We are dearer to Allaah, and nobler in His sight than you'?" [Ibn Jareer]

Verse Number 79

79- Then woe to those who write the Book with their own hands, and then say: "This is from Allaah," to traffic with it for a small price! Woe to them for what their hands do write, and for the gain they make thereby.

A narration on the authority of Ibn 'Abbaas [Allaah be pleased with them] that he said: This Quraanic Ayaah was revealed in connection with the people of Scripture. [An-Nasaa'i]

A narration on the authority of Ibn 'Abbaas [Allaah be pleased with them] that he said: This Quraanic Ayaah was revealed in connection with the rabbis of the Yahood: They found the attributes of the Prophet [peace and blessings of Allaah be upon him] written in the Torah: he was of big and beautiful eyes as if kohl was applied to them, medium size, curly hair and good-looking face. But they erased those attributes, out of envy and transgression, and rather said: "We find him very long, blue-complexioned, with lank hair". [Ibn Abu Haatim] Verse Number 80-81

80- And (when the Prophet [peace and blessings of Allaah be upon him] threatened them with the Hellfire) they said: "The Fire shall not touch us but for a few numbered days": say (O Muhammad): "Have you taken a promise from Allaah, for He never breaks His promise? Or is it that you say of Allaah what you do not know?"

81- Nay, he who gains Evil and is girt round by his sins, they are dwellers of the Fire (Hell): therein shall they abide (forever).

A narration on the authority of Ibn 'Abbaas [Allaah be pleased with them] that he said: the Prophet [peace and blessings of Allaah be upon him] came to Madeenah and the Yahood were saying: "The duration of this world is no more than seven thousand years; and the people will be punished for each thousand years according to the time of the world only one day in the Fire according to the days of the hereafter. The duration of punishment then will be no more than seven days, after which it will cease". On that occasion, Allaah Almighty (the Most High) Revealed those Quraanic Aayaat. [At-Tabaraani in his Al-Kabeer; Ibn Jareer and Ibn Abu Haatim]

A narration on the authority of Ibn 'Abbaas [Allaah be pleased with them] that he said: The Yahood said: "We shall not enter the Fire except as a result of Allaah's absolving the oath (in which Allaah Says what means: {And there is none of you except that he will come to it. This is upon your Lord (Rabb) an inevitability decreed}. [Maryam, verse 71]). We worshipped the calf for forty days; and if they finish, the torment will cease from us". On that occasion these Noble Aayaat were revealed. [Ibn Jareer]

Verse Number 89

89- And when there comes to them a Book (the Noble Quraan) from Allaah, confirming what is with them (the Torah) - although from of old they had prayed for victory against the disbelieverswhen there comes to them (the truth) that they (should) have recognized, they disbelieved in it (out of envy and fear lest they would lose the authority and presidency). So let the curse of Allaah be upon the disbelievers (al-Kaafireen).

A narration on the authority of Ibn 'Abbaas [Allaah be pleased with them] that he said: The Yahood of Khaybar more often fought Ghatfaan, and whenever both parties met the Yahood would be defeated. The Yahood then would seek refuge in the following supplication: "O Allaah! We beseech You, by the right of Muhammad, the unlettered Prophet whom You promised to bring out to us towards the end of time, to give us victory over them (Ghatfaan)". Afterwards, whenever they met, they would supplicate with that supplication and thus defeat Ghatfaan. When the Prophet [peace and blessings of Allaah be upon him] was sent, they disbelieved in him. On that occasion, Allaah Almighty (the Most High) revealed this Quraanic Ayaah. [Al-Haakim in his Mustadrak; and Al-Bayhaqi in Ad-Dalaa'il: weak narration]

A narration on the authority of Ibn 'Abbaas [Allaah be pleased with them] that the Yahood had, more often, prayed for victory over the Aws and Khazraj with the help of the Prophet [peace and blessings of Allaah be upon him] before his Prophetic mission. But when Allaah Almighty (the Most High) sent him as a Prophet from among the Arabs, the Yahood disbelieved in him, and denied what they used to say about him. Both Mu'aadh Ibn Jabal and Bishr Ibn Al-Baraa' Ibn Ma'roor [Allaah be pleased with them] said to them: "O assembly of Yahood! Fear Allaah and embrace Islam. You used to pray for victory over us with the help of Muhammad [peace and blessings of Allaah be upon him] when we were polytheists, and you used to tell us that he would be sent as a Prophet, and describe him to us". Salaam Ibn Mishkam from Banu An-Nadeer said: "He brought nothing we know about him, and he is not the same one whom we had previously mentioned to you". [Ibn Abu Haatim]

Verse Number 94

94- Say: "If the Home of the hereafter (Paradise), with Allaahbe for you specially, and not for anyone else (as you falsely claim)then long you for death, if you are truthful." A narration on the authority of Abu Al-'AAliyah that he said: The Yahood said: "Only the Yahood shall enter Paradise". On that occasion, Allaah revealed this Quraanic Ayaah. [At-Tabari]

Verse Number 97

97- Say: Whoever is an enemy to Jibreel (Let him perish in rage) for he brings down the (Quraan) to your heart by Allaah's will, a confirmation of (the previous Scriptures such as the Torah and Gospel) that came before it, and a guidance (from error) and glad tidings (of Paradise) for the believers (al-Mumineen).

A narration on the authority of Anas [may Allaah be pleased with him] that he said: When the Prophet [peace and blessings of Allaah be upon him] arrived in Madeenah 'Abdullaah Ibn Salaam was picking up some dates from the garden of his family. Then he went to him to ask him about certain things, He said: "I am going to ask you about three things which only a

Prophet can answer: "What is the first sign of The Hour? What is the first food which the people of Paradise will eat? Why does a child attract the similarity to his father or to his mother?" The Prophet [peace and blessings of Allaah be upon him] replied: "Jibreel has just now informed me of that." Ibn Salaam said: "He (that is Jibreel) is the enemy of the Yahood from amongst the angels". On that occasion the Prophet [peace and blessings of Allaah be upon him] recited that Noble Ayaah. [Al-Bukhaari]

Commenting on that, Ibn Hajar says in his Al-Fath: What seems apparent from the context is that the Prophet [peace and blessings of Allaah be upon him] recited this Ayaah as a reply to the Yahood. But this does not mean that it had been revealed on that occasion. That is the valid opinion.

A narration on the authority of Ibn 'Abbaas [Allaah be pleased with them] that he said: Once, a pact amongst the Yahood visited the Prophet [peace and blessings of Allaah be upon him] and said to him: "O Muhammad! Tell us of four things we are going to ask you about, by which we would recognize your Prophethood and command the people to admit it". They asked him about the sexual discharge of both man and woman, and how a male or a female would come from it; the food Jacob forbade to himself before the Torah had been sent down; and about the Noble Spirit. When he told them that this was Jibreel [peace and blessings of Allaah be upon him], they said: "But he is our enemy O Muhammad, and he is an angel who always comes with severe commands and bloodshed; and were it not for that, if you had mentioned that he was Mikhail who always comes down with mercy and rainfall, we would have surely followed you". [Ahmad, At-Tirmidhi and An-Nasaa'i]

A narration on the authority of Ash-Sha'bi that 'Umar [may Allaah be pleased with him] used to go to the Yahood and listen to the Torah and wonder how it confirmed the Quraan. He said: Once, the Prophet [peace and blessings of Allaah be upon him] passed by them, thereupon I said: "I beseech you by Allaah to tell me: do you know that he is the Messenger of Allaah?" The literate one among them said: "Yes, we know well that he is the Messenger of Allaah". I said: "Then, why do you not follow him?" They said: "We asked him about the angel who brings the revelation to him and he told us that he was Jibreel, our enemy. He is our enemy because he always comes down with harshness, severity, war and destruction".

I said: "Then who is the source of your peace from amongst the angels?" They said: "Mikhail who always comes down with mercy and rain". I asked: "What is their position in the sight of their Lord (Rabb)?" They replied: "One of them is on His Right Side and the other is on the other side". I said: "It is unlawful for Jibreel to be the enemy of those for whom Mikhail is a source of peace; and it is unlawful for Mikhail to be peaceful with the enemies of Jibreel. Verily, I bear witness that they and their Lord (Rabb) are a source of peace for those who are at peace with them, and a source of war for those who wage war against them".

Then I went to the Prophet [peace and blessings of Allaah be upon him] with the intention to tell him. When I met him he said: "Should I not tell you of some Quraanic Aayaat which have been revealed to me?" I said: "Yes O Messenger of Allaah". He recited that Noble Ayaah after which I said: "O Messenger of Allaah! By Allaah, no sooner had I left the Yahood than I came to you to tell you of the dialogue that was between me and them. But I found out that Allaah has preceded me". [Ishaaq Ibn Rahawayh in his Musnad; and Ibn Jareer: although the Isnaad to Ash-Sha'bi is authentic, he did not see 'Umar]

A narration on the authority of 'Abd Ar-Rahmaan Ibn Abu Layla a Jew met 'Umar Ibn Al-Khattaab [may Allaah be pleased with him] and told him: "Jibreel, whom your companion (Muhammad) mentions, is our enemy". Therefore, 'Umar said: "Whoever is an enemy to Allaah, His angels and Messengers, Jibreel and Mikhail, then Allaah is an enemy to him". Thus this Ayaah was revealed on the tongue of 'Umar. Ibn Jareer related the consensus of the scholars that this was the occasion on which this Quraanic Ayaah was revealed. [Ibn Abu Haatim]

Verse Number 99-100

99- We have sent down to you (O Muhammad) manifest Signs; and none disbelieve in them but the perverse (who rebel against the command of Allaah Almighty). 100- Is it not (the case) that every time they make a Covenant (with Allaah Almighty (the Most High) to believe in the expected Prophet once he emerges, and not to assist the polytheists against him), a party among them throws it away (by repealing it)? Nay, most of them are disbelievers (al-Kaafireen).

A narration on the authority of Ibn 'Abbaas [Allaah be pleased with them] that he said: Ibn Sooryah said to the Prophet [peace and blessings of Allaah be upon him]: "O Muhammad! You have not brought to us anything we know, nor has Allaah revealed unto you a clear sign". On that, Allaah revealed this Quraanic Ayaah.

Furthermore, when the Prophet [peace and blessings of Allaah be upon him] was sent as a Prophet and a mention was made of the covenant that was taken from them concerning Muhammad [peace and blessings of Allaah be upon him], Maalik Ibn As-Sayf said: "By Allaah, nothing concerning Muhammad was given to us, nor was a covenant taken from us". On that occasion, Allaah revealed this Quraanic Ayaah. [Ibn Abu Haatim]

Verse Number 102

102- They (the Yahood) followed (the magic) which the devils gave out (falsely) during the reign of Solomon. It is not Solomon (who practiced magic which is disbelief) but (it is) the devils who disbelieved (by doing it), teaching men magic, and such things as came down to the angels Haaroot and Maaroot at Babylon. But neither of these taught anyone (such things) without saying: "We are only for trial; so do not disbelieve (by learning it)." They learned from them the means to sow discord between man and his wife. But they could not thus harm anyone except by Allaah's permission. They learned (magic) which harmed them (in the hereafter), and profited them not. They (Yahood) indeed knew that the buyers of (magic) would have no share in the happiness (Paradise) of the Hereafter. And vile was the price for which they did sell their souls, if they but knew!

A narration on the authority of Shahr Ibn Hawshab that he said: The Yahood declared: "Considering Muhammad, how he mixes truth with falsehood? He mentions Solomon among the Prophets. Was Solomon not a magician who used to ride the wind?" On that occasion, Allaah Almighty (the Most High) revealed this Quraanic Ayaah. [Ibn Jareer]

A narration on the authority of Abu Al-'AAliyah that the Yahood asked the Prophet [peace and blessings of Allaah be upon him] about things from the Torah, but they did not ask him about anything that Allaah Almighty (the Most High) revealed to him as the answer of what they asked for therewith the Prophet overpowered them in argument. Having seen that, they said: "This (Muhammad) has better knowledge of what was revealed to us than us". Once they asked him about sorcery and disputed with him concerning it. On that occasion, Allaah Almighty (the Most High) revealed to him the Quraanic Ayaah in issue. [Ibn Abu Haatim]

Verse Number 104

104- O you who believe! Say not (to the Prophet) 'Raa'ina', but (say (to him instead) 'Inthurna'; and hearken (to him): to the disbelievers (al-Kaafireen) is a painful torment (in the Hellfire).

A narration on the authority of As-Suddi that he said: Whenever Maalik Ibn As-Sayf and Rifaa'ah Ibn Zayd, among the Yahood, met the Prophet [peace and blessings of Allaah be upon him], they would say to him: "Hear but be not heard" and "Raa'ina." The Muslims, having thought those expressions had been used by the men of Scripture to exalt and honor their Prophets, said the same to the Prophet [peace and blessings of Allaah be upon him]. On that occasion, Allaah Almighty (the Most High) revealed this Quraanic Ayaah. [Ibn Al-Mundhir]

A narration on the authority of Ibn 'Abbaas [Allaah be pleased with them] that he said: Raa'ina according to the Yahood meant a bad abuse. When they heard the Companions of the Prophet [peace and blessings of Allaah be upon him] saying this to him, they used to say it and laugh among themselves. After this Quraanic Ayaah had been revealed, Sa'd Ibn Mu'aadh [may Allaah be pleased with him] heard it from them, thereupon he said to the Yahood: "O enemies of Allaah! If I hear this from anyone of you after this gathering, I would chop off his head". [Abu Na'eem in Ad-Dalaa'il]

Verse Number 106

106- None of our revelations do We abrogate or cause to be forgotten/postpone, but that We substitute something better or similar (in obligation and reward): do you not know that Allaah has power over all things?

A narration on the authority of Ibn 'Abbaas [Allaah be pleased with them] that he said: "It happened that sometimes the Prophet [peace and blessings of Allaah be upon him] received some revelations at night which he might forget by day. In this connection, Allaah Almighty (the Most High) revealed this Quraanic Ayaah. [Ibn Abu Haatim]

Verse Number 108

108- Or do you like to question your Messenger (Muhammad [peace and blessings of Allaah be upon him]) as Moses was questioned of old (by his people to show them Allaah manifestly, and others)? But whoever exchanges faith for disbelief (by avoiding meditation on the signs and rather proposing others instead), has strayed without doubt from the even way.

A narration on the authority of Ibn 'Abbaas [Allaah be pleased with them] that he said: Raafi' Ibn Huraymilah and Wahb Ibn Zayd told the Prophet [peace and blessings of Allaah be upon him]: "O Muhammad! Bring us a book to be sent down from heaven so that we would read it, or cause rivers to gush forth so that we would follow and believe in you". In this connection, Allaah Almighty (the Most High) revealed this Quraanic Ayaah. [Ibn Abu Haatim]

A narration on the authority of Mujaahid that he said: The Quraysh men asked the Prophet [peace and blessings of Allaah be upon him] to turn Safa mountain into a mountain of gold". He said: "Yes, but in this case, it would be for you like the Repast for the children of Israel if you disbelieve". For this reason they rejected and retracted from their demand. On that occasion, Allaah Almighty (the Most High) revealed this Quraanic Ayaah. [Ibn Jareer]

A narration on the authority of As-Suddi that he said: The Arabs asked the Prophet [peace and blessings of Allaah be upon him], to bring them Allaah to see Him face to face. In this connection this Quraanic Ayaah was revealed. [Ibn Jareer]

A narration on the authority of Abu Al-'AAliyah that he said: A man said to the Prophet [peace and blessings of Allaah be upon him]: "O Messenger of Allaah! Would that the expiations for our sins are like those of the children of Israel". The Prophet [peace and blessings of Allaah be upon him] replied: "No doubt, what Allaah has given you is better. Whenever anyone of the children of Israel sinned he would find his sin written on the gate of his door along with its expiation: if he did it, it would be a source of disgrace in this world; and if he did not do it, it would be a source of shame in the hereafter. Allaah has given you better than this. He Almighty says (what means): {And whoever does a wrong or wrongs himself but then seeks forgiveness of Allaah will find Allaah Forgiving and Merciful}. [An-Nisaa', verse 110] Verily, the five (obligatory) prayers, the Jumu'ah to the next Jumu'ah expiate (whatever sins are committed) between them". In this connection, Allaah Almighty (the Most High) revealed that Quraanic Ayaah. [Ibn Jareer]

Verse Number 109

109- Quite a number of the People of the Book (Yahood and Nasaara) wish they could turn you (people) back to infidelity after you have believed. Out of envy from their own selves (towards you because of their wickedness), after the Truth has become manifest unto them (in the Torah that Muhammad [peace and blessings of Allaah be upon him] is really the Messenger of Allaah). But forgive and overlook, till Allaah brings His command (of fighting them): for Allaah has power over all things.

A narration on the authority of Abu Al-'AAliyah that both Huyayy Ibn Akhtab and his brother Abu Yaasir Ibn Akhtab envied the Arabs most from among the Yahood, because Allaah Almighty (the Most High) favored the Arabs with His Messenger (Muhammad). They worked hard to avert people from Islam. On that occasion, Allaah revealed this Quraanic Ayaah. [Ibn Abu Haatim]

Verse Number 113

113- The Yahood say: "The Nasaara have nothing to follow"; and the Nasaara say: "The Yahood have nothing to follow." Yet they (profess to) recite the Scripture. Like unto their word do those who now not say; but Allaah ill judge between them on the Day of Resurrection about that over which they were in dispute.

A narration on the authority of Ibn 'Abbaas [Allaah be pleased with them] that he said: When the Nasaara of Najraan came to the Prophet [peace and blessings of Allaah be upon him], the Jewish rabbis came to them and both disputed.

Raafi Ibn Khuzaymah said: "You have no grounds (of religion to stand upon)". He disbelieved in Jesus and the Gospel. A man from Najraan said to the Yahood: "You have no grounds (of religion to stand upon)". He denied the Prophethood of Moses and disbelieved in the Torah. On that occasion, Allaah Almighty (the Most High) revealed that Quraanic Ayaah. [Ibn Abu Haatim]

Verse Number 114

114- And who is more unjust than he who forbids that Allaah's name be celebrated in Allaah's mosques, and strive to ruin them? It is not fitting that such should enter those (mosques) except in fear. For them there is nothing but disgrace in this world, and in the hereafter, they shall receive a grievous torment (in the fire).

A narration on the authority of Ibn 'Abbaas [Allaah be pleased with them] that the Quraysh people prevented the Prophet [peace and blessings of Allaah be upon him], from praying at the Ka'bah in Al-Masjid Al-

Haraam. On that occasion, Allaah Almighty (the Most High) revealed this Quraanic Ayaah. [Ibn Abu Haatim]

A narration on the authority of Ibn Zayd that he said: This Quraanic Ayaah was revealed in connection with the polytheists when they averted the Prophet [peace and blessings of Allaah be upon him] from Makkah in the year of Hudaybiyah. [Ibn Jareer]

Verse Number 115

115- To Allaah belong the East and the West: whithersoever you turn (your faces in prayer by His command), there is Allaah's countenance. For Allaah is All-Embracing, All-Knowing.

A narration on the authority of Ibn 'Umar [Allaah be pleased with them] that the Prophet [peace and blessings of Allaah be upon him] used to perform the voluntary prayers on his mount wherever it went with him while coming from Makkah to Madeenah. Then he recited this Quraanic Ayaah and told that it was revealed in this connection. [Muslim; At-Tirmidhi and

An-Nasaa'i] A narration on the authority of Ibn 'Abbaas [Allaah be pleased with them] that when the Prophet [peace and blessings of Allaah be upon him] emigrated to Madeenah Allaah ordered him to face Bayt Al-Maqdis in prayer. The Yahood rejoiced in that and he continued to face it for over ten months. But he liked the Qiblah of Abraham and invoked Allaah looking towards the sky for this purpose. On that, Allaah Almighty (the Most High) revealed (what means): {So, turn your face towards it (Al-Masjid Al-Haraam in prayer)} [Al-Baqarah, verse 144] thereupon the Yahood doubted and said: "What has turned them from the Qiblah on which they were?" On that occasion, Allaah Almighty (the Most High) revealed this Quraanic Ayaah. [Ibn Jareer and Ibn Abu Haatim]

Verse Number 118

118- And those without knowledge (that is the disbelievers (al-Kaafireen) of Makkah) say (to Muhammad [peace and blessings of Allaah be upon him]): "Why does Allaah not speak unto us (to tell us that you are really His Messenger)? Or why does no Sign (From the many signs we have proposed to you to confirm your truthfulness) come unto us?" So said the (disbelievers (al-Kaafireen)) who were before them (to their Prophets), words of similar import. Their hearts (Qalb) are alike (in disbelief and obstinacy). We have indeed made clear the Signs to a people who are certain (of faith that those are indeed signs thereupon they will believe in them).

A narration on the authority of Ibn 'Abbaas [Allaah be pleased with them] that he said: Raafi' Ibn Khuzaymah told the Prophet [peace and blessings of Allaah be upon him]: "If you are a Messenger sent from Allaah as you claim, ask Allaah to talk to us directly so that we would hear His speech". On that occasion, Allaah Almighty (the Most High) revealed this Quraanic Ayaah. [Ibn Jareer and Ibn Abu Haatim]

Verse Number 119

119- Verily, We have sent you (O Muhammad) in truth as a bearer of glad tidings (Of Paradise for those who respond to and accept your message and invitation) and a warner (Of the Hellfire for those who reject your invitation and message): but you shall not be asked about the Companions of the Blazing Fire. A narration on the authority of Muhammad Ibn Ka'b Al-Qurathi that the Prophet [peace and blessings of Allaah be upon him] said: "Would that I know what my parents did!" On that occasion, Allaah revealed this Quraanic Ayaah. ['Abd-Ar-Razzaaq: Mursal]

A narration on the authority of Daawood Ibn Abu 'AAsim that the Prophet [peace and blessings of Allaah be upon him] asked: "Where are my parents?" On that occasion this Quraanic Ayaah was revealed. [Ibn Jareer: Mursal, Weak]

Verse Number 120

120- Never will the Yahood or the Nasaara be pleased with you unless you follow their form of religion. Say: "The Guidance of Allaah (Islam), that is the (only) Guidance," were you to follow their desires after the knowledge which has reached you (through the divine revelation you have received from Allaah Almighty), then you would find neither Protector nor Helper against Allaah.

A narration on the authority of Ibn 'Abbaas [Allaah be pleased with them] that he said: The Yahood of

Madeenah and the Nasaara of Najraan wished that the Prophet [peace and blessings of Allaah be upon him] should pray to their Qiblah. When Allaah turned the Qiblah to the Ka'bah, this was difficult to them and they lost all hope that he would agree with them on their religion. On that occasion, Allaah Almighty (the Most High) revealed this Quraanic Ayaah. [Ath-Tha'labi]

Verse Number 125

125- And remember We made the House (Ka'bah) a place of resort for men (To visit from all directions and take as refuge) and a place of safety; and take you (O people) the Station of Abraham as a place of prayer; and We covenanted with Abraham and Ishmael, that they should purify My House (from the idols) for those who circumambulate it (perform Tawaaf), or stay in it (in I'tikaaf), or bow and prostrate themselves (therein in Prayer).

A narration on the authority of 'Umar Ibn Al-Khattaab [may Allaah be pleased with him] that he said: My Lord (Rabb) agreed with me in three things: I said: "O Allaah's Apostle, I wish we take the station of Abraham as our praying place (for some of our prayers). So did come Allaah's saying (what means): {And take you (people) the station of Abraham as a place of prayer}. [Al-Baqarah, verse 125] I said: "O Allaah's Apostle! I wish you order your wives to cover themselves from the men because good and bad ones talk to them". So the verse of Hijaab was revealed. Once the wives of The Prophet [peace and blessings of Allaah be upon him] made a united front against him and I said to them: "It may be that if he (The Prophet) divorced you (all) his Lord (Rabb) (Allaah) will give him instead of you wives better than you". So this verse (the same as I had said) was revealed." [At-Tahreem 5] [Al-Bukhaari and others]

Verse Number 130

130- And who turns away from the religion of Abraham but such as debases his soul with folly! We chose and rendered him pure in this world (To carry Our message and be Our intimate friend): and he will be in the Hereafter among the Righteous (that is those of the highest rank).

A narration on the authority of Ibn 'Uyaynah that 'Abdullaah Ibn Salaam [may Allaah be pleased with him] invited his nephews, Salamah and Muhajir to Islam saying to them: "You know well that Allaah Almighty (the Most High) says in the Torah: 'I am going to send, from the offspring of Ishmael, a Prophet named Ahmad': whoever believes in him will be guided to the right direction, and whoever disbelieves in him will be cursed". Salamah embraced Islam but Muhaajir rejected faith. In connection with him this Quraanic Ayaah was revealed.

Verse Number 135

135- "Be Yahood", they (the Yahood of Madeenah) said, or "be Nasaara", (the Nasaara of Najraan said) "so that you would be guided (to the right way)". Say

(O Muhammad to them): "Nay! (we would rather) the Religion of Abraham, inclining toward Truth (apart from all other religions), and he was not among the polytheists".

A narration on the authority of Ibn 'Abbaas [Allaah be pleased with them] that he said: Ibn Sooryah said to the Prophet [peace and blessings of Allaah be upon him]: "The right guidance is only that (religion) on which we are: so, follow us, O Muhammad, perchance you would be guided aright". The Nasaara said the same. In connection with them Allaah revealed that Quraanic Ayaah. [Ibn Abu Haatim]

Verse Number 142

142- The Fools among the people will say: "What has turned them from the Qiblah to which they were used?" Say: "To Allaah belong East and West: He guides whom He wills to a Way that is straight".

A narration on the authority of Al-Baraa' [may Allaah be pleased with him] that he said: the Prophet [peace and blessings of Allaah be upon him] prayed towards Bayt Al-Maqdis and more often looked at the sky waiting the command of Allaah. Then Allaah revealed (what means): {We have certainly seen the turning of your face (O Muhammad) toward the heaven, and We will surely turn you to a Qiblah with which you will be pleased. So turn your face toward al-Masjid al-Haraam}. [Al-Baqarah, verse 144]

One of the Muslims said: "Would that we know the fate of those among us who died before we were turned to this Qiblah. What is about our prayer towards Bayt Al-Maqdis?" On that occasion, Allaah revealed (what means): {And never would Allaah have caused you to lose your faith. Indeed Allaah is, to the people, Kind and Merciful}. [Al-Baqarah, verse 143]

The fools of people (that is the men of Scripture) said: "What has turned them from their Qiblah on which they were?" On that occasion, Allaah revealed this Quraanic Ayaah [142]. [Ibn Ishaaq] Verse Number 154

154- And say not of those who are slain in the way of Allaah: "They are dead." Nay, they are living, though you perceive (it) not.

A narration on the authority of Ibn 'Abbaas [Allaah be pleased with them] that he said: "On the day of Badr, 'Umayr Ibn Al-Humaam was killed". In connection with him and others, who were killed, this Quraanic Ayaah was revealed. [Ibn Mandah in As-Sahaabah]

Verse Number 158

158- Behold! Safa and Marwah (mountains in Makkah) are among the Symbols of Allaah. So whoever visits the House for Hajj or 'Umrah there is no sin on him to compass them round. And if any one does Good voluntarily, certainly Allaah is Ready to appreciate (the deed by giving reward for it), All-Knowing.

A narration on the authority of 'Urwah Ibn Az-Zubayr that he said: I asked 'AA'ishah [Allaah be pleased with her] -and I was still a young man- about the interpretation of Allaah's saying (what means): {Behold! Safa and Marwah (mountains in Makkah) are among the Symbols of Allaah. So whoever visits the House for Hajj or 'Umrah there is no sin on him to compass them round}. I think that (it is evident from this revelation that) there is no harm if one does not compass Safa and Marwah round".

'AA'ishah [Allaah be pleased with her] said: "How bad is your understanding, O son of my sister! Had this interpretation been correct, the statement of Allaah should have been: there is no sin on him if he does not compass them round. But in fact, this Quraanic Ayaah was revealed concerning the Ansaar who (in the pre-Islamic days) used to assume Ihraam for an idol called "Manaah" and whoever assumed Ihram (for the idol), would consider it not right to compass round Safa and Marwah. When they embraced Islam, they asked the Prophet [peace and blessings of Allaah be upon him] regarding it. So Allaah revealed (what means): {Behold! Safa and Marwah (mountains in Makkah) are among the Symbols of Allaah. So whoever visits the House for Hajj or 'Umrah there is no sin on him to compass them round}. [Al-Baqarah, verse 158] [Al-Bukhaari]

A narration on the authority of 'AAsim Ibn Sulaymaan that he said: I asked Anas Ibn Malik about (compassing round) Safa and Marwah. He said: "We considered it one of the ceremonies of the pre-Islamic days. When Islam came, we stopped doing it till Allaah revealed (what means): {Behold! Safa and Marwah (mountains in Makkah) are among the Symbols of Allaah. So whoever visits the House for Hajj or 'Umrah there is no sin on him to compass them round}. [Al-Baqarah, verse 158] [Al-Bukhaari]

A narration on the authority of Ibn 'Abbaas [Allaah be pleased with them] that he said: In the pre-Islamic days, devils used to compass round Safa and Marwah along the whole night, and between them there were idols belonging to them. When Islam came the Muslims said: "O Messenger of Allaah! We should not compass Safa and Marwah round since it is a thing we used to do in the pre-Islamic days". On that occasion, Allaah Almighty (the Most High) revealed this Quraanic Ayaah. [Al-Haakim]

Verse Number 159

159- Those (Yahood) who conceal the Clear Signs We have sent down, and the Guidance, after we have made it clear for the People in the Book (Torah), on them shall be Allaah's curse (By being rejected and moved far away from His mercy), and the curse of those entitled to curse.

A narration on the authority of Ibn 'Abbaas [Allaah be pleased with them] that he said: Mu'aadh Ibn Jabal, Sa'd Ibn Mu'aadh and Khaarijah Ibn Zayd [Allaah be pleased with them] asked some Jewish rabbis about something in the Torah, but they concealed it from them and rejected to tell them about it. In connection with them Allaah Almighty (the Most High) revealed this Quraanic Ayaah. [Ibn Jareer and Ibn Abu Haatim]

Verse Number 164

164- Behold! In the creation of the heavens and the earth (and what they contain of wonders); in the alternation of the Night and the Day; in the ships which sail through the Ocean for the profit of mankind; in the rain which Allaah sends down from the sky thereby He gives life to a land after its death; in the beasts of all kinds that He scatters through the earth; in the veering of winds and clouds which are held between the sky and the earth: indeed are Signs (indicating to Allaah's Oneness and Omnipotence) for a people who use reason.

A narration on the authority of Ibn Abu Ad-Duha that he said: Allaah revealed to His Prophet [peace and blessings of Allaah be upon him] (what means): {And your god is one God. There is no deity (worthy of worship) except Him, the Most Gracious, the Most Merciful}. [Al-Baqarah, verse 163] The polytheists wondered and said: "One God! If he is truthful, let him bring us a sign". On that, Allaah Almighty (the Most High) revealed this Quraanic Ayaah. [Sa'eed Ibn Mansoor in his Sunan; Al-Firyaabi in his Tafseer and Al-Bayhaqi in Shu'ab Al-EEmaan]

A narration on the authority of 'Ataa' that he said: the Prophet [peace and blessings of Allaah be upon him] received while being in Madinah Allaah's saying (what means): {And your god is one God. There is no deity (worthy of worship) except Him, the Most Gracious, the Most Merciful}. [Al-Baqarah, verse 163] Thereupon the disbelievers (al-Kaafireen) of Quraysh in Makkah said: "How could only one god extend over all the people?" On that occasion, Allaah Almighty (the Most High) revealed this Quraanic Ayaah [164] [Ibn Abu Haatim and Abu Ash-Shaykh in Al-'Athamah]

A narration on the authority of Ibn 'Abbaas [Allaah be pleased with them] that he said: The Quraysh people said to the Prophet [peace and blessings of Allaah be upon him]: "Invoke Allaah for us to make Safa a mountain of gold thereby we would be too strong to face our enemy". Allaah revealed to him: "I am going to give it to them: I will make Safa a mountain of gold. But if they disbelieve afterwards, I will punish them with such a punishment as I have never punished therewith any of the worlds". The Prophet [peace and blessings of Allaah be upon him] said: "O Lord (Rabb)! Leave me with my people to invite them (to Islam) step by step". On that occasion, Allaah revealed this Quraanic Ayaah. The point is that how do they ask you for Safa and they see of signs what is far greater? [Ibn Abu Haatim and Ibn Mardawayh]

Verse Number 170

170- When it is said to them (disbelievers (al-Kaafireen)): "Follow what Allaah has revealed," they say: "Nay! We shall follow the ways of our fathers." What! Even though their fathers were void of wisdom and guidance!

A narration on the authority of Ibn 'Abbaas [Allaah be pleased with them] that he said: the Prophet [peace and blessings of Allaah be upon him] invited the Yahood to Islam and exhorted them to follow it and warned them of Allaah's torment and wrath. Raafi' Ibn Huraymilah and Maalik Ibn 'Awf said: "Nay, we follow, O Muhammad, that on which we have found our forefathers, because they were more knowledgeable and better than us". On that occasion, Allaah revealed this Quraanic Ayaah. [Ibn Abu Haatim]

Verse Number 174

174- Those who conceal Allaah's revelations in the Book (concerning the attributes and characteristics of Muhammad [peace and blessings of Allaah be upon him] and those are the Yahood), and purchase a miserable profit therewith (in this world), they eat into their bellies Naught but Fire; Allaah will not speak to them on the Day of Resurrection (out of His anger with them), nor purify them (from the filth of sins), and their's will be a painful torment.

A narration on the authority of 'Ikrimah that this Quraanic Ayaah and AAl 'Imraan 77 were revealed in connection with the Yahood. [Ibn Jarir]

A narration on the authority of Ibn 'Abbaas [Allaah be pleased with them] that he said: This Quraanic Ayaah was revealed in connection with the chiefs and scholars of the Yahood: they used to get from the lowly gifts and dregs of food, hoping that the Prophet to be sent should be from among them. When Muhammad [peace and blessings of Allaah be upon him] was sent from a people (Arabs) other than them, they feared they might lose their privileges. So, they changed the attributes of Muhammad [peace and blessings of Allaah be upon him] in the Torah and then said: "That is the description of the Prophet who will appear towards the end of time: he is not similar to the one (Muhammad) who has appeared". On that occasion, Allaah revealed this Quraanic Ayaah. [Ath-Tha'labi]

Verse Number 177

177- Righteousness is not that you turn your faces (in prayer) towards East or West; but righteousness is to believe in Allaah, the Last Day, the Angels, the Book and the Messengers; to spend of your wealth, in spite of love for it, for your kin, for orphans, for the needy, for the wayfarer, for those who ask and for the ransom of slaves; to establish prayer, give Zakaah, and fulfill the contracts which you have made (with the people or with Allaah Almighty); and to be firmly patient in severe poverty and ailment, and at the time of fighting (in the Cause of Allaah). Such are true (to their faith and righteousness), the God-fearing.

A narration on the authority of Qataadah that he said: The Yahood used to pray towards the West and the Nasaara towards the East. On that occasion, Allaah revealed this Quraanic Ayaah. [Abd Ar-Razzaaq]

A narration on the authority of Qataadah that he said: It was mentioned to us that a man asked the Prophet [peace and blessings of Allaah be upon him] about righteousness thereupon Allaah revealed this Quraanic Ayaah. the Prophet [peace and blessings of Allaah be upon him] invited the man and recited it to him. Before imposing the obligatory duties, if a man bears witness that there is none worthy of worship except Allaah and that Muhammad [peace and blessings of Allaah be upon him] is the Prophet and then dies, good would be expected for him. It is reported that this Quraanic Ayaah was revealed in this connection. The Yahood, before that, used to face the West and the Nasaara the East (in their prayer). [Ibn Jarir and Ibn Al-Mundhir]

Verse Number 178

178- O you who believe! The legal retribution is prescribed to you in cases of murder: the free (should be killed in retribution) for (his killing) the free, the slave for the slave and the female for the female. But if anything is remitted for the murderer (by an heir) from (the blood of) his brother (the murdered, by giving up retribution), then (the blood claimants) should fairly adhere to that (forgiveness and demand the blood-money from the murderer without transgression), and (the murderer) should pay (the blood-money) to him with kindness (in the sense that he should neither procrastinate nor reduce from it). This (allowance to give up the legal retribution and adhere to the blood-money) is a concession and a Mercy from your Lord (Rabb). After this, whoever exceeds the due limits shall have a painful torment (in the world by being killed and in the hereafter by being admitted to the fire of Hell).

A narration on the authority of Sa'eed Ibn Jubayr that he said: Two of Arab tribes fought with each other during the pre-Islamic days, a short time before the emergence of Islam, leading to many casualties among them to the extent that slaves and women were killed. They kept on that state till they both embraced Islam. One of them boasted over the other, being greater in number of people and wealth.

They then swore that they would not make peace with them till they have killed a free person from the others in retaliation for every slave killed from among them and a man from the others in retaliation for each woman killed from among them. In connection with them, Allaah Almighty (the Most High) revealed this Quraanic Ayaah. [Ibn Abu Haatim]

Verse Number 184

184- (Fasting is) for a fixed number of days; but if any of you is ill, or on a journey, the prescribed number (should be made up) from days later. Due on those who can do it (with hardship), is a ransom, the feeding of an indigent; but if he gives more voluntarily, it will be better for him. And to fast is better for you (than to leave fast and give ransom) if you only knew.

A narration on the authority of Mujaahid that he said: This Quraanic Ayaah was revealed in connection with Qays Ibn As-Saa'ib, thereupon he left fasting and fed a needy person for each day he did not fast. [Ibn Sa'd in his Tabaqaat]

Verse Number 186

186- When My servants ask you concerning Me, (tell them that) I am indeed close (to them by My knowledge): I respond to the supplication of every supplicant when he calls on Me: let them also, with a will, respond to My call (by obedience), and believe in Me so that they may be led aright.

A narration on the authority of Mu'awiyah Ibn Haydah that he said: A Bedouin came to the Prophet [peace and blessings of Allaah be upon him] and said: "Is our Lord (Rabb) so much near (to us) that we could talk to Him privately, or is He far (from us) so that we should call Him out?" He kept silent and gave no reply. On that, Allaah Almighty (the Most High) revealed this Quraanic Ayaah. [Ibn Jareer; Ibn Abu Haatim; Ibn Mardawayh; Abu Ash-Shaykh and others]

A narration on the authority of Al-Hasan that he said: The Companions asked the Prophet [peace and blessings of Allaah be upon him]: "Where is our Lord (Rabb)?". On that occasion, Allaah Almighty (the Most High) revealed this Quraanic Ayaah. ['Abd-Ar-Razzaaq: Mursal]

A narration on the authority of 'Ali [may Allaah be pleased with him] that he said: the Prophet [peace and blessings of Allaah be upon him] said: "Do not fail to supplicate (Allaah). No doubt, Allaah has revealed to me (what means): {Invoke Me, so that I would answer your supplication}. [Ghaafir, verse 60] A man said: "O

Messenger of Allaah! Does our Lord (Rabb) hear the supplication?" On that, Allaah Almighty (the Most High) revealed this Quraanic Ayaah in issue. [Ibn 'Asaakir]

A narration on the authority of 'Ataa' that he was informed: When Allaah revealed (what means): {Invoke Me so that I would answer your supplication}, [Ghaafir, verse 60] they said: "We do not know at which hour we should supplicate (Him)". In this connection, Allaah Almighty (the Most High) revealed this Quraanic Ayaah. [Ibn Jareer]

Verse Number 187

187- It is made lawful for you, on the night of fasting, to have sexual intercourse with your wives. They are your garments and you are their's. Allaah knows what you used to do secretly among yourselves; but He turned to you (in repentance) and forgave you; so now (as it has been made lawful), have sexual relations with them, and seek what Allaah has ordained for you, and eat and drink until the white thread of dawn appear to you distinct from its black thread; then complete your fast (from dawn) till the night falls (at sunset); but do not have sexual relations with your wives while you are staying in I'tikaaf in masjids. Those are limits (set by) Allaah: so approach them not. Thus Allaah makes clear His Signs to men that they may restrain themselves.

A narration on the authority of Al-Baraa' [may Allaah be pleased with him] that he said: It was the habit of the Companions of Muhammad [peace and blessings of Allaah be upon him] that if any of them was fasting and the food was presented (for breaking his fast), but he slept before eating, he would not eat that night and the following day till sunset. Qays Ibn Sirmah Al-Ansaari was fasting and came to his wife at the time of breaking fast and asked her whether she had anything to eat. She replied: "No, but I would go and bring some for you." He used to do hard work during the day, so he was overtaken by sleep. When his wife came and saw him, she said: "Disappointment be for you." When it was midday on the following day, he fainted. The Prophet [peace and blessings of Allaah be upon him] was informed about the whole matter. On that occasion, Allaah revealed (what means): {and eat and drink, until the white thread of dawn appears to you distinct from its black thread}. They were overjoyed by it. [Al-Bukhaari]

A narration on the authority of Mu'aadh [may Allaah be pleased with him] that on the same day and after sleeping 'Umar had sexual intercourse with his wife and on the coming day he went and told the Prophet [peace and blessings of Allaah be upon him] about that. On that occasion, Allaah Almighty (the Most High) revealed (what means): {It is made lawful for you, on the night of fasting, to have sexual intercourse with your wives. They are your garments and you are their's}. [Ahmad; Abu Daawood and Al-Haakim]

A narration on the authority of Al-Baraa' [may Allaah be pleased with him] that he said: When the fasting of Ramadaan was enjoined they used not to approach their wives along the whole month. But some men used to deceive themselves. On that occasion, Allaah Almighty (the Most High) revealed (what means): {Allaah knows what you used to do secretly among yourselves; but He turned to you (in repentance) and forgave you; so now (as it has been made lawful), have sexual relations with them, and seek what Allaah has ordained for you}. [Al-Bukhaari]

A narration on the authority of Ka'b Ibn Maalik [may Allaah be pleased with him] that he said: It was the habit of the people in Ramadaan that if anyone of them fasted and evening came upon him and he slept, food, drink and sex were forbidden to him till the time of breaking fast of the coming day. One night, 'Umar returned from the Prophet [peace and blessings of Allaah be upon him] after having spent part of the night with him. He liked to have sexual intercourse with his wife, but she rejected under claim that she had slept. He said: "You have not slept yet". Then he had sexual relation with her. On the coming morning 'Umar went to the Prophet [peace and blessings of Allaah be upon him] and told him about that. In this connection this Quraanic Ayaah was revealed. [Ahmad; Ibn Jareer and Ibn Abu Haatim]

A narration on the authority of Sahl Ibn Sa'd [may Allaah be pleased with him] that he said: When the following verse was revealed (what means): {Eat and drink until the white thread appears to you, distinct from its black thread} and 'of dawn' was not revealed, some people who intended to fast tied black and white threads to their legs and went on eating till they could differentiate between the two. Allaah then revealed the words {of dawn} and it became clear that he meant night and day. [Al-Bukhaari]

A narration on the authority of Qataadah that he said: It was the habit that if anyone did I'tikaaf, he would come out of the masjid and have sexual intercourse with his wife/slave-girl if he so liked. But Allaah revealed (what means): {but do not have sexual relations with your wives while you are staying in I'tikaaf in masjids}. [Ibn Jareer]

Verse Number 188

188- And do not eat up your each other's property illegally, nor give wealth (in the form of bribery) to the judges, with intent to eat up sinfully some of (other) people's property and you know (That by doing so you are sinners and criminals).

A narration on the authority of Sa'eed Ibn Jubayr that he said: Both Imri' Al-Qays Ibn 'AAbis and 'Abdaan Ibn Ashoo' Al-Hadrami disputed over a piece of land, and Imri' Al-Qays liked him to take oath (to support his claim over it). In connection with him, this Quraanic Ayaah was revealed. [Ibn Abu Haatim]

Verse Number 189

189- They ask you (O Muhammad) concerning the New Moons. Say: They are but signs to mark fixed periods of time in (the affairs of) men, and for pilgrimage. It is not righteousness to enter your houses from the back: it is righteousness to fear Allaah. Enter houses through the proper doors: and fear Allaah that you may prosper.

A narration on the authority of Ibn 'Abbaas [Allaah be pleased with them] that he said: People asked the Prophet [peace and blessings of Allaah be upon him] about the new moons. On that occasion, Allaah revealed (what means): {They ask you (O Muhammad) concerning the New Moons. Say: They are but signs to mark fixed periods of time in (the affairs of) men, and for pilgrimage}. [Ibn Abu Haatim]

A narration on the authority of Abu Al-'AAliyah that he said: We were told that they said: "O Messenger of Allaah! Why have the new moons been created?" Thereone, Allaah revealed this Quraanic Ayaah. [Ibn Abu Haatim]

A narration on the authority of Ibn 'Abbaas [Allaah be pleased with them] that Mu'aadh Ibn Jabal and Tha'labah Ibn Ghanamah said: "O Messenger of Allaah! What is the matter that the new moon appears as thin as a thread and then increases till it becomes huge, ripe and round, and then decreases and becomes thinner gradually till it returns to its previous state? Why does it change from one state to another?" On that occasion, this Quraanic Ayaah was revealed. [Abu Na'eem in Al-Hilyah and Ibn 'Asaakir in Taareekh Dimashq]

A narration on the authority of Al-Baraa' [may Allaah be pleased with him] that he said: Whenever they assumed Ihraam in the pre-Islamic days, they would go to the House from its back. On that occasion, Allaah Almighty (the Most High) revealed (what means): {It is not righteousness to enter your houses from the back: it is righteousness to fear Allaah. Enter houses through the proper doors}. [Al-Bukhari]

A narration on the authority of Jaabir [may Allaah be pleased with him] that he said: The Quraysh people were named Hums, and they used to enter through the gates while being in the state of Ihraam. Whereas the Ansaar and all other Arabs did not enter through any gate while being in that state. While the Prophet [peace and blessings of Allaah be upon him] was in a garden he came out of the gate and with him came Qutbah Ibn 'AAmir Al-Ansaari. They said: "O Messenger of Allaah! Qutbah Ibn 'AAmir is a merchant and has come out with you from the gate". He said: "What has led you to do what you have done?" He replied: "Having seen you doing it, I have done it accordingly". He declared: "I am a man from Hums". He replied: "No doubt, my religion is yours". On that occasion, Allaah revealed this Quraanic Ayaah. [Ibn Abu Haatim and Al-Haakim who renders it Saheeh]

A narration on the authority of Al-Baraa' [may Allaah be pleased with him] that he said: It was the habit of the Ansaar that if they came back from journey, one would not enter from the gate of his house. On that occasion, Allaah revealed this Quraanic Ayaah. [At-Tayaalisi in his Musnad]

Verse Number 190-194

190- Fight in the cause of Allaah (to make superior His religion) those (disbelievers (al-Kaafireen)) who fight you, but do not transgress limits; for Allaah loves not transgressors (who always exceed the due limits in dealing with other people). 191- And slay them wherever you catch them, and drive them out from where they have drove you out; for Fitnah is worse than killing; but fight them not at Al-Masjid Al-Haraam unless they (first) fight you there; and if they fight you, slay them. Such (that is killing them and turning them out of Makkah) is the reward of the disbelievers (al-Kaafireen). 192- But if they cease (from polytheism, disbelief and obstinacy, it should be known that) Allaah is Oft-forgiving, Most Merciful. 193- And fight them until there is no more Fitnah (disbelief and polytheism) and (all and every kind of) worship is for Allaah (Alone). But if they cease, let there be no transgression (by killing or any kind of hostilities) except against the wrongdoers. 194- [Fighting in] the sacred month is for (aggression committed in) the sacred month, and for (all) violations is legal retribution. So whoever assaults you, then assaulted him in the same way as he assaults you. And fear Allaah and know that Allaah is with those who fear Him.

A narration on the authority of Ibn 'Abbaas [Allaah be pleased with them] that he said: These Quraanic Aayaat were revealed in connection with Hudaybiyah treaty. When the Prophet [peace and blessings of Allaah be upon him] and his Companions were averted from the House, they slaughtered their sacrificial animals at Hudaybiyah. Then the polytheists made peace with him on condition that he should return this year and come in the next year, and they would leave Makkah to him three days to perform Tawaaf round the House and do what he liked to do.

When it was the coming year, the Prophet [peace and blessings of Allaah be upon him] and his Companions got ready for the compensatory 'Umrah, and feared lest the Quraysh men would not fulfill the condition, and would rather avert them from Al-Masjid Al-Haraam and fight them. The Companions did not like to fight them in the sacred month. On that occasion, Allaah Almighty (the Most High) revealed (what means): {Fight in the way of Allaah those who fight you but do not transgress}. [Al-Waahidi]

A narration on the authority of Qataadah that he said: the Prophet [peace and blessings of Allaah be upon him] and his Companions came, having assumed Ihraam for 'Umrah in Dhul-Qa'dah bringing the Hadiy with them, till when they were in Hudaybiyah the polytheists averted them and the Prophet [peace and blessings of Allaah be upon him] made peace treaty with them on condition that he would return this year and come back in the next year (to perform compensatory 'Umrah).

When it was the next year, he and his Companions came and entered Makkah as performers of 'Umrah in Dhul-Qa'dah, where he spent three days. The polytheists had already boasted over him when they returned him (in the last year). But Allaah made him take retribution from them by having him enter

Makkah in the same month in which they had already returned him. In this connection, Allaah Almighty revealed (what means): {(Fighting in) the sacred month is for (aggression committed in) the sacred month, and for (all) violations is legal retribution}. [Ibn Jareer]

Verse Number 195

195- And spend in the Cause (obedience) of Allaah and do not throw yourselves into destruction, and do good. Truly, Allaah loves the doers of good (by rewarding them for their spending in His cause).

A narration on the authority of Hudhayfah [may Allaah be pleased with him] that he said: This was revealed in connection with spending. [Al-Bukhaari]

A narration on the authority of Abu Ayyoob Al-Ansaari [may Allaah be pleased with him] that he said: this Quraanic Ayaah was revealed concerning us, the community of Ansaar. When Allaah Almighty (the Most High) empowered Islam and his supporters increased in number, we said to each other in secret: "Our property has been damaged and Allaah has indeed empowered Islam. Would that we stay besides our property to repair what has been damaged thereof". On that, Allaah revealed the same we said (what means): {And spend in the Cause (obedience) of Allaah and do not throw yourselves into destruction, and do good. Truly, Allaah loves the doers of good). The destruction was thus to stay besides our property and leave fighting (in Allaah's cause). [Abu Daawood;

At-Tirmidhi and rendered Saheeh by Ibn Hibbaan and others]

A narration on the authority of Abu Jabeerah Ibn Ad-Dahhaak that he said: The Ansaar were in the habit of giving in charity as much as Allaah willed. But they were befallen by a famine year thereupon they withheld their charity. On that occasion, Allaah Almighty (the Most High) revealed this Quraanic Ayaah. [At-Tabaraani]

A narration on the authority of An-Nu'maan Ibn Basheer [may Allaah be pleased with him] that he said: Whenever a man committed a sin he would say: "It would not be forgiven for me". On that occasion, Allaah Almighty (the Most High) revealed this Quraanic Ayaah. [At-Tabaraani]

The same is narrated on the authority of Al-Baraa' [may Allaah be pleased with him]. [Al-Haakim]

Verse Number 196

196- And complete Hajj and 'Umrah for Allaah. But if you are prevented (from completing them by virtue of an enemy or any such impediment), sacrifice a Had'y such as you can afford, and do not shave your heads until the Had'y reaches the place of sacrifice. And whosoever of you is ill or has an ailment in his scalp, he must pay a ransom of either fasting or giving in charity or offering sacrifice. Then if you are in safety (from the enemy in case there is any) and whosoever avails himself of (performing) 'Umrah followed by

Hajj, due on him is such a Had'y as he can obtain, but if he cannot obtain it, due on him is three fasts during Hajj and seven days after his return (to his home), making ten days in all. This (ruling applies) to him whose family is not resident at Al-Masjid Al-Haraam. And fear Allaah much and know that Allaah is Severe in punishment.

A narration on the authority of Safwaan Ibn Umayyah that he said: A man came to the Prophet [peace and blessings of Allaah be upon him] and he was scented with perfume and having a cloak on him. He said: "what do you order me to do O Prophet concerning my 'Umrah?" then Allaah Almighty (the Most High) revealed (what means): {And complete Hajj and 'Umrah for Allaah}. the Prophet [peace and blessings of Allaah be upon him] said: "Where is the one who asked about the 'Umrah?" The man replied: "Here I am". He told him: "Put off your garment, take Ghusl and snuff your nose with water as much as you can, and do in your 'Umrah the same as you do in your Hajj". [Ibn Abu Haatim]

A narration on the authority of 'Abdullaah Ibn Ma'qal that he said: I sat with Ka'b Ibn Ujrah and asked him about the ransom. He replied: "This revelation (what means): {And whosoever of you is ill or has an ailment in his scalp, he must pay a ransom of either fasting or giving in charity or offering sacrifice}, was sent down concerning my case especially, but it is also for you in general. I was carried to the Prophet [peace and blessings of Allaah be upon him] and the lice were falling in great number on my face. He said: "I have never thought that your ailment (or struggle) has reached to such an extent as I see. Can you afford for a sheep?" I replied in the negative. He then said: "Fast three days, or feed six poor persons each with half a Saa of food." [Al-Bukhaari]

A narration on the authority of Ka'b that he said: We were with the Prophet [peace and blessings of Allaah be upon him], in Hudaybiyah while being in the state of Ihraam and prevented (from performing 'Umrah) by the polytheists. I had long hair which caused lice to fall down on my face. the Prophet [peace and blessings of Allaah be upon him] passed by me and said: "Do the lice of your head trouble you?" He ordered him to shave his head. Then this Quraanic Ayaah was revealed. [Ahmad]

A narration on the authority of Ibn 'Abbaas [Allaah be pleased with them] that he said: When we descended in Hudaybiyah, Ka'b Ibn 'Ujrah came with lice scattered on his face. He said: "O Messenger of Allaah! Lice have troubled me so much". He replied: "Then shave your head and give a ransom for that". Ka'b then shaved his head and sacrificed a cow. On that occasion, Allaah Almighty (the Most High) revealed this Quraanic Ayaah. [Al-Waahidi]

Verse Number 197

197- (The time of) Hajj is the well-known (lunar) months. So whoever makes Hajj due on himself therein (by assuming Ihraam), then he should commit neither sexual intercourse (with his wife) nor sin nor dispute during Hajj. And whatever good (charity) you do, (be sure that) Allaah knows it (for which He would reward you). And take a provision (with you) for the journey, for surely the best provision is the guarding of oneself (from begging others); and fear Me (by safeguarding yourselves from My punishment) O men of understanding!

A narration on the authority of Ibn 'Abbaas [Allaah be pleased with them] that he said: The people of Yemen used to perform Hajj and take no provision with them, and say: "We are reliants (on Allaah)". Whenever they reached Makkah they would beg the people. On that occasion, Allaah Almighty (the Most High) revealed this Quraanic Ayaah. [Al-Bukhaari and others]

Verse Number 198

198- There is no blame upon you for seeking bounty from your Lord (Rabb) (during Hajj). But when you depart from 'Arafaat (after spending the night at Muzdalifah), remember Allaah at Al- Mash'ar Al-Haraam. And remember Him as He has guided you (to the principles and rules of His religion), for indeed, you were before that among those who went astray.

A narration on the authority of Ibn 'Abbaas [Allaah be pleased with them] that he said: 'Ukaath, Majaannah and Dhul-Majaaz were markets in the pre-Islamic days. The people felt that traffic is sinful during the season (of Hajj). They asked the Prophet [peace and blessings of Allaah be upon him] about that, thereupon Allaah revealed this Quraanic Ayaah. [Al-Bukhaari and others]

A narration on the authority of Abu Umaamah At-Taymi that he said: I asked Ibn 'Umar: "We are in the habit of hiring others (for work). Is Hajj held valid for us?" He said: "A man came to the Prophet [peace and blessings of Allaah be upon him], and asked him the same question you have just asked me so he gave him no reply till Jibreel [peace and blessings of Allaah be upon him] came down to him with this Quraanic Ayaah. the Prophet [peace and blessings of Allaah be upon him] invited him and told him: "You are regarded a pilgrim". [Ahmad; Ibn Abu Haatim; Ibn Jareer; Al-Haakim and others]

Verse Number 199

199- Then depart at a quick pace from the place whence it is usual for the people to depart and ask for forgiveness of Allaah. Indeed, Allaah is Oft-Forgiving, Most Merciful.

A narration on the authority of Ibn 'Abbaas [Allaah be pleased with them] that he said: The Arabs used to stand at 'Arafah and the Quraysh at Muzdalifah. In this connection, Allaah Almighty (the Most High) revealed this Quraanic Ayaah. [Ibn Jareer]

The same is narrated on the authority of Asmaa' Bint Abu Bakr [Allaah be pleased with them]. [Ibn Al-Mundhir]

200- So, when you have accomplished your (holy) rituals, then celebrate the praises of Allaah as you used to sing the praises of your fathers or (even) with far more Heart and soul. So, of mankind (there are) some who say: "Our Lord (Rabb), give us (our share) in the present (life)," and in the Hereafter he will have no share. 201- And of them there are some who say: "Our Lord (Rabb)! Give us in this world good (favor) and in the Hereafter good (reward of Paradise), and save us from the torment of the Fire!

A narration on the authority of Ibn 'Abbaas [Allaah be pleased with them] that he said: The people of the pre-Islamic days used to stand during the season and say to each other: "My father used to serve food to the needy, fulfill the debts of the debtors among them, and pay the blood-moneys of others", making a mention only of the good deeds of their forefathers. On that occasion, Allaah Almighty (the Most High) revealed (what means): {So, when you have accomplished your (holy) rituals, then celebrate the praises of Allaah as you used to sing the praises of your fathers or (even) with far more Heart and soul}. [Ibn Abu Haatim]

The same is narrated on the authority of Mujaahid. [Ibn Jareer]

A narration on the authority of Ibn 'Abbaas [Allaah be pleased with them] that he said: Some Arabs used to come to the standing place and say: "O Allaah! Make it a year of rain, fertility, allegiance and goodness", making no mention of the hereafter affairs. In connection with them Allaah revealed (what means): {So, of mankind (there are) some who say: "Our Lord (Rabb), give us (our share) in the present (life)," and in the Hereafter he will have no share}. Others among the believers (al-Mumineen) would come after them and say: "Our Lord (Rabb), give us in this world (that which is) good and in the Hereafter (that which is) good and protect us from the punishment of the Fire," and that was exactly what Allaah revealed. [Ibn Abu Haatim]

Verse Number 204

204- And of mankind there is he whose speech may please you (O Muhammad) in this worldly life, and he calls on Allaah to witness as to what is in his heart; yet he is the most contentious of adversaries.

A narration on the authority of Ibn 'Abbaas [Allaah be pleased with them] that he said: When the people of the expedition of 'AAsim and Marthad were killed, two hypocrites (al-Munaafiqeen) said: "Woe to those tempted men who were ruined as such: they neither sat among their families nor fulfilled the message of their companion (the Prophet [peace and blessings of Allaah be upon him])". On that occasion, Allaah Almighty (the Most High) revealed this Quraanic Ayaah. [Ibn Abu Haatim]

A narration on the authority of As-Suddi that he said: It was revealed in connection with Al-Akhnas Ibn

Shareeq: one day he went to the Prophet [peace and blessings of Allaah be upon him], and showed him that he was a Muslim, and his behavior pleased him. Then he came out and passed by a farm where there was some donkeys belonging to Muslims. He burnt the crops and hamstrung the donkeys. On that occasion, Allaah revealed this Quraanic Ayaah. [Ibn Jareer]

Verse Number 207

207- And of mankind is he who would sell himself, seeking the Pleasure of Allaah. And Allaah is full of Kindness to (His) slaves. A narration on the authority of Sa'eed Ibn Al-Musayyab that he said: Suhayb [may Allaah be pleased with him] set out as an emigrant to the Prophet [peace and blessings of Allaah be upon him], and was pursued by a group of Quraysh. He dismounted and took out the arrows which were in his quiver. Then he said to them: "O community of Quraysh! You know well that I am the best archer among you all. By Allaah, you will not harm me till I throw all arrows I have in my quiver and then strike with my sword as much as I could and then let you do what you are able to do. But if you so like, I can guide you to my property in Makkah provided that you should let me go". They accepted. When he went to the Prophet [peace and blessings of Allaah be upon him] in Madeenah (and told him the story), he told him: "Your trade has profited O Abu Yahya! Your trade has profited O Abu Yahya!" In this connection, this Quraanic Ayaah was revealed. [Al-Haarith Ibn Abu Usaamah in his Musnad; Ibn Abu Haatim and Al-Haakim]

A narration on the authority of 'Ikrimah that he said: It was revealed in connection with Suhayb, Abu Dharr and Jundub Ibn As-Sakan, a man belonging to the household of Abu Dharr. [Ibn Jareer]

Verse Number 208

208- O you who believe, enter into Islam completely (and wholeheartedly) and do not follow the footsteps (ways) of Satan. Indeed, he is to you an evident enemy.

A narration on the authority of 'Ikrimah that he said: 'Abdullah Ibn Salaam, Tha'labah, Ibn Yameen, Asad and Usayd, sons of Ka'b, Sa'eed Ibn 'Amr and Qays Ibn Zayd - and all of them were Yahood - told the Prophet [peace and blessings of Allaah be upon him]: "O Messenger of Allaah! We always sanctify Saturday: so, let us do our religious ceremonies during it. Furthermore, the Torah is the Book of Allaah: so, let us spend the night (in prayer) with it". On that, Allaah revealed this Quraanic Ayaah. [Ibn Jareer]

Verse Number 214

214- Or do you think that you shall enter Paradise without such (trials) as came to those who passed away before you? They were befallen with suffering and adversity (in the form of various calamities and ailments), and were so shaken in spirit that even the Messenger and those who believed with him cried: "When (will come) the help of Allaah?" Ah! Verily, the help of Allaah is nigh!

A narration on the authority of Qataadah that he said: This Quraanic Ayaah was revealed on the day of Al-Ahzaab where the Prophet [peace and blessings of Allaah be upon him] was afflicted by adversities and siege (on the part of the polytheists). ['Abd-Ar-Razzaaq]

Verse Number 215

215- They ask you (O Muhammad) what they should spend. Say: "Whatever you spend of good is (to be) for parents and relatives and orphans and the needy and the wayfarer. And whatever you do of good (be it spending or any deed of benefit), indeed Allaah knows it (and will, surely, give reward for it in the hereafter).

A narration on the authority of Ibn Jurayj that he said: The believers (al-Muminccn) asked the Prophet [peace and blessings of Allaah be upon him] where to spend their property. On that occasion, this Quraanic Ayaah was revealed. [Ibn Jarirl

The same is narrated on the authority of 'Amr Ibn Al-Jamooh [may Allaah be pleased with him]. [Ibn Al-Mundhir]

Verse Number 217-218

217- They ask you (O Muhammad) about fighting in the sacred month. Say: "Fighting therein is great (sin), but graver (sin) in the sight of Allaah is to avert [people] from the way of Allaah, disbelieve in Him and (prevent access to) al-Masjid al-Haraam, and expel its people therefrom; And fitnah (polytheism) is greater than killing." And they (the disbelievers (al-Kaafireen)) will continue to fight you until they turn you back from your religion if they are able. And whoever of you reverts from his religion (to disbelief) and dies while he is a disbeliever - for those, their (righteous) deeds have become worthless in this world and the Hereafter, and those are the inmates of the Fire therein they will abide forever. 218- Verily, those who have believed, and those who have emigrated (for Allaah's Religion) and have striven hard in the Way of Allaah, all these hope for Allaah's Mercy (and reward). And Allaah is Oft Forgiving, Most Merciful.

A narration on the authority of Jundub Ibn 'Abdullaah [may Allaah be pleased with him] that the Prophet [peace and blessings of Allaah be upon him] dispatched a group under leadership of 'Abdullaah Ibn Jahsh. On the way they met Ibn Al-Hadrami and killed him, not knowing whether this day (on which they killed him) was from Rajab or Jumaada. The polytheists said to the Muslims: "You have killed a man in the prohibited month". On that occasion, Allaah Almighty (the Most High) revealed (what means): {They ask you (O Muhammad) about fighting in the sacred month...} Some of them said: "It is true that they have committed no sin, yet they will have no reward". On that occasion, Allaah Almighty (the Most High) revealed (what means): {Verily, those who have believed, and those who have emigrated (for Allaah's Religion) and have striven hard in the Way of Allaah, all these hope for Allaah's Mercy (and reward)}. [Ibn

Jareer; Ibn Abu Haatim; At-Tabaraani in Al-Kabeer and Al-Bayhaqi in his Sunan]

Verse Number 219

219- They ask you (O Muhammad) about (the ruling on) wine and gambling. Say: "In them is a great sin, and (some) benefit for men, but the sin of them is greater than their benefit." And they ask you what they should spend. Say: "That which is beyond your needs." Thus Allaah makes clear to you His signs in order that you may give thought.

A narration on the authority of Ibn 'Abbaas [Allaah be pleased with them] that he said: A group of Companions, when they were ordered to spend in the cause of Allaah, they went to the Prophet [peace and blessings of Allaah be upon him] and said: "We do not know the spending we have been commanded by Allaah to spend. What should we spend?" On that occasion, Allaah revealed (what means): {And they ask you what they should spend. Say, " That which is beyond your needs."} [Ibn Abu Haatim]

Verse Number 220

220- (Their bearings) on this worldly life and in the Hereafter. And they ask you concerning orphans. Say: "The best thing is to invest their property, and if you mix your affairs with theirs, then they are your brothers. And Allaah knows (and distinguishes) the corrupter (who intends mischief by swallowing their property) from the reformer (who intends good by saving and investing their property for their benefit). And if Allaah had wished, He could have put you into difficulties. Truly, Allaah is All-Mighty, All-Wise.

A narration on the authority of Ibn 'Abbaas [Allaah be pleased with them] that when Allaah Almighty (the Most High) revealed (what means): {Come not nigh to the orphan's property except to improve it, until he attains the age of full strength}, [Al-Israa', verse 34] and: {Those who unjustly eat up the property of orphans, eat up a fire into their own bodies: they will soon be enduring a blazing fire}, [An-Nisaa', verse 10], everyone who had an orphan under his guardianship hurried and separated his food and drink from those of the guardian (and his family), and thus, whenever some food was leftover (after the orphan's having his meals), it would be kept until he might eat it later, otherwise it would putrefy. This became hard upon them (the guardians), and they mentioned that to the Prophet [peace and blessings of Allaah be upon him]. Thereupon, Allaah Almighty (the Most High) revealed this Quraanic Ayaah. [Ibn Jareer; Abu Daawood; An-Nasaa'i; Ibn Mardawayh and Al-Haakim]

Verse Number 221

221- And do not marry polytheistic women until they believe. And a believing slave woman is better than a polytheistic (free) woman, even though she (the latter) might please you. And do not marry (your women to) polytheistic men until they believe. And a believing slave is better than a polytheistic (free) man, even though he (the latter) might please you. Those (polytheists) invite (you) to the Fire, but Allaah invites to Paradise and to forgiveness, by His leave. And He makes clear His signs to the people perchance they may remember (Him and receive admonition).

A narration on the authority of Muqaatil that he said: This Quraanic Ayaah was revealed in connection with Abu Marthad Al-Ghanawi: he sought the permission of the Prophet [peace and blessings of Allaah be upon him] to marry 'Anaaq, and she was a polytheist, but endued with a great fortune of beauty. On that occasion, Allaah Almighty (the Most High) revealed (what means): {And a believing slave woman is better than a polytheistic (free) woman, even though she (the latter) might please you}. [Ibn Al-Mundhir; Ibn Abu Haatim and Al-Waahidi]

A narration on the authority of Ibn 'Abbaas [Allaah be pleased with them] that he said: This Quraanic Ayaah was revealed in connection with 'Abdullaah Ibn Rawaahah: he had a black slave woman, and one day, having grown angry with her, slapped her on the face. Having been scared about that, he went to the Prophet [peace and blessings of Allaah be upon him] and told him about it and said: "I am going to emancipate and then marry her", and he did accordingly. He was criticized by some people who said: "Is it fit for him to marry a slave woman?" On that occasion, Allaah Almighty (the Most High) revealed this Quraanic Ayaah. [Al-Waahidi and Ibn Jareer]

Verse Number 222

222- And they ask you about menstruation. Say: "It is harm (and pollution), so keep away from (sexual intercourse with) women during menstruation. And do not approach them (by sexual intercourse) until they are pure. And when they have purified themselves, then have sexual intercourse with them from where Allaah has commanded you. Indeed, Allaah loves these who are constantly repentant and loves those who always purify themselves.

A narration on the authority of Anas [may Allaah be pleased with him] that the habit of the Yahood was if a woman among them menstruated they would not share food nor live with her in the same house. The Companions asked the Prophet [peace and blessings of Allaah be upon him] about that thereupon Allaah Almighty (the Most High) revealed this Quraanic Ayaah.

Commenting on that, the Prophet [peace and blessings of Allaah be upon him] said: "Do everything with her except sexual intercourse". [Muslim and At-Tirmidhi]

Verse Number 223

223- Your women are a tilth for you; so come up to your tilth however you will, and send forward (good deeds) for yourselves; and fear Allaah (by complying with His commands and avoiding His forbiddances), and know that you will meet Him (on the Day of Resurrection so that He would reward you for your deeds). And give (O Muhammad) good tidings (of

Paradise) to the believers (al-Mumineen) (who fear Him).

A narration on the authority of Jaabir [may Allaah be pleased with him] that he said: The Yahood used to say: "If one has sexual intercourse with his wife from the back, then she will deliver a squint-eyed child." So this Ayaah was revealed. [Al-Bukhaari; Muslim; Abu Daawood and others]

A narration on the authority of Ibn 'Abbaas [Allaah be pleased with them] that he said: 'Umar came to the Prophet [peace and blessings of Allaah be upon him] and said: "O Messenger of Allaah! I have mistaken!" He asked him about the reason and 'Umar replied: "Tonight I had sexual intercourse with my wife from her back (rather than from the front)". He gave no reply at once. Later on, Allaah Almighty (the Most High) revealed this Quraanic Ayaah. That is, approach her from front or from the back, but avoid the anus and the time of menses. [Ahmad and At-Tirmidhi]

A narration on the authority of Ibn 'Abbaas [Allaah be pleased with them] that he said: Ibn 'Umar, may Allaah forgive Him, was mistaking. The inhabitants of this town (of Madeenah) from amongst the Ansaar who were idolaters (before Islam) lived side by side with the inhabitants of this city (of Madinah) from amongst the Yahood, who were people of Scripture. The Ansaar thought those (Yahood) had superiority to them with regard to their knowledge, and thus, they used to follow their steps in so many acts. It was the habit of the people of Scripture not to approach women but from the front, (while she was lying on her back) and this is the best state a woman might be in that respect. The inhabitants of this city amongst the Ansaar took this habit from them.

On the other hand, the people of Quraysh used to (approach women from every side as if they were to) slice them very badly, and they took pleasure in them from the front, from the back and as lying. When the Emigrants came to Madinah, one of them got married to a woman from amongst the Ansaar, and went on doing as such with her, but she rejected this act and said: "We used to be approached from the front while lying on our backs. So, you should do so, otherwise you might leave me". Their story was spread, and became known among the people until it reached the Prophet [peace and blessings of Allaah be upon him]. Then Allaah Almighty (the Most High) revealed (what means): {Your women are a tilth for you; so come up to your tilth however you will}, that is from the front, from the back, and as lying, but through the same (opening of the vagina, which leads to uterus), the place of the child. [Abu Daawood and Al-Haakim]

Verse Number 224

224- And do not make (your oath by) Allaah an excuse against being righteous and fearing Allaah and making peace among people. And Allaah is All-Hearing (of all your words), All-Knowing (of all your secrets).

A narration on the authority of Ibn Jurayj that he said: I was told that Allaah's saying (what means): {And do not make (your oath by) Allaah an excuse against being righteous...} was revealed in connection with Abu Bakr [may Allaah be pleased with him] concerning Mistah (Ibn Uthaathah, when he took an oath to not to spend on him after what he had said about 'AA'ishah [Allaah be pleased with her]). [Ibn Jareer]

Verse Number 228

228- And divorced women shall wait (as regards their marriage) for three menstrual periods, and it is not lawful for them to conceal what Allaah has created in their wombs (be it pregnancy or menstruation), if they really believe in Allaah and the Last Day. And their husbands have more right to take them back in that period, if they wish for reconciliation. And they (women) have rights (over their husbands) similar to those (of their husbands) over them according to what is reasonable, but men have a degree (of responsibility) over them. And Allaah is All-Mighty (Whose power extends over all things in His dominion), All-Wise (in all that he does in favor of His creation).

A narration on the authority of Asmaa' Bint Yazeed Ibn As-Sakan Al-Ansaariyyah [Allaah be pleased with her] that she said: During the lifetime of the Prophet [peace and blessings of Allaah be upon him] I was divorced and at that time the divorced woman had no 'Iddah (post-marriage waiting period). Then Allaah prescribed 'Iddah of divorce as revealed in this Quraanic Ayaah. [Abu Daawood and Ibn Abu Haatim]

A narration on the authority of Muqaatil that Isma'eel Ibn 'Abdullaah Al-Ghifaari divorced his wife Qutaylah during the lifetime of the Prophet [peace and blessings of Allaah be upon him], but knew nothing about her pregnancy. When he knew, he took her back (to his wedlock). She gave birth and died and the child also died. On that occasion, this Quraanic Ayaah was revealed. [Ath-Tha'labi]

Verse Number 229

229- (Revocable) divorce is (permissible) twice. Then, either keep (her) in an acceptable manner or release (her) with good treatment. And it is not lawful for you (O husbands in case of divorce) to take anything of (the dowry) that you have given them unless both (spouses) fear that they will not be able to keep (within) the limits of Allaah. But if you fear that they will not keep (within) the limits of Allaah, then there is no blame upon either of them concerning that (money) by which she ransoms herself (for divorce). These are the limits of Allaah, so do not transgress them. And whoever transgresses Allaah's limits - it is those who are the wrongdoers.

A narration on the authority of 'AA'ishah [Allaah be pleased with her] that she said: It was the habit of anyone to divorce his wife as many as he liked and could take her back before the expiration of her 'Iddah even if he divorced her more than one hundred times. A man once said to his wife: "By Allaah, I will neither divorce you with an irrevocable divorce, nor take you to my house". She said: "How is that?" He replied: "I divorce you and whenever your 'Iddah is about to finish I would take you back". The woman went and told the Prophet [peace and blessings of Allaah be upon him] about that, but he gave no reply till the following verse was revealed (what means): {(Revocable) divorce is (permissible) twice. Then, either keep (her) in an acceptable manner or release (her) with good treatment}. [At-Tirmidhi and Al-Haakim]

A narration on the authority of Ibn 'Abbaas [Allaah be pleased with them] that he said: It was the habit of a man to devour his wife's property from the dowry or the gift he had given her seeing no blame on him for this matter. On that occasion, Allaah Almighty (the Most High) revealed (what means): {And it is not lawful for you (O husbands in case of divorce) to take anything of (the dowry) that you have given thcm}. [Abu Daawood]

A narration on the authority of Ibn Jurayj that he said: This Quraanic Ayaah was revealed in connection with Thaabit Ibn Qays and his wife Habeebah. She made a complaint about him to the Prophet [peace and blessings of Allaah be upon him] who asked her: "Will you give him back his garden (so that he would divorce you)?" Therefore, she agreed. He invited him and made a mention of that to him. He said: "Will she do so willingly and gladly?" He declared her approval. So he said: "Then I have done (that is I have divorced her)". [Ibn Jareer]

230- And if he has divorced her (for the third time by which the divorce becomes irrevocable), then she is not lawful for him thereafter until she has married another husband. Then, if the other husband divorces her, it is no sin on both of them (the woman and the former husband) that they reunite (in marriage after the term of her 'Iddah (post-marriage waiting period) is over, provided they think that they can keep the limits ordained by Allaah. These are the limits of Allaah, which He makes plain for the people who have knowledge (by which they could reflect upon the limits and signs of Allaah).

A narration on the authority of Muqaatil Ibn Hayyaan that he said: This Noble Ayaah was revealed in connection with 'A'ishah Bint 'Abd-Ar-Rahmaan Ibn 'Ateek. She was the wife of Rifa'ah Ibn Wahb Ibn 'Ateek, her paternal cousin, before he divorced her irrevocably. After him, she was married to 'Abd-Ar-Rahmaan Ibn Az-Zubayr Al-Qurathi, who also divorced her. She went to the Prophet [peace and blessings of Allaah be upon him] and said: "He had divorced me but before having sexual relation with me. Shall I then return to my former husband (Rifaa'ah)?" He [peace and blessings of Allaah be upon him] replied: "No, till he (your second husband) has sexual relation with you". In connection with her, Allaah revealed this Quraanic Ayaah. [Ibn Al-Mundhir] Verse Number 231

231- When you divorce women, and they almost fulfill their prescribed term (of "Iddah), either take them back on equitable terms or set them free on equitable terms; but do not take them back to harm (or) transgress against them; and if any one does that, He wrongs his own soul (by exposing it to the severe punishment of Allaah). Do not take Allaah's Signs for mockery (by violating them), but solemnly rehearse Allaah's favor (of Islam) on you, and the fact that He sent down to you the Book (Quraan) and Wisdom, thereby to instruct you. And fear Allaah (by acting upon His laws and teachings as it should be), and know that Allaah is well acquainted with all things.

A narration on the authority of Ibn 'Abbaas [Allaah be pleased with them] that he said: It was the habit of a man to divorce his wife and then take her back before her 'Iddah was over, and then divorce her once again and take her back. He used to do so simply to do harm to her and prevent her from marrying others than him. On that occasion, Allaah revealed this Quraanic Ayaah. [Ibn Jareer]

A narration on the authority of As-Suddi that he said: This Quraanic Ayaah was revealed in connection with an Ansaari man called Thaabit Ibn Yasaar who divorced his wife, so he waited for only two or three days before the end of her term, he took her back and then divorced her once again simply to do harm to her. On that, Allaah revealed (what means): {but do not take them back to harm (or) transgress against them}. [Ibn Jareer]

A narration on the authority of Abu Ad-Dardaa' [may Allaah be pleased with him] that he said: A man used to divorce his wife and then say: "I was only jesting", and emancipate his slave and then say: "I was jesting". In this connection, Allaah revealed (what means): {Do not take Allaah's Signs for mockery (by violating them)}. [Ibn Abu 'Umar in his Musnad; and Ibn Mardawayh]

Verse Number 232

232- And when you divorce women and they have fulfilled their term (of 'Iddah), do not prevent them from remarrying their (former) husbands (who have previously divorced them) if they (the women and their former husbands) agree among themselves on an acceptable basis. That instruction is to admonish anyone among you who believes in Allaah and the Last Day. That is better and purer for you, and Allaah knows (What benefits you best and realizes your advantage) and you know not (What benefits you).

A narration on the authority of Ma'qal Ibn Yasaar [may Allaah be pleased with him] that he said: I had a sister, whom many proposed to marry, and when a paternal cousin of mine came and demanded her hand, I gave her in marriage to him but later he divorced her retrievably and left her until her term of 'Iddah elapsed. Then, he felt he had a desire for her and so she is. When many men demanded her hand from me he came and betrothed her from me, the pon told him: "O wicked man! I have honored you by allowing you to marry my sister and then you divorced her. No, by

Allaah, I will never allow you to marry her again". Allaah Almighty, having learnt his desire for her and hers for him, revealed this Quraanic Ayaah. Ma'qal invited him and allowed him again to marry her. [Al-Bukhaari; Abu Daawood; At-Tirmidhi and others]

Verse Number 238

238 Guard strictly the (five obligatory) prayers and (particularly) the middle prayer and stand (in prayer) before Allaah devoutly obedient (without talking to each other).

A narration on the authority of Zayd Ibn Thaabit [may Allaah be pleased with him] that the Prophet [peace and blessings of Allaah be upon him] used to perform Thuhr prayer at noon when it was very hot which was the heaviest time to his Companions. On that, Allaah revealed this Quraanic Ayaah. [Ahmad; Abu Daawood; Al-Bayhaqi and Ibn Jareer]

A narration on the authority of Zayd Ibn Thaabit [may Allaah be pleased with him] that the Prophet [peace and blessings of Allaah be upon him] used to pray Thuhr when it was very hot and no one stood behind him in prayer except a few, in one or two rows, while the others were busy in sleeping and trade. On that occasion, Allaah revealed (what means): {Guard strictly the (five obligatory) prayers and (particularly) the middle prayer}. [Ahmad; An-Nasaa'i and Ibn Jareer]

A narration on the authority of Zayd Ibn Arqam [may Allaah be pleased with him] that he said: In the lifetime of The Prophet [peace and blessings of Allaah be upon him] we used to speak while praying, and one of us would tell his needs to his companions. On that occasion, Allaah revealed (what means): {and stand before Allaah, devoutly obedient}. thus we were commanded to keep silent in prayer and forbidden to talk (to one another) during it. [Al-Bukhaari; Muslim; At-Tirmidhi; Abu Daawood; An-Nasa'i and Ibn Maajah]

Verse Number 240

240- And those who die among you and leave wives behind should make for their wives a bequest of a full year maintenance and residence without turning (them) out. But if they leave (of their own accord), then there is no blame upon you (O deceased's guardians) for what they do with themselves in an acceptable manner. And Allaah is Exalted in Might, Full of Wisdom.

A narration on the authority of Muqaatil Ibn Hayyaan that a man from Taa'if who had male and female children came to Madeenah, in addition to his parents and wife. He died in Madeenah and his case was raised to the Prophet [peace and blessings of Allaah be upon him] who gave his parents and children according to what is equitable and gave nothing to the wife. But they were commanded to spend on her from the property of her husband till a lunar year was over. In connection with him, this Quraanic Ayaah was revealed. [Ishaaq ibn Rahawayh in his Tafsir]

Verse Number 241

241- To divorced women a gift should be given on a reasonable (scale). This is a duty on these who fear Allaah.

A narration on the authority of Ibn Zayd that he said: When Allaah revealed (what means): {but give them (A gift of) compensation, the wealthy according to his means, and the poor according to his means;- A gift of a reasonable amount is due on the doers of good (who always obey Allaah Almighty)}, [Al-Baqarah, verse 236] a man said: "If I like to do a good thing, I will do it; and if I do not like to do so, I will not do it". On that occasion, Allaah revealed this Quraanic Ayaah. [Ibn Jareer]

Verse Number 245

245- Who is it that would loan Allaah a goodly loan so He may multiply it for him many times? And it is Allaah who (by way of testing) withholds (Sustenance from whomever He pleases) and grants (Provision to whomever He wills) in abundance, and to Him you will be returned.

A narration on the authority of Ibn 'Umar [Allaah be pleased with them] that he said: When Allaah revealed (what means): {The example of those who spend their wealth in the way of Allaah is like a seed (of grain) which grows seven spikes...} the Prophet [peace and blessings of Allaah be upon him] said: "O Lord (Rabb)! Give more to my ummah!" On that, Allaah revealed this Quraanic Ayaah. [Ibn Hibbaan; Ibn Abu Haatim and Ibn Mardawayh]

Verse Number 256

256- There is no compulsion in religion. Verily, the Right Path has become distinct from the wrong path. Whoever disbelieves in Taaghoot (devil/false deities) and believes in Allaah, then he has grasped the most trustworthy handhold that will never break.

And Allaah is All-Hearing (of words), All-Knowing (of states and secrets).

A narration on the authority of Ibn 'Abbaas [Allaah be pleased with them] that he said: Whenever there was a woman, for whom no child lived, she would take a vow that if a child lived for her, she would convert him to Judaism. When the tribe of Banu An-Nadir was expelled (from Madinah), from amongst them there were some belonging to the Ansaar, who said: "We should not leave our children (with them)". On that occasion, Allaah Almighty (the Most High) revealed this Quraanic Ayaah. [Abu Daawood; An-Nasaa'i and Ibn Hibbaan]

A narration on the authority of Ibn 'Abbaas [Allaah be pleased with them] that he said: This Quraanic Ayaah was revealed in connection with an Ansaari man from Banu Saalim Ibn 'Awf called Husayn: he had two

Christian children while he was a Muslim. He said to the Prophet [peace and blessings of Allaah be upon him]: "Should I not compel them to embrace Islam? They insist on adopting Christianity". [Ibn Jareer]

Verse Number 257

257- Allaah is the Protecting Guardian of those who believe: He brings them out from the depths of darkness (that is disbelief) into light (that is belief). But as for those who disbelieve, their protectors are Taaghoot (devils/false deities): they bring them out from light into the depths of darkness. Those are the dwellers of the Fire therein they will abide forever.

A narration on the authority of 'Abdah Ibn Abu Lubaabah that he said: Those who believe in this Quraanic Ayaah are the people who believed in Jesus [peace and blessings of Allaah be upon him], and when Muhammad [peace and blessings of Allaah be upon him] came as a Prophet they believed in him. In connection with them, this Quraanic Ayaah was revealed. [Ibn Jareer]

A narration on the authority of Mujaahid that he said: Some people believed in Jesus [peace and blessings of Allaah be upon him] and others disbelieved in him. When Muhammad [peace and blessings of Allaah be upon him] was sent as a Prophet those who disbelieved in Jesus believed in him, and those who believed in Jesus disbelieved in him. On that occasion, Allaah revealed this Quraanic Ayaah. [Ibn Jareer]

267- O you who believe! Spend (in charity) of the good things which you have (legally) earned, and of (the good things) that We have produced for you from the earth, and do not aim at that which is bad to spend from it, (though) you would not accept it save with disdain (and closed eyes). And know that Allaah is Free of want, Praiseworthy.

A narration on the authority of Al-Baraa' Ibn 'AAzib [may Allaah be pleased with him] that he said: This Quraanic Ayaah was revealed with regard to us, the community of Ansaar. We had date-palms and anyone of us brought from his fruits in accordance with the quantity he possessed. But anyone of those who had no desire for good, brought the bad fruits of inferior quality and hang that (in the pillars of the masjid). On that occasion, Allaah revealed (what means): {O you who believe! Spend (in charity) of the good things which you have (legally) earned, and of (the good things) that We have produced for you from the earth}. [Al-Haakim; At-Tirmidhi and Ibn Maajah]

A narration on the authority of Sahl Ibn Hunayf [may Allaah be pleased with him] that he said: The people aimed at the worst of their fruits to give in charity. On that occasion, Allaah revealed (what means): {and do not aim at that which is bad to spend from it, (though) you would not accept it save with disdain (and closed eyes)....} [Abu Daawood; An-Nasa'i and Al-Haakim]

A narration on the authority of Jaabir [may Allaah be pleased with him] that he said: the Prophet [peace and blessings of Allaah be upon him] commanded that Zakaat Al-Fitr should be given as a Saa of dates. A man brought very bad dates, thereupon Allaah revealed this Quraanic Ayaah. [Al-Haakim]

A narration on the authority of Ibn 'Abbaas [Allaah be pleased with them] that he said: The Companions of the Prophet [peace and blessings of Allaah be upon him] used to buy the cheap foodstuff and give it in charity. On that, Allaah revealed this Quraanic Ayaah. [Ibn Abu Haatim]

Verse Number 272

272- It is not your duty (O Muhammad) to guide them, but Allaah guides whom He wills. And whatever good you (believers (al-Mumineen)) spend is for your benefit (since its reward is for you only) given that you spend only seeking the countenance of Allaah. And whatever you spend of good - it will be repaid to you in full, and you will not be wronged.

A narration on the authority of Ibn 'Abbaas [Allaah be pleased with them] that he said: They disliked to give their relatives from among the polytheists. They asked about that and a concession was given to them in this respect. On that occasion, Allaah Almighty (the Most High) revealed this Quraanic Ayaah. [An-Nasaa'i; Al-Haakim; Al-Bazzaar; At-Tabaraani and others]

A narration on the authority of Ibn 'Abbaas [Allaah be pleased with them] that the Prophet [peace and blessings of Allaah be upon him] ordered that charity shall be given to the Muslims only. In this connection, Allaah revealed this Quraanic Ayaah, thereupon he [peace and blessings of Allaah be upon him] commanded that charity shall be given to anyone who asked for it regardless of his/her religion. [Ibn Abu Haatim]

Verse Number 274

274- Those who spend their wealth (in Allaah's Cause) by night and day, in secret and in public, they shall have their reward with their Lord (Rabb). On them shall be no fear, nor shall they grieve. A narration on the authority of Ibn 'Abbaas [Allaah be pleased with them] that he said: This Quraanic Ayaah was revealed in connection with 'Ali Ibn Abu Taalib [may Allaah be pleased with him]: He had four Dirhams of which he spent (in charity for Allaah's cause) a Dirham at night, a Dirham by the day, a Dirham in secret and a Dirham in public. ['Abd-Ar-Razzaaq; Ibn Jareer; Ibn Abu Haatim and At-Tabaraani with a weak Isnaad]

A narration on the authority of Ibn Al-Musayyab that he said: This Quraanic Ayaah was revealed in connection with 'Uthmaan Ibn 'Affaan and 'Abd-Ar-Rahmaan Ibn 'Awf [Allaah be pleased with them] with regard to their spending in the Army of Difficulty (which was prepared for the battle of Tabook). [Ibn Al-Mundhir]

Verse Number 278-279

278- O you who believe! Fear Allaah and give up what remains (due to you) from Riba if you are (really) believers (al-Mumineen). 279- And if you do not do so, then take notice of a war (against you) from Allaah and His Messenger. But if you repent, you may have the capital of your riches, (thus) you will not wrong (your debtors by asking for more than your capital), nor will you be wronged (by taking less than your capital).

A narration on the authority of Ibn 'Abbaas [Allaah be pleased with them] that he said: We have been informed that this Quraanic Ayaah was revealed in connection with Banu 'Amr Ibn 'Awf from Thaqif and Banu Al-Mugheerah. Banu Al-Mugheerah used to lend money with interest (Riba) to Thaqeef. When Allaah made His Messenger [peace and blessings of Allaah be upon him] conquer Makkah, the whole Riba was cancelled out. Banu 'Amr and Banu Al-Mugheerah went to 'Attaab Ibn Aseed, who was the governor of Makkah at that time and told him: "No doubt, Riba has made us the most wretched of people; and it has been cancelled out by others". Banu 'Amr said: "Our case has been settled on condition that we should take our Riba (from them)". "Attaab sent a message about that to the Prophet [peace and blessings of Allaah be upon him]. On that, those Quraanic Aayaat were revealed. [Abu Ya'la in his Musnad]

Verse Number 285-286

285- The Messenger (Muhammad) believes in (the Quraan) that has been sent down to him from his Lord (Rabb), and (so do) the believers (al-Mumineen). Each one believes in Allaah, His Angels, His Books, and His Messengers. They say: "We make no distinction between one another of His Messengers". And they say: "We hearken (and accept Your commands) and obey (You). (We seek) Your Forgiveness, our Lord (Rabb), and to You is the return (of all things)". 286- Allaah does not lay upon a soul (a burden) beyond its capacity. It will have (the reward of) what (good) it has gained, and it will bear (the sin of) what (evil) it has earned. (Say): "Our Lord (Rabb), do not punish us if we forget or err. Our Lord (Rabb), and lay not upon us a burden like that which You laid upon those before us. Our Lord (Rabb), and burden us not with (obligations and assignments) that we have no power to bear. And pardon us; and forgive us; and have mercy upon us. You are our protector, so give us victory over the disbelieving people.

A narration on the authority of Abu Hurayrah [may Allaah be pleased with him] that he said: When the following was revealed unto the Prophet [peace and blessings of Allaah be upon him]: {To Allaah belongs all that is in the heavens and all that is on earth, and whether you disclose what is in your own selves or conceal it, Allaah will call you to account for it}, [Al-Baqarah, verse 284] the Companions felt it hard and severe and they came to the Prophet [peace and blessings of Allaah be upon him] and sat down on their knees and said: "O Messenger of Allaah! We have been obligated duties which are within our capacity to perform, such as prayer, fasting, Jihaad, charity and so forth. Then this (the above mentioned) Ayaah was revealed to you and it is beyond our power to live up to it".

On that, the Prophet [peace and blessings of Allaah be upon him] said: "Do you want to say what the people of the two Scriptures (Yahood and Nasaara) said before you: 'We hear and disobey'? You should rather say: 'We hear and we obey, we seek forgiveness, our Lord (Rabb), and to You is the final return". They said it and when they went on reciting it and it smoothly flowed on their tongues, Allaah revealed immediately afterwards (what means): {The Messenger (Muhammad) believes in what has been sent down to him from his Lord (Rabb), and (so do) the believers (al-Mumineen). Each one believes in Allaah, His Angels, His Books, and His Messengers. (They say), "We make no distinction between one another of His Messengers", and they say, "We harken (and accept the commands), and we obey. (We seek) Your forgiveness, our Lord (Rabb), and to You is the final return (of all things)}. When they did that, Allaah abrogated (the ruling of) this (Ayaah mentioned above that is 284) and revealed (what means): {Allaah does not lay upon a soul (a burden) beyond its capacity. It will have (the reward of) what (good) it has gained, and it will bear (the sin of) what (evil) it has earned. ...} [Muslim; Ahmad and others]

Soorah AAl 'Imraan

A narration on the authority of Ar-Rabee' that the Nasaara came to the Prophet [peace and blessings of Allaah be upon him] and disputed with him over Jesus [peace and blessings of Allaah be upon him]. On that, Allaah Almighty (the Most High) revealed (what means): {Alif, Laam, Meem. Allaah - there is no deity except Him, the Ever-Living, the Sustainer of existence...} up to over the eightieth Ayaah of the Soorah. [Ibn Abu Haatim]

A narration on the authority of Muhammad Ibn Sahl Ibn Abu Umaamah that he said: When the Nasaara of Najraan came to the Prophet [peace and blessings of Allaah be upon him] to ask him about Jesus, son of Mary, the opening of AAl 'Imraan was revealed up to some Aayaat over eighty. [Al-Bayhaqi in Ad-Dalaa'il]

Verse Number 12

12- Say (O Muhammad) to those (Yahood) who disbelieve: "You will be defeated and gathered together to Hell, and worst indeed is that place to rest."

A narration on the authority of Ibn 'Abbaas [Allaah be pleased with them] that he said: When the Quraysh pagans were smitten by the Muslims with the help of Allaah Almighty (the Most High) on the day of (the battle of) Badr, the Prophet [peace and blessings of Allaah be upon him] gathered the Yahood of Banu Qaynuqaa' in the market of Madeenah and told them:

"O assembly of Yahood! Embrace Islam before Allaah Almighty (the Most High) dooms you to the same destiny as that of the Quraysh". They told him challengingly: "O Muhammad! Do not deceive yourself by the fact that you have killed a group of the Quraysh who were inexperienced and unskilled in war. Were you to fight us, you would come to know that we are really the people (who are adamant in fighting), and you would never meet the like of us". On that occasion, Allaah Almighty (the Most High) revealed this Quraanic Ayaah. [Abu Daawood and Al-Bayhaqi in Ad-Dalaa'il]

Verse Number 23

23- Have you not seen those (that is Yahood) who have been given a portion of the Scripture (the Torah)? They are being invited to the Book of Allaah to settle their dispute, then a party of them turn away, and they are averse.

A narration on the authority of Ibn 'Abbaas [Allaah be pleased with them] that he said: the Prophet [peace and blessings of Allaah be upon him] entered Bayt Al-Midraas where there were a group of Yahood, whom he invited to Allaah Almighty. An-Nu'maan Ibn 'Amr and Al-Haarith Ibn Zayd asked him: "Which religion do you adopt O Muhammad?" the Prophet [peace and blessings of Allaah be upon him] replied: "The religion of Abraham". They said: "Abraham then was a Jew". the Prophet [peace and blessings of Allaah be upon him] told them: "Then, let us appeal for the Torah to judge between us". But they rejected. On that occasion,

Allaah revealed this Quraanic Ayaah. [Ibn Abu Haatim and Ibn Al-Mundhir]

Verse Number 26

26- Say (O Muhammad): "O Allaah, possessor of dominion, You give dominion to whom You will, and You take dominion from whom You will, and You endue with honor whom You will, and You humiliate whom You will. In Your Hand is the good. Verily, You have the power to do all things.

A narration on the authority of Qataadah that he said: It was mentioned to us that the Prophet [peace and blessings of Allaah be upon him] asked his Lord (Rabb) to make the dominion of Byzantines and Persians in his ummah. On that occasion, Allaah revealed this Quraanic Ayaah. [Ibn Abu Haatim]

Verse Number 28

28- Let not the believers (al-Mumineen) take the disbelievers (al-Kaafireen) as allies instead of the believers (al-Mumineen), and whoever does so will never be helped by Allaah in any way, except if you indeed fear a danger from them. And Allaah warns you against Himself, and to Allaah is the final return.

A narration on the authority of Ibn 'Abbaas [Allaah be pleased with them] that he said: Al-Hajjaaj Ibn 'Amr was an ally of Ka'b Ibn Al-Ashraf, Ibn Abu Al-Huqayq, and Qays Ibn Zayd. They considered as intimate friends a group of Ansaar to turn them from their religion. Rifa'ah Ibn Al-Mundhir, 'Abdullaah Ibn Jubayr and Sa'd Ibn Hathmah told them: "Avoid those Yahood and beware of being intimate friends with them lest they would turn you from your religion". But they rejected. In connection with them, Allaah Almighty (the Most High) revealed this Quraanic Ayaah. [Ibn Jareer]

Verse Number 31

31- Say (O Muhammad): "If you (really) love Allaah then follow me, so that Allaah will love you and forgive you your sins. And Allaah is Oft-Forgiving, Most Merciful."

A narration on the authority of Al-Hasan that he said: During the lifetime of our Prophet [peace and blessings of Allaah be upon him], some people (from among the Yahood) said: "By Allaah, O Muhammad, we love our Lord (Rabb)". On that occasion, Allaah Almighty (the Most High) revealed this Quraanic Ayaah. [Ibn Al-Mundhir]

Verse Number 58

58- This (story of Jesus) is what We recite to you (O Muhammad) of the Aayaat and the Wise message (that is the Quraan). A narration on the authority of Al-Hasan that he said: The two monks of Najraan went to the Prophet [peace and blessings of Allaah be upon him] and one of them said: "Who is the father of Jesus?" It was the habit of the Prophet [peace and blessings of Allaah be upon him] not to give a hasty reply till he was commanded by his Lord (Rabb). On that occasion, this Quraanic Ayaah was revealed. [Ibn Abu Haatim]

Verse Number 59-62

59- Verily, the example of Jesus in the sight of Allaah is like that of AAdam. He created him from dust, then said to him: "Be!" - and he was. 60- (This (affair of Jesus [peace and blessings of Allaah be upon him] is) the truth from your Lord (Rabb), so be not of those who doubt. 61- Then whoever (of the Nasaara) disputes with you concerning him (Jesus) after (all this) knowledge that has come to you, say (O Muhammad): "Come, let us call our sons and your sons, our women and your women, ourselves and yourselves then we pray and invoke (sincerely) the Curse of Allaah upon those who lie." 62- Verily! This is the true narrative (about Jesus): there is none worthy of worship but Allaah. Indeed, Allaah is Exalted in might, Full of wisdom. -

A narration on the authority of Ibn 'Abbaas [Allaah be pleased with them] that he said: A group of Najraan including As-Sayyid and Al-'AAqib, came to the Prophet [peace and blessings of Allaah be upon him]. They said: "What is the matter with you that you make a mention of our companion?" He replied: "Who is it?" They said: "Jesus: you claim he is the slave of Allaah".

He said: "Yes". They asked him: "Have you seen or been informed about the like of Jesus?" They then left him and Jibreel [peace and blessings of Allaah be upon him] came to him and said: "Tell them, if they come to you, that {Verily, the example of Jesus in the sight of Allaah is like that of Adam} [Ibn Abu Haatim].

A narration on the authority of Maslamah Ibn 'Abd Yashoo' from his father, from his grandfather that the Prophet [peace and blessings of Allaah be upon him] sent to the people of Najraan before Soorah An-Naml was revealed to him: "In the Name of the God of Abraham, Isaac, Jacob. From Muhammad, the Prophet..." They sent him Sharhabeel Ibn Wadaa'ah Al-Hamdaani, 'Abdullaah Ibn Sharhabeel Al-Asbahi and Jabbaar Al-Harthi. They came to him and exchanged questions with him. They asked him: "What do you say about Jesus?" He replied: "I have nothing to say about him this day. So, wait till I tell you". When it was the morning of the coming day, Allaah revealed those Quraanic Aayaat. [Al-Bayhaqi in Ad-Dalaa'il]

A narration on the authority of Al-Azraq Ibn Qays that he said: The bishop of Najraan along with Al-'AAqib came to the Prophet [peace and blessings of Allaah be upon him], to propose them to embrace Islam. They said: "We were Muslims before you (have been sent as a Prophet)". He said: "You have told a lie. Three things have prevented you from embracing Islam: your claim that Allaah Almighty (the Most High) has taken a son [Exalted be Allaah far above what they ascribe to Him]; your eating the flesh of the swine and your prostration to the idol".

They said: "Who is the father of Jesus?" the Prophet [peace and blessings of Allaah be upon him] gave no reply till Allaah Almighty (the Most High) revealed those Quraanic Aayaat.

He invited them to invoke Allaah's curse upon the liar of them but they rejected and accepted to give the Jizyah and then returned home. [Ibn Sa'd in At-Tabaqaat]

Verse Number 65

65- O people of the Scripture (Yahood and Nasaara)! Why do you dispute about Abraham, while the Torah and the Gospel were not revealed till after him? Have you then no sense (To the fallacy of your argument and the falsehood of your statement)?

A narration on the authority of Ibn 'Abbaas [Allaah be pleased with them] that the Jewish rabbis and the Christian bishops of Najraan who gathered with the Prophet [peace and blessings of Allaah be upon him] disputed with each other over Abraham [peace and blessings of Allaah be upon him]. The Jewish rabbis said: "Abraham was but a Jew".

The Christian bishops of Najraan said: "No, Abraham was but a Christian". On that occasion, Allaah Almighty (the Most High) revealed this Quraanic Ayaah. [Ibn Ishaaq and Al-Bayhaqi in Ad-Dalaa'il]
Verse Number 71-73

71- O people of the Scripture! Why do you mix truth with falsehood and conceal the truth (About the Prophethood of Muhammad [peace and blessings of Allaah be upon him]) while you know (it with full certainty)? 72- And a party of the people of the Scripture (Yahood) say (to each other): "Believe in the morning in (the Quraan) that is revealed to the believers (al-Mumineen) (Muslims), and disbelieve in it at the end of the day, so that they may turn back. 73- And believe none but him who follows your religion". Say (O Muhammad): "Verily! The right guidance is the Guidance of Allaah." (They say): "and do not believe that anyone can receive like that which you have received (of Revelation) except when he follows your religion, otherwise they would engage you in argument before your Lord (Rabb)". Say (O Muhammad): "All the bounty is in the Hand of Allaah; He grants it to whom He wills. And Allaah is All-Embracing (in sufficiency for the needs of His servants), All-Knowing (of who among them deserves His bounty)."

A narration on the authority of Ibn 'Abbaas [Allaah be pleased with them] that he said: 'Abdullaah Ibn Sayfi, 'Adiyy Ibn Sayfi and Al-Haarith Ibn 'Awf said to each other: "Let us believe in what was revealed to Muhammad and his Companions in the morning, and disbelieve in it in the evening, in order that we would put them to confusion about their religion, perchance they would do the like of what we do, and revert from his religion". On that occasion, Allaah Almighty (the Most High) revealed (what means): {O you People of the Scripture! why do you mix Truth with falsehood, and conceal the Truth...?} [Ibn Ishaaq]

A narration on the authority of Abu Maalik that he said: The rabbis of the Yahood used to say to the laymen among them: "Believe only those who follow your religion". On that occasion, Allaah Almighty (the Most High) revealed (what means): {Say (O Muhammad): "Verily! The right guidance is the Guidance of Allaah."...} [Ibn Abu Haatim]

Verse Number 77

77- Verily, those who purchase a small gain at the cost of Allaah's Covenant and their oaths, they shall have no portion in the Hereafter, nor will Allaah speak to them (out of His anger with them), nor look at them (with the eye of mercy) on the Day of Resurrection, nor will He purify them, and they shall have a painful torment.

A narration on the authority of 'Abdullaah Ibn Mas'ood [may Allaah be pleased with him] that he said: the Prophet [peace and blessings of Allaah be upon him] said: "Whoever takes a false oath so as to take the property of a Muslim (illegally) will meet Allaah while He will be angry with him." Al-Ash'ath said: "By Allaah, that saying concerned me. I had a common land with a Jew but the Jew later on denied my ownership, so I took him to The Prophet [peace and blessings of Allaah be upon him] who asked me whether I had a proof of my ownership. When I replied in the negative, The Prophet [peace and blessings of Allaah be upon him] asked the Jew to take an oath. I said: "O Allaah's Apostle! He will take an oath and deprive me of my property." So, Allaah revealed this Quraanic verse. [Al-Bukhaari; Muslim and others]

A narration on the authority of 'Abdullaah Ibn Abu Awfa [may Allaah be pleased with him] that he said: A man displayed some goods in the market and swore by Allaah that he had been offered so much for that, that which was not offered, and he said so in order to cheat a Muslim. On that occasion, this Quraanic Ayaah was revealed. [Al-Bukhaari]

Commenting on it, Al-Haafith Ibn Hajar says in his Fath: "There is no contradiction between both Hadeeths because this Ayaah may, probably, have been sent down on the two occasions".

A narration on the authority of 'Ikrimah that he said: This Quraanic Ayaah was revealed in connection with Huyayy Ibn Akhtab and Ka'b Ibn Al-Ashraf and others from among the Yahood who concealed what Allaah revealed in the Torah and changed it and swore that it is from Allaah. [Ibn Jareer]

Commenting on that, Al-Haafith Ibn Hajar says that although the Ayaah may reveal this meaning, what is fundamental in this issue is that which has been proven in the authentic narrations (of Al-Bukhaari and Muslim).

Verse Number 79

79- It is not (fit) for any human being to whom Allaah has given the Book and authority to say to the people:

"Be my worshippers rather than Allaah's." On the contrary (he would say): "Be you pious scholars of the Lord (Rabb) because of what you teach and act upon your knowledge of the Book, and because of what you study."

A narration on the authority of Ibn 'Abbaas [Allaah be pleased with them] that he said: During the meeting of the Jewish rabbis and Christian bishops of Najraan with the Prophet [peace and blessings of Allaah be upon him], who invited them to Islam, Abu Raafi' Al-Qurathi said: "Do you like us, O Muhammad, to worship you just as the Nasaara worship Jesus, son of Mary?" A Christian from the delegate of Najraan called Ar-Rayyis or Ar-Ra'ees, said: "is it that which you want from us, O Muhammad, and invite us to?" the Prophet [peace and blessings of Allaah be upon him] replied: "Allaah forbid that I should worship anyone other than Allaah, or command anyone to worship others beside Him. It is not with this that Allaah sent or commanded me to do". On that occasion, Allaah Almighty (the Most High) revealed this Quraanic Ayaah. [Ibn Ishaaq and Al-Bayhaqi]

A narration on the authority of Al-Hasan that he said: I was informed that a man said: "O Messenger of Allaah! We greet you in the same way as we greet one another: should we not prostrate ourselves to you?" He said: "No, but you should rather honor your Prophet and recognize the right to those liable for it. It is not fit for people to prostrate themselves to anyone other than Allaah". On that occasion, Allaah revealed this Quraanic Ayaah. ['Abd-Ar-Razzaaq in his Tafseer]

86- How shall Allaah guide a people who disbelieved after their belief and after they testified that the Messenger (Muhammad) is true and after clear proofs had come unto them? And Allaah guides not the wrongdoing (disbelieving) people.

A narration on the authority of Ibn 'Abbaas [Allaah be pleased with them] that he said: An Ansaari man embraced Islam and then renegaded and showed regret for what he did. He sent a message to his people who sent to ask the Prophet [peace and blessings of Allaah be upon him], whether his repentance would be accepted if he repented. On that occasion, Allaah revealed this Quraanic Ayaah. His people sent that to him, thereupon he reverted to Islam. [An-Nasaa'i; Ibn Hibbaan and Al-Haakim]

A narration on the authority of Mujaahid that he said: Al-Haarith Ibn Suwayd came and embraced Islam with the Prophet [peace and blessings of Allaah be upon him]. But later he disbelieved and returned to his people. In connection with him, Allaah revealed this Quraanic Ayaah. A man from his people came to him and recited it to him. Al-Haarith said: "By Allaah, to the best of my knowledge, you are truthful; and the Prophet [peace and blessings of Allaah be upon him] is more truthful than you; and Allaah is the most truthful of them all". Then he reverted to Islam and was good in faith. [Musaddad in his Musnad; and 'Abd-Ar-Razzaaq].

Verse Number 97

97- In it are manifest signs (such as) the standing place of Abraham; and whosoever enters it shall be safe. And due to Allaah on mankind is Hajj (pilgrimage) to the House (Ka'bah), for whoever is able to find thereto a way; and whoever disbelieves, then indeed, Allaah is not in need of the worlds.

A narration on the authority of "Ikrimah that he said: When Allaah revealed (what means): {And whoever desires other than Islam as religion – never will it be accepted from him…}. [Al Imran, verse 85] the Yahood said: "Then, we are Muslims". the Prophet [peace and blessings of Allaah be upon him] said: "Verily, Allaah has enjoined upon the Muslims to perform Hajj to the House (that is the Ka'bah)". They said: "But it has not been decreed for us". They refused to perform Hajj. On that occasion, Allaah revealed (what means): {and whoever disbelieves, then indeed, Allaah is not in need of the worlds}. [Sa'eed Ibn Mansoor]

Verse Number 99-102

99- Say: "O people of the Scripture! Why do you avert those who have believed from the Path of Allaah, seeking to make it (the path) seem crooked, while you (yourselves) are witnesses (to the truth)? And Allaah is not unaware of what you do." 100- O you who believe! If you obey a group of those who were given the Scripture (Yahood and Nasaara), they would (indeed) render you disbelievers (al-Kaafireen) after you have believed! 101- And how would you disbelieve, while to you are recited Allaah's Aayaat, and among you is His Messenger (Muhammad)? And whoever holds firmly to Allaah, then he has indeed been guided to the Right Path. 102- O you who believe! Fear Allaah as He should be feared and die not except in a state of Islam (monotheists).

A narration on the authority of Ibn 'Abbaas [Allaah be pleased with them] that he said: During the pre-Islamic days, there were disputes between the Aws and Khazraj. (After they embraced Islam and) while they were sitting, they made a mention of the disputes which were between them to the extent that they grew angry and stood and raised the weapons against each other. On that occasio those Quraanic Aayaat were revealed. [Al-Firyaabi and Ibn Abu Haatim]

A narration on the authority of Zayd Ibn Aslam that he said: Shaas Ibn Qays, a very old man who despised and envied Muslims, passed by a group of the Companions of the Prophet [peace and blessings of Allaah be upon him] from Aws and Khazraj while they were talking. He was infuriated by their intimacy and unity and their agreement after their wars during the pre-Islamic days of Jaahiliyyah. He said: "Banu Qaylah (Aws and Khazraj) became united on this land. By Allaah, we will not be able to stay with them if they became united". He ordered a young man from the Yahood to sit with them and commanded him saying: "Go, sit with them and then mention the Day of Bu'aath and what was before it and let them hear some of the poems that they used to recite on that occasion". The Jewish young man did so. At this point, the people (of Aws and Khazraj) talked, disputed, contended and boasted over each other until two men: one from Aws, Aws Ibn Qaythi from Banu Haarithah Ibn Al-Haarith, and the other from Khazraj, Jabbaar Ibn Sakhr, quarreled. When the news of that reached the Prophet [peace and blessings of Allaah be upon him], he went to them in the company of a group of Muhaajiroon and instructed them. Realized that, it was incitement from Satan and a scheme from their enemy, the people cried, hugged each other and then departed while obeying the Prophet [peace and blessings of Allaah be upon him]. Allaah revealed in connection with Aws Ibn Qaythi and Jabbaar Ibn

Sakhr (what means): {O you who believe! If you obey a group of those who were given the Scripture (Yahood and Nasaara), they would (indeed) render you disbelievers (al-Kaafireen) after you have believed!} [verse 100] In connection with Shaas Ibn Qays Allaah revealed (what means): {Say: "O people of the Scripture! Why do you avert those who have believed from the Path of Allaah, seeking to make it (the path) seem crooked, while you (yourselves) are witnesses (to the truth)?"} [verse 99]

Verse Number 113

113- Not all of them (the people of Scripture) are alike; a party of the people of the Scripture stand for the right, and recite the Aayaat of Allaah during the hours of the night, prostrating themselves in prayer.

A narration on the authority of Ibn 'Abbaas [Allaah be pleased with them] that he said: When 'Abdullaah Ibn Salaam, Tha'labah Ibn Sa'yah, Usayd Ibn Tha'labah and Asad Ibn 'Abd embraced Islam along with those of Yahood who believed, and had a desire for Islam, the rabbis and disbelievers (al-Kaafireen) among Yahood said: "None believed in Muhammad but the worst among us; and had they been the best among us they would not have left the religion of their fathers for another". On that occasion, Allaah revealed this Quraanic Ayaah. [Ibn Abu Haatim and At-Tabaraani]

A narration on the authority of Ibn Mas'ood [may Allaah be pleased with him] that he said: One night the Prophet [peace and blessings of Allaah be upon him] delayed the 'Ishaa' prayer for some time after which he came out to the masjid and behold! The people were waiting the prayer. On that he said: "Verily, none among the men of all religions (on the surface of the earth) remembers Allaah at this hour other than you". In this connection, this Quraanic Ayaah were revealed. [Ahmad and others]

Verse Number 118

118- O you who believe! Take not as intimates those outside your religion since they will not fail to do their best to corrupt you. They desire you are in severe hardship. Hatred has already appeared from their mouths, but what their breasts conceal (of your enmity) is far worse. Indeed We have clarified to you the signs (of their hostility toward you) if you understand.

A narration on the authority of Ibn 'Abbaas [Allaah be pleased with them] that he said: some men from amongst the Muslims contacted men from amongst the Yahood due to the mutual rights of protection and alliance between them. Allaah forbade the Muslims to take them as intimate friends when He revealed this Quraanic Ayaah. [Ibn Jareer and Ibn Ishaaq]

Verse Number 121

121- And (remember O Muhammad) when you left your household in the morning to post the believers (al-Mumineen) at their stations for the battle (of Uhud). And Allaah is All-Hearer (of your words), All-Knower (of your states).

A narration on the authority of Al-Miswar Ibn Makhramah [may Allaah be pleased with him] that he said: I asked 'Abd-Ar-Rahmaan Ibn 'Awf about their story on the day of Uhud (battle). He said: "Recite, if you so like, from 121 of AAl 'Imraan, therein you would find our story.

{And (remember) when two parties among you were about to lose courage} [verse 122] refers to those who sought security from the polytheists.

{So if he was to die or be killed, would you turn back on your heels (to disbelief)} [verse 144] refers to the cry of Satan: "Muhammad was killed". [Ibn Abu Haatim and Ibn Abu Ya'li]

Verse Number 122

122- and (remember) when two parties among you were about to lose courage, but Allaah was their Supporter and Protector. And in Allaah (Alone) let the believers (al-Mumineen) put their trust.

A narration on the authority of Jaabir [may Allaah be pleased with him] that he said: It is in connection with us, Banu Salamah and Banu Haarithah, that Allaah Almighty (the Most High) revealed (what means): {And (remember) when two parties among you were about to lose courage}. [Al-Bukhaari and Muslim]

Verse Number 124

124- (Remember O Muhammad) when you said to the believers (al-Mumineen) (by way of promising and reassuring them): "Is it not enough for you that your Lord (Rabb) (Allaah) should help you with three thousand angels sent down?"

A narration on the authority of Ash-Sha'bi that on the day of the battle of Badr, the Muslims were informed that Karz Ibn Jaabir AlMuhaaribi was providing the polytheists with forces, thereupon it was difficult on them. On that occasion, Allaah revealed this Quraanic Ayaah. So, when the news of defeat reached Karz he did not send supplies to the polytheists, and, consequently, the Muslims did not receive the supplies of five thousand (angels). [Ibn Abu Shaybah in Al-Musannaf; and Ibn Abu Haatim]

Verse Number 128

128-Not for you (O Muhammad but for Allaah) is the decision; whether He turns in mercy to them or punishes them; verily, they are wrongdoers (by their disbelief).

A narration on the authority of Anas [may Allaah be pleased with him] that he said: On the day of Uhud the canine tooth of the Prophet [peace and blessings of Allaah be upon him] was broken and his face was injured so much that blood flowed on his face. He said: "How should a people prosper who have done this (harm) to their Prophet while he was inviting them to their Lord (Rabb)?" On that occasion, Allaah Almighty (the Most High) revealed this Quraanic Ayaah. [Muslim and Ahmad]

A narration on the authority of Ibn 'Umar and Abu Hurayrah [Allaah be pleased with them] that they said: I heard the Prophet [peace and blessings of Allaah be upon him] having said: "O Allaah! Curse so and so! O Allaah! Curse Al-Haarith Ibn Hishaam! O Allaah! Curse Suhayl Ibn 'Amr! O Allaah! Curse Safwaan Ibn Umayyah!" In this connection, Allaah revealed this Quraanic Ayaah. Consequently, all of those repented (and embraced Islam) and their repentance was accepted (by Allaah). [Ahmad and Al-Bukhaari]

Commenting on that Ibn Hajar says: Those two Hadeeths may be combined by the fact that he [peace and blessings of Allaah be upon him] invoked curse upon those men in his prayer after he had been afflicted in the battle; and thus the Quraanic Ayaah was revealed in connection with both events: that is what afflicted him and the invocation of evil against him afterwards.

But even, it is narrated by Muslim on the authority of Abu Hurayrah [may Allaah be pleased with him] that he [peace and blessings of Allaah be upon him] said in Fajr prayer: "O Allaah! Curse Ra'l, Dhakwaan and 'Usayyah", till Allaah revealed unto him this Quraanic Ayaah.

The problem here lies in the fact that this Quraanic Ayaah was revealed in connection with the story of Uhud whereas the story of Ra'l and Dhakwaan took place after it. However, the event of Ra'l might, probably, have happened a short time after the battle of Uhud and the Quraanic Ayaah was sent down after both events.

Verse Number 130

130- O you who believe! Eat not Ribaa (usury) doubled and multiplied, but fear Allaah (by avoiding it) that you may prosper. A narration on the authority of Mujaahid that he said: They used to buy and sell on credit to a specific term; and once it came they would prolong the term in return for increasing the interest. On that occasion, Allaah Almighty (the Most High) revealed that Quraanic Ayaah. [Al-Firyaabi]

A narration on the authority of 'Ataa' that he said: Thaqif (of Taa'if) used to lend money to Banu An-

Nadeer to a specific term during the pre-Islamic days; and if the term came they would say to them: "Should we give you usury and you postpone the time of payment for us?" On that occasion, Allaah revealed that Quraanic Ayaah. [Al-Firyaabi]

Verse Number 140

140- If a wound has touched you (in Uhud), be sure a similar wound had (already) touched the others (in Badr). And so the days (of varying conditions), We alternate between men by turns, in order that Allaah may make evident those who believe, and take (to Himself) witnesses (or martyrs) from among you. And Allaah likes not the wrongdoers.

A narration on the authority of 'Ikrimah that he said: When the news (of the Uhud battle) was too slow to reach the women, they came out and behold! Two men riding a camel appeared. A woman said: "What has happened to the Prophet [peace and blessings of Allaah be upon him]?" One of them said: "He is still living". She said: "Then, I am careless that Allaah should take witnesses/martyrs from among His servants". The Quraan was revealed in agreement with this sentence (what means): {and take (to Himself) witnesses (or martyrs) from among you}. [Ibn Abu Haatim] Verse Number 143

143- You did indeed wish for death (through martyrdom) before you met it. Now you have seen it openly with your own eyes.

A narration on the authority of Ibn 'Abbaas [Allaah be pleased with them] that some Companions said: "Would that we should be killed as Badr warriors were killed; or would that we should have a day like the day of Badr to fight the polytheists, and do good on it or seek to attain martyrdom and Paradise, or life and provisions". Then Allaah made them attend Uhud (battle), thereupon they did not remain steadfast except such of them as Allaah willed. On that occasion, Allaah revealed this Quraanic Ayaah. [Ibn Abu Haatim]

Verse Number 144

144- Muhammad is no more than a Messenger, and indeed (many) Messengers have passed away before him. If he dies or is killed, will you then turn back on your heels (as disbelievers (al-Kaafireen))? And he who turns back on his heels, he will cause no harm to Allaah in the least; and Allaah will give reward to those who are grateful.

A narration on the authority of 'Umar Ibn Al-Khattaab [may Allaah be pleased with him] that he said: We left the Prophet [peace and blessings of Allaah be upon him] on the day of Uhud (battle), and when I ascended the mountain I heard the Yahood saying: "Muhammad was killed". I said: "I would chop off the head of anyone whom I hear saying that Muhammad was killed". I looked and behold! the Prophet [peace and blessings of Allaah be upon him] and the people were returning. On that occasion, Allaah Almighty (the

Most High) revealed this Quraanic Ayaah. [Ibn Al-Mundhir]

A narration on the authority of Ar-Rabee' that he said: When they were afflicted by the wound they received on the day of Uhud (battle), and they called each other that the Prophet of Allaah [peace and blessings of Allaah be upon him] was killed, some said: "Had he been a Prophet, he would not have been killed". Others said: "Fight (your enemies) on the same religion on which your Prophet fought till Allaah makes you victorious or you join him". In this connection, Allaah Almighty (the Most High) revealed this Quraanic Ayaah. [Ibn Abu Haatim]

A narration on the authority of Abu Najeeh that a man from the Muhaajiroon came upon an Ansaari man while being agitated in his blood.

He said: "Have you learnt that Muhammad was killed?" He replied: "If Muhammad was killed, (you should know that) he has really conveyed (Allaah's Message): so, fight in defense of your religion". On that occasion, this Quraanic Ayaah was revealed. [Al-Bayhaqi in Ad-Dalaa'il]

A narration on the authority of Ibn Shihaab Az-Zuhri that Ka'b Ibn Maalik [may Allaah be pleased with him] was the first to recognize the Prophet [peace and blessings of Allaah be upon him] after the defeat, and the spread of rumor that he had been killed. Ka'b said: "I saw his eyes glowing from underneath the helmet, thereupon I cried at the top of my voice: "O assembly of Muslims! That is the Prophet [peace and blessings of Allaah be upon him] (still living)". On that occasion, Allaah revealed this Quraanic Ayaah. [Ibn Rahawayh in his Musnad; and Ibn Ishaaq]

Verse Number 154

154- Then after the distress, He sent down security on you. Slumber overtook a party of you, while another party worried about themselves and assumed wrongly of Allaah - the assumption of ignorance. They said: "Have we any part in the affair?" Say you (O Muhammad): "Indeed the affair belongs wholly to Allaah." They hide within themselves what they dare not disclose to you, saying: "If we had anything to do with the affair, none of us would have been killed here." Say: "Even if you had remained in your homes, those for whom death was decreed would certainly have gone forth to the place of their death." But (He Almighty did what He did in the battle of Uhud) so that Allaah might test what is in your breasts (of sincerity and hypocrisy) and distinguish what is in your hearts (Qalb), and Allaah is All-Knower of what is in (your) breasts.

A narration on the authority of Az-Zubayr [may Allaah be pleased with him] that he said: On the day of Uhud (battle) when we were in a state of severe fear and overwhelmed by slumber, there was none of us but that his chin fell in his breast. By Allaah, I heard, as if it were a dream, the statement of Mu'tib Ibn Qushayr: "If we had anything to do with the affair, none of us would have been killed here." [154] I memorized it and later on Allaah Almighty (the Most High) revealed that Quraanic Ayaah. [Ibn Rahawayh]

Verse Number 161

161- It is not fit for any Prophet to misappropriate a part of booty, and whosoever takes anything illegally of the booty, shall bring forth on the Day of Resurrection that which he misappropriated. Then every person shall be paid in full what he has earned, and they shall not be dealt with unjustly.

A narration on the authority of Ibn 'Abbaas [Allaah be pleased with them] that he said: This Quraanic Ayaah was revealed in connection with a piece of red amaranth which was lost on the day of Badr (Battle), thereupon some said: "Perhaps The Prophet [peace and blessings of Allaah be upon him] has taken it". [Abu Daawood and At-Tirmidhi who renders it Hasan]

A narration on the authority of Ibn 'Abbaas [Allaah be pleased with them] that he said: the Prophet [peace and blessings of Allaah be upon him] dispatched an army but it was defeated. Then it was dispatched once again and then defeated. It was dispatched (for the third time) and defeated because of misappropriating a head of golden gazelle. On that occasion, Allaah revealed that Quraanic Ayaah. [At-Tabaraani in Al-Kabeer with a reliable chain of narrators]

Verse Number 165

165- (What is the matter with you) that when a single disaster smites you (in Uhud), although you smote (your enemies in Badr) with one twice as great, you say: "From where does this come to us?" Say (O Muhammad to them): "It is from yourselves." And Allaah has power over all things.

A narration on the authority of 'Umar Ibn Al-Khattaab [may Allaah be pleased with him] that he said: They received penalty on the day of Uhud (battle) for what they did on the day of Badr (battle), as they accepted the ransom. (on the day of Uhud) seventy of them were killed, and the Companions of the Prophet [peace and blessings of Allaah be upon him] were put to flight, and his canine tooth was broken, the helmet was crushed on his head and the blood flowed over his face. On that occasion, Allaah revealed this Quraanic Ayaah. [Ibn Abu Haatim]

Verse Number 169-170

169- Think not of those who are killed in the Way of Allaah as dead. Nay, they are alive, with their Lord (Rabb) receiving provision. 170They rejoice in what Allaah has bestowed upon them of His Bounty and rejoice for the sake of those who have not yet joined them, but are left behind (not yet martyred) that on them there shall be no fear, nor shall they grieve (in the hereafter).

A narration on the authority of Ibn 'Abbaas [Allaah be pleased with them] that he said: the Prophet [peace and blessings of Allaah be upon him] said: "When your brothers fell as martyrs on the day of (the battle of) Uhud, Allaah Almighty (the Most High) placed their souls in the bodies of green birds, which come to drink from the rivers of the Garden, eat of its fruits and then nestle to chandeliers of gold in the shade of the Throne (of Majesty). When they found that their food and drink were sweet, and their end was good, they said: "Would that our (living) brothers know what Allaah Almighty (the Most High) had done with us, so that they would not refrain from setting out for Jihad, nor fail to fight (in the Cause of Allaah)". Allaah Almighty (the Most High) said: "I would inform them on your behalf". Therefore, on that occasion, Allaah Almighty (the Most High) revealed those Quraanic Aayaat. [Abu Daawood; Ahmad and At-Tirmidhi on the authority of Jaabir]

Verse Number 172-174

172- Those who answered (the Call of) Allaah and the Messenger (Muhammad) after being wounded (in Uhud): for those of them who did good deeds and feared Allaah, there is a great reward (Paradise). 173- Those unto whom the people said: "Verily, the people have gathered against you (a great army to exterminate you), therefore, fear them." But it (only) increased them in Faith, and they said: "Allaah (Alone) is Sufficient for us, and He is the Best Disposer of affairs (for us)." 174- So they returned (from Badr) with Grace and Bounty from Allaah; and no harm touched them; and they followed the good Pleasure of Allaah. And Allaah is the Owner of Great Bounty.

A narration on the authority of Ibn 'Abbaas [Allaah be pleased with them] that he said: Allaah cast terror into the heart of Abu Sufyaan on the day of Uhud (battle) after (he decided to engage in fighting the Muslims once again) thereupon he returned to Makkah. the Prophet [peace and blessings of Allaah be upon him] said: "Abu Sufyaan had intended to strike you but he returned after Allaah had cast terror into his heart".

The battle of Uhud took place in Shawwaal and the merchants used to come to Madinah in Dhul-Qa'dah and camp at Badr, the Lesser. After the battle of Uhud they came and the Muslims had been stricken with severe wound of which they made a complaint. the Prophet [peace and blessings of Allaah be upon him] exhorted the people to come out with him, but Satan came and frightened his allies and said: "No doubt, the people (disbelievers (al-Kaafireen)) have gathered (their forces) for you". Consequently, the people rejected to follow the Prophet [peace and blessings of Allaah be upon him]. He said then: "Then, I will go alone even if none has followed me". He took with him Abu Bakr, 'Umar, 'Uthmaan, 'Ali, Az-Zubayr, Sa'd, Talhah, Abd-Ar-Ar-Rahmaan Ibn 'Awf, 'Abdullaah Ibn Mas'ood, Hudhayfah Ibn Al-Yamaan and Abu Ubaydah Ibn Al-Jarraah [Allaah be pleased with them], among seventy men. They went in pursuit of Abu Sufyaan till when they reached Safraa', Allaah revealed that Quraanic Ayaah. [Ibn Jareer At-Tabari]

A narration on the authority of Ibn 'Abbaas [Allaah be pleased with them] that he said: When the polytheists returned from Uhud they said: "You have neither killed Muhammad nor taken women with you (as captives). How evil is that which you have done! Return (and fight Muhammad once again)". Having heard the news, the Prophet [peace and blessings of Allaah be upon him] exhorted the Muslims to set out with him and they did accordingly till they reached Hamraa' Al-Asad or the well of Abu 'Utbah. On that occasion, Allaah Almighty (the Most High) revealed (what means): {Those who answered (the Call of) Allaah and the Messenger (Muhammad) after being wounded (in Uhud) ...} [172] Abu Sufyaan had already said to the Prophet [peace and blessings of Allaah be upon him]: "Your appointment will be in the season of Badr where you killed our companions".

As for the coward, he returned, whereas the brave got ready for fighting and traffic. Having found none there when they reached it, they then made shopping. On that occasion, Allaah revealed (what means): {So they returned with favor from Allaah and bounty, no harm having touched them. And they pursued the pleasure of Allaah, and Allaah is the possessor of great bounty}. [174] [At-Tabaraani]

A narration on the authority of Abu Raafi' [may Allaah be pleased with him] that the Prophet [peace and blessings of Allaah be upon him] dispatched 'Ali leading a group of men in pursuit of Abu Sufyaan (and the polytheists).

On the way they met a Bedouin from Khuzaa'ah who said to them: "Indeed, the people have gathered against you, so fear them." But it [merely] increased them in faith, and they said, "Sufficient for us is Allaah, and He is the best Disposer of affairs." On that occasion, Allaah Almighty (the Most High) revealed this Quraanic Ayaah [173] [Ibn Mardawayh]

Verse Number 181

181- Indeed, Allaah has heard the statement of those (Yahood) who say: "Truly, Allaah is poor and we are rich!" We shall record hat they have said and their killing of the Prophets with no just cause, and We shall say: "Taste you the torment of the burning (Fire)."

A narration on the authority of Ibn 'Abbaas [Allaah be pleased with them] that he said: Abu Bakr [Allaah Be Pleased with him] entered Bayt Al-Midraas (the place where the Yahood study the Torah) and found many of them gathering around someone called Finhaas, who was one of their scholars and rabbis with someone called Ashya'.

Abu Bakr [Allaah Be Pleased with him] said to Finhaas: "Woe to you, fear Allaah. By Allaah, you know that Muhammad [peace and blessings of Allaah be upon him] is the Prophet who came with the truth from Allaah and you can find that in your Torah and Gospel". Finhaas said to Abu Bakr [Allaah Be Pleased with him]: "By Allaah, O Abu Bakr, we are not in need of Allaah; it is He Who Is in need of us. We do not invoke Him as He Invokes us. We are rich and He Is not, for had He Been rich, He Would not Have Borrowed our property as your Prophet claims. He Forbids you from usury and Permits us to deal in it. If

He Had Been rich, He Would not Have Permitted us to deal in usury".

Abu Bakr [Allaah Be Pleased with him] became angry and slapped the face of Finhaas and said: "By The One in Whose Hand my soul is, had it not been for the covenant between us and you, I would have smashed your head, O enemy of Allaah". Finhaas, accordingly, went to the Prophet [peace and blessings of Allaah be upon him] and said: "O Muhammad, look what your Companion (Abu Bakr) has done to me".

The Prophet [peace and blessings of Allaah be upon him] said: "What drove you to do so, O Abu Bakr?" Abu Bakr [Allaah Be Pleased with him] replied: "This enemy of Allaah said a grave saying: he claimed that Allaah Almighty (the Most High) Is in need for them and that they are rich. When he said so, I became angry for the Sake of Allaah Almighty (the Most High) and slapped his face".

Therefore, Finhaas denied this and said: "I did not say so". On that occasion, Allaah Almighty (the Most High) Revealed this Quraanic Ayaah. [Ibn Ishaaq and Ibn Abu Haatim]

A narration on the authority of Ibn 'Abbaas [Allaah be pleased with them] that he said: The Yahood came to the Prophet [peace and blessings of Allaah be upon him] when Allaah revealed (what means): {Who is it that would loan Allaah a goodly loan so He may multiply it for him many times over?} [Al-Baqarah, verse 245] They said to him: "O Muhammad! Has your

Lord (Rabb) become in need so that He begs of His servants?" On that occasion, Allaah revealed this Quraanic Ayaah. [Ibn Abu Haatim]

Verse Number 186

186- You shall certainly be tried and tested in your wealth and properties and in your own selves, and you shall certainly hear much that will grieve you from those who received the Scripture before you (Yahood and Nasaara) and from those who ascribe partners to Allaah; but if you persevere patiently, and become righteous then verily, that will be a determining factor in all affairs.

A narration on the authority of Ibn 'Abbaas [Allaah be pleased with them] that this Quraanic Ayaah was revealed in connection with the quarrel that broke up between Abu Bakr [may Allaah be pleased with him] and Finhaas when the latter said: "Indeed, Allaah is poor, while we are rich." [Ibn Abu Haatim and Ibn Al-Mundhir with a good chain of narrators]

But according to the narration of 'Abd-Ar-Razzaaq on the authority of 'Abd-Ar-Rahmaan Ibn Ka'b Ibn Maalik, it was revealed in connection with Ka'b Ibn Al-Ashraf's poetry with which he lampooned the Prophet [peace and blessings of Allaah be upon him] and his Companions. ['Abd-Ar-Razzaaq] Verse Number 188

188- Think not that those who rejoice in what they have done (or brought about), and love to be praised for what they have not done, think not you that they are rescued from the punishment, and for them is a painful torment (in the hereafter).

A narration on the authority of Humayd Ibn 'Abd-Ar-Rahmaan Ibn 'Awf that Marwaan said to his porter: O Raafi'! Go to Ibn 'Abbaas and say to him: "If everybody who rejoices in what he has done, and likes to be praised for what he has not done, will be punished, then all of us will be punished."

Ibn 'Abbaas [Allaah be pleased with them] said: "What is your business with this case? It was only that The Prophet [peace and blessings of Allaah be upon him] called the Yahood and asked them about something. But they hid the truth and told him something else, showing him that they deserved praise for the favor of telling him the answer to his question. Thus, they became happy with what they had concealed". On that occasion, Allaah revealed this Quraanic Ayaah. [Al-Bukhaari, Muslim and others]

A narration on the authority of Abu Sa'eed Al-Khudri [may Allaah be pleased with him] that he said: During the lifetime of the Prophet [peace and blessings of Allaah be upon him], some hypocrites (al-Munaafiqeen) used to remain behind whenever he went out for a battle and they would be pleased to stay at home behind the Prophet [peace and blessings of Allaah be upon him].

Whenever he returned (from the battle) they would put forward (false) excuses and take oaths, wishing to be praised for what they had not done. So this

Quraanic verse was revealed. [Al-Bukhaari and Muslim]

A narration on the authority of Zayd Ibn Aslam that Raafi' Ibn Khadij and Zayd Ibn Thaabit [Allaah be pleased with them] were with Marwaan who said: "O Raafi'! On which occasion was this Quraanic Ayaah was revealed?" He recited (what means): {Think not that those who rejoice in what they have done (or brought about), and love to be praised for what they have not done,- think not you that they are rescued from the punishment, and for them is a painful torment (in the hereafter)}. [188]

He said: "It was revealed in connection with some hypocrites (al-Munaafiqeen): it was their habit that whenever the Prophet [peace and blessings of Allaah be upon him] set out for a battle they would apologize for not going out with him and say: "Nothing has kept us from coming out with you except our business. Would that we were with you!" In connection with them Allaah revealed this Quraanic Ayaah.

It seemed as if Marwaan denied this thereupon Raafi' got scared and asked Zayd Ibn Thaabit: "I beseech you by Allaah to tell me: do you know that which I have said?" Zayd answered in the affirmative. ['Abd-Ar-Razzaaq in his Tafsir]

Verse Number 190

190- Verily! In the creation of the heavens and the earth, and in the alternation of night and day, there are indeed signs for men of understanding.

A narration on the authority of Ibn 'Abbaas [Allaah be pleased with them] that he said: The Quraysh people went to the Yahood and said: "Which miracle did Moses bring to you?" They replied: "The staff (which turned into a serpent) and his hand which seemed shining to the beholders (whenever he took it out of his bosom)".

They went to the Nasaara and asked them: "What did Jesus bring to you?" They replied: "He used to cure the blind and the leper and quicken the dead".

Then, they went to the Prophet [peace and blessings of Allaah be upon him] and said: "Invoke your Lord (Rabb) to turn Safa (mountain) into gold". He invoked his Lord (Rabb) thereupon this Quraanic Ayaah was revealed. [At-Tabaraani and Ibn Abu Haatim]

Verse Number 195

195- So their Lord (Rabb) accepted of them (their supplication and answered them): "Never will I allow to be lost the work of any of you, be he male or female. You are (members) one of another, so those who emigrated (from Makkah to Madeenah) and were driven out from their homes, and suffered harm in My Cause, and who fought (the disbelievers (al-Kaafireen)), and were killed (in My Cause), verily, I will remove from them their evil deeds and admit them into Gardens under which rivers flow (in Paradise); a reward from Allaah, and with Allaah is the best of rewards."

A narration on the authority of Umm Salamah [Allaah be pleased with her] that she said: "O Messenger of Allaah! I do not hear that Allaah has mentioned anything about women concerning emigration". On that occasion, Allaah revealed this Quraanic Ayaah. ['Abd-Ar-Razzaaq; Sa'eed Ibn Mansoor; At-Tirmidhi; Al-Haakim and Ibn Abu Haatim]

Verse Number 199

199- And there are, certainly, among the people of the Scripture (Yahood and Nasaara), those who believe in Allaah and in that which has been revealed to you (that is the Quraan), and in that which has been revealed to them (that is the Torah and the Gospel), humbling themselves before Allaah. They do not sell the Aayaat of Allaah for a little price, for them is a reward with their Lord (Rabb). Surely, Allaah is Swift in account.

A narration on the authority of Anas Ibn Maalik [may Allaah be pleased with him] that he said: When the death news of the Negus came, the Prophet [peace and blessings of Allaah be upon him] said: "Perform funeral prayer on him".

They said: "O Messenger of Allaah! Should we perform funeral prayer on an Abyssinian slave?" On that occasion, Allaah Almighty (the Most High) revealed this Quraanic Ayaah. [An-Nasaa'i]

The same is narrated on the authority of Jaabir [may Allaah be pleased with him]. [Ibn Jareer]

A narration on the authority of 'Abdullaah Ibn Az-Zubayr [Allaah be pleased with them] that he said: This Quraanic Ayaah was revealed in connection with the Negus. [Al-Haakim in Al-Mustadrak]

Soorah An-Nisaa'

Verse Number 2

2- And give unto orphans their property and do not exchange the evil (and unlawful) for the good (and lawful); and devour not their substance (by adding it) to your substance. Surely, this is a great sin.

A narration on the authority of Abu Saalih that he said: The habit was to a man, if he gave his daughter in marriage, he would take her dowry for himself. Allaah Almighty (the Most High) forbade them to do so by revealing this Quraanic Ayaah. [Ibn Abu Haatim]

Verse Number 7

7- There is a share for men and a share for women from what is left by parents and nearest relatives, whether the property be small or large - a legal share.

A narration on the authority of Ibn 'Abbaas [Allaah be pleased with them] that he said: The men of pre-Islamic days did not allow girls to inherit the property of the deceased and also the children till they would attain maturity. One of the Ansaar called Aws Ibn Thaabit died and left behind two daughters and a small male child. His two paternal cousins, Khaalid and Urfatah, a pact, took all his legacy. His wife came to the Prophet [peace and blessings of Allaah be upon him] and made a mention of that to him. He said to her: "In fact, I do not know what to say (to you)". On that occasion, this Quraanic Ayaah was revealed. [Abu Ash-Shaykh and Ibn Hibbaan in Al-Faraa'id]

Verse Number 11-12

11- Allaah commands you as regards your children's (inheritance): to the male, a portion equal to that of two females; if (there are) only daughters, two or more, their share is two-thirds of the inheritance; if only one (daughter), her share is half. For parents, a sixth share of inheritance to each if the deceased left children; if there are no children, and the parents are the (only) heirs, the mother has a third; if the deceased left_brothers (or sisters), the mother has a sixth. (The distribution in all cases is) after the payment of legacies he may have bequeathed or debts. You know not which of them, whether your parents or your children, are nearest to you in benefit; (these fixed shares) are ordained by Allaah. And ever is Allaah All-Knowing, All-Wise. 12- In that which your wives leave, your share is a half if they have no child; but if they leave a child, you get a fourth of that which they leave after payment of legacies that they may have bequeathed or debts. In that which you leave, their (your wives) share is a fourth if you leave no child; but if you leave a child, they get an eighth of that which you leave after payment of legacies that you may have bequeathed or debts. If the man or woman whose inheritance is in question has left neither ascendants nor descendants, but has left a brother or a sister, each one of the two gets a sixth; but if they are more than two, they share in a third, after payment of legacies he (or she) may have bequeathed or debts, so that no loss is caused (to the heirs). This is a Commandment from Allaah; and ever is Allaah All-Knowing, Most-Forbearing.

A narration on the authority of Jaabir Ibn 'Abdullaah [Allaah be pleased with them] that he said: the Prophet [peace and blessings of Allaah be upon him] and Abu Bakr came walking to pay me a visit (during my illness) at Banu Salamah's (dwellings). The Prophet [peace and blessings of Allaah be upon him] found me unconscious, so he asked for water and performed the ablution from it and sprinkled some water over me. I came to my senses and said: "O Messenger of Allaah! What do you order me to do as regards my wealth?" On that occasion, those Quraanic Aayaat were revealed. [Al-Bukhaari; Muslim; At-Tirmidhi; Abu Daawood; An-Nasa'i and Ibn Majah]

A narration on the authority of Jaabir Ibn 'Abdullaah [Allaah be pleased with them] that he said: The wife of Sa'd Ibn Ar-Rabee' brought two daughters to the Prophet [peace and blessings of Allaah be upon him] and said: "O Messenger of Allaah! Both are the daughters of Sa'd Ibn Ar-Rabee', who was killed when he was fighting beside you in (the battle of) Uhud; and their paternal uncle usurped all of their property and heritage, and left nothing (belonging to their father) but that he took it; and it is known that they would not be married (in most cases) but on account of their property". the Prophet [peace and blessings of Allaah be upon him] said: "Allaah will definitely decide the matter". Then, the Quraanic Aayaat of the inheritance were revealed. [Abu Daawood; Ahmad; At-Tirmidhi and Al-Haakim]

Commenting on that Ibn Hajar tells that those two Quraanic Aayaat may, possibly, have been revealed in both cases, in the sense that the first part, that is {Allaah commands you as regards your children's (inheritance): to the male, a portion equal to that of two females...} [verse 11] was revealed in connection with Jaabir [may Allaah be pleased with him]; and the concluding part, that is {If the man or woman whose inheritance is in question has left neither ascendants nor descendants, but has left a brother or a sister...} [verse 12] in connection with Sa'd Ibn Ar-Rabee' [may Allaah be pleased with him].

A third occasion for this Quraanic Ayaah is mentioned: A narration on the authority of As-Suddi that he said: It was the habit of the people of the pre-Islamic days not to make the girls and weak males to inherit the property of the deceased; and none among the deceased's sons would inherit his property except such as was able to fight. 'Abd-Ar-Rahmaan, the brother of Hassaan (Ibn Thaabit), the poet, died and left behind a woman (his wife) called Umm Kahhah and five daughters. The heirs came to take his legacy, thereupon Umm Kahhah made a complaint to the Prophet [peace and blessings of Allaah be upon him]. On that, Allaah Almighty (the Most High) revealed (what means): {if (there are) only daughters, two or more, their share is two-thirds of the inheritance}. [verse 11] Concerning Umm Kahhah, He said (what means): {In that which you leave, their (your wives) share is a fourth if you leave no child; but if you leave a child, they get an eighth of that which you leave}. [verse 12] [Ibn Jareer] Verse Number 19

19- O you who believe! It is unlawful for you to inherit women against their will; nor to prevent (your previous wives whom you divorce) from marrying others than you, in order that you may take away part of the dower you have given them, unless they commit evident immorality; And live with them honorably. If you dislike them (be patient), it may be that you dislike a thing and Allaah brings through it a great deal of good.

A narration on the authority of Ibn 'Abbaas [Allaah be pleased with them] that he said: It was the habit that if a man died, his heirs would have more right over his wife, anyone of them could marry her if he so liked and they could give her in marriage if they so liked which means that they had more right over her than her family. On that occasion, this Quraanic Ayaah was revealed. [Al-Bukhaari; Abu Daawood and An-Nasaa'i]

A narration on the authority of Abu Umaamah Ibn Sahl Ibn Hunayf that he said: When Abu Qays Ibn Al-Aslat died, his son liked to marry his wife and during the pre-Islamic day, they had a right to do such thing. On that occasion, Allaah Almighty (the Most High) revealed (what means): {O you who believe! It is unlawful for you to inherit women against their will}. [Ibn Jareer and Ibn Abu Haatim]

Verse Number 22

22- And marry not women whom your fathers married, except what has already passed; indeed it (marrying such women) was shameful and most hateful (in the sight of Allaah), and an evil way.

A narration on the authority of 'Adiyy Ibn Thaabit from an Ansaari man that he said: Abu Qays Ibn Al-Aslat died, and he was one of the righteous among the Ansaar. His son proposed marriage to his wife who said to him: "No doubt, I consider you as one of my children and you are one of the righteous among your people". She came to the Prophet [peace and blessings of Allaah be upon him] and made a mention of that to him. He said: "Return to your home". No sooner had she returned than Allaah revealed (what means): {And marry not women whom your fathers married, except what has already passed}. [Ibn Abu Haatim; Al-Firyaabi and At-Tabaraani]

The same is narrated on the authority of Muhammad Ibn Ka'b Al-Qurathi. [Ibn Sa'd in At-Tabaqaat]

A narration on the authority of Az-Zuhri that he said: This Quraanic Ayaah was revealed in connection with some of the Ansaar: whenever anyone of them died, his heir would have the most claim over his wife and he would keep her (at home without enabling her to marry) till she would die. [Ibn Sa'd]

Verse Number 23

23- Forbidden to you (for marriage) are: your mothers, your daughters, your sisters, your father's sisters, your mother's sisters, your brother's daughters, your sister's daughters, your foster mother who gave you suck, your foster milk suckling sisters, your wives' mothers, your step-daughters under your guardianship, born of your wives to whom you have gone in - but there is no sin on you if you have not gone in them (to marry their daughters if you divorce their mothers), - the wives of your sons who (spring) from your own loins, and two sisters in wedlock at the same time, except for what has already passed; verily, Allaah is Oft-Forgiving, Most Merciful.

A narration on the authority of Ibn Jurayj that he said: I asked 'Ataa' about Allaah's saying (what means): {And (also forbidden to you for marriage are) the wives of your sons who (spring) from your own loins}. He said: We said to one another that it was revealed in connection with Muhammad [peace and blessings of Allaah be upon him] when he married the wife of Zayd Ibn Haarithah [may Allaah be pleased with him] about which polytheists talked badly. On that occasion, this Quraanic Ayaah was revealed.

In addition, Allaah Almighty (the Most High) revealed (what means): {And he has not made your adopted sons your (true) sons}. [Al-Ahzaab, verse 4] And: {Muhammad is not the father of (any) one of your men, but (he is) the Prophet and last of the prophets}. [Al-Ahzaab, verse 40] [Ibn Jareer]

Verse Number 24

24- Also (forbidden for marriage) are the married women, except those whom your right hands possess. Thus has Allaah ordained for you. All others are lawful, provided you seek (them in marriage) with dowry from your property, desiring chastity through marriage, not committing illegal sexual intercourse. So to those of whom you have enjoyed sexual relations, give them their dowry as prescribed; and there is no sin on you, if after a dowry is prescribed you agree mutually on something else. Surely, ever is Allaah All-Knowing, All-Wise.

A narration on the authority of Abu Sa'id Al-Khudri [may Allaah be pleased with him] that he said: We got female captives from Awtaas who had husbands. It seemed that some of the companions of the Prophet [peace and blessings of Allaah be upon him] felt it difficult upon themselves to have sexual relations with them on account of their husbands are from the infidels. We asked the Prophet [peace and blessings of Allaah be upon him] about that thereupon Allaah revealed (what means): {Also (forbidden for marriage) are the married women, except those whom your right hands possess}. By this, they became lawful for us (once the term of their 'Iddah elapsed). [Abu Daawood; At-Tirmidhi and An-Nasaa'i]

A narration on the authority of Ibn 'Abbaas [Allaah be pleased with them] that he said: When it was the day of Hunayn (battle) and Allaah Almighty (the Most High) helped the Muslims conquer Hunayn, the Muslims got female captives from the people of

Scripture. If a man liked to have sexual intercourse with any woman (of them whom his right hand possessed) she would say to him: "I have a husband". the Prophet [peace and blessings of Allaah be upon him] was asked about that, thereupon Allaah revealed this Quraanic Ayaah. [At-Tabaraani]

A narration on the authority of Ma'mar from Sulaymaan that he said: Al-Hadrami claimed that men used to fix a dowry and might, probably, become insolvent (and unable to give it). On that, Allaah revealed (what means): {and there is no sin on you, if after a dowry is prescribed you agree mutually on something else}. [Ibn Jareer]

Verse Number 32

32- And wish not for the things in which Allaah has made some of you excel others. For men there is reward for what they have earned, and (likewise) for women there is reward for what they have earned, and ask Allaah of His Bounty. Surely, ever is Allaah All-Knower of everything.

A narration on the authority of Umm Salamah [Allaah be pleased with her] that she said: "Men always take part in fight but women do not do; and we (women) have only half the men's share (of inheritance)". On that occasion, Allaah revealed this Quraanic Ayaah. [At-Tirmidhi and Al-Haakim]

A narration on the authority of Ibn 'Abbaas [Allaah be pleased with them] that he said: A woman came to the

Prophet [peace and blessings of Allaah be upon him] and said: "O Prophet of Allaah! The male's share of inheritance is equal to two females; and the witness of two females is equal to the witness of one male. would we (women) be dealt with as such in the deed? That is, if a woman does a good deed, would it be written down only a half good deed in her account?" On that occasion, Allaah revealed this Quraanic Ayaah. [Ibn Abu Haatim]

Verse Number 33

33- And to every one (of men and women), We have appointed heirs of what is left by parents and relatives. To those also with whom you have made a (bond of brotherhood through) pledge, give them their due portion (by bequest). Truly, ever is Allaah a Witness over all things.

A narration on the authority of Daawood Ibn Al-Haseen that he said: I was reciting to the mother of Sa'd Ibn Ar-Rabee' the Quraan and she was living under the guardianship of Abu Bakr. I recited to her (what means): {To those also with whom you have made a (bond of brotherhood through) pledge, give them their due portion (by bequest)}. On that, she said: "No doubt, this Quraanic Ayaah was revealed in connection with Abu Bakr and his son ('Abd-Ar-Rahmaan) when the latter rejected to embrace Islam. Abu Bakr swore not to make him inherit of his property. But when he embraced Islam, he asked him to give him his share of inheritance. [Abu Daawood in his Sunan]

34- Men are in charge of women, because Allaah has made one of them excel the other, and because they spend (to support them) from their means. Therefore the righteous women are devoutly obedient (to Allaah and to their husbands), and guard the husband's absence by what Allaah guards for them. As to those women on whose part you see ill-conduct, admonish them (first), (then), forsake them in their beds, (then) beat them (lightly and gently); but if they return to obedience, seek not a mean against them. Surely, ever is Allaah Most High, Most Great.

A narration on the authority of Al-Hasan that he said: A woman came to the Prophet [peace and blessings of Allaah be upon him] complaining of her husband because he had slapped her (on the face). The Messenger of Allaah [peace and blessings of Allaah be upon him] said: "The legal retribution should be enforced". On that occasion, Allaah revealed this Quraanic Ayaah. She returned without taking the legal retribution from him. [Ibn Abu Haatim and Ibn Jareer]

A narration on the authority of 'Ali [may Allaah be pleased with him] that he said: An Ansaari man came to the Prophet [peace and blessings of Allaah be upon him] with his wife. She said: "O Messenger of Allaah! He has struck me and injured my face". the Prophet [peace and blessings of Allaah be upon him] said: "It is not fit for him to do so". On that occasion, Allaah revealed this Quraanic Ayaah. [Ibn Mardawayh]

37- Those who are miserly and enjoin miserliness on other men and hide what Allaah has bestowed upon them of His Bounties. And We have prepared for the disbelievers (al-Kaafireen) a disgraceful torment.

A narration on the authority of Sa'eed Ibn Jubayr that he said: The scholars of the children of Israel used to withhold the knowledge they had. In connection with them, Allaah Almighty (the Most High) revealed this Quraanic Ayaah. [Ibn Abu Haatim]

A narration on the authority of Ibn 'Abbaas [Allaah be pleased with them] that he said: Qardam Ibn Qays, the ally of Ka'b Ibn Al-Ashraf, Usaamah Ibn Habeeb, Naafi' Ibn Abu Naafi', Bahri Ibn 'Amr, Huyayy Ibn Akhtab and Rifaa'ah Ibn Zayd Ibn At-Taaboot, used to frequent some men of the Ansaar with whom they mixed from among the Companions of the Prophet [peace and blessings of Allaah be upon him], with the intention to advise them. They used to tell them: "Spend not your wealth, because we fear poverty for you by losing it, nor hasten in spending, since you do not know what will happen in the morrow". In connection with them, Allaah revealed this Quraanic Ayaah. [Ibn Abu Haatim]

Verse Number 43

43- O you who believe! Approach (perform) not the prayer when you are in a drunken state until you know (the meaning) of what you utter, nor when you are in a state of Janaabah, except when travelling on the road, till you wash your whole body. And if you are ill, or on a journey, or anyone of you comes after answering the call of nature, or you have been in contact with women and you find no water, perform Tayammum with clean earth and rub therewith your faces and hands. Truly, ever is Allaah Oft-Pardoning, Oft-Forgiving.

A narration on the authority of 'Ali Ibn Abu Taalib [may Allaah be pleased with him] that a man from amongst the Ansaar invited him and 'Abd Ar-Rahmaan Ibn 'Awf, he served them with wine before it was prohibited. When the prayer was due they made 'Ali lead them in the prayer, in which he recited: {Say: O you disbelievers (al-Kaafireen)!} but he was put to confusion while reciting it. On that occasion, Allaah Almighty (the Most High) revealed this Quraanic Ayaah. [Abu Daawood]

A narration on the authority of Al-Asla' Ibn Shurayk that he said: I was in charge of preparing the she-camel of the Prophet [peace and blessings of Allaah be upon him] when I became in a state of Janaabah on a very cold night. I felt afraid of taking Ghusl with the cold water lest I would die or at least be sick. I made a mention of that to the Prophet [peace and blessings of Allaah be upon him], thereupon Allaah revealed this Quraanic Ayaah. [Ibn Mardawayh]

A narration on the authority of Al-Asla' that he said: I used to serve the Prophet [peace and blessings of

Allaah be upon him] and prepare his mount. One day he told me: "O Asla'! Stand and prepare the mount". I replied: "O Messenger of Allaah! I have become in a state of Janaabah". the Prophet [peace and blessings of Allaah be upon him] kept silent and then Jibreel came to him with the Quraanic Ayaah of doing Tayammum with the clean earth. the Prophet [peace and blessings of Allaah be upon him] said: "O Asla'! Stand and do Tayammum (dry ablution)". He showed me how to do Tayammum: to strike the face and the hands up to the elbows with one strike each. I stood and did Tayammum and then prepared the riding mount for him. [At-Tabaraani]

A narration on the authority of Yazeed Ibn Abu Habeeb that some Ansaari men had the gates of their houses open to the masjid. Sometimes they might become in a state of Janaabah and they had no water; and if they liked to get water they would have no way but to pass through the masjid. On that occasion, Allaah revealed (what means): {nor when you are in a state of Janaabah, except when travelling on the road, till you wash your whole body} [verse 43]. [Ibn Jareer]

A narration on the authority of Mujaahid that he said: This Quraanic Ayaah was revealed in connection with an Ansaari man: he was sick and unable to stand to perform ablution (for prayer), and had no servant to bring him water. He made a mention of that to the Prophet [peace and blessings of Allaah be upon him], thereupon Allaah revealed (what means): {And if you are ill...} [Ibn Abu Haatim]

A narration on the authority of Ibraaheem An-Nakh'i that he said: the Companions of the Prophet [peace and blessings of Allaah be upon him] received severe wounds and, further, were afflicted with Janaabah. They made a complaint of that to the Prophet [peace and blessings of Allaah be upon him], thereupon Allaah revealed (what means): {And if you are ill...} [Ibn Jareer]

Verse Number 44

44- Have you not seen those who were given a portion of the book (the Yahood), purchasing the error (in exchange for guidance), and wish that you should go astray?

A narration on the authority of Ibn 'Abbaas [Allaah be pleased with them] that he said: Whenever Rifaa'ah Ibn Zayd Ibn At-Taaboot, one of the chiefs of the Yahood, talked to the Prophet [peace and blessings of Allaah be upon him] he would twist his tongue and say: "Raa'ina (that is give us your ear), O Muhammad, so that we could understand you". Then, he slandered and severely criticized Islam. On that occasion, Allaah revealed this Quraanic Ayaah. [Ibn Ishaaq]

Verse Number 47

47- O you who have been given the Scripture (Yahood and Nasaara)! Believe in what We have revealed (of the Quraan) confirming what is (already) with you (of Torah and Gospel), before We efface faces and turn them hindwards, or curse them as We cursed the

Sabbath-breakers. And ever is the Commandment of Allaah accomplished.

A narration on the authority of Ibn 'Abbaas [Allaah be pleased with them] that he said: the Prophet [peace and blessings of Allaah be upon him] talked to some leading Jewish rabbis, including 'Abdullaah Ibn Sooriyah, the one-eyed, and Ka'b Ibn Asad, and told them: "O community of Yahood! Fear Allaah and embrace Islam, for by Allaah, you know well that what I have brought to you is the truth". They said: "We do not know this O Muhammad". Thus, they denied what they knew of the truth, and insisted on disbelief. In connection with them Allaah revealed this Quraanic Ayaah. [Ibn Ishaaq]

Verse Number 48

48- Verily, Allaah forgives not association (of partners with Him in worship), but He forgives what is less than that (of sins) to whom He wills; and whoever associates partners with Allaah (in worship), he has indeed invented a tremendous sin.

A narration on the authority of Abu Ayyoob Al-Ansaari [may Allaah be pleased with him] that he said: A man went to the Prophet [peace and blessings of Allaah be upon him] and said: "I have a nephew of mine and he does not cease to do the unlawful". He asked him: "What is his religion?" He replied: "He prays and worships Allaah Alone". He said: "Then, let him grant you his religion and if he rejects, then buy it from him". The man asked his nephew to do so but he rejected. He went to the Prophet [peace and blessings of Allaah be upon him] and told him saying: "I have found him too stingy to leave his religion". On that, Allaah revealed this Quraanic Ayaah. [Ibn Abu Haatim and At-Tabaraani]

Verse Number 49

49- Have you not seen those (Yahood) who claim sanctity for themselves. Nay, but Allaah sanctifies whom He wills, and they will not be dealt with unjustly even as much as a thread (in a date-stone). A narration on the authority of Ibn 'Abbaas [Allaah be pleased with them] that he said: The Yahood used to put forward their children to lead them in prayer and present the offerings on behalf of them under claim that they were sinless. On that occasion, Allaah revealed this Quraanic Ayaah. [Ibn Abu Haatim and Ibn Jareer]

Verse Number 51

51- Have you not seen those who were given a portion of the Scripture? They believe in Jibt (superstitions) and Taaghoot (false objects of worship)and say to the disbelievers (al-Kaafireen) that they are better guided as regards the way than the believers (al-Mumineen) (Muslims).

A narration on the authority of Ibn 'Abbaas [Allaah be pleased with them] that he said: When Ka'b Ibn Al-Ashraf came to Makkah, the Quraysh men said to him: "Do you not see this man who is cut off from his people? He claims that he is better than us even though we are the people of Hajj, the custodians of the Ka'bah and the providers of water (to the pilgrims)". He said: "No doubt, you are better than him". In connection with them, Allaah revealed (what means): {Indeed, your enemy is cut off}. [Al-Kawthar, verse 3] Allaah also revealed this Quraanic Ayaah in issue. [Ahmad and Ibn Abu Haatim]

A narration on the authority of Ibn 'Abbaas [Allaah be pleased with them] that he said: Those who took the lead of gathering the confederates against the Muslims, from among the Quraysh, Ghatfân and Banu Quraythah, were Huyayy Ibn Akhtab, Salaam Ibn Abu Al-Huqayq, Ar-Rabee' Ibn Ar-Rabee' Ibn Abu Al-Huqayq, Abu 'Ammaar, Wahwah Ibn 'AAmir and Hawdhah Ibn Qays and they were from Banu Waa'il and Banu An-Nadeer. When they went to the Quraysh, the disbelievers (al-Kaafireen) said to each other: "Those are the Jewish rabbis who have knowledge of the previous Scripture. Ask them whether your religion or the religion of Muhammad is better". They asked them and the Yahood replied: "Nay! Your religion is better than his, and you are more guided than him and his followers". In connection with them, Allaah Almighty (the Most High) revealed this Quraanic Ayaah. [Ibn Ishaaq]

Verse Number 54

54- Or do they envy men (Muhammad and his followers) for what Allaah has given them of His Bounty? Then We had already given the family of

Abraham the Book and wisdom, and conferred upon them a great kingdom.

A narration on the authority of Ibn 'Abbaas [Allaah be pleased with them] that he said: The people of Scripture said: "Muhammad claims that he has been given what he has been given; yet he is humble. But he has nine wives and his main concern is to have sexual intercourse (with his wives). Which dominion is better than this?" On that occasion, Allaah revealed this Quraanic Ayaah. [Ibn Abu Haatim]

Verse Number 58

58- Verily! Allaah commands that you should render back the trusts to those to whom they are due; and that when you judge between men, you judge with justice. Verily, how excellent is the teaching which He (Allaah) gives you! Truly, ever is Allaah All-Hearing, All-Seeing.

A narration on the authority of Ibn 'Abbaas [Allaah be pleased with them] that he said: When the Prophet [peace and blessings of Allaah be upon him] conquered Makkah, he invited 'Uthmaan Ibn Talhah so when he came to him he said: "Give me the key (of the Ka'bah)". He brought it to him and when he stretched his hand to him to take it Al-'Abbaas stood up and said: 'O Messenger of Allaah! Let my father and mother sacrifice their lives for you! Give it to me besides Siqaayah!" 'Uthmaan withdrew his hand. the Prophet [peace and blessings of Allaah be upon him] told him: "Give me the key O 'Uthmaan!" He told him:

"Here it is the trust of Allaah". the Prophet [peace and blessings of Allaah be upon him] stood and opened the Ka'bah and then came out and performed Tawaaf around the House. Jibreel then revealed to him to give back the key (to 'Uthmaan). He invited 'Uthmaan Ibn Talhah once again and gave him the key and then recited (Allaah's saying what means): {Verily, Allaah commands that you should render back the trust to those to whom they are due...} [verse 58] [Ibn Mardawayh].

Verse Number 59

59- O you who believe! Obey Allaah and obey the Messenger (Muhammad) and those in authority among you. If you dispute in anything amongst yourselves, refer it to (the Book of) Allaah and His Messenger, if you believe in Allaah and in the Last Day. That is better and more suitable in conclusion.

A narration on the authority of Ibn 'Abbaas [Allaah be pleased with them] that this Quraanic Ayaah was revealed in connection with 'Abdullaah Ibn Hudhaafah whom the Prophet [peace and blessings of Allaah be upon him] appointed a leader of a military expedition. Having grown angry with his soldiers, he kindled a fire and asked them to throw themselves into it. They were put to confusion and some of them intended to do while others rejected the command. [Al-Bukhaari]

Commenting on that, Ibn Hajar argues that the point in this story is Allaah's saying (what means): {If you dispute in anything amongst yourselves, refer it to (the Book of) Allaah and His Messenger} [verse 59], which refers to their dispute as to whether or not they should comply with the command of the leader. For this reason, the revelation came to guide them to what to do when they dispute over anything: it is to refer the matter to (the Book of) Allaah and His Messenger [peace and blessings of Allaah be upon him].

Verse Number 60

60- Have you seen those (hypocrites (al-Munaafiqeen)) who claim that they believe in that which has been sent down to you, and that which was sent down before you, and they wish to go for judgment (in their disputes) to the Taaghoot while they have been ordered to disbelieve in them. But Satan wishes to lead them far astray (from the truth).

A narration on the authority of Ibn 'Abbaas [Allaah be pleased with them] that he said: Abu Barzah Al-Aslami was a soothsayer and used to judge between the Yahood whenever they appealed to him for judgment. One day some Muslims appealed to him for judgment, thereupon Allaah revealed this Quraanic Ayaah. [Ibn Abu Haatim and At-Tabaraani with an authentic chain of narrators]

A narration on the authority of Ibn 'Abbaas [Allaah be pleased with them] that he said: Al-Julaas Ibn As-Saamit, Mu'tib Ibn Qushayr, Raafi' Ibn Zayd and Bishr claimed to be Muslims. They disputed with some Muslims over something, thereupon, they were invited to the Prophet [peace and blessings of Allaah be upon him] to judge between them. But they invited them to the soothsayers, who used to judge between the people in the pre-Islamic days. In connection with them, Allaah Almighty (the Most High) revealed this Quraanic Ayaah. [Ibn Abu Haatim]

A narration on the authority of Ash-Sha'bi that he said: There was a dispute between a Jew and a hypocrite, the Jew told him: "Let me appeal to the men of your religion to judge between you and me", or he told "to the Prophet", because he knew that he did not accept bribe in judgment. But they differed and agreed to go to a soothsayer in Juhaynah. [Ibn Jareer]

Verse Number 65

65- But no, by your Lord (Rabb), they can have no Faith, until they make you (O Muhammad) judge in all disputes between them, and find in themselves no discomfort from your decisions, and accept (them) with full submission.

A narration on the authority of 'Abdullaah Ibn Az-Zubayr [Allaah be pleased with them] that he said: An Ansaari man quarreled with Az-Zubayr in the presence of The Prophet [peace and blessings of Allaah be upon him] about the Harrah Canals which were used for irrigating the date-palms. The Ansaari man told Az-Zubayr: "Let the water pass", but Az-Zubayr refused to do so. So, the case was brought to The Prophet [peace and blessings of Allaah be upon him] who said to Az-Zubayr: "O Zubayr! Irrigate (your land) and then let the water pass to your neighbor." On that, the Ansaari got angry and told The Prophet [peace and blessings of Allaah be upon him]: "Is it because he (that is Zubayr) is your aunt's son?" On that, the color of the face of the Prophet [peace and blessings of Allaah be upon him] changed (because of anger) and he said: "O Zubayr! Irrigate (your land) and then withhold the water till it reaches the walls between the pits round the trees." Az-Zubayr said: "By Allaah, I think that this Quraanic verse was revealed on this occasion. [Al-Bukhaari; Muslim; At-Tirmidhi; Ibn Maajah; Abu Daawood and An-Nasaa'i]

The same is narrated on the authority of Umm Salamah [Allaah be pleased with her]. [At-Tabaraani in Al-Kabeer]

A narration on the authority of Abu Al-Aswad that he said: Two men appealed to the Prophet [peace and blessings of Allaah be upon him] to judge between them and he did accordingly. The one against whom he gave his judgment said: "Let us go to 'Umar Ibn Al-Khattaab (to judge between us)". They went to him and the man said: "the Prophet [peace and blessings of Allaah be upon him] gave a judgment in my favor against this man but he said: 'Let us go to 'Umar to judge between us". 'Umar said: "Has he done so?" He said yes. On that, 'Umar said: "Remain in your places till I come out and judge between you". He came to them taking up his sword, therewith, he killed the one who asked his opponent to go to 'Umar. On that occasion, Allaah revealed this Quraanic Ayaah. [Ibn

Mardawayh: Mursal and its chain of narrators is strange.]

Verse Number 66

66- And if We had decreed upon them (the command): "Kill yourselves or leave your homes," they would not have done it except for a very few of them; but if they had done what they were instructed to do, it would have been better for them, and would have strengthened their (Faith).

A narration on the authority of As-Suddi that he said: When Allaah revealed (what means): {And if We had decreed upon them (the command): "Kill yourselves" or "Leave your homes," they would not have done it, except for a very few of them} [verse 66], Thaabit Ibn Qays Ibn Shamaas and a Jew vied in glory with each other. The Jew said: "By Allaah, Allaah decreed upon us to kill ourselves and we actually killed ourselves". Thaabit said: "By Allaah, if Allaah decreed upon us to kill ourselves, we would kill ourselves". On that occasion, Allaah revealed (what means): {But if they had done what they were instructed to do, it would have been better for them, and would have strengthened their (Faith)} [verse 66]. [Ibn Jareer]

Verse Number 69

69- And whosoever obey Allaah and the Messenger (Muhammad) then they will be in the company of those on whom Allaah has bestowed His favor, of the Prophets, the sincere affirmers of truth, the martyrs and the righteous. And how excellent are these for companions!

A narration on the authority of 'AA'ishah [Allaah be pleased with her] that she said: A man came to the Prophet [peace and blessings of Allaah be upon him] and said: "O Messenger of Allaah! You are indeed dearer to me than myself and my children. Sometimes, I remember you while I am at home and I cannot help going out to see you. I feel afraid when I remember that you and I will die, as I know that when you enter Paradise you will be in the highest place with the prophets, and that if I enter Paradise I will not be able to see you (d to your being in that high status)". The Prophet [peace and blessings of Allaah be upon him] gave no reply until Allaah Almighty (the Most High) revealed this Quraanic Ayaah. [At-Tabaraani and Ibn Mardawayh]

A narration on the authority of Masrooq that he said: The Companions of Muhammad [peace and blessings of Allaah be upon him] told him: "O Messenger of Allaah! It is not fit for us to leave you. Verily, if you die, you will be raised above us, and we will not be able to see you". On that occasion, Allaah revealed this Quraanic Ayaah. [Ibn Abu Haatim]

A narration on the authority of 'Ikrimah that he said: A young man came to the Prophet [peace and blessings of Allaah be upon him] and said: "O Prophet of Allaah! We, in this world, are able to see you, but on the Day of Resurrection, we will not be able to see you because you will be in the highest rank in Paradise". On that occasion, Allaah revealed this Quraanic Ayaah. the Prophet [peace and blessings of Allaah be upon him] said to him: "You will be with me in Paradise, Allaah willing". [Ibn Abu Haatim]

Verse Number 77

77- Have you not seen those who were told to hold back their hands and establish prayer, and give Zakaah, but when the fighting was ordained for them, behold! A section of them fear men as they fear (the punishment of) Allaah or even more. They say: "Our Lord (Rabb)! Why have You ordained for us fighting? Would that You had granted us respite for a short period?" Say: "Short is the enjoyment of this world (Paradise in) the Hereafter is (far) better for him who fears Allaah, and you shall not be dealt with unjustly even as much as a thread in a date-stone.

A narration on the authority of Ibn 'Abbaas [Allaah be pleased with them] that 'Abd-Ar-Rahmaan Ibn 'Awf and some of his companions went to the Prophet [peace and blessings of Allaah be upon him] (while they were still in Makkah) and said: "O Prophet of Allaah! When we were polytheists, we were living in honor and power but when we believed, we became humiliated". He said: "I have been commanded to pardon (people): so do not fight them". When Allaah turned him to Madeenah, He commanded him to fight (the polytheists and disbelievers (al-Kaafireen)), thereupon they (those Muslims) withheld (their hands from fighting). On that occasion, Allaah Almighty (the

Most High) revealed this Quraanic Ayaah. [An-Nasa'i and Al-Haakim]

Verse Number 83

83- When there comes to them some matter touching (public) safety (because of victory) or fear (because of defeat), they make it known (among the people); if only they had referred it to the Messenger or to those charged with authority among them, the proper investigators would have understood it from them (directly). Had it not been for Allaah's Grace and Mercy upon you, you would have followed Satan, save a few of you.

A narration on the authority of 'Umar Ibn Al-Khattaab [may Allaah be pleased with him] that he said: When the Prophet [peace and blessings of Allaah be upon him] kept aloof from his wives, I entered the mosque and behold! People were striking the ground with pebbles and saying: "the Prophet [peace and blessings of Allaah be upon him] has divorced his wives". I stood near the gate of the mosque and called, at the top of my voice: "the Prophet [peace and blessings of Allaah be upon him] has not divorced his wives". On that occasion, this Quraanic Ayaah was revealed. I was of those who drew correct conclusions from this matter. [Muslim]

Verse Number 88

88- Then what is the matter with you that you are divided into two parties about the hypocrites (al-

Munaafiqeen)? Allaah has cast them back (to disbelief) because of what they have earned (of mistrust and sins). Do you want to guide him whom Allaah has made to go astray? And he whom Allaah has made to go astray, you will never find for him any way (of guidance).

A narration on the authority of Zayd Ibn Thaabit [may Allaah be pleased with him] that he said: When the Prophet [peace and blessings of Allaah be upon him] set out for the battle of Uhud, some people of those who set out with him returned. The Companions of the Prophet [peace and blessings of Allaah be upon him] had two opinions about them: a party was of the opinion that they should be killed and another party adopted the opinion that they should not be killed. On that occasion, Allaah Almighty (the Most High) revealed this Quraanic Ayaah. [Al-Bukhaari; Muslim and others]

A narration on the authority of Sa'd Ibn Mu'aadh [may Allaah be pleased with him] that he said: the Prophet [peace and blessings of Allaah be upon him] addressed the people saying: "Who could support me against him who harms me and gathers in his house those who do harm to me?" Sa'd Ibn Mu'aadh said: "If he is from the Aws (tribe), then we would kill him and if he is from our brothers of Khazraj (tribe), you then should command us and we would obey you". Sa'd Ibn 'Ubaadah stood and said: "No doubt, by so saying, O Mu'aadh, you do not seek to obey the Prophet [peace and blessings of Allaah be upon him], since you know well that this (man) does not belong to your (tribe)".

Usayd Ibn Hudayr stood and said: "Verily, You O Ibn 'Ubaadah are a hypocrite and love the hypocrites (al-Munaafiqeen)". Muhammad Ibn Maslamah stood and said: "Keep silent O people because the Prophet [peace and blessings of Allaah be upon him] is among us; so, let him command us and we shall carry out his command". On that occasion, Allaah revealed this Quraanic Ayaah. [Sa'eed Ibn Mansoor]

Verse Number 90

90- Except those who take refuge to a group, between you and whom there is a treaty (of peace), or those who approach you with their breasts restraining from fighting you (beside their people) as well as fighting their own people (beside you). Had Allaah willed, indeed He would have given them power over you, and they would have fought you. So if they withdraw from you, and fight not against you, and offer you peace, then Allaah has made for you no cause (of seizing or fighting) against them.

A narration on the authority of Al-Hasan that Suraaqah Ibn Malik Al-Mudliji related to them: When the Prophet [peace and blessings of Allaah be upon him] emerged victorious over the people of Badr and Uhud, and people around him embraced Islam, I was informed that he intended to send Khalid Ibn Al-Waleed (to fight) my people, Banu Mudlij. I went to him and said: "I beseech you by the blessing!" The people told me to keep silent. the Prophet [peace and blessings of Allaah be upon him] said: "Let him! What do you want?" I said: "I was informed that you intend to send (Khaalid Ibn Al-Waleed) to (fight) my people, and I see that you should make a peace treaty with them. If your people (the Quraysh) embraced Islam, they would embrace Islam with them, and if they did not do, then, your people would not treat them harshly". the Prophet [peace and blessings of Allaah be upon him] caught hold of the hand of Khalid Ibn Al-Waleed and told him: "Go with him and do what he wants". Khalid made a peace treaty with them, on the condition that they should assist none against the Prophet [peace and blessings of Allaah be upon him] and that if the Quraysh embraced Islam, they would embrace Islam with them. On that occasion, Allaah Almighty (the Most High) revealed this Quraanic Ayaah. [Ibn Abu Haatim and Ibn Mardawayh]

A narration on the authority of Mujaahid that he said: This Quraanic Ayaah was revealed in connection with Hilaal Ibn 'Uwaymir Al-Aslami between whom and the Muslims there was a treaty. Some of his people came to him (seeking his protection) thereupon he disliked to fight The Prophet [peace and blessings of Allaah be upon him] and also his people. [Ibn Abu Haatim]

Verse Number 92

92- It is not fit for a believer to kill a believer except (that it be) by mistake; and whosoever kills a believer by mistake, (it is ordained that) he must set free a believing slave and a compensation be given to the deceased's family (heirs), unless they remit it. If the deceased belonged to a people at war with you and he was a believer, the freeing of a believing slave (is prescribed); and if he belonged to a people with whom you have a treaty of mutual alliance, a compensation must be paid to his family, and a believing slave must be freed. And whosoever could not afford for this (freeing a slave), the fasts of two consecutive months will be due on him in order to seek repentance from Allaah. And ever is Allaah All-Knowing, All-Wise.

A narration on the authority of 'Ikrimah that he said: Al-Haarith Ibn Yazeed, from Banu 'AAmir Ibn Lu'ayy used to torment 'Ayyaash Ibn Abu Rabi'ah with Abu Jahl. Later on, he set out as an emigrant to the Prophet [peace and blessings of Allaah be upon him] whereupon 'Ayyaash met him at Al-Harrah and struck him with the sword, thinking him to be a disbeliever.

Then, he went to the Prophet [peace and blessings of Allaah be upon him] and told him what happened. On that occasion, Allaah revealed this Quraanic Ayaah. [Ibn Jareer]

Verse Number 93

93- And whoever kills a believer intentionally, his recompense is Hell to abide therein; and the Wrath and the Curse of Allaah are upon him, and a great punishment is prepared for him. A narration on the authority of 'Ikrimah that an Ansaari man killed the brother of Miqyas Ibn Sabaabah, so the Prophet [peace and blessings of Allaah be upon him] gave him (Miqyas) the compensation and he accepted it. Then he jumped over the killer of his brother and killed him. On that, the Prophet [peace and blessings of Allaah be upon him] said: "I will never give him security, whether outside or inside the Sanctuary". Then he was killed on the day of the conquest (of Makkah). In connection with him, this Quraanic Ayaah was revealed. [Ibn Jareer]

Verse Number 94

94- O you who believe! When you go (to fight) in the Cause of Allaah, verify (the truth), and say not to anyone who greets you (with peace): "You are not a believer"; seeking the perishable goods of the worldly life. There are much more profits and booties with Allaah. Even as he is now, so were you yourselves before till Allaah conferred on you His Favor (of embracing Islam). Therefore, be cautious in discrimination. Ever is Allaah Well-Aware of what you do.

A narration on the authority of Ibn 'Abbaas [Allaah be pleased with them] that he said: A man from Banu Sulaym came upon a group of the Companions of the Prophet [peace and blessings of Allaah be upon him], while he was driving some sheep belonging to him. He greeted them but they said: "He has greeted us only to seek refuge from us". They then killed him and brought his sheep to the Prophet [peace and blessings of Allaah be upon him]. On that occasion, Allaah revealed this Quraanic Ayaah. [Al-Bukhaari; At-Tirmidhi; Al-Haakim and others]

A narration on the authority of Ibn 'Abbaas [Allaah be pleased with them] that he said: the Prophet [peace

and blessings of Allaah be upon him] dispatched a military expedition including Al-Miqdaad. They arrived by the time the enemies had dispersed except for one man who had an abundant possessions. He said: "I testify that there is none worthy of worship but Allaah". But Al-Miqdaad killed him. On that, the Prophet [peace and blessings of Allaah be upon him] told him: "How do you do with (his statement) 'I testify that there is none worthy of worship but Allaah' tomorrow (in the hereafter)?" On that occasion, Allaah revealed this Quraanic Ayaah. [Al-Bazzaar]

A narration on the authority of 'Abdullah Ibn Abu Hadrad: the Prophet [peace and blessings of Allaah be upon him] sent us to Idaam, and I set out in the company of some Muslims, including Abu Qataadah, Al-Haarith Ibn Rib'i and Muhallam Ibn Jaththaamah Ibn Qays. We proceeded until we reached the valley of Idaam, 'AAmir Ibn Adbat Al-Ashja'i met us, riding a camel and having two young camels. When he came upon us, he saluted us.

We did not harm him but Muhallam Ibn Jaththaamah attacked and killed him for some (mutual) hatred which was between them. He then took his belongings. When we returned to the Prophet [peace and blessings of Allaah be upon him] and told him about what happened, Allaah revealed in connection with us this Quraanic Ayaah. [Ahmad; At-Tabaraani and others]

According to the narration of Ath-Tha'labi the name of the murdered is Mirdaas Ibn Naheek from Fadak, the killer is Usaamah Ibn Zayd and the commander of the expedition is Ghaalib Ibn Fadaalah Al-Laythi.

A narration on the authority of Juz' Ibn Al-Hadrajaan that he said: The brother of Al-Miqdaad came to the Prophet [peace and blessings of Allaah be upon him] from Yemen and was met by the military expedition of the Prophet [peace and blessings of Allaah be upon him]. He told them: "I am a believer".

But they did not accept it from him and killed him. (Al-Miqdaad said) Having been informed, I went to the Prophet [peace and blessings of Allaah be upon him] (and made a mention of that to him). On that occasion, Allaah revealed this Quraanic Ayaah.

The Prophet [peace and blessings of Allaah be upon him] gave me the compensation of my (killed) brother. [Ibn Mandah]

Verse Number 95

95- Not equal are those of the believers (al-Mumineen) who sit (at home), except those who are disabled, and those who strive hard and fight in the Cause of Allaah with their wealth and their lives. Allaah has preferred those who strive hard and fight with their wealth and their lives above those who sit (at home) in degrees. Unto each, Allaah has promised good (Paradise), but Allaah has preferred those who strive hard and fight, above those who sit (at home) by a great reward.

A narration on the authority of Al-Baraa' [may Allaah be pleased with him] that he said: When Allaah Almighty (the Most High) revealed: {Not equal are those Believers who sit (at home), and those who strive and fight in the Cause of Allaah with their wealth and their lives} The Prophet [peace and blessings of Allaah be upon him] said: "Call so-and-so (Zayd Ibn Thaabit)", who came with an ink-pot and a shoulder-blade. the Prophet [peace and blessings of Allaah be upon him] said: "Write: {Not equal are those Believers who sit (at home), and those who strive and fight in the Cause of Allaah with their wealth and their lives}[verse 95]. Ibn Umm Maktoom (the blind) was behind The Prophet [peace and blessings of Allaah be upon him]. He said: "O Messenger of Allaah! I am blind (and cannot take part in Jihad)". On that occasion, Allaah revealed instead (what means): {Not equal are those believers (al-Mumineen) who sit (at home), except those who are disabled, and those who strive hard and fight in the Cause of Allaah with their wealth and their lives}. [Al-Bukhaari]

Verse Number 97

97- Verily! As for those whom the angels take (in death) while they are wronging themselves, they (angels) say (to them): "In what (condition) were you?" They reply: "We were weak and oppressed on earth." They (angels) say: "Was not the earth of Allaah spacious enough for you to emigrate therein?" Such men will find their abode in Hell - What an evil destination!

A narration on the authority of Ibn 'Abbaas [Allaah be pleased with them] that he said: some Muslim people were with the pagans, increasing the number of the pagans against Allaah's Apostle [peace and blessings of Allaah be upon him]. An arrow used to be shot which would hit one of them (the Muslims in the company of the pagans) and kill him, or he would be struck and killed (with a sword). On that occasion, Allaah Almighty (the Most High) revealed this Quraanic Ayaah. [Al-Bukhaari]

According to the narration of Ibn Mardawayh, those included Qays Ibn Al-Waleed Ibn Al-Mugheerah, Abu Qays Ibn Al-Faakih Ibn Al-Mugheerah, Al-Waleed Ibn 'Utbah Ibn Rabee'ah, 'Amr Ibn Umayyah Ibn Sufyaan and 'Ali Ibn Umayyah Ibn Khalaf. They came to Badr (battle) and when they saw the Muslims as few in number, they fell in doubt and said: "Those (Muslims) have been deceived by their religion." Then they were killed in Badr.

A narration on the authority of Ibn 'Abbaas [Allaah be pleased with them] that he said: Some people in Makkah embraced Islam. When the Prophet [peace and blessings of Allaah be upon him] emigrated from Makkah they disliked to emigrate with him out of fear. In connection with them, Allaah revealed this Quraanic Ayaah. [At-Tabaraani]

A narration on the authority of Ibn 'Abbaas [Allaah be pleased with them] that he said: Some people from Makkah embraced Islam but they used not to take it seriously. So, on the day of (the battle of) Badr, the infidels made them set out (for fighting) beside them. Some of those (Muslims) were killed. Upon this, the Muslims (of Madinah) said: "Indeed, those (of Mecca) companions of us were Muslims, and they were forced (to set out for fighting). So, ask for Allaah's forgiveness for them". They asked for Allaah's forgiveness for them, and on that occasion, Allaah revealed this Quraanic Ayaah. Then, the remaining Muslims (in Makkah) were informed that they would have no excuse (to stay there and be forced to do the same once again) in accordance with this Quraanic Ayaah. So, they set out (with the intention of migration) but the infidels joined them and succeeded to seduce them. On that, Allaah revealed (what means): {Of the people there are some who say: "We believe in Allaah and the Last day;" but they do not (really) believe}. [Al-Baqarah 8] [Ibn Abu Haatim] Verse Number 100

100- He who emigrates (from his home) in the Cause of Allaah, will find on earth many dwelling places and plenty (of sustenance) to live by. And whosoever leaves his home as an emigrant unto Allaah and His Messenger, and death overtakes him, his reward is then surely incumbent upon Allaah. And ever is Allaah Oft-Forgiving, Most Merciful.

A narration on the authority of Ibn 'Abbaas [Allaah be pleased with them] that he said: Damrah Ibn Jundub set out (with the intention to emigrate) to the Prophet [peace and blessings of Allaah be upon him], and on his way, he died before reaching the Prophet [peace and blessings of Allaah be upon him]. On that occasion, Allaah revealed this Quraanic Ayaah. [Ibn Ab Haatim]

A narration on the authority of Abu Damrah Az-Zuraqi and he was in Makkah when Allaah revealed (what means): {Except for the oppressed among men, women and children who cannot devise a plan} [verse 98] He said: "I am rich and can devise a plan (to emigrate)". He got ready with the intention to emigrate to the Prophet [peace and blessings of Allaah be upon him] but death overtook him at At-Tan'eem. On that occasion, Allaah Almighty (the Most High) revealed this Quraanic Ayaah. [Ibn Abu Haatim]

A narration on the authority of Yazeed Ibn 'Abdullaah Ibn Qusayt that Jundub Ibn Damrah Ad-Damri was in Makkah when he fell ill. He said to his sons: "Take me out of Makkah since its anxieties have killed me". They asked him: "Where will you like to go?" He beckoned with his hand to Madeenah, thereby intending emigration. They took him out and when they reached Adaah Banu Ghifaar, he died. In connection with him, Allaah revealed this Quraanic Ayaah. [Ibn Sa'd in At-Tabaqaat]

A narration on the authority of Hishaam Ibn 'Urwah from his father that Az-Zubayr Ibn Al-'Awwaam [may Allaah be pleased with him] said: Khaalid Ibn Hizaam emigrated to Abyssinia and on the way, a serpent bit him and caused him death. In connection with him, Allaah revealed this Quraanic Ayaah. [Ibn Abu Haatim and others]

Verse Number 101

101- And when you (Muslims) travel in the land, there is no sin on you to shorten the prayer if you fear that the disbelievers (al-Kaafireen) may put you to trial. Verily, ever are the disbelievers (al-Kaafireen) unto you open enemies.

A narration on the authority of 'Ali [may Allaah be pleased with him] that he said: Some men from Banu An-Najjaar asked the Prophet [peace and blessings of Allaah be upon him] saying: "O Messenger of Allaah! We always travel through the earth: then how should we pray?" On that occasion, Allaah revealed this Quraanic Ayaah.

The divine revelation then stopped for some time and when it was a year later, the Prophet [peace and blessings of Allaah be upon him] set out for fighting and performed Thuhr prayer. The polytheists said: "Verily, Muhammad and his Companions exposed their backs to you: would you then attack them?" One of them said: "They will pray another one (that is 'Asr) following it". In the interval between both prayers (of Thuhr and 'Asr), Allaah revealed this and the succeeding Quraanic Aayaat. In this way, the command of the Fear prayer was sent down. [Ibn Jareer]

A narration on the authority of Abu 'Ayyaash Az-Zuraqi that he said: We were with the Prophet [peace and blessings of Allaah be upon him] in 'Usfaan when we faced the infidels under the leadership of Khalid

Ibn Al-Waleed, while they were standing between us and the Qiblah. When the Prophet [peace and blessings of Allaah be upon him] led us in the Thuhr prayer, they (the infidels) told one another: "They were in such a state as if we had taken them by surprise (we would have overpowered them)". They said (in reply to this): "Now, a prayer (that is Asr) will come upon them, which is much dearer to them than their offspring and themselves". Then, during the period between Thuhr and 'Asr, Jibreel [peace and blessings of Allaah be upon him] came with this and the succeeding Quraanic Aayaat. When it was the prayer's due time, the Prophet [peace and blessings of Allaah be upon him] ordered us to take arms, and then, he aligned us in two rows behind him. When he bowed, we all bowed after him. When he raised (his head) we raised (ours). Then, the Prophet [peace and blessings of Allaah be upon him] fell in prostration with the row next to him, while the people of the other were standing to safeguard them (who prostrated). When they rose and sat, these (of the other row) sat and prostrated in their places. Then, those in the rear came forward and took the places of those who were in the front, who, in turn, came back to take the places of those in the rear. When the Prophet [peace and blessings of Allaah be upon him] bowed, they all bowed. When he raised (his head) they all raised (theirs). Then, the Prophet [peace and blessings of Allaah be upon him] fell in prostration with the row next to him, while the others were standing to safeguard them. When they (rose and) sat, the others (who were standing) sat and then prostrated. Then, the Prophet [peace and blessings of Allaah be upon him] concluded (the prayer) with the End Salutation and turned away. the Prophet [peace and blessings of Allaah be upon him] offered this (Fear) prayer twice: one in 'Usfaan, and the other near the dwellings of Banu Sulaym. [Ahmad and Al-Haakim and rendered Saheeh by Al-Bayhaqi in Ad-Dalaa'il]

Verse Number 102

102- When you (O Muhammad) are among them, and lead them in prayer, let a party of them stand up (in prayer) with you taking their arms with them; when they fall in prostration, let them (the other party) take their positions in the rear of you and let the other party come up which have not yet prayed, and let them pray with you taking all their precautions and bearing arms. Those who disbelieve wish, if you were negligent of your arms and your baggage, to attack you in a single rush, but there is no sin on you if you put away your arms because of the inconvenience of rain or because you are ill, but take every precaution for yourselves. Verily, Allaah has prepared a humiliating torment for the disbelievers (al-Kaafireen).

A narration on the authority of Ibn 'Abbaas [Allaah be pleased with them] that he said: This Quraanic Ayaah was revealed in connection with 'Abd-Ar-Rahmaan Ibn 'Awf as was ounded. [Al-Bukhaari]

Verse Number 105

105- Surely, We have sent down to you (O Muhammad) the Book (Quraan) in truth that you may judge between men by that which Allaah has shown you. So be not a pleader for the treacherous.

A narration on the authority of Qataadah Ibn An-Nu'maan [may Allaah be pleased with him] that he said: We had a household among us called Banu Ubayriq: Bishr, Basheer and Mubashshir. Basheer was a hypocrite and used to compose poetry lampooning the Companions of the Prophet [peace and blessings of Allaah be upon him] and attribute it to some Arabs. They were a poor and needy family before and even after the appearance of Islam. Dates and barley formed the main food of the inhabitants of Madeenah. My uncle Rifaa'ah Ibn Zayd bought a camel's load of foodstuff and stored it in an attic upper room containing arms. Then it was attacked from below and the foodstuff and weapons were taken from the upper room.

In the morning my uncle Rifaa'ah came to me and said: "O my nephew! Tonight we have been attacked and our upper room was dug and our foodstuff and weapons were taken". After investigation, we were informed that Banu Ubayriq kindled fire on that night and to the best of our knowledge, they did so with part of our foodstuff". Banu Ubayriq said: "By Allaah, we do not think except that the one who has done so is Labeed Ibn Sahl, a man from among us who is righteous and good in faith". Having heard about that, Labeed took up his sword and said: "Is it that I steal? By Allaah, I will kill you with this sword or you should make evident this theft". They said: "Leave us O man: it is unfit for you to do so".

We investigated once again till we came to know, with certainty, that it is those who committed it. My uncle told me: "O my nephew! Would that you go to the Prophet [peace and blessings of Allaah be upon him] and make a mention of that to him!" I went to him and said: "A household from among us aimed at my uncle and dug an attic room belonging to him and took his weapons and foodstuff. Let them give back to us our weapons; and as for the foodstuff, we have no need for it". the Prophet [peace and blessings of Allaah be upon him] said: "I will consider the matter".

Having heard about that, Banu Ubayriq went to a man from among them called Usayr Ibn 'Urwah and talked to him with respect to that. Some men of the household gathered for this purpose and said: "O Messenger of Allaah! Qataadah Ibn An-Nu'maan and his uncle aimed at a household from among us recognized for their good faith and righteousness and accused them of stealing with no evidence". Qataadah said: I went to the Prophet [peace and blessings of Allaah be upon him] and he said: "Have you aimed at a household of Muslims and accused them of stealing with no evidence?" I came back and told my uncle who said: "It is Allaah Whose aid is sought".

Shortly Allaah revealed (what means): {Indeed, We have revealed to you (O Muhammad) the Book (Quraan) in truth so you may judge between the people by that which Allaah has shown you. And be not a pleader for the treacherous}. [verse 105]

Concerning Banu Ubayriq, Allaah revealed (what means): {And seek forgiveness of Allaah (from what you have said to Qataadah) ...} up to {then We are going to give him a great reward}. [verse 106-114]

When this revelation came down, the Prophet [peace and blessings of Allaah be upon him] brought the weaponry and gave it back to Rifa'ah. Basheer joined the polytheists and descended in the house of Sulaafah Bint Sa'd. On that occasion, Allaah revealed (what means): {And whoever opposes the Messenger ...} up to {has certainly gone far astray}. [verse 115-116] [At-Tirmidhi; Al-Haakim and others]

Verse Number 123-124

123- It does not go back to your desires (Muslims), nor to those of the people of the Scripture (Yahood and Nasaara), whosoever works evil will have the recompense thereof, and he will not find any protector or helper besides Allaah. 124- And whoever does deeds of righteousness, be he male or female, and is a (faithful) believer, such will enter Paradise and not be dealt with unjustly in the least even as much as a speck on the back of a date-stone.

A narration on the authority of Ibn 'Abbaas [Allaah be pleased with them] that he said: The Yahood said: "None other than us will enter Paradise". The Quraysh people also said: "We shall not be resurrected after death". On that occasion, Allaah Almighty (the Most High) revealed this Quraanic Ayaah. [Ibn Abu Haatim]

A narration on the authority of Masrooq that he said: The Nasaara and Muslims vied in glory and each party claimed that they were better than the other. On that occasion, Allaah Almighty (the Most High) revealed this Quraanic Ayaah. [Ibn Jareer]

A narration on the authority of Masrooq that he said: When Allaah revealed (what means): { It does not go back to your desires (Muslims), nor to those of the people of the Scripture (Yahood and Nasaara)...} [verse 123], the people of Scripture said (to the Muslims): "We and you are equal (in rank)". Allaah revealed (what means): {And whoever does deeds of righteousness, be he male or female, and is a (faithful) believer, such will enter Paradise and not be dealt with unjustly in the least even as much as a speck on the back of a date-stone}. [verse 124] [Ibn Abu Haatim]

Verse Number 127

127- They ask your legal instruction concerning women, say: Allaah instructs you about them, and about what is recited unto you in the Book (Quraan) concerning the orphan girls to whom you (their guardians) give not their prescribed shares (Of dowry and inheritance) and disdain to marry, and (concerning) the weak and oppressed children, and (instructs you) to stand firm for justice to orphans. And whatever good you do, ever is Allaah All-Knowing of it.

A narration on the authority of 'AA'ishah [Allaah be pleased with her] that she said: "This is about the orphan girl who lives with her guardian and shares his property. Her wealth and beauty may tempt him to marry her without giving her an adequate dowry which might have been given by another suitor. So, such guardians were forbidden to marry those orphan girls unless they treated them justly and gave them the most suitable dowry; otherwise they were ordered to marry any other woman. 11

'AA'ishah [Allaah be pleased with her] further said: "After that Quraanic verse had been revealed (that is Allaah's saying what means): {And if you that you shall not able to deal justly with the orphan-girls...} [verse 3], the people again asked The Prophet [peace and blessings of Allaah be upon him] (about the marriage with orphan girls), so Allaah revealed (what means): {They ask your legal instruction concerning women, say: Allaah instructs you about them, and about what is recited unto you in the Book (Quraan) concerning the orphan girls to whom you (their guardians) give not their prescribed shares (Of dowry and inheritance) and disdain to marry} [Al-Bukhaari]

A narration on the authority of As-Suddi that he said: Jabir had an ugly paternal female cousin but she had wealth which she inherited from her father. Jabir did not desire to marry her but, at the same time, did not like to give her in marriage to anyone for fear her husband would take her property. On that occasion, this Quraanic Ayaah was revealed. [Ibn Abu Haatim]

Verse Number 128

128- And if a woman fears arrogance or desertion on her husband's part, there is no sin on them both if they make terms of peace between them; and reconciliation is better. And human inner-selves are swayed by stinginess. But if you do good and ward off evil, verily, ever is Allaah Well-Acquainted with what you do.

A narration on the authority of 'AA'ishah [Allaah be pleased with her] that she said: Sawdah (Bint Zam'ah) felt afraid lest the Prophet [peace and blessings of Allaah be upon him] would leave her when she grew very old, thereupon she said: "I grant my day-and-night turn to 'AA'ishah (provided that you should not divorce me)". On that occasion, this Quraanic Ayaah was revealed. [Abu Daawood and Al-Haakim]

A narration on the authority of Ibn Al-Musayyab that the daughter of Muhammad Ibn Maslamah was the wife of Raafi' Ibn Khadij, who disliked something about her, so he wanted to divorce her but she told him: "Do not divorce me and fix in me whatever seems more suitable to you".

On that occasion, Allaah Almighty (the Most High) revealed this Quraanic Ayaah.

[Sa'eed Ibn Mansoor and Al-Haakim on the authority of Raafi' Ibn Khadij] A narration on the authority of 'AA'ishah [Allaah be pleased with her] that she said: Allaah's statement (what means): {and reconciliation is better} was revealed in connection with a man who had a wife from whom he had children and he liked to replace her with another. She seduced him to remain with him and ceded her day-and-night turn. [Al-Haakim]

A narration on the authority of Sa'eed Ibn Jubayr that he said: When this Quraanic Ayaah was revealed, a woman came to her husband and said: "I want you to assign to me my financial maintenance".

She had already accepted to give up her day-and-night turn provided that he should keep her in wedlock. On that occasion, Allaah revealed (what means): {And human inner-selves are swayed by stinginess}. [verse 128] [Ibn Jareer]

Verse Number 135

135- O you who believe! Stand out firmly for justice, as witnesses to Allaah, even though it be against yourselves, or your parents, or your kin; and if he (the witnessed) is rich or poor, Allaah is Worthier of both (than you). So follow not (your) inclination, lest you avoid justice; and if you distort your witness or refuse to give it, verily, ever is Allaah Well-Acquainted with what you do.

A narration on the authority of As-Suddi that he said: When this Quraanic Ayaah was revealed to the Prophet [peace and blessings of Allaah be upon him], two men, a rich and a poor, appealed to him to judge between them. the Prophet [peace and blessings of Allaah be upon him] took sides with the poor, seeing that in no way could the poor be unjust to the rich. But Allaah Almighty (the Most High) insisted that he should stand out with justice between both. [Ibn Abu Haatim]

Verse Number 148

148- Allah does not like the public mention of evil except by him who has been wronged. And ever is Allaah All-Hearing, All-Knowing.

A narration on the authority of Mujaahid that he said: This Quraanic Ayaah was revealed in connection with a man who received somebody as a guest in Madeenah but dealt with him badly. The guest left him and complained of the bad treatment he received from him. So, one was given concession to complain of the bad treatment he receives from another. [Hannaad Ibn As-Sari]

Verse Number 153-156

153- The people of the Scripture (Yahood) ask you (O Muhammad) to bring down a book upon them from heaven. Indeed they asked Moses for even greater than that, when they said: "Show us Allaah in public," but they were struck with thunderclap and lightning for their wickedness. Then they worshipped the calf even after clear proofs had come to them. (Even) so We forgave them. And We gave Moses a clear proof of authority. 154- And We raised over them the Mount for (breaking) their covenant, and said: "Enter the gate (of the town) prostrating (or bowing) with humility;" and We commanded them: "Transgress not on the Sabbath." And We took from them a solemn covenant.

155- (We have cursed them) because of their breaking the covenant, disbelief in the signs of Allaah, and killing the Prophets with no just cause, and saying (to the Prophet Muhammad): "Our hearts (Qalb) are wrapped." Nay, Allaah has set a seal upon their hearts (Qalb) because of their disbelief, so they believe not but a few. 156- And because of their disbelief (in Jesus) and launching against Mary a grave false charge;

A narration on the authority of Muhammad Ibn Ka'b Al-Qurathi, Qataadah and As-Suddi that they said: The Yahood asked the Prophet [peace and blessings of Allaah be upon him] to (ask Allaah to) send down the Book from the heaven, the same as the Torah was sent down in written form upon Moses [peace and blessings of Allaah be upon him]. On that occasion, Allaah revealed those Quraanic Aayaat. A Jew knelt and said: "Allaah has not sent down any revelation to you, to Moses, to Jesus nor to anyone". On that occasion, Allaah revealed (what means): {And they did not appraise Allaah with true appraisal when they said, "Allaah did not reveal to a human being anything."} [Al-An'aam, verse 91] [Ibn Jareer]

Verse Number 163

163- Verily, We have revealed to you (O Muhammad) as We had revealed to Noah and the Prophets after him; We (also) revealed to Abraham, Ishmael and Isaac (his sons), Jacob (Isaac's son), his (Jacob's) offspring, Jesus, Job, Jonah, Aaron, and Solomon, and to David (Solomon's father) We gave Psalms.

A narration on the authority of Ibn 'Abbaas [Allaah be pleased with them] that he said: 'Adiyy Ibn Zayd said: "We do not know that Allaah sent down any revelation to any human being after Moses". On that occasion, Allaah revealed this Quraanic Ayaah. [Ibn Ishaaq]

Verse Number 166

166- But Allaah bears witness to (your Prophethood by) that which He has sent down (of the Quraan) unto you (O Muhammad): He has sent it down with His Knowledge, and the angels bear witness (to the same). And sufficient is Allaah as a Witness.

A narration on the authority of Ibn 'Abbaas [Allaah be pleased with them] that he said: A group of Yahood visited the Prophet [peace and blessings of Allaah be upon him] to whom he said: "By Allaah, I know well that you have been learnes that I am the Messenger of Allaah". They said: "We did not learn this". On that occasion, Allaah revealed this Quraanic Ayaah. [Ibn Ishaaq]

Verse Number 176

176- They ask you for a legal verdict. Say: "Allaah instructs you about such as leaves neither descendants nor ascendants (as heirs). If it is a man that dies leaving a sister, but not a child (nor a father), she shall have half the inheritance. If (such a deceased is) a woman, leaving (a brother but) no child, her brother shall take all her inheritance. If there are two sisters (and above), they shall have two-thirds of the inheritance; if they (the heirs) are brothers and sisters, the male shall have twice the share of the female. (Thus) does Allaah make clear to you (His Law) lest you go astray. And Allaah has knowledge of all things."

A narration on the authority of Jaabir Ibn 'Abdullaah [Allaah be pleased with them] that he said: The Prophet [peace and blessings of Allaah be upon him] came to me while I was sick. He performed ablution and poured the remaining water on me (or said: "Pour it on him") When I came to my senses I said: "O Allaah's Apostle! I have no son or father to inherit me, should I make a bequest to my sisters with one-third?" He said: "Be kind!" I said: "Then, should it be with the half?" He said: "Be kind!" Then he left and when he came in this Quraanic Ayaah was revealed according to which two-thirds the legacy should be assigned to the sisters if they are more than one. [An-Nasaa'i]

A narration on the authority of 'Umar [may Allaah be pleased with him] that he said: I asked the Prophet [peace and blessings of Allaah be upon him] about the deceased who leaves neither descendants nor ascendants as heirs, thereupon he said: "The Noble Ayaah revealed in summer is sufficient (to explain the matter) for you". However, had I asked the Prophet [peace and blessings of Allaah be upon him] about that, it would have been much dearer to me than to have in possession the red camels. [Ibn Mardawayh]

Soorah Al-Ma'idah

Verse Number 2

2- O you who believe! Violate not the Symbols of Allaah, nor the sanctity of the Sacred Month, nor the Had'y, nor (harm) the garlanded (people, animals or others) nor (encroach upon the safety of) the people coming to Al-Bayt Al-Haraam (in Makkah), seeking their Lord (Rabb)'s bounty (by trade) and good pleasure. But when you finish the Ihraam (of Hajj or 'Umrah), you may hunt, and let not the hatred of some people in (once) stopping you from Al-Masjid-al-Haraam (at Makkah) lead you to transgression (and hostility on your part). Cooperate in righteousness and piety; but do not cooperate in sin and transgression. And fear Allaah. Verily, Allaah is Severe in punishment.

A narration on the authority of 'Ikrimah that he said: Al-Hatn Ibn Hind Al-Bakri came to Madeenah with a caravan of foodstuff belonging to him which he sold. Then he entered upon the Prophet [peace and blessings of Allaah be upon him] and gave him the pledge of allegiance for Islam. When he turned his back (to leave), the Prophet [peace and blessings of Allaah be upon him] looked at him and said to those who were present with him: "This man has entered upon me with an impious face and turned his back with a treacherous nape". When he arrived in Yamaamah he renegaded from Islam. When it was the month of Dhul-Qa'dah, he came out with a caravan of foodstuff with the intention to go to Makkah. Having heard about him, a group of emigrants and Ansaar among the Companions of the Prophet [peace and blessings of Allaah be upon him] got ready to set out and take hold of him along with his caravan. On that occasion, Allaah revealed (what means): {O you who believe, Violate not the Symbols of Allaah, nor the sanctity of the Sacred Month}. They then desisted (and did not come out). [Ibn Jareer]

A narration on the authority of Zayd Ibn Aslam that he said: the Prophet [peace and blessings of Allaah be upon him] was at Hudaybiyah along with his Companions when the polytheists averted them from the House; which is was very hard on them. In the meantime, some polytheists from the people of the East came upon them with the intention to perform 'Umrah. The Companions of the Prophet [peace and blessings of Allaah be upon him] said: "Let us avert those as they (the polytheists of Makkah) had already averted our companions". On that occasion, Allaah revealed (what means): {and let not the hatred of some people in (once) stopping you from Al-Masjid-al-Haraam (at Makkah) lead you to transgression (and hostility on your part}. [Ibn Abu Haatim]

Verse Number 3

3- Forbidden to you (for food) are: the dead (animals), blood, the flesh of swine, and that on which Allaah's Name has not been mentioned while slaughtering, and that which has been killed by strangling, or by a violent blow, or by a head-long fall, or by the goring of horns, and that which has been (partly) eaten by a wild animal unless you are able to slaughter it (before its death) and that which is sacrificed (slaughtered) on stone altars. (Forbidden) also is to seek decision (or fortune) through divining arrows: (all) that is defiant disobedience (of Allaah). This day, those who disbelieved have given up all hope of your religion; so fear them not, but fear Me. This day, I have perfected your religion for you, completed My Favor upon you, and have chosen for you Islam as your religion. But as for him who is forced by severe hunger, with no inclination to sin then surely, Allaah is Oft-Forgiving, Most Merciful.

A narration on the authority of Hibbaan Ibn Hujr that he said: We were with the Prophet [peace and blessings of Allaah be upon him] when I was cooking the flesh of a dead in a boiling vessel. Then, the prohibition of the flesh of the dead was revealed thereupon, I turned over the boiling vessel. [Ibn Mandah in Kitaab As-Sahaabah]

Verse Number 4

4- They ask you (O Muhammad) what is lawful for them (as food). Say: "Lawful unto you are edibles (which Allaah has made permissible). And game (caught by) hunting animals which you have trained as hounds in the manner Allaah taught you; so eat of what they catch for you, but pronounce the Name of Allaah over it, and fear Allaah. Verily, Allaah is Swift in reckoning."

A narration on the authority of Abu Raafi' [may Allaah be pleased with him] that he said: Jibreel [peace and blessings of Allaah be upon him] came to the Prophet [peace and blessings of Allaah be upon him] and sought his permission and he was admitted. But he did not come in. the Prophet [peace and blessings of Allaah be upon him] took his garment and went out to meet him and he was standing at the door. He said: "We have admitted you". Jibreel said: "Yes, but we (angels) never enter a house in which there is a picture or a dog". They looked and behold! There was a puppy in one of their (the Prophet's wives') chambers. He [peace and blessings of Allaah be upon him] then commanded Abu Raafi' not to leave a dog in Madeenah but that he should kill it. The people came to him and said: "O Messenger of Allaah! What is lawful for us from this sect (of dogs) you have commanded to be killed?" On that occasion, Allaah revealed this Quraanic Ayaah. [At-Tabaraani; Al-Haakim; Al-Bayhaqi and others]

A narration on the authority of 'Ad Ibn Haatim At-Taa'i that he said: A man went to the Prophet [peace and blessings of Allaah be upon him] to ask him about hunting with the help of dogs and he [peace and blessings of Allaah be upon him] did not know what to say to him till Allaah revealed (what means): {"Lawful unto you are edibles (which Allaah has made permissible). And game (caught by) hunting animals which you have trained as hounds in the manner Allaah taught you"}. [verse 4] [Ibn Jareer]

A narration on the authority of Sa'eed Ibn Jubayr that 'Adiyy Ibn Haatim and Zayd Ibn Al-Muhalhil from Tayyi' asked the Prophet [peace and blessings of Allaah be upon him]: "O Messenger of Allaah! We are a people who hunt with dogs and falcons; and the dogs always catch hold of cows, onagers and gazelles; and Allaah has forbidden the flesh of the dead (animals). So, what is lawful for us from all this?"

On that occasion, Allaah revealed (what means): {They ask you (O Muhammad) what is lawful for them (as food). Say: "Lawful unto you are edibles (which Allaah has made permissible...} [verse 4] [Ibn Abu Haatim]

Verse Number 6

6- O you who believe! When you intend to establish prayer, wash your faces and your hands (forearms) up to the elbows, rub (by passing wet hands over) your heads, and (wash) your feet up to ankles. If you are in a state of Janaabah, purify yourself (by a ceremonial bath). But if you are ill or on a journey, or any of you comes after answering the call of nature, or you have been in contact with women (through sexual intercourse), and you find no water, then perform Tayammum with clean earth and rub therewith your faces and hands (forearms up to the elbows). Allaah does not want to put you to difficulty, but He wants to purify you (from sins), and to complete His Favor on you that you may be thankful.

A narration on the authority of 'AA'ishah [Allaah be pleased with her] that she said: A necklace of mine was lost at Al-Baydaa when we were on our way to Madinah. The Prophet [peace and blessings of Allaah be upon him] made his camel kneel down. Then he dismounted and laid his head on my lap and slept. Abu Bakr came and hit me violently on the chest and said: "You have detained the people because of a necklace." I kept as motionless as a dead person because of the position of the Prophet [peace and blessings of Allaah be upon him] (on my lap) although Abu Bakr had hurt me. Then, The Prophet [peace and blessings of Allaah be upon him] woke up and it was the time for the morning (prayer). Water was sought for, but in vain; so this Quraanic Ayaah was revealed. Usayd Ibn Hudayr said: "Allaah has blessed the people for your sake, O the family of Abu Bakr. You are but a blessing for them." [Al-Bukhaari]

A narration on the authority of 'AA'ishah [Allaah be pleased with her] that she said: After the story of my necklace had taken place and the men of the false speech (fabricated about me) had said what they said, I set out in the company of the Prophet [peace and blessings of Allaah be upon him] in another battle, and once again my necklace fell down from me and he detained the people in order to search for it. Abu Bakr said to me: "O my daughter! You always become a source of suffering and trial for the people in each journey". On that occasion, Allaah revealed the Quraanic Ayaah of Tayammum. On that Abu Bakr said: "No doubt, you are a blessed woman". [At-Tabaraani]

Verse Number 11

11- O you who believe! Remember the Favor of Allaah unto you when some people (the Quraysh) intended to stretch out their hands to (harm) you, but He (Allaah) held back their hands from you. So fear Allaah; and on Allaah let the believers (al-Mumineen) rely.

A narration on the authority of 'Ikrimah, Yazeed Ibn Abu Ziyaad and others that the Prophet [peace and blessings of Allaah be upon him] set out in the company of Abu Bakr, 'Umar, 'Uthmaan, 'Ali, Talhah, and 'Abd-Ar-Rahmaan Ibn 'Awf and entered upon Ka'b Ibn Al-Ashraf and the Yahood of Banu An-Nadeer, to seek their aid to pay the blood compensation due upon the Muslims. They said: "Yes, sit till we serve you food and then give you what you have asked for". He sat and Huyayy Ibn Akhtab said to his companions: "You will not see him nearer to you than he is now. Throw upon him a stone to kill him and then you will receive no evil afterwards". They got a huge millstone to throw over him. But Allaah held back their hands from him till Jibreel [peace and blessings of Allaah be upon him] came and caused him to leave the place immediately. On that occasion, Allaah revealed this Quraanic Ayaah. [Ibn Jareer]

A narration on the authority of Qataadah that he said: It was mentioned to us that this Quraanic Ayaah was revealed to the Prophet [peace and blessings of Allaah be upon him], while he was amid the palm-trees in the seventh battle, where Banu Tha'labah and Banu Al-Haarith intended to kill the Prophet [peace and blessings of Allaah be upon him] thereupon they sent to him the Bedouin, that is who came to him while he was sleeping and took the sword and said: "Who can prevent me from killing you?" [Ibn Jareer]

A narration on the authority of Jaabir, may may Allaah be pleased with him, that a man from Banu Muhaarib called Ghawrath Ibn Al-Haarith proposed to kill the Prophet [peace and blessings of Allaah be upon him], to his people asked him how he would do so, thereupon he said: "I will murder him". He went to the Prophet [peace and blessings of Allaah be upon him] while he was sitting with his sword on his lap. He told him: "O Muhammad! Let me have a look at this sword of yours!" He said: "Well". It was adorned with silver as mentioned by Ibn Hishaam. He then took the sword and unsheathed it and shook it with the intention of killing him, but Allaah Disappointed him. He asked him: "O Muhammad! Do you not fear me?" The Prophet [peace and blessings of Allaah be upon him] replied: "No, why should I fear you?" He asked him: "Do you not fear me and there is a sword in my hand?" The Prophet [peace and blessings of Allaah be upon him] replied: "No, for Allaah Protects me from you". Then, he sheathed the sword and gave it back to the Prophet [peace and blessings of Allaah be upon him]. On that occasion, Allaah Almighty (the Most High) Revealed this Quraanic Ayaah. [Abu Na'eem in Ad-Dalaa'il]

Verse Number 15

15- O people of the Scripture (Yahood and Nasaara)! Now has come to you Our Messenger (Muhammad) explaining to you much of that which you used to hide from the Scripture and passing over much. Indeed, there has come to you from Allaah a light (Prophet Muhammad) and a plain Book (this Quraan).

A narration on the authority of 'Ikrimah that he said: the Prophet [peace and blessings of Allaah be upon him] was visited by the Yahood to ask him about stoning (to death), thereupon he said: "Who among you has the best knowledge (in the Torah)?" They beckoned to Ibn Sooriyah. He besought him with (Allaah) Who sent down the Torah upon Moses, and raised up the Mount over them and also by the covenant taken from them (to tell him the truth), till at the end he said to him: "When illegal sexual intercourse became spread among us, we then passed the judgment of giving one hundred lashes and shaving the heads". But he [peace and blessings of Allaah be upon him] judged that they (the adulterers) should be stoned to death. On that occasion, Allaah revealed this Quraanic Ayaah. [Ibn Jareer]

Verse Number 18

18- And (both) Yahood and Nasaara say: "We are the children of Allaah and His loved ones." Say: "Why then does He punish you for your sins?" Nay, you are but human beings, of those He has created, He forgives whom He wills and He punishes whom He wills. And to Allaah belongs the dominion of the heavens and the earth and all that is between them; and to Him is the return (of all).

A narration on the authority of Ibn 'Abbaas [Allaah be pleased with them] that he said: An-Nu'maan Ibn Adaa', Bahri Ibn 'Amr and Shaas Ibn 'Adiyy came to the Prophet [peace and blessings of Allaah be upon him] and exchanged talks with him. The Messenger Allaah [peace and blessings of Allaah be upon him] invited them to Allaah Almighty, and warned them of His wrath. They said: "From which do you frighten us O Muhammad? By Allaah, we are the sons and beloved of Allaah". They said just like what the Nasaara say. On that occasion, Allaah revealed this Quraanic Ayaah. [Ibn Ishaaq]

Verse Number 19

19- O people of Scripture! Now has come to you Our Messenger (Muhammad) making clear unto you (the rites of religion), after a break in (the series of) Messengers, lest you say: "There came unto us no bringer of glad tidings and no warner". But now has come unto you a bringer of glad tidings and a warner. And Allaah is Able to do all things.

A narration on the authority of Ibn 'Abbaas [Allaah be pleased with them] that he said: the Prophet [peace and blessings of Allaah be upon him] invited the Yahood to Islam, exhorted them to believe in it, warned them of worshipping others than Allaah and frightened them of His punishment. But they did not accept his invitation, but they disbelieved in what he brought to them. Mu'aadh Ibn Jabal, Sa'd Ibn 'Ubaadah and 'Uqbah Ibn Wahb [Allaah be pleased with them] told them: "O community of Yahood! Fear Allaah! By Allaah, you know well that he is the Prophet [peace and blessings of Allaah be upon him] whom you mentioned and described to us before his Prophetic mission". Raafi' Ibn Huraymilah and Wahb Ibn Yahoodhah said: "We have never said that to you nor has Allaah revealed a Book after Moses nor has He sent a warner or a bearer of glad tidings after him". On that occasion, Allaah Almighty (the Most High) revealed this Quraanic Ayaah. [Ibn Ishaaq]

Verse Number 33

33- There is no recompense for those who wage war against Allaah and His Messenger (by fighting the Muslims) and do mischief on earth (by intercepting the travelers) but to be killed or crucified or their hands and their feet be cut off from opposite sides, or be exiled from the land. That is their disgrace in this world, and a great torment (in the Hellfire) is theirs in the Hereafter.

A narration on the authority of Yazeed Ibn Abu Habeeb that 'Abdul-Malik Ibn Marwaan sent to Anas a letter [may Allaah be pleased with him] asking him about this Quraanic Ayaah. Anas told him that it was revealed in connection with those of 'Uraynah who renegaded from Islam, killed the shepherd (of the Prophet [peace and blessings of Allaah be upon him]) and drove the mulch camels with them... [Ibn Jareer]

The same is narrated on the authority of Abu Hurayrah [may Allaah be pleased with him]. ['Abd-Ar-Razzaaq]

Verse Number 38-39

38- And (as for) the male thief and the female, cut off (from the wrist joint) their (right) hand as a recompense for that which they committed, a deterrent (punishment) from Allaah. And Allaah is Exalted in Might, Full of Wisdom. 39- But whosoever repents after his crime and amends (his deeds), then verily, Allaah will pardon him (accept his repentance). Verily, Allaah is Oft-Forgiving, Most Merciful.

A narration on the authority of 'Abdullaah Ibn 'Amr [may Allaah be pleased with him] that a woman committed theft during the lifetime of the Prophet [peace and blessings of Allaah be upon him], so her right hand was cut off (in implementation of the corporal punishment prescribed for this crime in this Ayaah). She said: "O Messenger of Allaah! Is there a repentance for me?" On that occasion, Allaah revealed (what means): {But whosoever repents after his crime and amends (his deeds), then verily, Allaah will pardon him (accept his repentance). Verily, Allaah is Oft-Forgiving, Most Merciful} Ayaah. [Ahmad and others]

Verse Number 41

41- O Messenger! Let not those who hurry to fall into disbelief grieve you, of such who say: "We believe" with their mouths but their hearts (Qalb) have no faith. And of the Yahood are men who listen much and eagerly to lies - listen (from you on behalf of) others who have not come to you. They change the words from their places; they say: "If you are given this, take (and accept) it, but if you are not given this, then beware (of accepting it)!" And whomsoever Allaah wants to put to temptation, you can do nothing for him against Allaah. Those are the ones whose hearts (Qalb) Allaah does not want to purify (from disbelief and hypocrisy); for them there is a disgrace in this world, and in the Hereafter a great torment.

A narration on the authority of Ibn 'Abbaas [Allaah be pleased with them] that Allaah's saying (what means): {If any do fail to judge by (the light of) what Allaah hath revealed, they are (no more than) Unbelievers... they are (no more than) wrongdoers... they are (no more than) those who rebel".} [Al-Maa'idah, verse 41]: "Allaah Almighty (the Most High) revealed that with regard to two sects of Yahood, one of which oppressed the other in the pre-Islamic days, and then they agreed that if the more powerful sect killed anyone from the oppressed one, his blood-money would be fifty Wasqs, and if the weak one killed anyone from the victorious sect, his blood-money would be one hundred Wasqs. They remained as such until the Prophet [peace and blessings of Allaah be upon him] came to Madinah.

Then, it happened that one from the weak sect killed another from the powerful sect whose members sent to the weak sect, asking them to give one hundred Wasqs (for the blood-money). The weak sect replied by saying: "Is it convenient that both sects of the same religion, blood relations and town have the habit that the blood-money of anyone from this sect is only half the blood-money of anyone from the other? Indeed, we conceded that to you in the past as a result of your oppression and aggression against us. But, since Muhammad came to Madinah, we are not going to give you such a concession". In this way, the war was about to break up between them. But they agreed to appeal to the Prophet [peace and blessings of Allaah be upon him] to judge between them.

Then, the people of the powerful sect told one another: "By Allah, Muhammad will never give you from them twice what he will give them from you. Indeed, these (of the weak sect) have told the truth. They did not give us that concession but because of our oppressing and wronging them. So, you should let somebody (other than you) know from Muhammad his opinion: if he is to give you what you want, then let him judge between you, otherwise, beware of making him judge the case". Thus, they let some of the hypocrites (al-Munaafiqeen) go in order to detect the opinion of the Prophet [peace and blessings of Allaah be upon him]. When they came to the Prophet [peace and blessings of Allaah be upon him], Allaah Almighty (the Most High) told him of the whole matter and what they planned to do. In connection with them, Allaah Almighty (the Most High) revealed this Quraanic Ayaah. [Ahmad and Abu Daawood]

A narration on the authority of Al-Baraa' Ibn 'AAzib [may Allaah be pleased with him] that he said: There came upon the Prophet [peace and blessings of Allaah be upon him] a Jew with his face charcoaled and he was being whipped. the Prophet [peace and blessings of Allaah be upon him] called those (Yahood who were punishing him) and asked: "Is it thus that you find the legal punishment of fornication in your Book (of Torah)?" He called one of their learnt men and asked him: "I beseech you by Allaah Who sent down the Torah upon (The Prophet) Moses to tell me: Is it thus that you find the legal punishment of the adulterer in your Book (of Torah)?" He said: "No, and had you not besought me by Allaah to tell you the truth, I would never have told you. We find that it is the stoning to death. But it (the practice of adultery) has been prevalent among our great men. So, it became a habit that whenever we took one belonging to a high social class from among us, (who had committed adultery), we would leave him (without executing such a legal punishment) and whenever we took a poor one (in such a state), we would execute such a legal punishment on him. So, we said: Let's agree upon something, which we could execute on both the rich and the poor one. Then, we substituted (the punishment of) charcoaling the face and lashing for (the punishment of) stoning to death". Upon this the

Prophet [peace and blessings of Allaah be upon him] said: "O Allaah! I would be the first to revive a tradition which they (abandoned and subsequently) caused to die". He ordered (that the adulterer should be stoned) and he was stoned to death. On that occasion, Allaah Almighty (the Most High) revealed this Quraanic Ayaah up to His saying (what means): {And whoever does not judge by what Allaah has revealed - then it is those who are the wrongdoers}. [verse 45] [Abu Daawood and Muslim]

Verse Number 42

42- (They like to) listen to falsehood, to devour anything forbidden. So if they come to you (O Muhammad for judgment) either judge between them, or turn away from them. If you turn away from them, they cannot hurt you in the least. And if you judge, judge with justice between them. Verily, Allaah loves those who do justice.

A narration on the authority of Jabir Ibn 'Abdullaah [Allaah be pleased with them] that he said: A man from the inhabitants of Fadak committed adultery, therefore, the people there sent a message to the Yahood of Madinah, requiring them to ask Muhammad about that: "If he orders you to lash him, then accept it from him, but if he orders you to stone him to death, then, do not admit it from him". When they asked him about that, he said to them: "Send to me the most two learnt men among you".

They sent to him a one-eyed man called Ibn Sooriyah, accompanied by another one. the Prophet [peace and blessings of Allaah be upon him] told them: "Are you the most knowledgeable men from among your people?" They replied: "As such our people describe us". The Messenger of Allaah [peace and blessings of Allaah be upon him] told them: "Do you not have the Torah, containing the commandments of Allaah?" They replied in the affirmative. the Prophet [peace and blessings of Allaah be upon him] said: "I beseech you by Him, Who divided the sea for the children of Israel (in order to cross it), shaded you with the cloud, saved you from the people of Pharaoh and sent manna and quails unto the children of Israel to tell me: what do you find in the Torah concerning the matter of stoning (the adulterer) to death?" One of them told the other one: "No doubt, I've never been besought as such before". They replied him: "Indeed, we find that repeating the glances (of anyone of either gender upon the other) is regarded as (a portion of) adultery, (man's) embracing (the woman) is (a portion of) adultery, kissing is also (a part of) adultery and if four persons witness that they saw one getting his male organ into a woman's female organ repeatedly (that is having sexual intercourse with her), then, stoning to death would be binding". On that, the Prophet [peace and blessings of Allaah be upon him] said: "It is so". He ordered that they (the adulterer and the adulteress) should be stoned to death. On this occasion, Allaah Almighty (the Most High) revealed (what means): {So if they come to you (O Muhammad for judgment) either judge between them, or turn away from them...} [Al-Humaydi]

Verse Number 49

49- And so judge you (O Muhammad) among them by what Allaah has revealed and follow not their vain desires, but beware of them lest they turn you far away from some of that which Allaah has sent down to you. And if they turn away, then know that Allaah's Will is to punish them for some sins of theirs. And truly, most of men are rebellious disobedient.

A narration on the authority of Ibn 'Abbaas [Allaah be pleased with them] that he said: Ka'b Ibn Asad, Ibn Saloobah, 'Abdullaah Ibn Sooryah and Shaas Ibn Qays told each other: "Let us go to Muhammad and tempt him to make changes in his religion: he is but a human being". They went to him and said: "O Muhammad! You know well that we are the rabbis, noble men and chiefs of Yahood, and if we follow you, all the Yahood will follow you accordingly, and will not oppose us.

However, there is a dispute between us and some of our people: should we send them to trial before you, so that you would pass a judgment in our favor against them, with the result that we would believe in and give trust to you?" the Prophet [peace and blessings of Allaah be upon him] rejected their offer. On that occasion, Allaah revealed this Quraanic Ayaah. [Ibn Ishaaq]

Verse Number 51

51- O you who believe! Take not the Yahood and the Nasaara as allies (to befriend rather than the believers (al-Mumineen)), they are but allies of one another. And if any amongst you takes them (as allies), then surely he is one of them. Verily, Allaah guides not a people who are wrongdoers.

A narration on the authority of 'Ubaadah Ibn Al-Waleed Ibn 'Ubaadah Ibn As-Saamit that he said: When Banu Qaynuqaa fought the Muslims, 'Abdullaah Ibn Ubayy Ibn Salool was faithful to them, and did his best to protect them. But 'Ubaadah Ibn As-Saamit [may Allaah be pleased with him], one of Banu 'Amr Ibn 'Awf, who had the same degree of alliance with Banu Qaynuqaa as 'Abdullaah Ibn Ubayy, went to the Prophet [peace and blessings of Allaah be upon him] and declared in front of him his disassociation from their alliance before Allaah and His Messenger [peace and blessings of Allaah be upon him] saying: "O Messenger of Allaah! I take as allies Allaah, His Messenger [peace and blessings of Allaah be upon him] and the faithful believers (al-Mumineen) and disassociate myself from the alliance of disbelievers (al-Kaafireen)." In connection with him and 'Abdullaah Ibn Ubayy, Allaah Almighty (the Most High) revealed this Quraanic Ayaah. [Ibn Ishaaq; Ibn Jareer; Ibn Abu Haatim and Al-Bayhaqi]

Verse Number 55

55- Verily, your ally is none other than Allaah, His Messenger, and the believers (al-Mumineen) - those who establish prayer and give Zakaah, and bow down (humbly to Allaah in worship). A narration on the authority of 'Ammaar Ibn Yaasir [may Allaah be pleased with him] that he said: A beggar stood upon 'Ali Ibn Abu Taalib while he was bowing in a voluntary prayer, thereupon he took off his ring and gave it to him. On that occasion, Allaah revealed this Quraanic Ayaah. [At-Tabaraani in Al-Awsat]

Verse Number 57

57- O you who believe! Take not as allies those who take your religion in mockery and as a plaything from among those who were given the Scripture (Yahood and Nasaara) before you, nor

the disbelievers (al-Kaafireen); and fear Allaah if you indeed are true believers (al-Mumineen). A narration on the authority of Ibn 'Abbaas [Allaah be pleased with them] that he said: Rifaa'ah Ibn Zayd Ibn At-Taaboot and Suwayd Ibn Al-Haarith showed that they had embraced Islam even though they were hypocrites (al-Munaafiqeen); and, at the same time, a man from the Muslims had affection for them. On that occasion, Allaah Almighty (the Most High) revealed this Quraanic Ayaah. [Abu Ash-Shaykh and Ibn Hibbaan]

Verse Number 59

59- Say: "O people of the Scripture (Yahood)! Do you find fault with us for no other reason than that we believe in Allaah, and in (the revelation) which has been sent down to us and in that which has been sent down before (us), and that most of you are rebellious disobedient?"

A narration on the authority of Ibn 'Abbaas [Allaah be pleased with them] that he said: A group of Yahood including Abu Yaasir Ibn Akhtab, Naafi Ibn Abu Naafi' and Ghaazi Ibn 'Umar came to the Prophet [peace and blessings of Allaah be upon him] and asked him about the Prophets in whom he believed. He recited (what means): {"We have believed in Allaah and in what was revealed to us and what was revealed to Abraham, Ishmael, Isaac, Jacob, and the Descendants, and in what was given to Moses and Jesus and to the prophets from their Lord (Rabb). We make no distinction between any of them, and we are Muslims (submitting) to Him."} [AAl 'Imraan, verse 84] When he mentioned Jesus they rejected his Prophethood and said: "We do not believe in Jesus and in such who believes in him". In connection with them, Allaah revealed this Quraanic Ayaah. [Abu Ash-Shaykh and Ibn Hibbaan]

Verse Number 64

64- The Yahood say: "Allaah's Hand is tied up." Let their hands be tied up (from doing good) and let them be accursed for what they uttered. Nay, both His Hands are widely outstretched. He spends (out of His Bounty) as He wills. Verily, the Revelation (this Quraan) that has come to you from (Allaah) your Lord (Rabb) increases most of them in inordinacy and disbelief. We have cast enmity and hatred amongst them till the Day of Resurrection. Every time they kindled the fire of war (against the Prophet Muhammad), Allaah extinguished it; and they (ever) strive to make mischief on the earth (by committing sins). And Allaah does not like the mischief-makers.

A narration on the authority of Ibn 'Abbaas [Allaah be pleased with them] that he said: A man from the Yahood called An-Nabbaash Ibn Qays said: "Your Lord (Rabb) is stingy and does not spend". On that occasion, Allaah revealed this Quraanic Ayaah. [At-Tabaraani]

A narration on the authority of Ibn 'Abbaas [Allaah be pleased with them] that he said: This Quraanic Ayaah was revealed in connection with Finhaas, the head of the Yahood of Qaynuqaa'. [Abu Ash-Shaykh]

Verse Number 67

67- O Messenger (Muhammad)! Proclaim (the Message) which has been sent down to you from your Lord (Rabb). And if you do not, then you have not conveyed His Message. Allaah will protect you from mankind. Verily, Allaah guides not the disbelieving people.

A narration on the authority of Al-Hasan that he said: the Prophet [peace and blessings of Allaah be upon him] said: "Verily, Allaah sent me with a Message by which I have been burdened, and known that the people would give lie to me. But Allaah threatened me: either I should proclaim it, or He would punish me".

On that occasion, this Quraanic Ayaah was revealed. [Abu Ash-Shaykh]

A narration on the authority of Mujaahid that he said: When Allaah revealed (what means): {O Messenger (Muhammad)! Proclaim (the Message) which has been sent down to you from your Lord (Rabb)}, the Prophet [peace and blessings of Allaah be upon him] said: "O Lord (Rabb)! How should I do it and I am only an individual and they could stand against me". On that occasion, Allaah revealed (what means): {and if you do not, then you have not conveyed His message}. [Ibn Abu Haatim]

A narration on the authority of 'AA'ishah [Allaah be pleased with her] that she said: the Prophet [peace and blessings of Allaah be upon him] was guarded by the people till Allaah Almighty (the Most High) revealed (what means): {Allaah will protect you from mankind. Verily, Allaah guides not the disbelieving people}. Then he brought his head out of the tent and said: "O people! you can go because Allaah has protected me". [Al-Haakim and At-Tirmidhi]

This Hadeeth indicates that this Quraanic Ayaah was revealed at night and when the Prophet [peace and blessings of Allaah be upon him] was in bed.

A narration on the authority of Abu Hurayrah [may Allaah be pleased with him] that he said: Whenever we set out on journey in the company of the Prophet [peace and blessings of Allaah be upon him] (and alighted on the way for rest), we would choose for him the hugest and shadiest tree to sit beneath. Once, he sat under the shade of a tree, and hung his sword on it. Then, one came and took the sword and said to him: "O Muhammad! Who could protect you from me now?" the Prophet [peace and blessings of Allaah be upon him] said: "Allaah protects me from you. You should put down the sword!" so he put it down. Then, Allaah revealed (what means): {Allaah will protect you from mankind}. [Ibn Hibbaan in his Saheeh]

A narration on the authority of Jaabir Ibn 'Abdullaah [Allaah be pleased with them] that during a military expedition Ghawrath ibn Al-Haarith declared that he would kill Muhammad [peace and blessings of Allaah be upon him]. When his companions asked him how he would kill him, he said that he would ask the Prophet [peace and blessings of Allaah be upon him] to give him his sword, which he would take and kill him with. Thus, he went to the Prophet [peace and blessings of Allaah be upon him] and asked him to give him his sword to smell, and the Prophet [peace and blessings of Allaah be upon him] gave it to him. When he held the sword, his hand trembled and the sword dropped. Hence, the Prophet [peace and blessings of Allaah be upon him] said: "Allaah Has Prevented you from doing what you wanted to do". [Ibn Abu Haatim and Ibn Mardawayh]

Verse Number 68

68- Say (O Muhammad): "O people of the Scripture! You stand on nothing (of religion) till you act upon (the laws of) the Torah, the Gospel, and what has (now) been sent down to you from your Lord (Rabb)." Verily, that which has been sent down to you (the Quraan) from your Lord (Rabb) increases most of them in inordinacy and disbelief. So grieve not over the people who disbelieve.

A narration on the authority of Ibn 'Abbaas [Allaah be pleased with them] that he said: Raafi' and Salaam Ibn Mishkam and Maalik Ibn As-Sayf came and said: "O Muhammad! Do you not pretend that you are on the religion of Abraham, and believe in what we have (of the Scripture)?" He said: "Yes, but you have made changes in it, denied what it contains and concealed what you have been commanded to disclose to the people". They replied: "We act upon what we have: verily, we are on the right guidance and truth". On that occasion, Allaah Almighty (the Most High) revealed this Quraanic Ayaah. [Ibn Abu Haatim] Verse Number 82

82- Verily, you (O Muhammad) will find the strongest among men in enmity to the believers (al-Mumineen) (Muslims) the Yahood and those who associate partners (with Allaah in worship), and you will find the nearest in love to the believers (al-Mumineen) (Muslims) those who say: "We are Nasaara." That is because amongst them are priests (scholars) and monks (worshippers) and (because) they are not proud.

A narration on the authority of Sa'eed Ibn Jubayr that he said: The Negus of Abyssinia sent thirty of his best companions to the Prophet [peace and blessings of

Allaah be upon him], to whom he recited Soorah Yaa-Seen, thereupon they went on weeping. In connection with them, Allaah revealed this Quraanic Ayaah. [Ibn Abu Haatim] Verse Number 83

83- And when they (who call themselves Nasaara) listen to what has been sent down to the Messenger (the Quraan) you see their eyes overflowing with tears because of the truth they have recognized. They say: "Our Lord (Rabb)! We believe; so write us down among the witnesses.

A narration on the authority of 'Abdullaah Ibn Az-Zubayr [Allaah be pleased with them] that he said: This Quraanic Ayaah was revealed in connection with the Negus and his companions. [An-Nasa'i] The same is narrated on the authority of Ibn 'Abbaas [Allaah be pleased with them]. [At-Tabaraani]

Verse Number 87

87- O you who believe! Make not unlawful the good things which Allaah has made lawful to you, and transgress not. Verily, Allaah does not like the transgressors.

A narration on the authority of Ibn 'Abbaas [Allaah be pleased with them] that he said: A man came to the Prophet [peace and blessings of Allaah be upon him] and said: "O Messenger of Allaah! Whenever I eat flesh, my sexual desire for women becomes more powerful, and that is why I have forbidden meat to myself". On that occasion, Allaah revealed this Quraanic Ayaah. [At-Tirmidhi and others]

A narration on the authority of Ibn 'Abbaas [Allaah be pleased with them] that some men including 'Uthmaan Ibn Math'oon forbade women and meat to themselves and were about to remove their testicles in order to devote themselves to worship. On that occasion, this Quraanic Ayaah was revealed. [Ibn Jareer]

A narration on the authority of Ibn 'Abbaas [Allaah be pleased with them] that he said: 'Uthmaan Ibn Math'oon, 'Ali Ibn Abu Taalib, Ibn Mas'ood, Al-Miqdaad Ibn Al-Aswad and Saalim, the freed slave of Abu Hudhayfah [Allaah be pleased with them], decided to live in celibacy, stay in their homes in seclusion from women, put on sackcloth and forbid to themselves the good kinds of food and clothes except for what is eaten and dressed by the wandering people among the children of Israel. They also intended to get themselves castrated, stand for supererogatory prayers during the whole night and observe fast every day. On that occasion, this Quraanic Ayaah was revealed. [Ibn 'Asaakir in his Taareekh and others]

A narration on the authority of Zayd Ibn Aslam that 'Abdullaah Ibn Rawaahah [may Allaah be pleased with him] had guests in his house while he was still with the Prophet [peace and blessings of Allaah be upon him]. But when he went back to his family, he found that his wife had not served the guest food but she waited him to come. On that he grew angry and said: "Have you not served my guests (with food) for my sake? I have forbidden this (food) to myself". His wife (and guests) said: "Then, we also have forbidden it to ourselves". He then stretched his hand to the food and said to them: "Let us eat, in the Name of Allaah". On that occasion, this Quraanic Ayaah was revealed. [Ibn Abu Haatim]

Verse Number 90-93

90- O you who believe! Intoxicants, gambling, (sacrificing on) stone alters (to other than Allaah), and divining arrows are but abomination from the work of Satan, so avoid it that you may prosper. 91- Satan wants only to excite enmity and hatred between you with intoxicants and gambling, and hinder you from the remembrance of Allaah and from the prayer. So, will you not then abstain? 92- And obey Allaah and the Messenger and beware (of committing sins) and fear Allaah. Then if you turn away, you should know that Our Messenger's duty is only to convey (the Message) in the clearest way. 93- There is no sin on those who believe and do righteous deeds for what they ate (in the past), if they ward off (what is forbidden), and believe and do righteous deeds, and then ward off (evil) and believe, and again ward off (sin) and do good. And Allaah loves the doers of good.

A narration on the authority of Abu Hurayrah [may Allaah be pleased with him] that he said: The prohibition of wine came upon three stages: when the Prophet [peace and blessings of Allaah be upon him] immigrated to Madinah, the people there used to drink wine and eat up (the money gained through) gambling.

When they asked the Prophet [peace and blessings of Allaah be upon him] about them, Allaah revealed (what means): {They ask you concerning wine and gambling. Say: in them is great sin, and some profit for men; but their sin is greater than their profit}. [Al-Baqarah, verse 219] But the people said then: "It has not yet prohibited from us, since Allaah says (what means): {in them is great sin}."

So, they kept drinking it until one day, when one of the Emigrants led the prayer and he was confused in reciting. Then, Allaah revealed a Ayaah severer than this, in which He said (what means): {O you who believe! Approach (perform) not the prayer when you are in a drunken state until you know (the meaning) of what you utter}. (An-Nisaa', verse 43) But the people continued drinking, putting in consideration that they shall come to the prayer in a state of full consciousness.

Later, Allaah revealed a Ayaah, far severer and more decisive in prohibition than that, in which He said (what means): {O you who believe! Intoxicants, gambling, (sacrificing on) stone alters (to other than Allaah), and divining arrows are but abomination from the work of Satan, so avoid it that you may prosper}. [Al-Maa'idah Ayaah 90] Then, they said: "O our Lord (Rabb)! We desist".

They said: "O Messenger of Allaah! Some people were killed in the Way of Allaah, and others died on bed, and they used to drink wine and eat up the (earnings of) gambling, which Allaah has made now an abomination of Satan's work (what will their destination be?)" On that, Allaah revealed (what means): {There is no sin on those who believe and do righteous deeds for what they ate (in the past), if they ward off (what is forbidden), and believe and do righteous deeds, and then ward off (evil) and believe, and again ward off (sin) and do good. And Allaah loves the doers of good}. [Al-Maa'idah, verse 93] the Prophet [peace and blessings of Allaah be upon him] said: "Had it been forbidden to them (when they were still alive), surely, they would have left that as you do now". [Ahmad]

A narration on the authority of Ibn 'Abbaas [Allaah be pleased with them] that the Quraanic Ayaah pertaining to the prohibition of wine was revealed in connection with two tribes among the Ansaar, who drank, and when they were intoxicated, they went on hurting (by way of playing) one another.

When they became conscious, the man saw the effect (of injury) on his face, his head and his beard, and then said: "My brother so and so did this to me. By Allaah, had he been merciful and kind to me, surely, he would not have done this to me". Indeed, before this, they were brothers in whose hearts (Qalb) there was neither enmity nor hatred towards one another.

But after this their hearts (Qalb) came to be filled with grudges and feelings of resentment towards one another. On that occasion, Allaah revealed those Quraanic Aayaat [90-91].

Some people who used to make things difficult upon themselves and others said: "It is then an abomination and it was in the stomach of so and so who was killed on the day of (the battle of) Uhud". Then, Allaah revealed: {On those who believe and do righteous deeds for what they ate...} [verse 93] [Al-Bayhaqi and An-Nasaa'i].

Verse Number 100

100- Say: "Not equal are the bad (the unlawful) and the good (the lawful) even though the abundance of the bad may please you." So fear Allaah O men of understanding in order that you may prosper.

A narration on the authority of Jaabir [may Allaah be pleased with him] that the Prophet [peace and blessings of Allaah be upon him] made a mention of the prohibition of wine. A Bedouin stood and said: "(Selling wine) was my trade from which I earned money: should I use this money if I comply with the command of Allaah?" the Prophet [peace and blessings of Allaah be upon him] said: "No doubt, Allaah never accepts but what is good (and lawful)". In confirmation of His Messenger [peace and blessings of Allaah be upon him] Allaah revealed this Quraanic Ayaah. [Al-Waahidi and Al-Asbahaani]

Verse Number 101

101- O you who believe! Ask not about things which, if made plain to you, may cause you trouble. But if you ask about them while the Quraan is being revealed, they will be made plain to you. Allaah has forgiven that, and Allaah is Oft-Forgiving, Most Forbearing.

A narration on the authority of Anas [may Allaah be pleased with him] that he said: The Prophet [peace and blessings of Allaah be upon him] delivered a sermon the like of which I had never heard before. He said: "If you but knew what I know then you would laugh little and weep much." On hearing that, the companions of The Prophet [peace and blessings of Allaah be upon him] covered their faces and the sound of their weeping was heard. A man said: "Who is my father?" The Prophet [peace and blessings of Allaah be upon him] said: "So-and-so." On that occasion, this Quraanic Ayaah was revealed. [Al-Bukhaari and Muslim]

A narration on the authority of 'Ali [may Allaah be pleased with him] that when Allaah revealed (what means): {And (due) to Allaah from the people is a pilgrimage to the House - for whoever is able to find thereto a way}, [AAl 'Imraan, verse 97] they asked: "O Messenger of Allaah! Is it obligatory every year?" He kept silent". They asked him once again thereupon he said: "If I answered in the affirmative, it would be enjoined upon you (to perform Hajj every year)". On that occasion, Allaah revealed this Quraanic Ayaah. [Ahmad; At-Tirmidhi and Al-Haakim]

Verse Number 106

106- O you who believe! When death approaches any of you, and you make a bequest, then take the testimony of two just men of your own folk or two others from outside, while you are travelling through the land and the calamity of death befalls you. Detain them both after the ('Asr) prayer, (then) if you are in doubt (about their truthfulness), let them both swear by Allaah (saying): "never do we exchange our oath for a little price, even though he be our near relative. We shall not hide the Testimony of Allaah, for then (if we conceal it) indeed we should be of the sinful."

A narration on the authority of Ibn 'Abbaas [Allaah be pleased with them] that he said: A man from (the tribe of) Sahm went out on a journey with Tameem Ad-Daari and 'Adiyy Ibn Badaa'ah. He died in a town, which had none of Muslims. His two companions returned with his heritage, from which a cup of silver inscribed with gold was lost. The Prophet [peace and blessings of Allaah be upon him] got them swear (that they did not take it). Later, this cup was found in Makkah. When The Prophet [peace and blessings of Allaah be upon him] asked about it, people of Makkah answered that they had purchased it from both 'Adiyy and Tameem. Two heirs of the deceased man of Sahm stood up and said to The Prophet [peace and blessings of Allaah be upon him]: "By Allaah! Our witness is more reliable than theirs". They confirmed that the cup belonged to their deceased companion. In connection with them, this Quraanic Ayaah was revealed. [At-Tirmidhi who renders it weak]

Soorah Al-Anaam

Verse Number 19

19- Say: "What thing is the greatest in witness?" Say: "Allaah is Witness between me and you; and this Quraan has been revealed to me that I may therewith warn you and whomsoever it may reach (of men and jinn). Can you testify that besides Allaah there are other deities?" Say: "I never testify (to that)!" Say: "But truly He (Allaah) is the only one God. And truly I am disassociated from what you join in worship with Him."

A narration on the authority of Ibn 'Abbaas [Allaah be pleased with them] that he said: A delegate of Yahood, including An-Nahhaam Ibn Zayd, Qardam Ibn Ka'b and Bahri Ibn 'Amr came to the Prophet [peace and blessings of Allaah be upon him] and said: "O Muhammad! Do you not know that there is another god with Allaah?" the Prophet [peace and blessings of Allaah be upon him] said: "There is no deity to be worshipped except Allaah: with that (message) I have been sent, and to which I invite (the people)". In this connection, Allaah Almighty (the Most High) revealed this Quraanic Ayaah. [Ibn Ishaaq and Ibn Jareer]

Verse Number 26

26- And they avert people from him and they themselves keep away from him, and (by keeping away from him) they destroy not but their own selves, yet they perceive (it) not.

A narration on the authority of Ibn 'Abbaas [Allaah be pleased with them] that he said: This Quraanic Ayaah was revealed in connection with Abu Taalib: he used to forbid the polytheists to do harm to the Prophet [peace and blessings of Allaah be upon him], and, at the same time, he himself used to keep himself far from his religion. [Al-Haakim and others]

A narration on the authority of Sa'eed Ibn Abu Hilaal that he said: It was revealed in connection with the paternal uncles of The Messenger of Allah [peace and blessings of Allaah be upon him]: they were ten men. In public, they were the strongest with him (against the Quraysh), and in secret the strongest against him. [Ibn Abu Haatim]

Verse Number 33

33- We know indeed how their words certainly grieve you (O Muhammad): it is not you that they reject, but it is the revelations (the Quraan) of Allaah that the wrongdoers deny. A narration on the authority of 'Ali [may Allaah be pleased with him] that he said: Abu Jahl said to the Prophet [peace and blessings of Allaah be upon him]: "No doubt, we do not belie you: but we rather give lie to that which you have brought (that is this Quraan)". On that occasion, Allaah Almighty (the Most High) revealed this Quraanic Ayaah. [At-Tirmidhi and Al-Haakim]

51- And warn therewith (the Quraan) those who fear that they will be gathered before their Lord (Rabb), when there will be neither a protector nor an intercessor for them besides Him, so that they may fear Allaah. 52- And drive not away those who invoke their Lord (Rabb), morning and evening seeking His Countenance. You are accountable for them in nothing, and they are accountable for you in nothing, that you may turn them away, and thus become of the wrongdoers. 53- Thus We have tried some of them with others, that they (the noble and wealthy) might say: "Is it these (poor and lowly) that Allaah has favored from amongst us?" Does not Allaah know best those who are grateful?

A narration on the authority of Sa'd Ibn Abu Waqqaas [may Allaah be pleased with him] that he said: This Quraanic Ayaah was revealed in connection with six: I, 'Abdullaah Ibn Mas'ood and other four said to the Prophet [peace and blessings of Allaah be upon him]: "Drive away (those indigent from you), because we feel shy to be your followers like those". the Prophet [peace and blessings of Allaah be upon him] felt something within himself which none knew but Allaah Almighty. On that occasion, Allaah Almighty (the Most High) revealed (what means): {And drive not away those who invoke their Lord (Rabb) Does not Allaah know best those who are grateful?} [verse 52-53] [Ibn Hibbaan and Al-Haakim]

A narration on the authority of Ibn Mas'ood [may Allaah be pleased with him] that once, a group of the (chiefs of) Quraysh came upon the Prophet [peace and blessings of Allaah be upon him], while he was sitting with Khabbaab Ibn Al-Aratt, Suhayb, 'Ammaar and Bilaal, in addition to others from among the weak Muslims. They told him: "O Muhammad! Are you pleased with sitting in the company of those people? Are they those whom Allaah favored from amongst us? Shall we be followers to those? Drive them away from you, and if you do, perchance we might follow you". On that occasion, Allaah Almighty (the Most High) revealed those Quraanic Aayaat [51-54]. [Ahmad; At-Tabaraani and Ibn Abu Haatim]

A narration on the authority of 'Ikrimah that he said: 'Utbah and Shaybah, sons of Rabee'ah, Mut'im Ibn 'Adiyy, Al-Haarith Ibn Nawfal, and others from among the nobles of 'Abd-Manaaf who were disbelievers (al-Kaafireen), came to Abu Taalib and said: "If your nephew sends away those slaves, this will be greater in our hearts (Qalb), and we may be more obedient to him and more closer to follow him". Abu Taalib talked to the Prophet [peace and blessings of Allaah be upon him], thereupon 'Umar Ibn Al-Khattaab [may Allaah be pleased with him] said: "Would that you do so, in order that we would see what they like". On that occasion, Allaah revealed those Quraanic Aayaat [51-53]. These (intended men) were Bilaal, 'Ammaar Ibn Yaasir, Saalim, the freed slave of Abu Hudhayfah, Saalih, the freed slave of Usayd, Ibn Mas'ood, Al-Miqdaad Ibn 'Abdullaah, Waaqid Ibn 'Abdullaah Ibn Al-Hanthali and others. 'Umar [may Allaah be pleased with him] came and apologized for his statement. Then Allaah revealed Ayaah no. 54. [Ibn Jareer]

Verse Number 54

54- If those who believe in Our revelations come to you, say: "Peace be upon you"; your Lord (Rabb) has ordained Mercy to Himself, so that if any of you does evil in ignorance, and thereafter repents and does righteous deeds, then surely, He is Oft-Forgiving, Most Merciful.

A narration on the authority of Maahaan that he said: Some people came to the Prophet [peace and blessings of Allaah be upon him] and said: "We have committed grave sins". But the Prophet [peace and blessings of Allaah be upon him] gave no reply. On that occasion, Allaah revealed this Quraanic Ayaah. [Al-Firyaabi and Ibn Abu Haatim]

Verse Number 65-67

65- Say: "He has power to send torment on you from above or from under your feet, or to cover you with confusion in party strife, and make you to taste the violence of one another." See how variously We diversify the signs so that they may understand. 66But your people (O Muhammad) have rejected it (the Quraan) though it is the truth. Say: "I am not in charge of your affairs." 67- For every news there is a term and you will come to know.

A narration on the authority of Zayd Ibn Aslam that he said: When Allaah revealed (what means): {Say: "He has power to send torment on you from above or from under your feet...} the Prophet [peace and blessings of Allaah be upon him] said: "Do not return, after me, as disbelievers (al-Kaafireen), striking each other with swords". They said: "We testify that there is none worthy of worship except Allaah, and that you [peace be upon you] are the Messenger of Allaah". Some said: "That will never come to pass: we shall never kill one another while we are Muslims". On that occasion, Allaah revealed (what means): {See how variously We diversify the signs so that they may understand...} up to Ayaah no. 67. [Ibn Abu Haatim]

Verse Number 82

82- It is those who believe and confuse not their belief with injustice, for them (only) there is security and they are the guided.

A narration on the authority of Bakr Ibn Sawaadah that he said: A man from the enemies attacked the Muslims and killed a man. He attacked them once again and killed another man. He attacked them for the third time and killed a man. Then he said: "Will my embracing Islam avail me after all this?" the Prophet [peace and blessings of Allaah be upon him] said: "Yes". He struck his horse and broke into the rows of his fellows and attacked them and killed a man and then another from among them. Then he was killed. It is thought that in connection with him this Quraanic Ayaah was revealed. [Ibn Abu Haatim]

Verse Number 91

91- They (the Yahood) did not estimate Allaah with a due estimation when they said: "Nothing did Allaah send down to any human being (by way of revelation)." Say (to them): "Who then sent down the Book which Moses brought, a light and a guidance to mankind which you have made into (separate) sheets, disclosing (some of it) and concealing much. And you (Yahood) were taught (through the Quraan) that which neither you nor your fathers knew." Say: "Allaah (sent it down)." Then leave them to play in their vain discourse.

A narration on the authority of Sa'eed Ibn Jubayr that he said: A Jew, called Maalik Ibn As-Sayf, came to the Prophet [peace and blessings of Allaah be upon him] and engaged in argument with him. the Prophet [peace and blessings of Allaah be upon him] told him: "I beseech you by Allaah Who sent down the Torah to Moses to tell me: do you find in the Torah that Allaah dislikes the fat rabbi?" This Jew was a fat rabbi. He grew angry and said: "Allaah has never revealed aught unto any human beings". His fellows said to him: "Woe to you, and not even unto Moses?" On that, Allaah revealed this Quraanic Ayaah. [Ibn Abu Haatim: Mursal]

A similar one is narrated on the authority of 'Ikrimah. [Ibn Jareer]

A narration on the authority of Ibn 'Abbaas [Allaah be pleased with them] that he said: The Yahood said: "By Allaah, Allaah never sent down a Book from the heaven". On that occasion, Allaah revealed this Quraanic Ayaah. [Ibn Jareer]

Verse Number 93

93- And who can be more unjust than he who invents a lie against Allaah, or says: "a revelation has come to me" whereas no revelation has come to him in aught; and who says: "I will reveal the like of what Allaah has revealed"? And if you (O Muhammad) could but see when the wrongdoers are in the agonies of death, while the angels are stretching forth their hands (saying): "Deliver your souls! This day you shall be recompensed with the torment of degradation because of what you used to tell lies against Allaah. And you used to deny His revelations arrogantly!"

A narration on the authority of 'Ikrimah that Allaah's saying (what means): {And who can be more unjust than he who invents a lie against Allaah, or says: "a revelation has come to me" whereas no revelation has come to him...} was revealed in connection with Musaylamah (Al-Kadhdhaab). As for His saying (what means): {and who says: "I will reveal the like of what Allaah has revealed"}, was revealed in connection with 'Abdullaah Ibn Sa'd Ibn Abu Sarh: he used to write the divine revelation to the Prophet [peace and blessings of Allaah be upon him].

When he renegaded from Islam and went to the Quraysh people, he told that whenever the Prophet dictated to him: {Exalted in Might, Full of Wisdom}, he would change it for {Oft-Forgiving, Most Merciful}, and claim that the Prophet [peace and blessings of Allaah be upon him] would approve. [Ibn Jareer]

The same is narrated on the authority of As-Suddi, with the following addition: he used to say: "If Muhammad is being divinely revealed, then, I also have been divinely revealed; and if Allaah sends down (this Quraan), I also have sent down the same as Allaah has sent down. Muhammad says: {All-Hearing, All-Knowing}, and I say: "All-Knowing, All-Wise". [Ibn Jareer]

Verse Number 94

94- And truly you have come unto Us alone as We created you for the first time. You have left behind you all that which We had bestowed on you. We see not with you your intercessors whom you claimed to be partners with Allaah (in worship). Now all relations between you and them have been cut off, and all that you used to claim has vanished from you.

A narration on the authority of 'Ikrimah that he said: An-Nadr Ibn Al-Haarith said: "Verily, Al-Laat and Al-'Uzza will intercede for me (in the hereafter, if there is any)". On that occasion, Allaah revealed this Quraanic Ayaah. [Ibn Jareer and others]

Verse Number 108

108- And insult not those whom they (disbelievers (al-Kaafireen)) invoke besides Allaah, lest they would insult Allaah in enmity and injustice without knowledge. Thus We have made alluring to each people its own doings; then to their Lord (Rabb) is their return and He shall then inform them of all that they used to do.

A narration on the authority of Qataadah that he said: The Muslims used to abuse the idols of the disbelievers (al-Kaafireen) thereupon the disbelievers (al-Kaafireen) would abuse Allaah. On that occasion, Allaah revealed this Quraanic Ayaah. ['Abd-Ar-Razzaaq]

Verse Number 109-111

109- And they (disbelievers (al-Kaafireen)) swear their strongest oaths by Allaah, that if there came to them a sign, they would surely believe therein. Say: "Signs are but with Allaah; and what will make you (Muslims) perceive that (even) if it (the sign) came, they will not believe?" 110- And We shall turn their hearts (Qalb) and their eyes away (from the truth), as they refused to believe therein for the first time, and We shall leave them in their trespass blindly wandering in distraction. 111- And even if We had sent down unto them angels, and the dead had spoken unto them, and We had gathered together all things before their very eyes, they would not have believed, unless Allaah willed, but most of them are ignorant (of this fact).

A narration on the authority of Muhammad Ibn Ka'b Al-Qurathi that he said: the Prophet [peace and blessings of Allaah be upon him] talked to the men of Quraysh (calling them to believe in Islam), thereupon they told him: "O Muhammad! You tell us that Moses had a rod, with which he struck the rock, therefrom twelve springs (of water) gushed forth; that Jesus used to raise the dead and that the tribe of Thamood had a (marvelous) she-camel. So, bring us (special miraculous) signs like those, in order that we might believe you". the Prophet [peace and blessings of Allaah be upon him] asked them: "Which sign do you like me to bring you?" They replied: "Turn the (mountain of) Safa into (a mountain of) gold". He told them: "Then, if I do so, will you believe me?" They said: "Yes, by god, we all will follow you".

The Prophet [peace and blessings of Allaah be upon him] stood (for prayer) and invoked (Allaah for that). But Jibreel [peace and blessings of Allaah be upon him] came to him and said to him: "What do you like? If you like, it will turn into gold. But in this case, if He (Allaah) sends a (special) sign and they do not believe, then, He will be hasty to punish them. If you like, I might leave them (without such a sign) until the one destined to repent among them might turn in repentance (to Allaah)". On that, the Prophet [peace and blessings of Allaah be upon him] said: "No, but (let them) until the one destined to repent among them might turn in repentance (to Allaah)". In this connection, Allaah Almighty (the Most High) revealed those Quraanic Aayaat. [Ibn Jareer]

Verse Number 118-121

118- So eat of that (meat of the animal) on which Allaah's Name has been pronounced (while slaughtering), if you are believers (al-Mumineen) in His signs. 119- And why should you not eat of that (meat of the animal) on which Allaah's Name has been pronounced (at the time of slaughtering), while He has explained to you in detail what is forbidden to you, excepting that to which you are forced by necessity? And surely many do lead (mankind) astray by their own desires without knowledge. Certainly your Lord (Rabb) knows best the transgressors. 120- Eschew (O man) sin, what is apparent and what is hidden thereof. Verily, those who commit sin will be recompensed (in the hereafter) for that which they used to commit. 121- Eat not of that (meat of the animal) on which Allaah's Name has not been mentioned (at the time of slaughtering), for sure it is a grave disobedience. And certainly, the devils inspire their friends (from mankind) to dispute with you, and if you obey them (by making it lawful), then you would indeed be polytheists.

A narration on the authority of Ibn 'Abbaas [Allaah be pleased with them] that he said: Some people came to the Prophet [peace and blessings of Allaah be upon him] and said: "O Messenger of Allaah! Should we eat what we kill and not what is killed by Allaah?" On that occasion, Allaah revealed those Quraanic Aayaat. [Abu Daawood and At-Tirmidhi]

A narration on the authority of Ibn 'Abbaas [Allaah be pleased with them] that he said: They commented on Allaah's saying (what means): {And certainly, the devils inspire their friends (from mankind) to dispute with you} [verse 121]: "Eat not what Allaah kills, and eat only what you kill". On that occasion, Allaah revealed this Quraanic Ayaah [118]. [Abu Daawood; Al-Haakim and others]

A narration on the authority of Ibn 'Abbaas [Allaah be pleased with them] that he said: When Allaah revealed (what means): {And do not eat of that upon which the name of Allaah has not been mentioned}, the Persians sent to the Quraysh a message asking them to argue with Muhammad saying: "What you slaughter by yourself with a knife is lawful; and what Allaah kills (that is causes to die) is unlawful". On that occasion, Allaah revealed (what means): {And certainly, the devils inspire their friends (from mankind) to dispute with you}. [verse 121] The devils stands for the Persians, and the Quraysh people are their allies. [At-Tabaraani and others]

Verse Number 122

122- Is he who was dead (without Faith by ignorance and disbelief) and We gave him life (by knowledge and Faith) and set for him a light (of Belief) whereby he can walk amongst men - like him who is in the darkness (of disbelief) from which he can never come out? Thus it is made fair-seeming to the disbelievers (al-Kaafireen) that which they used to do.

A narration on the authority of Ibn 'Abbaas [Allaah be pleased with them] that this Quraanic Ayaah was revealed in connection with 'Umar and Abu Jahl. [Abu Ash-Shaykh]

Verse Number 141

141- And it is He Who produces gardens trellised and untrellised, and date-palms and crops whose seeds and fruits are different (in shape and taste), and olives, and pomegranates, similar (in kind) and different (in taste and size). Eat of their fruit when they yield, but pay its due (Zakaah) on the day of its harvest, and waste not by extravagance. Verily, He likes not those who waste by extravagance.

A narration on the authority of Abu Al-'AAliyah that he said: They used to give something to the poor other than Zakaah and then indulged in that. On that occasion, Allaah revealed this Quraanic Ayaah. [Ibn Jareer]

According to the narration of Ibn Jurayj, it was revealed in connection with Thaabit Ibn Qays Ibn Shamaas [may Allaah be pleased with him]: he had a date-palm from which he kept feeding the poor till evening came upon him so he had no fruits at all.

Soorah Al-Araaf

Verse Number 31-33

31- O Children of Adam! Take your adornment (by wearing clothes to screen your private parts) in every place of worship and eat and drink but waste not by excess: surely, He (Allaah) likes not the wasters. 32- Say: "Who has forbidden the adornment of Allaah which He has produced for His slaves, and the good (lawful pleasant) provision?" Say: "They are, in the life of this world, for those who believe, (and) exclusively for them on the Day of Resurrection. Thus We explain the revelations in detail for people who know. 33- Say: "Indeed my Lord (Rabb) has forbidden only the immoralities (major evils) what is apparent and what is hidden thereof, sins, oppression against the truth, association of partners (in worship) with Allaah for which He has sent down no authority, and saying things about Allaah of which you have no knowledge."

A narration on the authority of Ibn 'Abbaas [Allaah be pleased with them] that he said: During the pre-Islamic days, the woman used to perform Tawaaf round the House as naked, putting a cloth over her private parts and saying: "Today there seems the whole or a part (of my body), and I will not make lawful (for men) what seems thereof". On that occasion, Allaah revealed these Quraanic Aayaat. [Muslim]

Verse Number 184

184- Do they not reflect? There is no madness in their companion (Muhammad) (and that) he is but a plain warner. A narration on the authority of Qataadah that he said: It was mentioned to us that the Prophet [peace and blessings of Allaah be upon him] stood at Safa mountain and went on calling the tribes and clans of Quraysh in name one by one, and warning them of Allaah's punishment (if they did not believe in Allaah). One of them said: "Verily, your companion (Muhammad) is a madman. He kept calling out till morning". On that occasion, Allaah Almighty (the Most High) revealed this Quraanic Ayaah. [Ibn Abu Haatim and Abu Ash-Shaykh]

Verse Number 187

187- They ask you about the (Final) Hour: "When will be its appointed time?" Say: "The knowledge thereof is with my Lord (Rabb) (Alone). None can reveal its time but He. Heavy is its burden through the heavens and the earth. It shall not come upon you except all of a sudden." They ask you as if you were eagerly in search of it. Say: "The knowledge thereof is with Allaah (Alone) but most of people know not."

A narration on the authority of Ibn 'Abbaas [Allaah be pleased with them] that he said: Hamaalah Ibn Qushayr and Samaw'al Ibn Zayd told the Prophet [peace and blessings of Allaah be upon him]: "Tell us about the time of the (final) Hour if you are really a Prophet: we indeed know it". On that occasion, Allaah revealed this Quraanic Ayaah. [Ibn Jareer and others]

Verse Number 204

204- So, when the Quraan is recited, listen to it, and be silent that you may receive mercy.

A narration on the authority of Abu Hurayrah [may Allaah be pleased with him] that he said: This Quraanic Ayaah was revealed in connection with raising the voices in prayer behind the Prophet [peace and blessings of Allaah be upon him]. [Ibn Abu Haatim and others]

It is narrated on the same authority that he said: They used to talk in the prayer (to one another), thereupon this Quraanic Ayaah was revealed. [Ibn Abu Haatim]

The same is narrated on the authority of 'Abdullaah Ibn Mughaffal and 'Abdullaah Ibn Mas'ood [Allaah be pleased with them]. [Ibn Jareer]

Soorah Al-Anfaal

Verse Number 1

1- They ask you (O Muhammad) about the spoils of war. Say: "The spoils of war belong to Allaah and the Messenger." So fear Allaah and amend what is between you, and obey Allaah and His Messenger if you are believers (al-Mumineen).

A narration on the authority of Ibn 'Abbaas [Allaah be pleased with them] that he said: When it was the day of (the battle of) Badr, the Prophet [peace and blessings of Allaah be upon him] said: "Whoever does such and such a thing (in fight) will have such and such a reward (of the booty)". The young men competed one another in that, while the old men remained under the flag (in view of their weakness and old age). At the time of distributing the spoils, the young men came to the Prophet [peace and blessings of Allaah be upon him] and asked him what they were promised.

On that, the old men said: "Do not give yourselves superiority over us in this matter. Indeed, we acted as protectors for you, and had you been exposed to defeat, surely, you would have returned to take shelter with us".

The young men refused and said: "No doubt, the Prophet [peace and blessings of Allaah be upon him] has (promised to) assign it to us". Both parties disputed over that until Allaah Almighty (the Most

High) revealed this Quraanic Ayaah. [Abu Daawood; An-Nasaa'i and Al-Haakim]

A narration on the authority of Sa'd Ibn Abu Waqqaas [may Allaah be pleased with him] that he said: When it was the day of (the battle of) Badr, on which my brother 'Umayr was killed, and I killed Sa'eed Ibn Al-'AAs, and took as booty his sword known as Dhul-Kateefah, I brought it to the Prophet [peace and blessings of Allaah be upon him] who ordered me to go and put it in the well (where all the spoils were put). I went and no one but Allaah knew in which state I was because of the killing of my brother and the taking of my booty. But, no sooner had I turned away than the Quraanic Ayaah of the Anfaal was revealed, thereupon the Prophet [peace and blessings of Allaah be upon him] ordered me to go and take my booty. [Ahmad]

A narration on the authority of Sa'd ibn Abu Waqqaas [may Allaah be pleased with him] that he said: I brought a sword to the Prophet [peace and blessings of Allaah be upon him] on the day of (the battle of) Badr and said: "O Messenger of Allaah! Allaah has quenched my thirst of revenge from the enemy: grant me this sword (in addition to my share of the booty)". He said: "Indeed, this sword is not at my disposal (so that I would give it to you), nor is it for you in particular". I went away while saying: "Today, this (sword) will be given to such as has not fought so much as I've done". While I was sitting a messenger came to me and asked me to respond to the invitation of the Prophet [peace and blessings of Allaah be upon him]. I thought something (of the Quraan) had been revealed in connection with me on account of my statement. I came to the Prophet [peace and blessings of Allaah be upon him] who told me: "You've asked me (to give you) this sword and it was not for you nor at my disposal; but Allaah Almighty (the Most High) has made it at my disposal, and I grant it to you". Then, he recited to me this Quraanic Ayaah. [Abu Daawood; At-Tirmidhi and An-Nasaa'i]

A narration on the authority of Mujaahid that they asked the Prophet [peace and blessings of Allaah be upon him] about (how to dispose of) the one-fifth after the four-fifths (to be assigned to the soldiers), thereupon this Quraanic Ayaah was revealed. [Ibn Jareer]

Verse Number 5

5- As your Lord (Rabb) caused you (O Muhammad) to go out from your home with the truth, even though verily, a party among the believers (al-Mumineen) disliked it.

A narration on the authority of Abu Ayyoob Al-Ansaari [may Allaah be pleased with him] that he said: While we were in Madeenah, the Prophet [peace and blessings of Allaah be upon him] told us: "I was told that the caravan of Abu Sufyaan is now on the way (from Sham to Makkah). Do you wish that we set out to meet it, perchance Allaah would cause us to get it as booty?" We answered in the affirmative. When we set out and proceeded on for one or two days, the Prophet [peace and blessings of Allaah be upon him] asked us:

"What do you see if you (are forced to) fight the (unbelieving) people? Indeed, they learnt of your setting out (and thus they went forth to protect the caravan)". We said: "No, by Allaah, we have no power to fight the enemy, but (we set out) with the intention to get the caravan". Then, he repeated the same question, and we gave the same reply. But Al-Miqdaad Ibn 'Amr said: "Then, (since there is fight), we never said to you what the people of Moses said to him, that is 'Go you, and your Lord (Rabb), and fight you two, while we sit here (and watch).'" Had we said the same as Al-Miqdaad had said, it would have been dearer to us than to have a great property. Then, Allaah Almighty (the Most High) revealed this Quraanic Ayaah. [Ibn Abu Haatim and Ibn Mardawayh]

A narration on the authority of 'Umar Ibn Al-Khattaab [may Allaah be pleased with him] that he said: When it was the day on which the Battle of Badr took place, the Prophet [peace and blessings of Allaah be upon him] cast a glance at the infidels, they were over one thousand while his own Companions were just over three hundred. The Prophet [peace and blessings of Allaah be upon him] turned (his face) towards the Qiblah, having his upper and lower garments on him, raised his hands and began his supplication to his Lord (Rabb): "O Allaah! Accomplish for me what You have promised me. O Allaah! Bring about what You have promised me. O Allaah! If this small group of Muslims is destroyed, You will not be worshipped on the earth." He continued his supplication to his Lord (Rabb), raising his hands, facing the Qiblah, until his upper garment slipped down from his shoulders. Abu Bakr came to him, picked up his upper garment and put it on his shoulders. Then he embraced him from behind and said: "O Prophet of Allaah! This supplication of yours to your Lord (Rabb) will be sufficient for you, and He will accomplish for you what He has promised you". On this occasion, Allaah revealed this Quraanic Ayaah. In this way, Allaah supported him with angels. [Ahmad; Abu Daawood and Muslim]

Verse Number 17

17- You killed them not, but Allaah killed them. And you (O Muhammad) threw not when you did throw, but Allaah threw, that He might test the believers (al-Mumineen) by a fair trial from Him. Verily, Allaah is All-Hearing, All-Knowing.

Verse Number 9

9- (Remember) when you sought help of your Lord (Rabb) and He answered you (saying): "I will help you with a thousand of the angels following one another in succession."

A narration on the authority of Ibn 'Abbaas and Jaabir [Allaah be pleased with them] that they said: On the day of (the battle of) Badr, the Prophet [peace and blessings of Allaah be upon him] raised both his hands and said (invoking): "O Lord (Rabb)! If this group (of Muslims) perish, then You will never be worshipped on earth afterwards". Jibreel [peace and blessings of Allaah be upon him] told him: "Take a handful of dust and throw their (the pagans') faces therewith". He took a handful of dust therewith he threw the faces of the pagans, and there was no one of them but that the dust of this handful harmed his eyes, nostrils and mouth. Consequently, they turned away and retreated. [Abu Ash-Shaykh; Ibn Jareer and Ibn Abu Haatim]

The same is narrated on the authority of Hakeem Ibn Hizaam [may Allaah be pleased with him]. [At-Tabaraani]

Verse Number 19

19- (O disbelievers (al-Kaafireen)) if you ask for a judgment, now has the judgment come unto you; and if you cease (from disbelief and war), it will be better for you, and if you return, so shall We return, and your forces will be of no avail to you, however numerous they be; and verily, Allaah is with the believers (al-Mumineen).

A narration on the authority of 'Abdullaah Ibn Tha'labah Ibn Su'ayr that it was Abu Jahl who prayed for victory first on the day of (the battle of) Badr. He said: "O Allah! Cause to perish in the morning the one who severs kinship ties more amongst us, and brings us that of wh we have no knowledge". However, this was a prayer for help and support on his part. On that occasion, this Quraanic Ayaah was revealed. [Al-Haakim]

A narration on the authority of 'Atiyyah that Abu Jahl said (on the day of (the battle of) Badr): "O Allaah! Give victory to the stronger of both factions and the more honored of the two parties". On that occasion, Allaah revealed this Quraanic Ayaah. [Ibn Abu Haatim]

Verse Number 27

27- O you who believe! Betray not Allaah and His Messenger, nor betray your trusts while you know (the consequences).

A narration on the authority of 'Abdullaah Ibn Abu Qataadah that this Quraanic Ayaah was revealed in connection with Abu Lubaabah Ibn Al-Mundhir when the Prophet [peace and blessings of Allaah be upon him] sent him to the Yahood of Quraythah in order to get them comply with the judgment issued by him upon them. When they asked for his opinion, he advised them that they should do so, that is to comply with his judgment, and he bcckoned to his throat, hinting that they would be slain. Then, Abu Lubaabah felt he had betrayed Allaah and His Messenger [peace and blessings of Allaah be upon him], thereupon he swore not to taste the food until he would die, otherwise Allaah would turn in repentance to him.

He went to the mosque of Madeenah, and fastened himself to one of its pillars, and kept as such for nine days (during which he never had any food) to the extent that he fell unconscious because of the great hunger he suffered, until Allaah Almighty (the Most High) revealed to His Messenger [peace and blessings of Allaah be upon him] that he turned in repentance to him and then the people came to give him the glad tidings. They intended to release him, but he swore that none other than the Prophet [peace and blessings of Allaah be upon him] should release him, so he did accordingly. [Sa'eed Ibn Mansoor and others]

A narration on the authority of As-Suddi that he said: Whenever the Companions heard anything from the Prophet [peace and blessings of Allaah be upon him], they would spread it till it would reach the polytheists. On that occasion, this Quraanic Ayaah was revealed. [Ibn Jareer]

Verse Number 30

30- And (remember O Muhammad) when the disbelievers (al-Kaafireen) plotted against you to imprison you, or to kill you, or to get you out (of Makkah); they were plotting and Allaah too was planning; and Allaah is the Best of planners.

A narration on the authority of Ibn 'Abbaas [Allaah be pleased with them] that the chiefs of every tribe of Quraysh met and they were about to enter Daar An-Nadwah when Iblees appeared to them in a form of a venerable man, whom they asked about his identity, thereupon he replied: "I'm an old man from Najd, and having learnt you would meet here, I wanted to take part with you, perchance my opinion and advice might be of benefit to you". They replied affirmatively, and allowed him to enter with them. When he entered with them, he said:

"Consider the affair of this man (that is the Prophet). By Allaah, he is about to take power from you with his matter (of religion)".

One of them said: "Let you imprison him in bonds, and then await for him some calamity (hatched) by Time until he dies and perishes, just as other poets like Zuhayr and An-Naabighah had perished before him. Indeed, he (the Prophet) is but like anyone of them". But Allaah's enemy, the old man of Najd (as he alleged) cried and said: "No, this is not a good opinion for you! By Allah, his Lord (Rabb) would cause him to get out of his prison to his companions, who would attack you until they would take him from your hands, and thus protect him against you. By Allaah, I feel afraid lest they afterwards would drive you out of your town. Consider another opinion".

Another one of them said: "Drive him away from amongst you so that you would be relieved of him. Once he comes out, whatever he does, and wherever he does it would not harm you. In this way, you would become far from his harm, since his matter would be with people other than you". The old man of Najd said: "By Allaah, this is not a good opinion for you. Do you not see the sweetness of his speech, the pleasantness of his words and the strong effect they have upon the hearts (Qalb) after hearing his speech? By Allaah, if you do so, he will then gather the Arabs who in turn will mobilize themselves against you, and then come to drive you out of your town and slay your chiefs". They said: "By Allaah, he has told the truth. Consider another opinion".

Abu Jahl said: "By Allaah, I'm going to suggest an opinion of which you've not thought yet". They asked him: "What is it?" He said: "Let us take from every tribe a strong, mighty young man, to each of whom a powerful sharp-edged sword should be given, and then they should strike him all at once as if it is a strike of a single man. If they kill him, his blood will be distributed among different tribes, and I do not think this clan of Banu Haashim will have power to fight all of Quraysh. When they see so, they will accept the blood-wet. In this way, we will be relieved of his harm". The old man of Najd said: "This, which the man has said, is, by Allaah, the right opinion, and there is no one (to be accepted) other than it". Then, they dispersed after all of them had agreed to carry out this opinion.

Jibreel [peace and blessings of Allaah be upon him] came and told the Prophet [peace and blessings of Allaah be upon him] of the matter and ordered him not to spend the night in his bed he used to sleep in. the Prophet [peace and blessings of Allaah be upon him] did not spend this night in his home and Allaah Almighty (the Most High) gave him permission to come out of Mecca as Emigrant. After his coming to Madinah, Allaah Almighty (the Most High) revealed to him the Surah of Al-Anfaal, in which He mentions His favors and blessings upon him (what means): {And (remember O Muhammad) when the disbelievers (al-Kaafireen) plotted against you to imprison you, or to kill you, or to get you out (of Makkah); they were plotting and Allaah too was planning; and Allaah is the Best of planners}. [verse 30]

Concerning their saying: "Let you imprison him in bonds, and then await for him some calamity (hatched) by time, until he dies and perishes, just as other poets like Zuhayr and An-Naabighah had perished before him. Indeed, he (the Prophet) is but like anyone of them", Allaah says (what means): {Or do they say: "A Poet! We await for him some calamity (hatched) by Time!"} (At-Toor, verse 30)

Concerning their intention to drive him away from the town, Allaah Almighty (the Most High) says (what means): {Their purpose was to drive you out of the land, in order to expel you: but in that case they would not have stayed (therein) after you, except for a little while}. (Al-Israa', verse 76) the Prophet [peace and blessings of Allaah be upon him] stayed (in Makkah) expecting for Allaah's order, until Quraysh gathered and made their plot against him, Jibreel [peace and blessings of Allaah be upon him] came to him and ordered him not to spend the night in the place where he used to sleep. the Prophet [peace and blessings of Allaah be upon him] invited 'Ali Ibn Abu Taalib [may Allaah be pleased with him] and asked him to spend the night in his bed, and wrap himself in a green mantle belonging to the Prophet, and he did accordingly. Then, the Prophet [peace and blessings of Allaah be upon him] came out, while they (the Quraysh) were standing at the gate of his house. He had with him a handful of dust, which he kept throwing their heads with and Allaah Almighty (the

Most High) took their sights away from His Messenger, while he was reciting (what means): {Yaa Seen. By the Quraan, Full of Wisdom, you are indeed one of the Messengers, On a Straight Way. It is a Revelation sent down by (Allaah), the Exalted in Might, Most Merciful, In order that you may admonish a people, whose fathers had received no admonition, and who therefore remain heedless (of the Signs of Allaah). The word is proved true against the greater part of them; for they do not believe. We have put yokes round their necks right up to their chins, so that their heads are forced up (and they cannot see). And We have put a bar in front of them and a bar behind them, and further, We have covered them up; so that they cannot see}. (Yaa Seen, verse 1-9]

When the Prophet [peace and blessings of Allaah be upon him] arrived in Madinah, Allaah Almighty (the Most High) revealed to him this Quraanic Ayaah [Al-Anfaal 30], reminding him of His favor on him and how He saved him from the disbelievers (al-Kaafireen). [Ibn Abu Haatim and Ibn Ishaaq]

Verse Number 31

31- And when Our Aayaat (of the Quraan) are recited to them, they say: "We have heard this (Quraan); if we wish we can say the like of this. This is nothing but the fables of the ancients." A narration on the authority of Sa'eed Ibn Jubayr that he said: On the day of (the battle of) Badr, the Prophet [peace and blessings of Allaah be upon him] ordered that three should be killed: 'Uqbah Ibn Abu Mu'ayt, Tu'aymah Ibn 'Adiyy and An-Nadr Ibn Al-Haarith. It was Al-Miqdaad who captured An-Nadr. When he commanded that he be killed Al-Miqdaad said: "O Messenger of Allaah! He is my captive". the Prophet [peace and blessings of Allaah be upon him] said: "He used to invent lies about the Book of Allaah". In connection with him, this Quraanic Ayaah was revealed. [Ibn Jareer]

Verse Number 32

32- And (remember) when they said: "O Allaah! If this (Quraan) is indeed the truth (revealed) from You, then rain down stones on us from the sky or bring on us a painful torment." A narration on the authority of Sa'eed Ibn Jubayr that he said: This Quraanic Ayaah was revealed in connection with An-Nadr Ibn Al-Haarith. [Ibn Jareer]

no. 33-34

33- And Allaah would not punish them while you (Muhammad) are amongst them, nor would He punish them while they seek (Allaah's) Forgiveness. 34- And why should not Allaah punish them while they keep (men) off Al-Masjid Al-Haraam, and they are not its guardians? None can be its guardian except the righteous, but most of them know not.

A narration on the authority of Anas [may Allaah be pleased with him] that he said: Abu Jahl used to say: "O Allaah! If this is indeed the Truth from You, rain down on us a shower of stones from the sky or send us a grievous Penalty". On that occasion, Allaah revealed this Quraanic Ayaah. [Al-Bukhaari]

A narration on the authority of Yazeed Ibn Roomaan and Muhammad Ibn Qays that the Quraysh men told one another: "Verily, Allaah has honored Muhammad from among us: O Allaah! If this is indeed the Truth from You, rain down on us a shower of stones from the sky, or send us a grievous Penalty". When the evening came, they showed regrets for what they had said and said: "O Allaah! Forgive for us!" On that, Allaah revealed those Quraanic Aayaat. [Ibn Jareer]

A narration on the authority of 'Abd-Ar-Rahmaan Ibn Abza that he said: When the Prophet [peace and blessings of Allaah be upon him] was in Makkah Allaah Almighty (the Most High) revealed (what means): {And Allaah would not punish them while you (Muhammad) are amongst them...} When the Prophet [peace and blessings of Allaah be upon him] left for Madinah, Allaah Almighty (the Most High) then revealed: {nor would He punish them while they seek (Allaah's) Forgiveness}.

The remaining part of Muslims who remained in Makkah were powerless, and they used to ask for Allaah's pardon. When they also emigrated (and left Makkah), Allaah Almighty (the Most High) revealed (what means): {And why should not Allaah punish them while they keep (men) off Al-Masjid Al-Haraam, and they are not its guardians? None can be its guardian except the righteous, but most of them know not}. thus, Allaah Almighty (the Most High) gave permission (to the Muslims) to conquer Mecca and this was the punishment He promised to send upon the pagans and disbelievers (al-Kaafireen). [Ibn Jareer]

Verse Number 35

35- Their prayer at the House (the Ka'bah) was nothing but whistling and clapping of hands. Therefore taste the punishment (at Badr) because you used to disbelieve. A narration on the authority of Ibn 'Umar [Allaah be pleased with them] that he said: They (the disbelievers (al-Kaafireen)) used to circumambulate the House while clapping their hands and whistling, thereupon this Quraanic Ayaah was revealed. [Al-Waahidi]

A narration on the authority of Sa'eed Ibn Jubayr that he said: The (disbelievers (al-Kaafireen) of the) Quraysh used to encounter the Prophet [peace and blessings of Allaah be upon him] during his Tawaaf (round the House) clapping and whistling, thereupon this Quraanic Ayaah was revealed. [Ibn Jareer]

Verse Number 36

36- Verily, those who disbelieve spend their wealth to hinder (men) from the Path of Allaah, and so will they continue to spend it; but in the end it will become a (source of) regret for them. Then they will be overcome (in this world). And (in the hereafter) those who disbelieve will be gathered (all) unto Hell.

A narration on the authority of Az-Zuhri and others that when the Quraysh men were afflicted on the day of (the battle of) Badr and returned to Makkah, 'Abdullaah Ibn Abu Rabee'ah, 'Ikrimah Ibn Abu Jahl, Safwaan Ibn Umayyah and other men from the Quraysh whose sons and fathers were killed in the battle, went to Abu Sufyaan and talked to him as well as to those of the Quraysh who had merchandise in this caravan.

They said: "O assembly of Quraysh! Muhammad has harmed you and killed the best among you. So, aid us with this wealth to fight him, perchance we would take our retaliation from him". They did accordingly. On that occasion, Allaah revealed this Quraanic Ayaah. [Ibn Ishaaq]

A narration on the authority of Al-Hakam Ibn 'Utaybah that he said: This Quraanic Ayaah was revealed in connection with Abu Sufyaan when he spent forty gold ounces upon the polytheists (to help them fight the Muslims). [Ibn Abu Haatim]

A narration on the authority of Sa'eed Ibn Jubayr that he said: This Quraanic Ayaah was revealed in connection with Abu Sufyaan when he, on the day of Uhud (battle) hired two thousands of the Ahaabeesh to take part in fighting the Prophet [peace and blessings of Allaah be upon him] and the Muslims. [Ibn Jareer]

Verse Number 47

47- And be not like those who come out of their homes boastfully and to be seen of men, and avert (men) from the Path of Allaah; and Allaah encompasses (in knowledge) all that they do.

A narration on the authority of Muhammad Ibn Ka'b Al-Qurathi that he said: When the men of Quraysh set out for the battle of Uhud they accompanied with them songstresses and tambourines. On that occasion, Allaah Almighty (the Most High) revealed this Quraanic Ayaah. [Ibn Jareer]

Verse Number 49

49- When the hypocrites (al-Munaafiqeen) and those in whose hearts (Qalb) was a disease (doubt) said: "These people (Muslims) are deceived by their religion." But whoever relies on Allaah, surely Allaah is Exalted in Might, Full of Wisdom.

A narration on the authority of Abu Hurayrah [may Allaah be pleased with him] that he said: When Allaah revealed to his Prophet in Makkah (what means): {(Their) assembly will be defeated, and they will turn their backs (in retreat)}, [Al-Qamar, verse 45] 'Umar Ibn Al-Khattaab [may Allaah be pleased with him] said: "O Messenger of Allaah! Which assembly is intended?" That was before (the battle of) Badr. When it was the day of (the battle of) Badr and Quraysh men were defeated, I ('Umar) looked at the Prophet [peace and blessings of Allaah be upon him] who was directing their sword towards them while they were fleeing, and he was reciting (what means): {(Their) assembly will be defeated, and they will turn their backs (in retreat)}. It then meant the day of (the battle of) Badr.

In connection with them, Allaah revealed (what means): {Until when We seize their affluent ones with punishment, at once they are crying (to Allaah) for help}. [Al-Mu'minoon, verse 64] He also revealed (what means): {Have you not considered those who exchanged the favor of Allaah for disbelief and settled their people (in) the home of ruin?} [Ibraaheem, verse 28]

The Prophet [peace and blessings of Allaah be upon him] threw them (with a handful of dust) and it extended over them all and filled their eyes and mouths to the extent that none of them was killed but that his eyes and mouth were covered with dust. On that occasion, Allaah revealed (what means): {You killed them not, but Allaah killed them. And you (O Muhammad) threw not when you did throw, but Allaah threw, that He might test the believers (al-Mumineen) by a fair trial from Him. Verily, Allaah is All-Hearing, All-Knowing}. [Al-Anfaal, verse 17]

In connection with Iblees He revealed (what means): {But when the two hosts came in sight of each other, he ran away and said: "Verily, I am disassociated from you. Verily! I see (of angels) what you see not. Verily! I fear Allaah (lest He would destroy me) for Allaah is Severe in punishment."} [Al-Anfaal, verse 48]

'Utbah Ibn Rabee'ah and other polytheists who were with him on the day of (the battle of) Badr said: "Those (Muslims) have been deceived by their religion". On that occasion, Allaah revealed (what means): {When the hypocrites (al-Munaafiqeen) and those in whose hearts (Qalb) was a disease (doubt) said: "These people (Muslims) are deceived by their religion."...} [verse 49] [At-Tabaraani in Al-Awsat with a weak chain of narrators]

Verse Number 55

55- Verily, The worst of living creatures in the Sight of Allaah are those who disbelieve; so they shall not believe.

A narration on the authority of Sa'eed Ibn Jubayr that he said: this Quraanic Ayaah was revealed in connection with six Yahood including Abu Al-Taaboot. [Abu Ash-Shaykh]

Verse Number 58

58- If you (O Muhammad) fear treachery from any people (with whom you make a covenant), throw back (their covenant) to them (so as to be) on equal terms (of information that there will be no covenant between you and them). Certainly Allaah likes not the treacherous.

A narration on the authority of Shihaab that he said: Jibreel [peace and blessings of Allaah be upon him] entered upon the Prophet [peace and blessings of

Allaah be upon him] and said: "Have you put down the arms while I am still ready to fight them? Verily, Allaah has given you permission to fight the Yahood of Quraythah". Then Allaah revealed this Quraanic Ayaah. [Abu Ash-Shaykh]

Verse Number 64

64- O Prophet! Sufficient for you is Allaah and the believers (al-Mumineen) who follow you.

A narration on the authority of Ibn 'Abbaas [Allaah be pleased with them] that he said: When thirty-nine men and women embraced Islam with the Prophet [peace and blessings of Allaah be upon him], and then 'Umar Ibn Al-Khattaab embraced Islam (raising the number to forty), Allaah revealed this Quraanic Ayaah. [At-Tabaraani and others]

A narration on the authority of Sa'eed Ibn Jubayr that he said: When thirty-three men and six women, along with 'Umar Ibn Al-Khattaab embraced Islam with the Prophet [peace and blessings of Allaah be upon him], Allaah Almighty (the Most High) revealed this Quraanic Ayaah. [Ibn Abu Haatim with an authentic chain of narrators]

A narration on the authority of Sa'eed Ibn Jubayr that he said: When 'Umar Ibn Al-Khattaab embraced Islam, Allaah Almighty (the Most High) revealed this Quraanic Ayaah. [Abu Ash-Shaykh] Verse Number 65-66

65- O Prophet! Urge the believers (al-Mumineen) to fight (the disbelievers (al-Kaafireen)). If there are twenty steadfast persons amongst you, they will overcome two hundred (of them), and if there be a hundred steadfast persons they will overcome a thousand of those who disbelieve, because they are people who do not understand. 66Now Allaah has lightened your (task), for He knows that there is weakness in you. So if there are of you a hundred steadfast persons, they shall overcome two hundred, and if there are a thousand of you, they shall overcome two thousand with the Leave of Allaah. And Allaah is with the patient.

A narration on the authority of 'Abdullaah Ibn 'Abbaas [Allaah be pleased with them] that when this Quraanic Ayaah was revealed, the Muslims felt it difficult, and it was hard on them that ten should fight one hundred, and one hundred should fight one thousand. So, Allaah lightened the burden from them, and abrogated it with His saying (what means): {Now Allaah has lightened your (task), for He knows that there is weakness in you...} [Al-Anfaal, verse 66] [Ishaaq Ibn Rahawayh]

Verse Number 67-68

67- It is not for a Prophet that he should have prisoners of war without having made a great slaughter (among the disbelievers (al-Kaafireen)) in the land. You desire the good of this world (by taking the money of ransom for freeing the captives), but Allaah desires (for you) the Hereafter. And Allaah is Exalted in Might, Full of

Wisdom. 68Were it not a previous ordainment from Allaah, a severe torment would have touched you for what you took (of the ransom).

A narration on the authority of Anas [may Allaah be pleased with him] that he said: the Prophet [peace and blessings of Allaah be upon him] consulted the people about the captives on the day of (the battle of) Badr. He said: "No doubt, Allaah has given you the power over them". 'Umar Ibn Al-Khattaab stood and said: "O Messenger of Allaah! Strike their necks (that is kill them)". But he turned away from him. Abu Bakr stood and said: "I see that you should pardon them and accept ransom from them". He pardoned them and accepted ransom from them. On that occasion, Allaah revealed (what means): {Were it not a previous ordainment from Allaah, a severe torment would have touched you...} [verse 68] [Ahmad and others]

A similar one is narrated on the authority of Ibn Mas'ood [may Allaah be pleased with him]. [Ahmad; At-Tirmidhi and others]

A narration on the authority of Abu Hurayrah [may Allaah be pleased with him] that he said: the Prophet [peace and blessings of Allaah be upon him] said: "The booty has not been made lawful for any people whose main property was sheep before you: but the fire would descend and devour it entirely". Then, when it was the day of (the battle of) Badr, and the Muslims emerged victorious, they took the booty and did not wait the command of Allaah. On that occasion, Allaah revealed (what means): {Were it not a previous ordainment from Allaah, a severe torment would have touched you...} [At-Tirmidhi]

Verse Number 70

70- O Prophet! Say to the captives that are in your hands: "If Allaah knows any good (sincere faith) in your hearts (Qalb), He will recompense you with something better than what has been taken from you (of ransom), and He will forgive you, and Allaah is OftForgiving, Most Merciful."

A narration on the authority of Ibn 'Abbaas [Allaah be pleased with them] that he said: Al-'Abbaas said: By Allaah, this Quraanic Ayaah was revealed when I told the Prophet [peace and blessings of Allaah be upon him] about my embracing Islam and asked him to account me with the twenty golden ounces found with me. He gave me, for it, twenty slaves each of whom trafficked in my wealth in his hand, besides what I expect of Allaah's forgiveness. [At-Tabaraani in Al-Awsat]

Verse Number 73

73- And those who disbelieve are allies of one another, (and) if you (Muslims) do not do so (that is take as allies the Muslims and suppress the disbelievers (al-Kaafireen)), there will be Fitnah on earth, and a great mischief (because of the emergence of disbelievers (al-Kaafireen) and weakness of Muslims).

A narration on the authority of Abu Maalik that he said: A man said: "Will we inherit the property of our kith and kin from among the polytheists?" On that occasion, this Quraanic Ayaah was revealed. [Ibn Jareer and Abu Ash-Shaykh]

Verse Number 75

75- And those who believed afterwards, and emigrated and strove hard along with you (in the Cause of Allaah), they are of you (O Muhaajiroon and Ansaar). But kindred by blood are nearer to one another (regarding inheritance) according to the ordinance of Allaah (in the Preserved Tablet). Verily, Allaah knows best all things.

A narration on the authority of Ibn Az-Zubayr [may Allaah be pleased with him] that he said: It was the habit that a man would make a contract with another to inherit the property of each other. On that occasion, this Quraanic Ayaah was revealed. [Ibn Jareer]

A narration on the authority of Hishaam Ibn 'Urwah from his father that he said: the Prophet [peace and blessings of Allaah be upon him] established a bond of brotherhood between Az-Zubayr Ibn Al-'Awwaam and Ka'b Ibn Maalik. Az-Zubayr said: "Having seen that Ka'b had been wounded in the battle of Uhud, I said to myself: "If he died then I would inherit his property". On that occasion, Allaah revealed this Quraanic Ayaah. After that, the inheritance then was established on the basis of the blood relation and not on the basis of the bond of brotherhood. [Ibn Sa'd]

Soorah At-Tawbah

Verse Number 14

14- Fight against them so that Allaah will punish them (by killing) at your hands and disgrace them (by captivity and oppression) and give you victory over them and heal the breasts of a believing people,

A narration on the authority of Qataadah that he said: It was mentioned to us that this Quraanic Ayaah was revealed in connection with Khuzaa'ah when they went on killing Banu Bakr. [Abu Ash-Shaykh]

The same is narrated on the authority of 'Ikrimah. [Abu Ash-Shaykh] A narration on the authority of As-Suddi that he said: Allaah's saying (what means): {and heal the breasts of a believing people}, was revealed in connection with Khuzaa'ah, the allies of the Prophet [peace and blessings of Allaah be upon him], who were made to heal their breasts (by taking retaliation) from Banu Bakr. [Abu Ash-Shaykh]

Verse Number 17-19

17- It is not for the polytheists to maintain the Mosques of Allaah (that is to enter and pray therein) while they witness against their own selves of disbelief. The deeds of such are fruitless and in Fire shall they abide. 18- The Mosques of Allaah shall be maintained only by those who believe in Allaah and the Last Day, establish prayer, and give Zakaah and fear none but

Allaah. It is those who are expected to be on true guidance. 19- Do you regard the providing of water to the pilgrims and the maintenance of Al-Masjid Al-Haraam equal to (the service of) him who believes in Allaah and the Last Day, and strives hard and fights in the Cause of Allaah? They are not equal in the sight of Allaah. And Allaah guides not the wrongdoing (disbelieving) people.

A narration on the authority of Ibn 'Abbaas [Allaah be pleased with them] that Al-'Abbaas said when he fell a captive in the battle of Badr: "If you have preceded us with Islam, emigration and striving (in Allaah's cause), then you should know that we used to maintain Al-Masjid Al-Haraam, provide the pilgrims with water and release the captives". On that occasion, Allaah revealed (what means): {Do you regard the providing of water to the pilgrims and the maintenance of Al-Masjid Al-Haraam equal to (the service of) him who believes in Allaah and the Last Day...} [verse 19] [Ibn Abu Haatim]

A narration on the authority of An-Nu'maan Ibn Bashir [may Allaah be pleased with him] that he said: While I was (sitting) near the pulpit of the Prophet [peace and blessings of Allaah be upon him], a man said: "I do not care if, after embracing Islam, I do not do any good deed except providing the pilgrims with water". Another said: "I do not care if, after embracing Islam, I do not do any good deed more than maintenance service to Al-Masjid Al-Haraam". A third one said: "Jihad in the cause of Allaah is better than what you said". 'Umar rebuked them and said: "Don't raise your voices near the pulpit of the Prophet [peace and blessings of Allaah be upon him] on Friday". After the prayer, I entered (the dwelling place of the Prophet) and asked for his verdict about that in which they had differed. It was on this occasion that Allaah revealed (what means): {Do you regard the providing of water to the pilgrims and the maintenance of Al-Masjid Al-Haraam equal to (the service of) him who believes in Allaah and the Last Day...} [verse 19] [Muslim; Ibn Hibbaan and Abu Daawood]

A narration on the authority of Ibn Seereen that he said: 'Ali Ibn Abu Taalib [may Allaah be pleased with him] arrived in Makkah and said to Al-'Abbaas: "O uncle! Will you not emigrate? Will you not join the Prophet [peace and blessings of Allaah be upon him]?" He said: "No: let me maintain Al-Masjid and be a custodian of the House". On that occasion, Allaah revealed (what means): {Do you regard the providing of water to the pilgrims and the maintenance of Al-Masjid Al-Haraam equal to (the service of) him who believes in Allaah and the Last Day...} [verse 19]

He said to other people whom he named: "Will you not emigrate? Will you not join the Prophet [peace and blessings of Allaah be upon him]?" They replied: "No, but we will live with our brothers and clansmen in our dwelling places". On that occasion, Allaah revealed (what means): {Say (O Muhammad): "If your fathers, your sons, your brothers, your wives...} [verse 24] [Al-Firyaabi]

A similar one is narrated on the authority of Ash-Sha'bi. ['Abd-Ar-Razzaaq] A narration on the authority of Muhammad Ibn Ka'b Al-Qurathi that he said: Talhah, 'Ali and Al-'Abbaas vied in glory with each other. Talhah said: "I am the guardian of the House, and its key is with me". Al-'Abbaas said: "I am responsible for providing the pilgrims with water". "Ali said: "I have prayed towards the Qiblah before the people and I have taken part in Jihaad (with the Prophet)". On that occasion, Allaah revealed (what means): {Do you regard the providing of water to the pilgrims and the maintenance of Al-Masjid Al-Haraam equal to (the service of) him who believes in Allaah and the Last Day...} [verse 19] [Ibn Jareer]

Verse Number 25

25- Truly Allaah has given you victory in many battlefields, and (remember your battle) on the Day of Hunayn when your great number elated you, but in naught it availed you, and the earth, withstanding its vastness, was straitened for you, then you turned back in flight.

A narration on the authority of Ar-Rabee' Ibn Anas that he said: On the day of (the battle of) Hunayn, a man said: "Today, we will not be defeated by a few number of people", and they (the Muslims) were twelve thousand. This saying was difficult on the Prophet [peace and blessings of Allaah be upon him], thereupon Allaah revealed this Quraanic Ayaah. [Al-Bayhaqi in Ad-Dalaa'il]

Verse Number 28

28- O you who believe! Verily, the polytheists are impure. So let them not approach Al-Masjid Al-Haraam after this year; and if you fear poverty, Allaah will enrich you if He wills, out of His Bounty. Surely, Allaah is All-Knowing, All-Wise.

A narration on the authority of Ibn 'Abbaas [Allaah be pleased with them] that he said: The polytheists used to go to the House with food to sell it. When they were forbidden to visit the House the Muslims said: "Then, from where should we get food?" On that occasion, Allaah revealed this Quraanic Ayaah. [Ibn Abu Haatim]

A narration on the authority of Sa'eed Ibn Jubayr that he said: When Allaah revealed (what means): {Verily, the polytheists are impure. So let them not approach Al-Masjid Al-Haraam after this year}, this was difficult on the Muslims who said: "Then, who shall bring us food and other things?" On that occasion, Allaah revealed (what means): {and if you fear poverty, Allaah will enrich you if He wills, out of His Bounty. Surely, Allaah is All-Knowing, All-Wise}. [Ibn Jareer and Abu Ash-Shaykh]

The same is narrated on the authority of 'Ikrimah, 'Atiyyah Al-'Awfi, Qataadah and others. [Ibn Jareer and Abu Ash-Shaykh]

Verse Number 30

30- And the Yahood say: Ezra is the son of Allaah, and the Nasaara say: The Messiah is the son of Allaah. That is their saying with their mouths, resembling the saying of those who disbelieved aforetime. Allaah's Curse be upon them, how they are deluded away from the truth!

A narration on the authority of Ibn 'Abbaas [Allaah be pleased with them] that he said: Salaam Ibn Mishkam, Nu'maan Ibn Abu Awfa, Abu Anas, Mahmood Ibn Dihyah, Shaas Ibn Qays, and Maalik Ibn Sayfi came to the Prophet [peace and blessings of Allaah be upon him] and said: "How should we follow you, given that you have abandoned our Qiblah and do not claim that Ezra is the son of Allaah?" In this connection, Allaah revealed this Quraanic Ayaah. [Ibn Abu Haatim and Ibn Ishaaq]

Verse Number 37

187

37- Verily, the transposition (of Sacred Months) is indeed an increase in disbelief thereby the disbelievers (al-Kaafireen) are led astray, for they make it lawful one year and unlawful another year in order to adjust the number of months forbidden by Allaah, and (thus) render lawful what has been made unlawful by Allaah. The evil of their deeds is made pleasing to them. And Allaah guides not the people who disbelieve.

A narration on the authority of Abu Maalik that he said: They used to make the year thirteen months and make Muharram Safar and render lawful what is unlawful. On that occasion, Allaah revealed this Quraanic Ayaah. [Ibn Jareer]

Verse Number 38

38- O you who believe! What is the matter with you, that when you are invited to march forth in the Cause of Allaah (that is Jihaad) you cling heavily to the earth? Are you pleased with the life of this world rather than the Hereafter? But little is the enjoyment of the life of this world as compared to the Hereafter.

A narration on the authority of Mujaahid that he said: This Quraanic Ayaah was revealed When they were commanded to set out for the battle of Tabook after the conquest of Makkah, and the Prophet [peace and blessings of Allaah be upon him] commanded them to go forth in summer where fruits ripened and they had longing for the shade, thereupon it was difficult on them to set out (and leave all this blessing). In connection with them, Allaah revealed this Quraanic Ayaah. [Ibn Jareer]

no. 39

39- If you march not forth, He will punish you with a painful torment and will replace you by another people; and in naught can you harm Him (Allaah or His Messenger), and Allaah is Able to do all things.

A narration on the authority of Najdah Ibn Nufay' that he said: I asked Ibn 'Abbas [Allaah be pleased with them] about this Quraanic Ayaah and he said: the Prophet [peace and blessings of Allaah be upon him] asked some tribes from Arabs to go forth and they did not respond quickly and rather adhered heavily to the land. On that occasion, Allaah revealed this Quraanic Ayaah. Then He withheld rain from them and that was their punishment. [Ibn Abu Haatim]

Verse Number 41

41- March forth (to fight), whether you are light (being healthy, young and wealthy) or heavy (being ill, old and poor), strive hard with your property and lives in the Cause of Allaah. This is better for you, if you but knew.

A narration on the authority of Hadrami that it was mentioned to him that it was the habit of some people that if anyone of them was sick or old-aged he would say that he was sinful. On that occasion, Allaah revealed this Quraanic Ayaah. [Ibn Jareer]

Verse Number 43

43- May Allah forgive you (O Muhammad). Why did you grant them leave (to remain behind? Why you did not refrain from giving them permission) until those who told the truth (in their excuses) would seem to you in a clear light, and you know the liars?

A narration on the authority of 'Amr Ibn Maymoon Al-Azdi that he said: the Prophet [peace and blessings of Allaah be upon him] did two things in connection with which he received no command (from Allaah): he gave permission to the hypocrites (al-Munaafiqeen), and accepted ransom from the captives. On that occasion, Allaah revealed this Quraanic Ayaah. [Ibn Jarir]

Verse Number 49

49- And among them is he who says: "Give me permission (not to fight) and put me not into trial." Surely, they have fallen into trial. And verily, Hell is surrounding the disbelievers (al-Kaafireen).

A narration on the authority of Ibn 'Abbaas [Allaah be pleased with them] that he said: the Prophet [peace and blessings of Allaah be upon him] said to Al-Jadd Ibn Qays: "O Jadd! Would you (set out with us in order to) fight the Byzantines this year?" He replied: "O Messenger of Allaah! Would you please grant me exemption and put me not to trial? Indeed, my people know well that there is no man who admires women more than me, and I am afraid if I see women of the Byzantines, I could not resist (my desire for having sexual intercourse with) them". On that, the Prophet [peace and blessings of Allaah be upon him] turned away from him and told him: "I've granted you exemption". In connection with this Al-Jadd, this Quraanic Ayaah was revealed. Al-Jadd Ibn Qays was one of the chiefs of Banu Salamah.

According to a correct narration, the Prophet [peace and blessings of Allaah be upon him] asked them: "Who is your chief O Banu Salamah?" They said: "He is Al-Jadd Ibn Qays but we regard him as a miser". the

Prophet [peace and blessings of Allaah be upon him] said: "Then, which ailment is more grievous than niggardliness? But your chief should be this white-complexioned curly-haired young man, Al-Bishr Ibn Al-Bara Ibn Ma'roor". [At-Tabaraani; Abu Na'eem; Ibn Mardawayh and Ibn Ishaaq]

A similar one is narrated on the authority of Jaabir Ibn 'Abdullaah [Allaah be pleased with them]. [Ibn Abu Haatim and Ibn Mardawayh]

A narration on the authority of Ibn 'Abbaas [Allaah be pleased with them] that the Prophet [peace and blessings of Allaah be upon him] said: "Fight (in Allaah's cause) so that you would get as booty the females of the Byzantines". Some hypocrites (al-Munaafiqeen) said: "Consider how he (Muhammad) tempts you with women?" On that occasion, Allaah revealed this Quraanic Ayaah. [At-Tabaraani]

Verse Number 50

50- If good (victory/booty) befalls you (O Muhammad) it grieves them, but if a calamity overtakes you, they say: "We took our precaution beforehand," and they turn away rejoicing.

A narration on the authority of Jaabir Ibn 'Abdullaah [Allaah be pleased with them] that he said: When the Prophet [peace and blessings of Allaah be upon him] set out for the battle of Tabook, the hypocrites (al-Munaafiqeen) who remained behind in Madeenah went on spreading false news about him and his

Companions, that they encountered great difficulties in their journey. But when good news about him [peace and blessings of Allaah be upon him] and his Companions reached them in opposition to what they fabricated, they grieved for this so much. On that occasion, Allaah revealed this Quraanic Ayaah. [Ibn Abu Haatim]

Verse Number 53

53- Say: "Spend (in Allaah's Cause) willingly or unwillingly, it will not be accepted from you. Verily, you are ever a defiantly disobedient people."

A narration on the authority of Ibn Abbaas [Allaah be pleased with them] that he said: Al-Jadd Ibn Qays told the Prophet [peace and blessings of Allaah be upon him]: "Once I see women, I will soon be tempted by them. But I could help you with my money". In connection with him, this Quraanic Ayaah was revealed. [Ibn Jareer]

Verse Number 58

58- And of them are some who criticize you concerning (the distribution of) alms. If they are given thereof, they are pleased, but if they are not given thereof, at once they are angry! A narration on the authority of Abu Sa'eed Al-Khudri [may Allaah be pleased with him] that he said: While the Prophet [peace and blessings of Allaah be upon him] was distributing something among the people of DhulKhuwaysirah, a man with a thick beard, prominent cheeks, sunken eyes, a raised forehead and a shaven head, came (in front of The Prophet) and said: "Observe justice, O Muhammad!" The Prophet [peace and blessings of Allaah be upon him] said: "Woe to you! Who then could do justice if I do not observe justice?" On that occasion, this Quraanic Ayaah was revealed. [Al-Bukhaari]

A similar one is narrated on the authority of Jaabir [may Allaah be pleased with him]. [Ibn Abu Haatim]

Verse Number 61

61- And among them (the hypocrites (al-Munaafiqeen)) are men who molest the Prophet (by slandering him and transmitting his talks) and (whenever they are forbidden to do so lest this may reach him they will) say: "He is (lending his) ear (to every news)." Say: "(He lends his) ear to what is good for you; he believes in Allaah, and trusts the believers (al-Mumineen) (in what they tell him), and is a mercy to those of you who believe." But those who molest Allaah's Messenger will have a painful torment.

A narration on the authority of Ibn 'Abbaas [Allaah be pleased with them] that he said: Nabtal Ibn Al-Haarith used to go to the Prophet [peace and blessings of Allaah be upon him], talk to, and listen to him, and then transmit his talk to the other hypocrites (al-Munaafiqeen). It is he who said: "Muhammad is but (lending his) ear (to anyone) and believes anyone if he tells him about anything whatsoever". In connection with him, Allaah Almighty (the Most High) revealed this Quraanic Ayaah. [Ibn Abu Haatim]

Verse Number 65

65- If you ask them (about this), they say (excusing): "We were only talking idly and joking." Say: "Was it at Allaah and His revelations and His Messenger that you were mocking?"

A narration on the authority of 'Abdullaah Ibn 'Umar [Allaah be pleased with them] that he said: During the battle of Tabook, a man was sitting in a gathering and said: "I have never seen the like of these reciters of ours! They have the hungriest stomachs, the most lying tongues and are the most cowardly in battle". A man in that gathering said: "You are lying. You are a hypocrite, and I will inform the Prophet [peace and blessings of Allaah be upon him]". This statement was conveyed to the Prophet [peace and blessings of Allaah be upon him] and some verses of the Quran were revealed about it.

'Abdullah ibn 'Umar [Allaah be pleased with them] said: "I saw that man afterwards holding onto the rope of the Messenger's camel while stones were being hurled at him, declaring: "O Messenger of Allaah! We were only engaged in idle talk and jesting", while the Prophet [peace and blessings of Allaah be upon him] was reciting the verses in which Allaah Almighty (the Most High) Says (what means): {Say: "Was it at Allaah and His revelations and His Messenger that you were mocking?"} [verse 65]

A similar one is narrated on the same authority in which the hypocrite was referred to as 'Abdullaah Ibn Ubayy. [Ibn Abu Haatim]

A narration on the authority of Ka'b Ibn Maalik [may Allaah be pleased with him] that he said: A group of hypocrites (al-Munaafiqeen) including Wadee'ah Ibn Thaabit and Mukhashshan Ibn Humayyir talked badly indirectly about the Prophet [peace and blessings of Allaah be upon him]. Wadee'ah said, by way of dissuading and terrorizing the Muslims: "Do you think that fighting the Byzantines is like fighting the Arabs? By Allaah, I see as if you will be chained in fetters tomorrow". Mukhashshan said: "By Allaah, I like that anyone of us is given one hundred lashes and no Quraan will be revealed in connection with us because of this statement of yours". Meanwhile, the Prophet [peace and blessings of Allaah be upon him] told 'Ammaar Ibn Yaasir: "Catch up with the people because they have been burnt and ask them about what they had said, and if they denied say to them: "No, you have said such and such".

'Ammaar [may Allaah be pleased with him] went to them and told them as the Prophet [peace and blessings of Allaah be upon him] asked him to do, so they immediately came to the Prophet [peace and blessings of Allaah be upon him] to offer their excuses to him. While the Prophet [peace and blessings of Allaah be upon him] was standing on his she-camel and holding its nose-band, Wadee'ah Ibn Thaabit said: "O Messenger of Allaah! We just were playing and jesting". On that occasion, Allaah Almighty (the Most High) revealed (what means): {If you ask them (about this), they say (excusing): "We were only talking idly and joking." Say: "Was it at Allaah and His revelations and His Messenger that you were mocking?"} [verse 65]

It seems as if it was Mukhashshan Ibn Humayyir who was pardoned in this Quraanic Ayaah, thereupon he changed his name into 'Abd-Ar-Rahmaan and asked Allaah Almighty (the Most High) to be killed as a martyr and make unknown the place of his dead body. He was killed as a martyr in the battle of Yamaamah and the place of his dead body was unknown. [Ibn Ishaaq and Ibn Abu Haatim]

A narration on the authority of Qataadah that while the Prophet [peace and blessings of Allaah be upon him] was in the battle of Tabook, there were some hypocrites (al-Munaafiqeen) who said: "This man (that is the Prophet [peace and blessings of Allaah be upon him]) hopes to conquer the palaces and forts of Shaam. What a far hope he wishes for!" So, Allaah Informed His Prophet [peace and blessings of Allaah be upon him] about this and said: "Detain those people". He went to them and said: "You have said so and so. On that occasion, Allaah Revealed this and the preceding Quraanic Aayaat. [Ibn Jareer]

Verse Number 74

74- They (the hypocrites (al-Munaafiqeen)) swear by Allaah that they said nothing (offensive about the

Prophet), but really they said the word of disbelief, and they disbelieved after their (pretense of) Islam, and they resolved to do that which they were unable to carry out, and they had no cause for resentment except that Allaah and His Messenger had enriched them of (Allaah's) Bounty. If then they repent (from hypocrisy and believe in you), it will be better for them, but if they turn away (from faith), Allaah will punish them with a painful torment in this worldly life (by killing) and in the Hereafter (with the Fire of Hell); and they will have on earth none to protect or help them.

A narration on the authority of Ibn 'Abbaas [Allaah be pleased with them] that when Al-Julaas Ibn Suwayd Ibn As-Saamit remained behind The Prophet [peace and blessings of Allaah be upon him] in the battle of Tabook, he said: "If this man (Muhammad) is true, we should be worse than asses". This statement was raised to the Prophet [peace and blessings of Allaah be upon him] by 'Umayr Ibn Sa‘d, his step-son, who said to him: "By Allaah, You are, Julaas, the dearest of men to me, and the greatest benefactor to me, and it aggrieves me most that any harm should befall you. Verily, you have said something which, if I convey from you, I would disgrace you, and if I conceal it, I would breech my religion. Anyway, one of them is easier upon me than the other". He went to the Prophet [peace and blessings of Allaah be upon him] and made a mention to him of what Julaas said. Julaas, in turn, swore by Allaah, before the Prophet [peace and blessings of Allaah be upon him] that 'Umayr attributed lies to him and that he did not say what he had claimed about him. In connection with him, Allaah Almighty (the Most High) revealed this Quraanic Ayaah. They pretended that he repented and did good and was perfect in his faith in Islam. [Ibn Abu Haatim]

A similar one is narrated on the authority of Ka'b Ibn Maalik [may Allaah be pleased with him]. [Ibn Abu Haatim]

The same is narrated on the authority of 'Urwah. [Ibn Sa'd in At-Tabaqaat]

A narration on the authority of Anas Ibn Maalik [may Allaah be pleased with him] that he said: Zayd Ibn Arqam heard a man having said while the Prophet [peace and blessings of Allaah be upon him] was delivering a speech: "If this man (Muhammad) is true in what he says, then, we should be worse than donkeys". When this statement was raised to the Prophet [peace and blessings of Allaah be upon him], the hypocrite denied it thereupon Allaah revealed this Quraanic Ayaah. [Ibn Abu Haatim]

A narration on the authority of Ibn 'Abbaas [Allaah be pleased with them] that he said: While the Prophet [peace and blessings of Allaah be upon him] was sitting in the shade of a tree he said: "A while later a man will come and will look at you with the eye of a devil". Then a blue-complexioned man came whom the Prophet [peace and blessings of Allaah be upon him] invited and asked: "For which reason do you and your companions abuse me?" He replied: "Let me come to invite them to you". He left and after a short time returned with his companions and they all swore by Allaah that they had said nothing. On that occasion, Allaah Almighty (the Most High) revealed this Quraanic Ayaah. [Ibn Jareer]

A narration on the authority of Qataadah that he said: Two men fought: one from Juhaynah and the other from Ghifaar. At that time, the people of Juhaynah were the allies of the Ansaar. But the one from Ghifar won over the other from Juhaynah. On that 'Abdullaah Ibn Ubayy said: "Help your brother, for by Allaah, the example of us and Muhammad is but like the statement which reads: "Feed your dog (till when it becomes strong) it would eat you". If we return to Madeenah, the highest and the most powerful will drive away therefrom the lowest and the weakest". A Muslim person went to the Prophet [peace and blessings of Allaah be upon him] and informed him. When he [peace and blessings of Allaah be upon him] went to 'Abdullaah and asked him, he swore by Allaah that he had not said it. On that occasion, Allaah revealed this Quraanic Ayaah. [Ibn Jareer]

A narration on the authority of Ibn 'Abbaas [Allaah be pleased with them] that he said: A man called Al-Aswad intended to kill the Prophet [peace and blessings of Allaah be upon him], thereupon Allaah revealed (what means): {and they resolved to do that which they were unable to carry out...} [verse 74] [At-Tabaraani]

A narration on the authority of 'Ikrimah that a freed slave belonging to Banu 'Adiyy killed a man belonging to the Ansaar so the Prophet [peace and blessings of Allaah be upon him] judged that twelve thousand be given as blood compensation. In connection with that man, Allaah revealed (what means): {and they had no cause for resentment except that Allaah and His Messenger had enriched them of (Allaah's) Bounty...} [verse 74] [Ibn Jareer and Abu Ash-Shaykh]

Verse Number 75

75- And of them are some who made a covenant with Allaah (saying): "If He bestows on us of His Bounty, we will verily give in charity and will be certainly among the righteous."

A narration on the authority of Abu Umaamah that he said: Tha'labah Ibn Haatib said: "O Messenger of Allaah! Invoke Allaah to bestow upon me wealth". He said: "Woe to you O Tha'labah! No doubt, a little for which you show gratitude (to Allaah) is better than much for which you can give no thanks". He said: "By Allaah, if Allaah gives me wealth, I will give each one who has a right what is due to him". He invoked Allaah for him, thereupon Allaah bestowed upon him wealth and he had sheep which extended so much that the alleys of Madinah became narrow for him. He kept himself aside with them. He used to attend the prayer (in the masjid) and then go to them.

Then, they extended till it became difficult on him to graze them in the pastures of Madeenah. He kept far with them so much that he hardly attended the Jumu'ah prayer (in congregation) and then went to them. They extended more and more till he kept farther and farther from them. Then he abandoned congregational prayer entirely. On that occasion, Allaah revealed to His Messenger (what means): {Take alms from their wealth in order to purify them and sanctify them with it}. [verse 103]

He appointed two men to collect the obligatory charity and gave them a letter concerning that. They went to Tha'labah and read to him the letter of the Prophet [peace and blessings of Allaah be upon him]. He said: "Go to collect the objects of charity from the people and when you finish come back to me". They did accordingly. (When they came back to him) he told them: "This is but similar to Jizyah (tax). So, go away from me". On that occasion, Allaah Almighty (the Most High) revealed this Quraanic Ayaah. [At-Tabaraani; Ibn Mardawayh and Al-Bayhaqi in Ad-Dalaa'il]

A similar one is narrated on the authority of Ibn 'Abbaas [Allaah be pleased with them]. [Ibn Jareer and Ibn Mardawayh]

Verse Number 79

79- Those who defame such of the believers (al-Mumineen) as give in charity voluntarily, and those who could not find to give in charity except what is available to them - so they mock at them (believers (al-Mumineen)); Allaah will throw back their mockery on them, and they shall have a painful torment.

A narration on the authority of Abu Mas'ood Al-Ansari [may Allaah be pleased with him] that he said: When the Quraanic verses of charity were revealed, we used to work as porters. A man came and distributed objects of charity in abundance. And they (the hypocrites (al-Munaafiqeen)) said: "He is showing off." Another man came and gave a Saa' (a small measure of food grains); and they said: "Allaah is not in need of this small amount of charity." Then this Quraanic Ayaah was revealed. [Al-Bukhaari and Muslim]

Verse Number 81

81 Those who remained behind (from Tabook expedition) rejoiced in their staying behind the Messenger of Allaah; they hated to strive and fight with their properties and their lives in the Cause of Allaah, and they said (to one another): "Go not forth in the heat." Say: "The Fire of Hell is more intense in heat", if only they could understand (this fact, they would not have remained behind from Tabook expedition).

A narration on the authority of Ibn 'Abbaas [Allaah be pleased with them] that he said: the Prophet [peace and blessings of Allaah be upon him] ordered the people to set out with him and this was during summer. A man said: "O Messenger of Allaah! It is very hot and we could not come out. So do not go forth when it is hot (as such)". On that occasion, Allaah revealed (what means): {Say: "The Fire of Hell is more intense in heat", if only they could understand (this fact, they would not have remained behind from Tabook expedition)}. [verse 81] [Ibn Jareer]

A narration on the authority of Muhammad Ibn Ka'b Al-Qurathi that he said: the Prophet [peace and blessings of Allaah be upon him] set out for Tabook when it was very hot. A man from Banu Salamah said: "Do not go forth in the heat". On that occasion, Allaah revealed this Quraanic Ayaah. [Ibn Jareer]

A similar one is narrated by Al-Bayhaqi.

Verse Number 84

84- And never (O Muhammad) perform (funeral) prayer for any of them (hypocrites (al-Munaafiqeen)) who dies, nor stand at his grave (for burial or visiting). Certainly they disbelieved in Allaah and His Messenger, and died while they were defiantly disobedient (disbelievers (al-Kaafireen)).

A narration on the authority of Ibn 'Umar [Allaah be pleased with them] that he said: When 'Abdullaah Ibn Ubayy (the chief of hypocrites (al-Munaafiqeen)) died, his son came to The Prophet [peace and blessings of Allaah be upon him] and said: "O Messenger of Allaah! Please give me your shirt to shroud him in it". the Prophet [peace and blessings of Allaah be upon him] gave him his shirt. Then he asked The Prophet [peace and blessings of Allaah be upon him] to perform the funeral prayer for him.

When The Prophet [peace and blessings of Allaah be upon him] got up to offer the funeral prayer, 'Umar took hold of his garment and said: "O Messenger of Allaah! Would you offer the funeral prayer for him though Allaah has forbidden you to offer the funeral prayer for the hypocrites (al-Munaafiqeen)?" The Prophet [peace and blessings of Allaah be upon him] said: "I have been given by Allaah the freedom to choose to ask forgiveness for them or not, because Allaah said (what means): {Whether you ask forgiveness for them or not, (their sin is unpardonable): if you ask forgiveness for them seventy times, Allaah will never forgive them). Moreover, I will ask forgiveness for them more than seventy times". 'Umar said: "But he is a hypocrite". So The Prophet offered the funeral prayer. On that occasion, Allaah Almighty (the Most High) revealed this Quraanic Ayaah. [Al-Bukhaari and Muslim]

Verse Number 91-92

91- There is no difficulty on those who are weak (like the old-aged men) or ill (with such chronic diseases as blindness and lameness) or who find no resources to spend (in Jihaad, to remain behind) if they are sincere and true (in duty) to Allaah and His Messenger. There is no way (of blame) against the doers of good. And Allaah is Oft-Forgiving, Most Merciful. 92- Nor (is there any sin) on those who came to you to be provided with mounts, when you said: "I can find no mounts for you," they turned back, while their eyes overflowing with tears of grief that they could not find anything to spend (for Jihaad).

A narration on the authority of Zayd Ibn Thaabit [may Allaah be pleased with him] that he said: I used to write for the Prophet [peace and blessings of Allaah be upon him] the divine revelation, and while I was writing Soorah Baraa'ah and putting the pen on my ear, we were commanded to fight (the disbelievers (al-Kaafireen)). While the Prophet [peace and blessings of Allaah be upon him] was considering what had been revealed to him, a blind man came to him and said: "What about me, O Prophet given that I am blind?" On that occasion, Allaah revealed (what means): {There is no difficulty on those who are weak...} [verse 91]

A group of his Companions including 'Abdullaah Ibn Ma'qil Al-Muzni came to him and said: "O Messenger of Allaah! Provide us with means of transportation". He said: "By Allaah, I have nothing to transport you". They turned back with their eyes shedding tears, they felt it difficult that they would not take part in Jihaad and have no spending nor riding mounts. On that occasion, Allaah revealed (what means): {Nor (is there any sin) on those who came to you to be provided with mounts.....} [verse 92] Their names are mentioned in Al-Mubhamaat, in the comment on Allaah's saying (what means): {But among the Bedouins are some who believe in Allaah and the Last Day...} [verse 99] [Ibn Abu Haatim]

A narration on the authority of Mujaahid that it was revealed in connection with Banu Muqarrin who came to the Messenger of Allaah [peace and blessings of

Allaah be upon him] to provide them with means of transportation. [Ibn Jareer]

A narration on the authority of 'Abd-Ar-Rahmaan Ibn Ma'qil Al-Muzni that he said: We were ten belonging to Muqarrin and in connection with us this Quraanic Ayaah was revealed. [Ibn Jareer]

Verse Number 102

102- And (there are) others who have acknowledged their sins, they have mixed a righteous deed with another that was evil. It may be that Allaah will turn to them in repentance. Surely, Allaah is Oft-Forgiving, Most Merciful.

A narration on the authority of Ibn 'Abbaas [Allaah be pleased with them] that he said: the Prophet [peace and blessings of Allaah be upon him] set out for fighting and Abu Lubaabah and other five remained behind him. Abu Lubaabah and two men thought of their matter and regretted for what they did and were certain of destruction. They said: "How should we live in shade and satisfaction with women and the Prophet [peace and blessings of Allaah be upon him] and the believers (al-Mumineen) with him are striving (in Allaah's cause)? By Allaah, we will fasten ourselves to the pillars and would not release ourselves till the Prophet [peace and blessings of Allaah be upon him] does it by himself". They did accordingly and the remaining three did not do.

The Prophet [peace and blessings of Allaah be upon him] returned from his battle and said: "Who are those fastened to the pillars?" a man said: "Those are Abu Lubaabah and some men who remained behind from the battle with him. They promised Allaah not to release themselves till you come and do it by yourself". He said: "I will not release them till I am commanded to do so". On that occasion, Allaah revealed this Quraanic Ayaah. When it was revealed, he released them and accepted their excuses; and the case of the three who did not fasten themselves remained undecided. They are those in connection with whom Allaah Almighty (the Most High) said (what means): {And others (of those who stayed behind) are held in suspense (concerning their repentance) for Allaah's Decree, whether He will punish them or will forgive them (if He so likes)...} [verse 106]

Some people said: "They have been ruined sincc accepting their excuse was not revealed". Others said: "It may be that Allaah Almighty will turn to them in repentance". Later on, Allaah Almighty (the Most High) revealed (what means): {And (He accepted also the repentance of) the three till for them the earth, albeit its vastness, was straitened and their own selves were constricted to them, and they perceived that there is no fleeing from Allaah, and no refuge but with Him. Then, He accepted their repentance, that they might turn to Him. Verily, Allaah is Ever-Accepting of repentance, Most Merciful}. [verse 118] [Ibn Mardawayh and Ibn Abu Haatim]

The same is narrated on the authority of Ibn 'Abbaas [Allaah be pleased with them] with the following addition: Abu Lubaabah and his companions went to the Prophet [peace and blessings of Allaah be upon him] having their property with them and said: "O Messenger of Allaah! That is our property: take it and give it in charity on behalf of us, and ask for Allaah's forgiveness for us". He said: "I have not been commanded to take anything of your property". On that occasion, Allaah revealed (what means): {Take alms from their wealth in order to purify them...} [verse 103] [Ibn Jareer]

A narration on the authority of Sa'eed Ibn Jubayr that it was revealed in connection with those seven, four of whom fastened themselves to the pillars: Abu Lubaabah, Mirdaas, Aws Ibn Khizaam and Tha'labah Ibn Wadee'ah. [Ibn Jareer]

A narration on the authority of Jaabir [may Allaah be pleased with him] that he said: Six were of those who remained behind the Prophet [peace and blessings of Allaah be upon him]: Abu Lubaabah, Aws Ibn Khizaam, Tha'labah Ibn Wadee'ah, Ka'b Ibn Maalik, Miraarah Ibn Ar-Rabee' and Hilaal Ibn Umayyah. Abu Lubaabah, Aws and Tha'labah came and fastened themselves to the pillars, brought their property and said: "O Messenger of Allaah! Take this (wealth) which detained us from you". He said: "I will not make it lawful till there is fighting". On that occasion, this Quraanic Ayaah was revealed. [Abu Ash-Shaykh and Ibn Mandah in As-Sahaabah]

A narration on the authority of Umm Salamah [Allaah be pleased with her] that she said: The news of accepting the repentance of Abu Lubaabah was revealed in my house. At predawn time, I heard the Prophet [peace and blessings of Allaah be upon him] smiling. I asked him: "Why are you smiling may Allaah keep you smile forever O Messenger of Allaah?" He said: "Allaah has accepted the repentance of Abu Lubaabah". I said: "Should I not give him the glad tidings O Messenger of Allaah?" He said: "Yes if you so like". She stood at the gate of her chamber, and this was before Hijaab was imposed, and said: "O Abu Lubaabah! Receive the glad tidings: Allaah has accepted your repentance". When the people came to untie him he said: "No, by Allaah, till the Prophet [peace and blessings of Allaah be upon him] releases me with his own hand". On his way to perform the Morning prayer, the Prophet [peace and blessings of Allaah be upon him] released him. In connection with him this Quraanic Ayaah was revealed. [Ibn Mardawayh] Verse Number 107-108

107- And there are those who put up a mosque by way of causing harm and disbelief and to disunite the believers (al-Mumineen), and as an outpost for those who warred against Allaah and His Messenger aforetime, they will indeed swear that their intention is nothing but good. Allaah bears witness that they are certainly liars. 108Never stand you therein (for prayer). Verily, the mosque whose foundation was laid from the first day on piety is more worthy for you to stand therein (for prayer). In it are men (Ansaar) who love to purify themselves. And Allaah loves (and rewards) those who purify themselves.

A narration on the authority of Abu Ruhm, who was one of those who gave the pledge of allegiance to the Prophet [peace and blessings of Allaah be upon him] underneath the tree (in the year of Hudaybiyah), that he said: the owners of the masjid of mischief had previously come to the Prophet [peace and blessings of Allaah be upon him] while he was getting ready for the battle of Tabook and said: "O Messenger of Allaah! We have built a masjid for the one who has a need to fulfill and for prayer in the rainy and wintery nights and we like you to come and pray for us in it". He said: "No, I am busy in preparing myself for the journey (or similar words) but when we return, by Allaah's willing, we would come and pray for you in it".

When the Prophet [peace and blessings of Allaah be upon him] camped at Dhu-'Awaan, he was informed about the masjid thereupon he invited Maalik Ibn Ad-Dukhshum and Ma'n Ibn 'Adiyy or his brother 'AAsim Ibn 'Adiyy, and said: "Go to this masjid whose owners are wrongful, and ruin and burn it". They went out quickly and came to the dwelling places of Banu Saalim Ibn 'Awf, the clansmen of Maalik Ibn Ad-Dukhshum who said to Ma'n: "Give me a respite till I bring you a piece of fire from my family". He entered into his family and took some leafstalks and kindled fire in them and then they both ran quickly to the masjid and burnt it upon its men and ruined it, and its men dispersed and left it. In connection with them, Allaah Almighty (the Most High) revealed this

Quraanic Ayaah. [Ibn Mardawayh depending on the narration of Ibn Ishaaq]

A narration on the authority of Ibn 'Abbaas [Allaah be pleased with them] that he said: When the Prophet [peace and blessings of Allaah be upon him] built the masjid of Qubaa', some men from Ansaar including Yakhdaj came out and built the mosque of hypocrisy. the Prophet [peace and blessings of Allaah be upon him] told him: "Woe to you! What have you intended by that which I see?" He said: "O Messenger of Allaah! I have not intended but good". On that occasion, Allaah revealed this Quraanic Ayaah. [Ibn Abu Haatim and Ibn Mardawayh]

A narration on the authority of Ibn 'Abbaas [Allaah be pleased with them] that he said: Some people from Ansaar built a mosque and Abu 'AAmir told them: "Build your mosque and strengthen yourselves with much force and weapons as you can. I will go to Caesar or the Byzantines and bring soldiers to drive out Muhammad and his Companions". When they finished from their mosque, they went to the Prophet [peace and blessings of Allaah be upon him] and said: "We have finished from building our mosque, and we like you to pray in it". On that occasion, Allaah revealed this Quraanic Ayaah. [Ibn Mardawayh]

A narration on the authority of Sa'd Ibn Abu Waqqaas [may Allaah be pleased with him] that he said: The hypocrites (al-Munaafiqeen) offered Abu 'AAmir Ar-Raahib the idea of building a mosque to be rival to the mosque of Qubaa', and suggested him to be their leader if he came. When they finished from building it, they went to the Prophet [peace and blessings of Allaah be upon him] and said: "We have built a mosque: so, would that you perform prayer in it!" On that occasion, Allaah Almighty (the Most High) revealed this Quraanic Ayaah. [Al-Waahidi]

A narration on the authority of Abu Hurayrah [may Allaah be pleased with him] that he said: This Quraanic Ayaah (what means): {In it are men (Ansaar) who love to purify themselves. And Allaah loves (and rewards) those who purify themselves}, [verse 108] was revealed in connection with the men of Qubaa': they used to wash their private parts with water. [At-Tirmidhi]

The same is narrated on the authority of Yahya Ibn Sahl Al-Ansaari from his father. ['Umar Ibn Shaybah in Akhbaar Al-Madinah]

A narration on the authority of 'Ataa' that he said: The men of Qubaa' broke their ablution thereupon washed their private parts with water and then performed ablution. In connection with them Allaah revealed (what means): {In it are men (Ansaar) who love to purify themselves. And Allaah loves (and rewards) those who purify themselves}. [verse 108] [Ibn Jareer]

Verse Number 111

111- Verily, Allaah has purchased from the believers (al-Mumineen) their lives and their properties for (the price) that theirs shall be the Paradise. They fight in

Allaah's Cause, so they kill (enemies) and are killed. It is a promise in truth which is binding on Him in the Torah and the Gospel and the Quraan. And who is truer to his covenant than Allaah? Then rejoice in the bargain which you have concluded. Such is the great success.

A narration on the authority of Muhammad Ibn Ka'b Al-Qurathi that 'Abdullaah Ibn Rawaahah told the Prophet [peace and blessings of Allaah be upon him]: "Put what you like of conditions for your Lord (Rabb) and for you". the Prophet [peace and blessings of Allaah be upon him] said: "As for my Lord (Rabb), I put condition that you should worship Him and associate no partner with Him in worship; and as for me, I put condition that you should protect me from the same from which you protect yourselves and your property". They said: "Then, if we do so, what shall we have?" the Prophet [peace and blessings of Allaah be upon him] said: "You shall have Paradise". They said: "Verily, the trade has profited. We will never leave it, nor seek to abandon it". On that occasion, Allaah revealed this Quraanic Ayaah. [Ibn Jareer]

Verse Number 113-114

113- It is not (fitting) for the Prophet and those who believe to ask Forgiveness for the polytheists even though they be near of kin (to them), after it has become clear to them that they are the dwellers of the Fire (because they died in a state of polytheism). 114- And Abraham's prayer for forgiveness of his father was only because of a promise he had made to him (his father). But when it became clear to him that he (his father) is an enemy of Allaah, he dissociated himself from him (and ceased to ask forgiveness for him). Verily Abraham was tenderhearted, forbearing.

A narration on the authority of Sa'eed Ibn Al-Musayyab from his father that he said: When Abu Taalib was in his deathbed, The Prophet [peace and blessings of Allaah be upon him] went to him while Abu Jahl and 'Abdullaah Ibn Abu Umayyah were sitting beside him. The Prophet [peace and blessings of Allaah be upon him] said: "O my uncle! Say: "There is none worthy of worship except Allaah, an expression therewith I will defend your case before Allaah." Abu Jahl and 'Abdullaah Ibn Abu Umayyah said: "O Abu Taalib! Will you leave the religion of 'Abd Al-Muttalib?" They kept saying this to him so that the last statement he said to them (before he died) was: "I am on the religion of 'Abd Al-Muttalib." Then The Prophet [peace and blessings of Allaah be upon him] said: "I will keep asking Allaah's Forgiveness for you unless I am forbidden to do so." Then Allaah revealed (what means): {It is not (fitting) for the Prophet and those who believe...} [verse 113] [Al-Bukhaari and Muslim]

A narration on the authority of 'Ali Ibn Abu Taalib [may Allaah be pleased with him] that he said: I heard a man asking Allaah's forgiveness for his parents and they were polytheists, thereupon I asked him: "Do you ask Allaah's forgiveness for your parents and they were polytheists?" He replied: "Which harm lies in this? Abraham [peace and blessings of Allaah be upon him] asked Allaah's forgiveness for his father and he was a polytheist". I made a mention of that to the Prophet [peace and blessings of Allaah be upon him], thereupon Allaah Almighty (the Most High) revealed those Quraanic Aayaat. [At-Tirmidhi who renders it Hasan and Al-Haakim]

A narration on the authority of 'Abdullaah Ibn Mas'ood [may Allaah be pleased with him] that he said: One day, the Prophet [peace and blessings of Allaah be upon him] came out to the graveyard and sat near one of the graves and talked privately for a long time after which he wept and I wept for his weeping. Then he said: "The grave near which I have sat is the grave of my mother; and I sought permission of my Lord (Rabb) to ask His forgiveness for my mother and He gave me no permission". On that occasion, Allaah revealed those Quraanic Aayaat. [Al-Haakim and Al-Bayhaqi in Ad-Dalaa'il]

A narration on the authority of Buraydah [may Allaah be pleased with him] that he said: I was with the Prophet [peace and blessings of Allaah be upon him] in 'Usfaan when he saw the grave of his mother. He performed ablution then prayed and went on weeping. Then he said: "I sought permission of my Lord (Rabb) to ask forgiveness for my mother and I was forbidden to do so". On that occasion, Allaah Almighty (the Most High) revealed those Quraanic Aayaat. [Ahmad and Ibn Mardawayh]

A narration on the authority of Ibn 'Abbaas [Allaah be pleased with them] that this event took place after his return from Tabook where he went to perform 'Umrah and descended at the side of 'Usfaan. [At-Tabaraani and Ibn Mardawayh]

Commenting on that, Ibn Hajar argues that there might be different occasions for the revelation of those Quraanic Aayaat.

Verse Number 117-118

117- Allaah has turned in repentance to the Prophet and the Muhaajiroon (emigrants) and the Ansaar (Helpers) who followed him (the Prophet) at the time of difficulty, after the hearts (Qalb) of a party of them had nearly deviated (from the Right Path), but He accepted their repentance. Certainly, He is unto them full of Kindness, Most Merciful. 118- And (He accepted also the repentance of) the three till for them the earth, albeit its vastness, was straitened and their own selves were constricted to them, and they perceived that there is no fleeing from Allaah, and no refuge but with Him. Then, He accepted their repentance, that they might turn to Him. Verily, ever is Allaah-Accepting of repentance, Most Merciful. A narration on the authority of 'Abdullaah Ibn Ka'b Ibn Maalik who, from amongst Ka'b's sons, was the guide of Ka'b when he became blind, that he said: I heard Ka'b Ibn Maalik narrating the story of (The Battle of) Tabook in which he did not participate. Ka'b said: "I did not remain behind the Prophet [peace and blessings of Allaah be upon him] in any battle that he fought except the battle of Tabook and I failed to take part in the battle of Badr, but Allaah did not admonish anyone who had not participated in it, for in fact, the Prophet [peace and blessings of Allaah be upon him] had gone out in search of the caravan of the Quraysh till Allaah made them (Muslims) and their enemy meet without any appointment. I witnessed the night of Al-'Aqabah (pledge) with the Prophet [peace and blessings of Allaah be upon him] when we gave the pledge of allegiance for Islam and I would not exchange it for the Badr battle although the Badr battle is more popular amongst the people than it (Al-'Aqabah's pledge).

As for my news (in this battle of Tabook), I had never been stronger or wealthier than I was when I remained behind The Prophet [peace and blessings of Allaah be upon him] in that battle. By Allaah, never had I two she-camels before, but I had then at the time of this Battle. Whenever the Prophet [peace and blessings of Allaah be upon him] wanted to make a battle, he used to hide his intention by apparently referring to a different Battle till it was the time of that Battle (of Tabook) which the Prophet [peace and blessings of Allaah be upon him] fought in severe heat, facing a long journey, desert and great number of enemy. For this reason, The Prophet [peace and blessings of Allaah be upon him] announced to the Muslims clearly (their destination) so that they might get prepared for their Battle. So he informed them explicitly of the destination he was going to. the Prophet [peace and blessings of Allaah be upon him] was accompanied by a large number of Muslims who could not be listed in a book, namely a register."

Ka'b added: "Any man who intended to be absent thought that the matter would remain hidden unless

Allaah revealed it through Divine Revelation. So the Prophet [peace and blessings of Allaah be upon him] fought that Battle at the time when the fruits had ripened and the shade looked pleasant. the Prophet [peace and blessings of Allaah be upon him] and his Companions prepared for the battle and I started to go out in order to get myself ready along with them but I returned without doing anything. I would say to myself: "I could do that". So I kept delaying it every now and then till the people got ready, the Prophet [peace and blessings of Allaah be upon him] and the Muslims along with him departed, but I had not prepared anything for my departure, and I said: "I will prepare myself (for departure) one or two days later, and then join them".

In the morning following their departure, I went out to get myself ready but returned having done nothing. Then again in the next morning, I went out to get ready but returned without doing anything. Such was the case with me till they hurried away and the battle was missed (by me). Even then I intended to depart to catch them. I wish I had done so! But I was unfortunate. So, after the departure of the Prophet [peace and blessings of Allaah be upon him], whenever I went out and walked amongst the people (who remained behind), it grieved me that I could see none around me but one accused of hypocrisy or one of those weak men whom Allaah had excused.

The Prophet [peace and blessings of Allaah be upon him] did not remember me till he reached Tabook. So while he was sitting amongst the people in Tabook, he said: "What has Ka'b done?" A man from Banu Salimah said: "O Messenger of Allaah! He has been stopped by his two garments and his looking at his own flanks with pride". Then Mu'adh Ibn Jabal said: "What a bad thing you have said! By Allaah! O Messenger of Allaah! We know nothing about him but good". On that, the Prophet [peace and blessings of Allaah be upon him] kept silent."

Ka'b Ibn Maalik added: "When I heard that the Prophet [peace and blessings of Allaah be upon him] was on his way back to Madeenah, I got dipped in my concern and began to think of false excuses, saying to myself: "How can I avoid his anger tomorrow?" I took the advice of wise members of my family in this matter. When it was said that the Prophet [peace and blessings of Allaah be upon him] had come near, all the evil false excuses went away from my mind and I knew well that I could never come out of this problem by forging a false statement. Then I decided firmly to speak the truth. So the Prophet [peace and blessings of Allaah be upon him] arrived in the morning, and whenever he returned from a journey, he used to visit the Mosque first of all and offer a two-Rak'ah prayer therein and then sit with the people. So when he had done all that, those who had failed to join the battle (of Tabook) came and started offering (false) excuses and taking oaths before him. They were over eighty men. the Prophet [peace and blessings of Allaah be upon him] accepted the excuses they had expressed, took their pledge of allegiance, asked Allaah's Forgiveness for them and left the secrets of their hearts (Qalb) for Allaah to judge.

Then I came to him but when I greeted him, he gave me a smile of an angry person and then said: "Come on". So I came walking till I sat before him. He said to me: "What has stopped you from joining us. Had you not purchased an animal for carrying you?" I answered: "Yes, O Messenger of Allaah! But by Allaah, had I sat before any person from among the people of the world other than you, I would have avoided his anger with an excuse. By Allaah, I have been endowed with the power of speaking fluently and eloquently, but by Allaah, I knew well that if today I tell you a lie to seek your favor, Allaah will surely make you angry with me in the near future, but if I tell you the truth, though you will get angry because of it, I hope for Allaah's Forgiveness. Really, by Allaah, there was no excuse for me. By Allaah, I had never been stronger or wealthier than I was when I remained behind you". Then the Prophet [peace and blessings of Allaah be upon him] said: "As regards this man, he has surely told the truth. So get up till Allaah Almighty (the Most High) decides your case".

I got up and many men of Banu Salimah followed me and told me: "By Allaah, we have never witnessed you doing any sin before this. Surely, you failed to offer excuse to the Prophet [peace and blessings of Allaah be upon him] as the others who did not join him have offered. The supplication of the Prophet [peace and blessings of Allaah be upon him] to Allaah to forgive you would have been sufficient for you". By Allaah, they continued blaming me so much that I intended to return (to The Prophet) and accuse myself of having told a lie, but I said to them: "Is there anybody else who has received the same fate as I have?" They replied: "Yes, there are two men who have said the same thing as you have, and both of them were given the same order as given to you". I said: "Who are they?" They replied: "Miraarah Ibn Ar-Rabee' Al-'Amri and Hilaal Ibn Umayyah Al-Waaqifi". By that, they mentioned to me two pious men who had attended the battle of Badr, and in whom there was an example for me. So I did not change my mind when they mentioned them to me.

The Prophet [peace and blessings of Allaah be upon him] forbade all the Muslims to talk to us, the three above-mentioned persons out of all those who had remained behind in that Battle. So we kept away from the people and they changed their attitude towards us till the very land (where I lived) appeared strange to me as if I did not know it. We remained in that condition for fifty nights.

As regards my two fellows, they remained in their houses and kept weeping but I was the youngest and the firmest of them, so I used to go out and witness the prayers along with the Muslims and roam about in the markets but none would talk to me, and I would come to the Prophet [peace and blessings of Allaah be upon him] and greet him while he was sitting in his gathering after the prayer, and I would wonder whether or not The Prophet [peace and blessings of Allaah be upon him] moved his lips in return to my greetings. I would offer my prayer near to him and look at him stealthily. Whenever I was busy with my prayer, he would turn his face towards me but whenever I turned my face to him, he would turn his face away from me.

When this harsh attitude of the people lasted long, I walked till I scaled the wall of the garden of Abu Qataadah who was my cousin and dearest person to me, and I offered my greetings to him. By Allaah, he did not return my greetings. I said: "O Abu Qataadah! I beseech you by Allaah to tell me! Do you know that I love Allaah and His Messenger?" He kept quiet. I asked him again, beseeching him by Allaah to tell me, but he remained silent.

Then I asked him again in the Name of Allaah. He said: "Allaah and His Messenger know best". Thereupon my eyes overflowed with tears and I returned and jumped over the wall."

Ka'b added: "While I was walking in the market of Madeenah, suddenly I saw a Christian farmer from Shaam who came to sell his grains in Madeenah, saying: "Who will lead me to Ka'b Ibn Maalik?" The people began to point (me) out for him till he came to me and handed me a letter from the king of Ghassaan in which the following was written: "To proceed, I have been informed that your friend (The Prophet) has treated you harshly. Anyhow, Allaah does not let you live at a place where you feel inferior and your right is lost. So join us, and we will console you." When I read it, I said to myself: "This is also a sort of test".

Then I took the letter to the oven therein I made a fire by burning it.

When forty out of the fifty nights elapsed, behold! There came to me the messenger of the Prophet [peace and blessings of Allaah be upon him] and said: "the Prophet [peace and blessings of Allaah be upon him] orders you to keep aloof from your wife". I said: "Should I divorce her; or else! What should I do?" He said: "No, only keep aloof from her and do not live together with her". The Prophet [peace and blessings of Allaah be upon him] sent the same message to my two fellows. Then I told my wife: "Go to your parents and remain with them till Allaah gives His Verdict in this 1199 matter."

Ka'b added: "The wife of Hilaal Ibn Umayyah came to the Prophet [peace and blessings of Allaah be upon him] and said: "O Messenger of Allaah! Hilaal Ibn Umayyah is a helpless old man who has no servant to attend on him. Do you dislike that I should serve him?" He said: "No (you can) but he should not approach you". She said: "By Allaah, he has no desire for anything. By Allaah, he has never ceased weeping since his case began up till this day". On that, some of my family members told me: "Will you also ask the Prophet [peace and blessings of Allaah be upon him] to permit your wife (to serve you) as he has permitted the wife of Hilaal Ibn Umayyah to serve him?" I said: "By Allaah, I will not ask the permission of the Prophet [peace and blessings of Allaah be upon him] regarding her, for I do not know what the Messenger of Allaah [peace and blessings of Allaah be upon him] will say if

I ask him to permit her (to serve me) while I am a young man".

Then I remained in that state for ten more nights till the period of fifty nights was completed starting from the time when the Prophet [peace and blessings of Allaah be upon him] prohibited the people from talking to us. I offered the Fajr prayer on the fiftieth morning on the roof of one of our houses. I was sitting in the condition which Allaah described (in the Quraan): My very soul seemed straitened to me and even the earth seemed narrow to me albeit its vastness, when I heard the voice of one who had ascended the mountain of Sala' calling at the top of his voice: "O Ka'b Ibn Maalik! Be happy (by receiving good tidings)". I fell down in prostration before Allaah, realizing that relief has come. the Prophet [peace and blessings of Allaah be upon him] announced the acceptance of our repentance by Allaah after he had offered the Fajr prayer. The people then went out to congratulate us. Some bearers of good tidings went out to my two fellows, a horseman came to me in haste and a man of Banu Aslam came running and ascended the mountain and his voice was swifter than the horse.

When he (The man) whose voice I had heard came to me conveying the good tidings, I took off my garments with which I dressed him; and by Allaah, I owned no other garments than them on that day. Then I borrowed two garments and wore them and went to the Prophet [peace and blessings of Allaah be upon him]. The people started receiving me in batches, congratulating me on Allaah's Acceptance of my repentance, saying: "We congratulate you on Allaah's Acceptance of your repentance." 1199

Ka'b added: "When I entered the Mosque, I saw the Prophet [peace and blessings of Allaah be upon him] sitting with the people around him. Talhah Ibn 'Ubaydullaah swiftly came to me, shook hands with me and congratulated me.

By Allaah, none of the Emigrants (Muhaajiroon) got up for me except him, and I will never forget this for Talhah."

Ka'b added: "When I greeted the Prophet [peace and blessings of Allaah be upon him], he, with his face being joyfully bright, said: "Be happy with the best day that you have got ever since your mother delivered you.' 1199

Ka'b added: "I told The Prophet [peace be upon him]: "Is this forgiveness from you or from Allaah?" He said: "No, it is from Allaah". Whenever the Prophet [peace and blessings of Allaah be upon him] became happy, his face would shine as if it were a piece of moon, and we all knew that characteristic of him. When I sat before him, I said: "O Messenger of Allaah! Because of the acceptance of my repentance I will give up all my wealth as charity for the Sake of Allaah and His Messenger".

The Prophet [peace and blessings of Allaah be upon him] said: "Keep some of your wealth, as it will be better for you". I said: "I will keep my share from Khaybar with me".

I added: "O Messenger of Allaah! Allaah has saved me for telling the truth; so it is part of my repentance not to tell but the truth as long as I am alive". By Allaah, I do not know anyone of the Muslims whom Allaah has helped foretelling the truth more than me. Since I mentioned that truth to the Prophet [peace and blessings of Allaah be upon him] till today, I have never intended to tell a lie. I hope that Allaah will also save me (from telling lies) during the rest of my life.

So Allaah revealed to His Messenger [peace and blessings of Allaah be upon him] the Quraanic Aayaat 117-118. [Al-Bukhaari] Verse Number 122

122- And it is not (fitting) for the believers (al-Mumineen) to go out to fight (in Allaah's Cause) all together. Of every troop of them, a party only should go forth, that they (who are left behind) may receive instructions in (Islamic) religion, and that they may warn their (fighting) people when they return to them (of what escaped them of teachings), that they may beware (of Allaah's punishment and abide by His rulings).

A narration on the authority of 'Ikrimah that he said: When Allaah revealed (what means): {If you do not go forth, He will punish you with a painful punishment and will replace you with another people, and you will not harm Him at all}, [verse 39] and, at the same time, some had remained behind him in the desert to instruct their people in the religion, the hypocrites (al-Munaafiqeen) said: "Some people remained behind in the desert: those who remained behind in the desert have been ruined". On that occasion, this Quraanic Ayaah was revealed. [Ibn Abu Haatim]

A narration on the authority of 'Abdullaah Ibn 'Ubayd Ibn 'Umayr that he said: It was the habit of the believers (al-Mumineen), because of their keenness on striving in Allaah's cause, that if the Prophet [peace and blessings of Allaah be upon him] dispatched a military expedition, they would set out and leave the Prophet [peace and blessings of Allaah be upon him] in Madeenah along with the weak people. On that occasion, Allaah Almighty (the Most High) revealed this Quraanic Ayaah. [Ibn Abu Haatim]

Soorah Yoonus

Verse Number 2

2- Is it a matter of wonderment for men that We have revealed to a man from among themselves (that is Prophet Muhammad) (saying): "Warn mankind (the disbelievers (al-Kaafireen) among them of torment), and give glad tidings to those who believe that they shall have a sure footing with their Lord (Rabb)?" (But) the disbelievers (al-Kaafireen) say: "This (Quraan) is indeed an evident magic!

A narration on the authority of Ibn 'Abbaas [Allaah be pleased with them] that he said: When Allaah sent Muhammad [peace and blessings of Allaah be upon him] as a Messenger, the Arabs denied this and said: "Verily, Allaah is too great to send a human being as His Messenger". On that occasion, Allaah revealed this Quraanic Ayaah. He also revealed (what means): {And We sent not before you (O Muhammad) except men to whom We revealed (the message), so ask the people of the message if you do not know}. [Al-Anbiyaa', verse 7] When Allaah repeated His arguments to them they said: "And even should he be a human being, then, another one would have more right than Muhammad to receive the Message". Allaah said relating this from them (what means): {And they said: "Why was this Quraan not sent down upon a great man from (one of) the two cities?"} [Az-Zukhruf, verse 31]

By those nobler than Muhammad they mean Al-Waleed Ibn Al-Mugheerah from Makkah and Mas'ood Ibn 'Amr Ath-Thaqafi from Taa'if. In reply to them, Allaah revealed (what means): {Do they distribute the mercy of your Lord (Rabb)? It is We who have apportioned among them their livelihood in the life of this world and have raised some of them above others in degrees (of rank) that they may make use of one another for service. But the mercy of your Lord (Rabb) is better than whatever they accumulate}. [Az-Zukhruf, verse 32] [Ibn Jareer]

Soorah Hood

5- No doubt! They did fold up their breasts, that they may hide from Him. Surely, even when they cover themselves with their garments, He knows what they conceal and what they reveal. Verily, He has the best knowledge of the (innermost secrets) of the breasts.

A narration on the authority of Ibn 'Abbaas [Allaah be pleased with them] that he said: Some people felt shy of entering the privy or having sexual intercourse (with their wives) as naked with their private parts exposed to the sky.

In connection with them, Allaah revealed (what means): {Surely, even when they cover themselves with their garments, He knows what they conceal and what they reveal}. [Al-Bukhaari]

A narration on the authority of 'Abdullaah Ibn Shaddaad that he said: It was the habit of anyone of them (disbelievers (al-Kaafireen)) that whenever he passed by the Prophet [peace and blessings of Allaah be upon him], he would turn away his breast in order that he would not see him.

On that occasion, Allaah revealed (what means): {No doubt! They (disbelievers (al-Kaafireen)) did fold up their breasts, that they may hide from Him}. [Ibn Jareer and others]

Verse Number 8

8- And if We delay the torment for them till a specific term, they are sure to say (mockingly): "What does keep it back?" Verily, on the day it comes to them, nothing will turn it away from them, and they will be encircled by that (torment) at which they used to mock!

A narration on the authority of Qataadah that he said: When Allaah revealed (what means): {(The time of) their account has approached for the people, while they are in heedlessness turning away}, [Al-Anbiyaa', verse 1] some people said: "It seems that the (final) Hour has become near".

Then they desisted (from evil) for a short time after which they returned to their evil plots.

On that occasion, Allaah revealed this Quraanic Ayaah. [Ibn Abu Haatim and Ibn Jareer on the authority of Ibn Jurayj] Verse Number 114

114- And establish prayer at the two ends of the day (Fajr, Thuhr and 'Asr) and in some hours of the night (Maghrib and 'Ishaa'). Verily, the good deeds (such as the five compulsory prayers) remove the evil deeds (minor sins). That is a reminder for these who accept the reminder.

A narration on the authority of Ibn Mas'ood [may Allaah be pleased with him] that a man kissed a woman and then went and made a mention of that to the Prophet [peace and blessings of Allaah be upon him]. On that occasion, Allaah revealed this Quraanic Ayaah.

The man asked: "Is this specific to me only?" the Prophet [peace and blessings of Allaah be upon him] said: "It is common to all of my followers". [Al-Bukhaari and Muslim]

A narration on the authority of Abu Al-Yusr that he said: A woman came to buy dates from me and I told her that I had in the house dates that are better than that".

When she came with me I jumped over her and kissed her.

Then I went to the Prophet [peace and blessings of Allaah be upon him] and made a mention of that to him.

The Prophet [peace and blessings of Allaah be upon him] said: "Have you done like this with the family of a fighter in the cause of Allaah instead of looking after them in his absence?"

He then lowered his head for a long time till Allaah Almighty (the Most High) revealed to him this Quraanic Ayaah. [At-Tirmidhi and others]

The same is narrated on the authority of Abu Umaamah, Mu'aadh Ibn Jabal, Ibn 'Abbaas, Buraydah and others. [At-Tirmidhi and others]

Soorah Yoosuf

Verse Number 3

3- We relate unto you (O Muhammad) the best of stories in what we have revealed to you, of this Quraan. And before this (revelation), you were among the heedless (of the Quraan).

A narration on the authority of Sa'd Ibn Abu Waqqaas [may Allaah be pleased with him] that he said: The Quraan was revealed to the Prophet [peace and blessings of Allaah be upon him], and he kept reciting to them for some time before they said to him: "O Messenger of Allaah! Would that you talk to us (in something else)!" On that occasion, Allaah revealed (what means): {Allaah has sent down the best statement: a consistent Book wherein is reiteration}. [Az-Zumar, verse 23] [Al-Haakim and others]

A similar one is narrated on the same authority with the following addition: They said: "O Messenger of Allaah! Would that you remind us!" On that occasion, Allaah revealed (what means): {Has the time not come for those who have believed that their hearts (Qalb) should become humbly submissive at the remembrance of Allaah and what has come down of the truth?} [Al-Hadeed, verse 16] [Ibn Abu Haatim]

A narration on the authority of Ibn 'Abbaas [Allaah be pleased with them] that he said: They said: "O Messenger of Allaah! Would that you relate stories to us!" On that occasion, Allaah revealed this Quraanic Ayaah [Yoosuf 3]. [Ibn Jareer]

The same is narrated on the authority of Ibn Mas'ood [may Allaah be pleased with him]. [Ibn Mardawayh]

Soorah Ar-Raa'd

8- Allaah knows well what every female bears, and by how much the wombs lose (prematurely) or exceed (beyond their time). Everything with Him is in (due) proportion (which it cannot surpass or fall short of).

A narration on the authority of Ibn 'Abbaas [Allaah be pleased with them] that both Arbad Ibn Qays and 'AAmir Ibn At-Tufayl came to Madinah to visit the Prophet [peace and blessings of Allaah be upon him]. 'AAmir said: "O Muhammad! What will you give me if I embrace Islam?" He said: "You will have the rights and obligations of the Muslims". He asked him: "Will you give me the matter (of ruling) after you?" He replied: "That will not be to you nor to your people".

When, they left him, 'AAmir told Arbad: "I will talk to Muhammad to divert his face from you and then you can strike him with the sword". They returned to the Prophet [peace and blessings of Allaah be upon him] once again so 'AAmir told him: "O Muhammad! Stand with me to talk to you". the Prophet [peace and blessings of Allaah be upon him] stood with him and he talked to him and Arbad unsheathed the sword. When he took hold of the handle of the sword, his hand stiffened and the Prophet [peace and blessings of Allaah be upon him] turned his face and saw him thereupon he left them. They went away till when they were in Ar-Raqm, Allaah sent a thunderbolt on Arbad and it killed him. On that occasion, Allaah revealed the Quraanic Aayaat 8-13. [At-Tabaraani and others]

Verse Number 13

13- And thunder exalts His (Allaah's) praises, and so do the angels because of His Awe, He sends the thunderbolts, and therewith He strikes whom He wills, yet they (disbelievers (al-Kaafireen)) dispute (the Prophet) about Allaah. And He is Mighty in strength and Severe in punishment.

A narration on the authority of Anas [may Allaah be pleased with him] that he said: the Prophet [peace and blessings of Allaah be upon him] sent a man to one of the chiefs of disbelievers (al-Kaafireen) in the pre-Islamic days to invite him to Islam. The disbeliever asked him: "What is your lord to whom you invite me? Is he made of iron, copper, silver or gold?" The man returned to the Prophet [peace and blessings of Allaah be upon him], and made a mention of that to him. He sent this man to him once again and returned with the same reply, and for the third time and he also returned with the same reply. Then Allaah sent a thunderbolt on that disbeliever which burnt him. On that occasion, Allaah revealed this Quraanic Ayaah. [An-Nasaa'i and Al-Bazzaar]

Verse Number 31

31- And if there had been a Quraan with which mountains could be moved (from their places), or the earth could be cloven asunder, or the dead could be (raised and) made to speak (they would not have believed). But the decision of all things is certainly with Allaah. Have not then those who believe yet known that had Allaah willed, He could have guided all people (even without a sign)? And a disaster will not cease to strike those who disbelieved (with all trials of killing, war, captivity or draught) because of their (evil) deeds (disbelief), or you (O Muhammad with your army) should come close to their homes (in Makkah), until the Promise of Allaah (of your victory over them) comes to pass. Certainly, Allaah never fails in His Promise.

A narration on the authority of Ibn 'Abbaas [Allaah be pleased with them] that he said: The polytheists said to the Prophet [peace and blessings of Allaah be upon him]: "If that which you have brought is true, then show us our old men (who died) to talk to them and ask them about it; and also make the land of Makkah spacious upon us because those mountains have squeezed us". On that occasion, Allaah revealed this Quraanic Ayaah. [At-Tabaraani and others]

A narration on the authority of 'Atiyyah Al-'Awfi that he said: The disbelievers (al-Kaafireen) told the Prophet [peace and blessings of Allaah be upon him]: "Would that you remove the mountains of Makkah till it becomes spacious and we can cultivate it; and would that you cut the land for us as Solomon cut the land for his people with the help of wind; and would that you quicken the dead as Jesus gave life to the dead for his people!" On that occasion, Allaah revealed this

Quraanic Ayaah. [Ibn Abu Haatim and Ibn Mardawayh]

Verse Number 38-39

38- And indeed We sent Messengers before you (O Muhammad) and made for them wives and offspring. And it was not for a Messenger to bring a sign except by Allaah's Leave. (For) every term there is a Decree (and time prescribed by Allaah). 39Allaah blots out what He wills and confirms (what He wills of rulings and judgments). And with Him is the Mother of the Book (the Preserved Tablet which never changes).

A narration on the authority of Mujaahid that he said: When Allaah revealed (what means): {And it was not for a Messenger to bring a sign except by Allaah's Leave}, [verse 38] the Quraysh men told the Prophet [peace and blessings of Allaah be upon him]: "We think, O Muhammad, that you have nothing (to bring to us). The matter than is over". On that occasion, Allaah revealed (what means): {Allaah blots out what He wills and confirms (what He wills of rulings and judgments). And with Him is the Mother of the Book}. [verse 39] [Ibn Abu Haatim]

Soorah Ibraaheem

Verse Number 28

28- Have you not seen those who have changed the (gratitude they were supposed to show for the) favor of Allaah into disbelief (ungratefulness by rejecting the Prophethood of Muhammad), and drove their people (by misleading them) to the abode of perdition?

A narration on the authority of 'Ataa' Ibn Yasaar that he said: This Quraanic Ayaah was revealed in connection with those who were killed on the day of the battle of Badr. [Ibn Jareer]

Soorah Al-Hijr

Verse Number 24

24-And indeed, We know those among you who come forward, and indeed, We know those who remain behind.

A narration on the authority of Ibn 'Abbaas [Allaah be pleased with them] that he said: One of the prettiest women used to pray (in congregation) behind the Prophet [peace and blessings of Allaah be upon him], and some men used to go forward to be in the first row in order not to see her, and others used to remain behind to pray in the last row so that whenever anyone prostrated he would look at her from underneath his armpits. On that occasion, Allaah revealed this Quraanic Ayaah. [At-Tirmidhi; An-Nasaa'i; Al-Haakim and others]

A narration on the authority of Daawood Ibn Saalih that he asked Sahl Ibn Hunayf Al-Ansaari about this Quraanic Ayaah: was it revealed in connection with Jihaad in the cause of Allaah? He said: "No, it was revealed in connection with the rows of praying people". [Ibn Mardawayh]

Verse Number 45

45- Truly! The righteous will be amidst Gardens and water-springs (flowing therein in Paradise).

A narration on the authority of Salmaan Al-Faaris [may Allaah be pleased with him] that when he heard Allaah's saying (what means): {And indeed, Hell is the promised place for them all}, [verse 43] he kept wandering for three days out of fear. Then he was brought to the Prophet [peace and blessings of Allaah be upon him] whom he asked: "O Messenger of Allaah! Has this Quraanic Ayaah been really revealed? By Him Who sent you with the truth, it has cut the strings of my heart". On that occasion, Allaah revealed this Quraanic Ayaah. [Ath-Tha'labi]

Verse Number 47

47- And We shall remove from their breasts any feeling of resentment (they may have so that they will be like) brothers facing each other on thrones.

A narration on the authority of 'Ali Ibn Al-Husayn that he said: This Quraanic Ayaah was revealed in connection with Abu Bakr and 'Umar [Allaah be pleased with them]. He was asked: "Which resentment?" He said: "The resentment of the pre-Islamic days. During the pre-Islamic days, there was animosity between Banu Tameem, Banu 'Adiyy and Banu Haashim. When those people embraced Islam, they loved each other. Once, Abu Bakr was afflicted with a pain in his flank, thereupon 'Ali went on warming up his hand to heat therewith the flank of Abu Bakr, thereupon this Quraanic Ayaah was revealed. [Ibn Abu Haatim]

Verse Number 49-50

49- Inform (O Muhammad) My slaves, that truly, I am the Oft-Forgiving, Most-Merciful (towards the believers (al-Mumineen)). 50- And that My Torment (therewith I shall touch the sinners) is indeed the most painful torment.

A narration on the authority of 'Abdullaah Ibn Az-Zubayr [Allaah be pleased with them] that once, the Prophet [peace and blessings of Allaah be upon him] passed by a group of his Companions and they were laughing. On that he said to them: "Are you laughing and the mention of Paradise and Fire is ahead of you?"

In this connection, Allaah Almighty (the Most High) revealed those Quraanic Aayaat. [At-Tabaraani]

A narration on the authority of one of the Companions of the Prophet [peace and blessings of Allaah be upon him] that once the Prophet [peace and blessings of Allaah be upon him] came out to them from the gate through which Banu Shaybah enter, and told them: "I do not like to see you laughing". Then he turned away and a while later he retreated and said to them: "No sooner had I reached Al-Hijr that Jibreel met me and said: "O Muhammad! Your Lord (Rabb) asks you: "Why do you cause My servants to despair? {Inform My slaves, that truly, I am the Oft-Forgiving, Most-Merciful (towards the believers (al-Mumineen)). And that My Torment (therewith I shall touch the sinners) is indeed the most painful torment}. [Ibn Mardawayh]

Verse Number 95

95- Truly! We will suffice you against the scoffers.

A narration on the authority of Anas Ibn Maalik [may Allaah be pleased with him] that once, the Prophet [peace and blessings of Allaah be upon him] came upon some disbelievers (al-Kaafireen) in Makkah and they went on poking him in his nape and saying: "That is the one who claims to be a Prophet". Jibreel was with him: he poked them with his fingers bringing about in their bodies something like sores which putrefied, and none of them was able to approach him. On that occasion, Allaah Almighty (the Most High) revealed this Quraanic Ayaah. [At-Tabaraani and Al-Bazzaar]

Soorah An-Nahl

Verse Number 1

1- The command of Allaah (that is the final Hour and the punishment of the disbelievers (al-Kaafireen) and polytheists) will come to pass, so seek not to hasten it (before its due time since it is inescapable). Exalted be He above all that they associate as partners with Him.

A narration on the authority of Ibn 'Abbaas [Allaah be pleased with them] that he said: When Allaah revealed (what means): {The command of Allaah will come to pass}, the Companions of the Prophet [peace and blessings of Allaah be upon him] were scared, thereupon Allaah revealed (what means): {so seek not to hasten it (before its due time since it is inescapable)}. Then they became calm. [Ibn Mardawayh; 'Abdullaah Ibn Ahmad; Ibn Jareer and Ibn Abu Haatim on the authority of Abu Bakr Ibn Hafs]

Verse Number 38

38- And they swear by Allaah their strongest oaths, that Allaah will not raise up him who dies. Nay! (He will raise them up), - a promise (binding) upon Him in truth, but most men (that is disbelievers (al-Kaafireen)) know not.

A narration on the authority of Abu Al-'AAliyah that he said: One of the Muslims had a debt with one of the polytheists, and while exchanging talks in which the Muslim said: "...and after death I hope for such and such good things". The polytheist told him: "Do you claim that you will be resurrected after death?" The Muslim took a strong oath that Allaah will resurrect him who dies". On that occasion, this Quraanic Ayaah was revealed. [Ibn Jareer and Ibn Abu Haatim]

Verse Number 41

41- And as for those who emigrated in the Cause of Allaah (to establish His religion), after they had been wronged (by the disbelievers (al-Kaafireen) of Makkah who harmed them severely), We will certainly give them goodly residence in this world (that is Madeenah), but indeed the reward of the Hereafter (that is Paradise) will be greater; if they but knew!

A narration on the authority of Daawood Ibn Abu Hind that this Quraanic Ayaah was revealed in connection with Abu Jandal Ibn Suhayl Ibn 'Amr. [Ibn Jareer]
Verse Number 75-76

75- Allaah sets forth an example (of two) a slave under the possession of another, he has no power of any sort, and a (free) man on whom We have bestowed a good provision from Us, and he spends thereof secretly and openly. Can they be equal? (Of course not). All perfect praise be to Allaah. Nay! (But) most of them know not (the torment that will afflict them thereupon they associate partners with Allaah). 76- And Allaah puts forward (another) example of two men, one of them dumb and has no power over anything (because he understands nothing and cannot be understandable), and he is a burden on his master, whichever way he directs him, he brings no good. Is such a man equal to one who commands justice and is himself on the Straight Path?

A narration on the authority of Ibn 'Abbaas [Allaah be pleased with them] that he said: Allaah's saying (what means): {Allaah sets forth an example (of two) a slave under the possession of another, he has no power of any sort...} [verse 75] was revealed in connection with a man from the Quraysh and his slave. Allaah's saying (what means): {And Allaah puts forward (another) example of two men, one of them dumb and has no power over anything...} [verse 76] was revealed in connection with 'Uthmaan [may Allaah be pleased with him] and one of his slaves who disliked Islam and rejected to embrace it: he further used to forbid him to give in charity and do good. [Ibn Jareer]

Verse Number 83

83- They acknowledge the favor of Allaah, yet they deny it (by associating partners with Allaah in worship) and most of them are the disbelievers (al-Kaafireen) (in Allaah)

A narration on the authority of Mujaahid that a Bedouin came to the Prophet [peace and blessings of Allaah be upon him] and begged him, thereupon he recited to him (what means): {And Allaah has made for you from your homes a place of rest}. the Bedouin said: "Yes". He recited to him (what means): {and made for you from the hides of the animals tents which you find light on your day of travel and your day of encampment}. [verse 81] the Bedouin said: "Yes". Whenever he recited to him the Bedouin would answer in the affirmative till he came to Allaah's saying (what means): {Thus does He complete His favor upon you that you might submit (to Him)}. [verse 82]. Then the Bedouin turned away. On that occasion, Allaah revealed this Quraanic Ayaah [83]. [Ibn Abu Haatim]

Verse Number 91

91- And fulfill the Covenant of Allaah (concerning transactions, oaths, etc.) when you have covenanted, and break not the oaths after you have confirmed them - and indeed you have made Allaah your surety (of fulfilling your covenant when You have sworn by Him). Verily! Allaah knows what you do (and will reward you according to it).

A narration on the authority of Buraydah [may Allaah be pleased with him] that he said: This Quraanic Ayaah was revealed in connection with the pledge of allegiance given to the Prophet [peace and blessings of Allaah be upon him]. [Ibn Jareer]

Verse Number 92

92- And be not like her who undoes the thread which she has spun after it has become strong, by taking your oaths as means of deception among yourselves, lest a community may be more numerous than another community. Allaah only tests you by this (command to fulfill your covenant, to distinguish him who obeys Allaah and fulfills His Covenant from him who disobeys Allaah and breaks His Covenant). And on the Day of Resurrection, He will certainly make clear to you that wherein you used to differ (in this world concerning the covenants so that He would punish the breaker and reward the fulfiller).

A narration on the authority of Abu Bakr Ibn Hafs that he said: Sa'idah Al-Asadiyyah was a madwoman and used to gather hair and fibers. In connection with her Allaah Almighty (the Most High) revealed this Quraanic Ayaah. [Ibn Abu Haatim]

Verse Number 103

103- And indeed We know that they (disbelievers (al-Kaafireen)) say: "It is only a human being who teaches him (Muhammad)." The tongue of the man they refer to is foreign, while this (Quraan) is a clear Arabic tongue (and it is beyond the capacity of such a non-Arab to teach it).

A narration on the authority of 'Abdullaah Ibn Muslim Al-Hadrami that he said: We had two slaves of Sicilian origin, and they used to read their book and teach their knowledge, and the Prophet [peace and blessings of Allaah be upon him] happened to pass by them and listen to their recitation. The disbelievers (al-Kaafireen) said: "He seems to be taught by those (slaves)". On that occasion, Allaah revealed this Quraanic Ayaah. [Ibn Abu Haatim]

106- Whoever disbelieves in Allaah after his belief, except him who is forced thereto (to pronounce the word of disbelief) and whose heart is at rest with Faith (will have a severe torment); but such as open their breasts to disbelief (that is accept it gladly), on them is wrath from Allaah, and theirs will be a great torment.

A narration on the authority of Ibn 'Abbaas [Allaah be pleased with them] that he said: When the Prophet [peace and blessings of Allaah be upon him] intended to emigrate to Madeenah, the polytheists took hold of Bilaal, Khabbaab and 'Ammaar and detained them. As for 'Ammaar, he told them a word that appealed to them. When he returned to the Prophet [peace and blessings of Allaah be upon him] and made a mention of that to him, he asked him: "When you said it, has your heart been expanded with it?" He answered in the negative, thereupon Allaah revealed this Quraanic Ayaah. [Ibn Abu Haatim]

A narration on the authority of Mujaahid that this Quraanic Ayaah was revealed in connection with some Muslims who embraced Islam and concealed their faith and when they were told by the Companions in Madinah to emigrate and they really came out, the men of Quraysh caught up with them and temped them thereupon they disbelieved under compulsion. [Ibn Abu Haatim]

A narration on the authority of 'Umar Ibn Al-Hakam that 'Ammaar Ibn Yaasir, Suhayb, Abu Fakeehah,

Bilaal, 'AAmir Ibn Fuhayrah and others were punished so much that they did not know what they were saying. In connection with them this Quraanic Ayaah was revealed up to Allaah's saying (what means): {indeed, your Lord (Rabb), after that, is Forgiving and Merciful}. [verse 110] [Ibn Sa'd In At-Tabaqaat]

Verse Number 126

126- And if you punish (your enemy), then punish them with the like of that with which you were afflicted. But if you patiently persevere (and leave retribution), verily, is better for the patient.

A narration on the authority of Abu Hurayrah [may Allaah be pleased with him] that he said: the Prophet [peace and blessings of Allaah be upon him] stood by the dead body of Hamzah [may Allaah be pleased with him] when he fell a martyr and his dead body was mutilated on the day of the battle of Uhud and said: "Verily, I will mutilate seventy of them (the polytheists) in place of you". No sooner had he said so than Jibreel [peace and blessings of Allaah be upon him] descended with the concluding Aayaat of Soorah An-Nahl [126-128]. Then the Prophet [peace and blessings of Allaah be upon him] changed his mind and abandoned this idea. [Al-Haakim; Al-Bayhaqi in Ad-Dalaa'il and Al-Bazzaar]

A narration on the authority of Ubayy Ibn Ka'b [may Allaah be pleased with him] that he said: On the day of the battle of Uhud the Ansaar lost sixty-four and the Muhaajirs lost six and the polytheists mutilated their dead bodies. The Ansaar said: "If Allaah enabled us to defeat them as they have done today, we will mutilate more of their dead bodies". Then, when it was the day of the conquest of Makkah, Allaah revealed this Quraanic Ayaah. [At-Tirmidhi who renders it Hasan]

This requires that the Quraanic Ayaah should have been revealed on the day of the conquest of Makkah, whereas according to the previous narration, it was revealed on the day of Uhud. Ibn Al-Hassaar replies that this Quraanic Ayaah might, possibly, have been revealed three times: one in Makkah, another on the day of Uhud and the third time on the day of the conquest of Makkah, so that Allaah would remind the believers (al-Mumineen).

Soorah Al-Israa'

Verse Number 15

15- Whoever receives guidance, then he receives guidance only for the benefit of his own self. And whoever goes astray, then he goes astray to his own loss. No bearer of burdens (that is sinner) can bear the burdens (sins) of another. And We never punish (anyone) until We have sent a Messenger (to clarify to him what is due on him to do).

A narration on the authority of 'AA'ishah [Allaah be pleased with her] that Khadijah [Allaah be pleased with her] asked the Prophet [peace and blessings of Allaah be upon him] about the destiny of the offspring of the disbelievers (al-Kaafireen) and he said: "They belong to their fathers". Then she asked him once again at a later time and he said: "Allaah Alone knows what will happen to them". For a third time she asked him after Islam had become strong thereupon this Quraanic Ayaah was revealed. Then the Prophet [peace and blessings of Allaah be upon him] said: "They will remain on the sound innate nature on which Allaah has created them", or "They will be in Paradise". [Ibn 'Abdul-Barr with a weak chain of narrators]

Verse Number 28

28- And if you turn away from them and you are awaiting a mercy (that is sustenance) from your Lord

(Rabb) for which you hope (to give them therefrom), then, speak unto them a soft kind word.

A narration on the authority of 'Ataa' Al-Khuraasaani that a group of people came to the Prophet [peace and blessings of Allaah be upon him] and asked him to provide them with mounts to ride (in order to set out for a certain battle), and the Prophet [peace and blessings of Allaah be upon him] said to them: "I have nothing for you to ride". They turned away with their eyes shedding tears, thinking that the Prophet [peace and blessings of Allaah be upon him] (did not give them mounts because he) was angry with them. On that occasion, Allaah revealed this Quraanic Ayaah. [Sa'eed Ibn Mansoor]

A narration on the authority of Ad-Dahhaak that it was revealed in connection with the poor who begged the Prophet [peace and blessings of Allaah be upon him]. [Ibn Jareer]

Verse Number 29

29- And let not your hand be tied (like a miser) to your neck, nor stretch it forth to its utmost reach (like a spendthrift), so that you become blameworthy (and that is the state of the miser) and insolvent (and that is the state of the spendthrift).

A narration on the authority of Sayyaar Abu Al-Hakam that once, some clothes were brought to the Prophet [peace and blessings of Allaah be upon him], and he was very generous. He distributed all this before a group of the poor came to him and found out that he had finished it. On that occasion, Allaah revealed this Quraanic Ayaah. [Sa'eed Ibn Mansoor]

A narration on the authority of Ibn Mas'ood [may Allaah be pleased with him] that he said: A woman sent her child to the Prophet [peace and blessings of Allaah be upon him] to beg something from him and he said: "We have nothing today". He said: "Then my mother asks you to dress her in your shirt". He took it off and gave it to her and sat naked in the house. On that occasion, Allaah revealed this Quraanic Ayaah. [Ibn Mardawayh and others]

Verse Number 45

45- And when you (O Muhammad) recite the Quraan, We put between you and those who believe not in the Hereafter a veil (to make you) invisible (from their eyes).

A narration on the authority of Shihaab that whenever the Prophet [peace and blessings of Allaah be upon him] recited the Quraan to the polytheists of Makkah and invited them to the Book of Allaah, they would say, in ridicule: "There are coverings over our hearts (Qalb) so that we would not understand that to which you invite us, there is deafness in our ears and between you and us there is a partition". On that occasion, Allaah revealed this Quraanic Ayaah. [Ibn Al-Mundhir]

Verse Number 56

56- Say (to them): "Invoke those whom you pretend (to be gods) besides Him (like angels, Jesus, Ezra, and others). They have no power to remove the adversity from you nor even to shift it from you to others."

A narration on the authority of Ibn Mas'ood [may Allaah be pleased with him] that he said: Some people used to worship many from among the jinn. The latter embraced Islam but the former did not cease to worship them. On that occasion, Allaah revealed this Quraanic Ayaah. [Al-Bukhaari]

Verse Number 59

59- And nothing prevents Us from sending the miracles (proposed and demanded by the Makkans) except that the people of old denied them (when they were sent unto them thereupon We destroyed them). And We sent the she-camel to (the people of) Thamood as a clear sign, but they were wrongdoers (by slaying) of her (thereupon they were ruined). And We sent not the miracles except to warn and frighten (people of the adverse consequences of disbelief so that they would believe).

A narration on the authority of Ibn 'Abbaas [Allaah be pleased with them] that he said: The polytheists of the Quraysh asked the Prophet [peace and blessings of Allaah be upon him] to turn Safa (mount) into gold and to move away the mountains surrounding Makkah to make it more spacious so that they would cultivate it. It was said to the Prophet [peace and blessings of Allaah be upon him]: "You can give them respite if you so like, or respond to their request if you so like, but in this case, if they disbelieve afterwards, they will be destroyed immediately as those before them were destroyed". the Prophet [peace and blessings of Allaah be upon him] said: "No, I will give them respite". On that occasion, Allaah revealed this Quraanic Ayaah. [Ibn Mardawayh; At-Tabaraani and others]

Verse Number 60

60- And (remember) when We told you: "Verily! Your Lord (Rabb) has encompassed people (in knowledge and power that they are in His Grip: so, proclaim the Message and fear none because Allaah protects you from them)." And We made not the vision which we showed you (actually with your own eyes and not as a dream on the night of Al-Israa') but a trial for people, and (also) the accursed tree (of Zaqqoom mentioned) in the Quraan (which grows at the bottom of the Hellfire). We thereby frighten them but it only increases them in enormous transgression.

A narration on the authority of Umm Haani' [Allaah be pleased with her] that when it was the night on which the Prophet [peace and blessings of Allaah be upon him] was taken on a night journey from Al-Masjid Al-Haraam to Al-Masjid Al-Aqsa, he related that to the people in the morning who went on mocking at him. They asked him to bring a sign so he described to them Bayt Al-Maqdis, and mentioned to them the story of the caravan (he had seen in the way). Al-Waleed Ibn Al-Mugheerah said: "He is a sorcerer". On that occasion, Allaah revealed this Quraanic Ayaah. [Abu Ya'li]

A narration on the authority of 'Ali Ibn Al-Husayn that one morning, the Prophet [peace and blessings of Allaah be upon him] became anxious, thereupon it was said to him: "What is the matter with you O Messenger of Allaah? Do not be anxious! Verily, the vision you have seen is but a trial to them". On that occasion, Allaah revealed this Quraanic Ayaah. [Ibn Mardawayh]

A narration on the authority of Ibn 'Abbaas [Allaah be pleased with them] that when Allaah Almighty (the Most High) made a mention of the tree of Zaqqoom by way of frightening the disbelievers (al-Kaafireen) and polytheists, Abu Jahl told the people: "O community of Quraysh! Do you know what the tree of Zaqqoom is, by which Muhammad frightens you?" They answered in the negative, thereupon he said: "It is the 'Ajwah dates of Yathrib, mixed with butter. By Allaah, should we get hold of it, we would eat of it greedily". On that occasion, Allaah Almighty (the Most High) revealed (what means): {and (also) the accursed tree (of Zaqqoom mentioned) in the Quraan (which grows at the bottom of the Hellfire). We thereby frighten them but it only increases them in enormous transgression}. [verse 60] He also revealed (what means): {Verily the tree of Zaqqoom Will be the food of the Sinful, Like molten brass; it will boil in their insides, Like the boiling of scalding water}. [Ad-Dukhaan, verse 43-46] [Ibn Abu Haatim and Al-Bayhaqi]

Verse Number 73

73- Verily, they were about to tempt you away from that which We revealed to you to fabricate something other than it against Us, and (had you done so) then they would surely have taken you an intimate friend!

A narration on the authority of Ibn 'Abbaas [Allaah be pleased with them] that he said: One day Umayyah Ibn Khalaf, Abu Jahl Ibn Hishaam and other men from Quraysh came out and met the Prophet [peace and blessings of Allaah be upon him] and said: "O Muhammad! Come to please our deities so that we would enter your religion". the Prophet [peace and blessings of Allaah be upon him], out of love for his people's reversion to Islam, did not reject their demand strongly. On that occasion, Allaah revealed this Quraanic Ayaah. [Ibn Mardawayh and Ibn Abu Haatim]

A narration on the authority of Sa'eed Ibn Jubayr that once the Prophet [peace and blessings of Allaah be upon him] was performing Tawaaf and intended to receive the (Black) Stone thereupon the polytheists of the Quraysh told him: "We will not leave you receive the Stone till you please our gods". the Prophet [peace and blessings of Allaah be upon him] said: "What harm shall befall me if I do since Allaah knows that I am averse to that?" On that occasion, Allaah revealed this Quraanic Ayaah. [Abu Ash-Shaykh]

A similar one is narrated by him on the authority of Ibn Shihab.

A narration on the authority of Jubayr Ibn Nufayr that he said: The chiefs of the Quraysh came to the Prophet [peace and blessings of Allaah be upon him] and said: "If you send to us to sit with you, then drive away those lowly and freed slaves from you so that we would be your sitters".

He [peace and blessings of Allaah be upon him] responded to them, thereupon Allaah revealed this Quraanic Ayaah. [Abu Ash-Shaykh]

A narration on the authority of Muhammad Ibn Ka'b Al-Qurathi that the Prophet [peace and blessings of Allaah be upon him] recited Soorah An-Najm to Allaah's saying (what means): {So have you considered al-Laat and al-'Uzza? And Manaat, the third - the other one?} [An-Najm, verse 19-20] Then Satan inspired him to say: "Those are the high goddesses whose intercession is expected". Then Allaah revealed (what means): {Verily, they were about to tempt you away from that which We revealed to you to fabricate something other than it against Us, and (had you done so) then they would surely have taken you an intimate friend! And if We had not strengthened you, you would have almost inclined to them a little}. [Al-Israa', verse 73-74] the Prophet [peace and blessings of Allaah be upon him] then kept distressed till Allaah revealed (what means): {And We did not send before you any messenger or prophet except that when he spoke (or recited), Satan threw into it (his recitation some misunderstanding). But Allaah abolishes that which Satan throws in; then Allaah makes precise His verses.

And Allaah is Knowing and Wise}. [Al-Hajj, verse 52] [Abu Ash-Shaykh]

Verse Number 76

76- And Verily, they were about to frighten you so much as to drive you out from the land (of Madeenah). But in that case (had they succeeded to expel you) they would not have stayed (therein) after you, except for a little (that is a short while, then they would have perished).

A narration on the authority of 'Abd-Ar-Rahmaan Ibn Ghunm that some Yahood came to the Prophet [peace and blessings of Allaah be upon him] and said: "If you are really a Prophet, then go to Shaam since it is the place of resurrection and the Prophets before you". the Prophet [peace and blessings of Allaah be upon him] believed them and set out for Shaam and when he reached Tabook Allaah Almighty (the Most High) revealed to him those Quraanic Aayaat [73-76] even after the Soorah had been revealed to its end in Makkah. Then He commanded him, through Jibreel [peace and blessings of Allaah be upon him], to return.

Jibreel [peace and blessings of Allaah be upon him] further said to him: "Verily, every Prophet has an invocation". the Prophet [peace and blessings of Allaah be upon him] asked: "What do you command me to invoke?" He recited to him (what means): {And say: "My Lord (Rabb)! Let my entry (to Madeenah) be by the gate of truth and honor (which causes me nothing to dislike), and (likewise) my exit (from

Makkah) be by the gate of truth and honor (and cause my heart not to be attached to it). And grant me from You a power of authority to help me (against Your and my enemies)}. [verse 80] [Ibn Abu Haatim and Al-Bayhaqi in Ad-Dalaa'il]

Verse Number 80

80- And say: "My Lord (Rabb)! Let my entry (to Madeenah) be by the gate of truth and honor (which causes me nothing to dislike), and (likewise) my exit (from Makkah) be by the gate of truth and honor (and cause my heart not to be attached to it). And grant me from You a power of authority to help me (against Your and my enemies).

A narration on the authority of Ibn 'Abbaas [Allaah be pleased with them] that while the Prophet [peace and blessings of Allaah be upon him] was in Makkah he was commanded to emigrate (to Madeenah, and on that occasion, Allaah revealed this Quraanic Ayaah. [At-Tirmidhi]

This means that this Quraanic Ayaah was revealed in Makkah.

no. 85

85- And they (the Yahood) ask you (O Muhammad) concerning the Spirit (which gives life to man); Say: "The Spirit is one of the affairs (whose knowledge is only with) my Lord (Rabb). And of knowledge, you (mankind) have been given only a little (in comparison with Allaah's)."

A narration on the authority of Ibn Mas'ood [may Allaah be pleased with him] that he said: While I was in the company of The Prophet [peace and blessings of Allaah be upon him] on a farm and he was reclining on a palm leave stalk, some Yahood passed by. Some of them told the others: "Would that you ask him (The Prophet) about the spirit!" One of them said: "What urges you to ask him about it?"

Another said: "(Don't do) lest he should give you a reply which you dislike." But they said: "Ask him." So they asked him about the Spirit.

The Prophet [peace and blessings of Allaah be upon him] kept quiet and did not give them any answer. Having known that he was being divinely inspired, I stayed at my place. When the divine inspiration was over, The Prophet [peace and blessings of Allaah be upon him] recited this Quraanic Ayaah. [Al-Bukhaari]

A narration on the authority of Ibn 'Abbaas [Allaah be pleased with them] that he said: The polytheists of Quraysh told the Yahood: "Tell us about something to ask him (Muhammad) about". They said: "Ask him about the spirit". They asked him thereupon Allaah Almighty (the Most High) revealed this Quraanic Ayaah. [At-Tirmidhi]

Verse Number 88

88- Say: "Were men and jinn to gather together to produce the like of this Quraan (in its inimitable eloquence), they could not produce the like thereof, even if they helped one another." A narration on the authority of Ibn 'Abbaas [Allaah be pleased with them] that he said: Salaam Ibn Mishkam, Nu'maan Ibn Abu Awfa: Abu Anas, Mahmood Ibn Dihyah, Shaas Ibn Qays, and Maalik Ibn Sayfi came to the Prophet [peace and blessings of Allaah be upon him] and said: "How should we follow you, given that you have abandoned our Qiblah? Moreover, what you have brought, is, in our sight, not as consistent as the Torah.

So, send down upon us a Book which we know, otherwise we will bring you the like of what you bring". In this connection, Allaah revealed this Quraanic Ayaah. [Ibn Ishaaq and Ibn Jareer] Verse Number 90-93

90- And they say: "We shall not believe in you (O Muhammad) until you cause a spring to gush forth (with water) from the earth for us; 91- Or you have a garden of date-palms and grapes, and cause rivers to gush forth in their midst abundantly; 92- Or you cause the heaven to fall upon us in pieces, as you have pretended, or you bring Allaah and the angels before (us) face to face (to see with our own eyes); 93- Or you have a house of pure gold, or you ascend up into the sky, and even then we will put no faith in your ascension until you bring down for us a Book that we could read." Say (O Muhammad to them) "Exalted be (Allaah) my Lord (Rabb)! Am I but a man, sent as a

Messenger (like all Messengers before me who brought no miracle but by Allaah's leave)?"

A narration on the authority of 'Abdullaah Ibn 'Abbaas [Allaah be pleased with them] that he said: 'Utbah and Shaybah, sons of Rabee'ah, Abu Sufyaan Ibn Harb, An-Nadr Ibn Al-Haarith Ibn Kaladah, the brother of Banu 'Abd-Ad-Daar, Abu Al-Bakhtari Ibn Hishaam, Al-Aswad Ibn Al-Muttalib, Zam'ah Ibn Al-Aswad, Abu Jahl, 'Amr Ibn Hishaam, Al-Waleed Ibn Al-Mugheerah, 'Abdullaah Ibn Abu Umayyah, Umayyah Ibn Khalaf, Al-'AAs Ibn Waa'il, Nubayh and Munabbih, sons of Al-Hajjaaj, or those among them who gathered at that time, assembled together after the sunset near the back of the Ka'bah and one of them said to the others: "Send (somebody) to Muhammad (with a message to come to you), talk to him and argue with him, so that you should have an excuse against him". They sent to him (a message): "The chiefs of your people gathered together in order to talk to you".

Soon, the Prophet [peace and blessings of Allaah be upon him] came to them, thinking that they might have started to see something significant in his matter (of calling them to Allaah). Indeed, he [peace and blessings of Allaah be upon him] was keen on their guidance, and it aggrieved him to see their obstinacy and rejection of the truth.

When he sat with them, they told him: "O Muhammad! We've sent to you (to come) so that we should talk to you. Indeed, by god, never have we known a man from among the Arabs, who brought to his people the like of what you have brought to your people: you've insulted the fathers, taxed the minds with error, abused the religion, disgraced the gods and divided the group; and there is no wicked matter but that you have done with us (or words similar to that). If you seek, with this speech of yours, for property and wealth, we should gather for you from our wealth and property so much until you become the wealthiest and the richest among us; and if your intention is to have the honor among us, we should make you the chief of all of us; and if your plan is to achieve authority over us, we shall make you a king over us; and if that which is revealed to you comes from a companion among the jinns, by whom you've been seized, we should afford as much as we could for medicine, seeking for your treatment until you recover from that state in which you are: otherwise, we should have an excuse against you".

On that, the Prophet [peace and blessings of Allaah be upon him] said: "I am not (seized by a companion from jinns) as you say, nor have I brought you that with which I've come to you in order to take your property, nor to have the honor among you, nor to gain authority over you. On the contrary, Allaah Almighty (the Most High) has sent me as a Messenger to you and revealed a Book unto me, and ordered me to be a giver of glad tidings (of Paradise for the believers (al-Mumineen) among you) and a warner (of the Hellfire for those who reject faith); and I've conveyed to you the Message of my Lord (Rabb), and given you good counsel: if you accept that with which I've come to you, then, it is your (good) share in the world as well as in the hereafter; and if you reject it, then, I will keep patient on the command of Allaah, until Allaah Almighty (the Most High) judges between you and me" or words similar to what the Prophet [peace and blessings of Allaah be upon him] said.

They said to him: "O Muhammad! If you are not going to accept any of those things we've offered to you, then, you know well that there is no people, whose town is narrower than ours, who have water lesser in quantity than we have who suffer from hardship of life more than we suffer: so, ask your Lord (Rabb) Who has sent you with that (revelation) with which He has sent you to remove from our town these (surrounding) mountains which make it narrow, to expand it for us, and cause rivers like those of Shaam and Iraq to gosh forth therein and to resurrect for us our forefathers who passed away, including Qusayy Ibn Kilaab, for indeed, he was a truthful glorious man, so that we might ask them about the reality of that which you say: whether it is true or false.

If you did what we asked you to do, and those (resurrected forefathers) trusted you, surely, we should trust you, and know the high position you have with Allaah, and that He has sent you as a Messenger as you say".

On that, the Prophet [peace and blessings of Allaah be upon him] said: "Never have I been sent with that (which you asked me to do): I have come to you (as a Messenger) from Allaah only with what He has sent me; and I've conveyed to you the Message with which I've been sent: if you accept that which I've brought to you, then, it is your (good) share in the world as well as in the hereafter; and if you reject it, then, I will keep patient on the command of Allaah, until Allaah Almighty (the Most High) judges between you and me".

They told him: "If you are not going to do so, then, support yourself: ask your Lord (Rabb) to send an angel with you in order to trust you in what you say, and argue us on your behalf.

Ask Him also to assign to you gardens, treasures and palaces of gold and silver, therewith you have no need of seeking for your earnings as we see you: indeed, you practice traffic in the markets and seek for sustenance as we do. By so doing we should know your position with your Lord (Rabb): whether you're a Messenger as you claim".

The Prophet [peace and blessings of Allaah be upon him] said to them: "I'm not going to do so, and I'm not going to ask my Lord (Rabb) about that, and I've not been sent to you with that: I've been sent only as a bringer of glad tidings (of Paradise) and a warner (of the Fire): if you accept that with which I've come to you, then, it is your (good) share in the world as well as in the hereafter but if you reject it, then, I will keep patient on the command of Allaah, until Allaah Almighty (the Most High) judges between you and me".

They told him: "Then, cause the sky to fall in pieces upon us as you pretend that if it is your Lord (Rabb)'s plan, He could do so: indeed, never shall we believe in you unless you do so".

The Prophet [peace and blessings of Allaah be upon him] said: "It is up to Allaah Almighty (the Most High) to do that with you if He so wills".

They said: "O Muhammad! Has your Lord (Rabb) not know that we would sit with you and demand from you what we've demanded and asked for what we've asked for, so that He might guide and instruct you how to argue with us in this matter, and tell you what He is going to do with us in this respect if we did not accept from you that with which you've come to us?

Indeed, we've been informed that this (revelation) is taught to you by a man living in Yamaamah, called Rahmaan, and never shall we, by god, believe in this Rahmaan. Of a surety, we now have our excuse against you O Muhammad: by god, never shall we let you do what you are doing with us until we destroy you or otherwise you destroy us". One of them said: "We do worship angels, who are the daughters of Allaah". Another said: "Never shall we believe in you until you bring both Allaah and the angels face to face".

When they said what they said, the Prophet [peace and blessings of Allaah be upon him] stood up and turned away from them, and there stood with him 'Abdullaah Ibn Abu Umayyah Ibn Al-Mugheerah Ibn 'Abdullaah Ibn 'Umar Ibn Makhzoom, the son of his paternal aunt: 'AAtikah bint 'Abd-Al-Muttalib, and told him: "O Muhammad! Your people offered you many things which you did not accept, and they asked you for many things therewith they would know your position with Allaah which you claim, and trust and follow you; but you did not respond to them, then, they asked you to support yourself with many things, therewith they would know your superiority over them, and your position with Allaah, but you did not do, and then, they asked you to hasten on some of the punishment with which you frighten them (or words similar to that): as to me, by Allaah, never shall I believe in you until you mount a ladder right to the sky, in which you ascend to it while I'm seeing till you reach it, and then return with four angels to witness that you're really (a Messenger) as you claim: but, by Allaah, even if you do so, I think I shall not trust you". Then, he turned away from the Prophet [peace and blessings of Allaah be upon him] who, in turn, went home in a state of sadness and grief because of losing his hope for getting his people bclieve in Allaah Almighty (the Most High) which aroused in him when they invited him (to talk to him), and in view of their deviation from him. On that occasion, Allaah Almighty (the Most High) revealed those Quraanic Aayaat. [Ibn Ishaaq and Ibn Jareer]

Verse Number 110

110- Say (to them): "Invoke Allaah or invoke the Most Gracious, by whatever name you invoke Him (it is the same), for to Him belong the Best Names. And establish your prayer neither too aloud (to be heard by the polytheists who might abuse you, the Quraan and (Allaah) Who revealed it), nor in a low voice (so that your Companions would benefit from it), but follow a way between (both extremities).

A narration on the authority of Ibn 'Abbaas [Allaah be pleased with them] that he said: While the Prophet [peace and blessings of Allaah be upon him] was at Makkah one day, he invoked Allaah saying: "O Allaah! O Rahmaan (Most Gracious)!" Having heard this, the polytheists said: "Do you consider this inventor of the new religion! He forbids us to invoke more than one god whereas he invokes two gods: Allaah and Ar-Rahmaan". On that occasion, Allaah revealed this Quraanic Ayaah. [Ibn Mardawayh and others]

A narration on the authority of Ibn 'Abbaas [Allaah be pleased with them] that he said: this Quraanic Ayaah was revealed while the Prophet [peace and blessings of Allaah be upon him] was hiding himself in Mecca. When he prayed with his companions, he used to raise his voice with the recitation of Quraan and if the pagans happened to hear him, they would abuse the Quraan, the One (Allaah) who revealed it and the one (the Prophet) who brought it. Allaah said to His Prophet (what means): {And establish your prayer neither too aloud.....} that is do not recite aloud lest the pagans should hear you, but follow a way between. [Al-Bukhaari]

A narration on the authority of 'AA'ishah [Allaah be pleased with her] that it was revealed in connection with supplication. [Al-Bukhaari] Although the former narration of Al-Bukhaari is more preponderant and more authentic, Ibn Hajar is of the opinion that it might be revealed in connection with the supplication in prayer.

A narration on the authority of Abu Hurayrah [may Allaah be pleased with him] that he said: It was the habit of the Prophet [peace and blessings of Allaah be upon him] that whenever he prayed at the House (Ka'bah) he would supplicate Allaah aloud. On that occasion, this Quraanic Ayaah was revealed. {Ibn Mardawayh]

A narration on the authority of 'AA'ishah [Allaah be pleased with her] that this Quraanic Ayaah was revealed in connection with Tashahhud. [Ibn Jareer] This clarifies (and confirms) her statement in the previous narration on her authority.

A narration on the authority of Ibn 'Abbaas [Allaah be pleased with them] that he said: They used to raise their voices in supplication: "O Allaah! Have mercy upon me!"

Then they were commanded not to recite aloud nor to recite in a very low tone: and rather to follow a middle way between both extremes. [Ibn Manee']

Verse Number 111

111- And say: "All perfect praise be to Allaah, Who has not begotten a son (nor an offspring), and Who has no partner in (His) Dominion, nor He is low to have a helper (to protect Him). And glorify Him with all magnificence (that is to say Allaahu Akbar (Allaah is the Greatest))."

A narration on the authority of Muhammad Ibn Ka'b Al-Qurathi that he said: The Yahood and Nasaara said: "Verily, Allaah has taken a son (that is Ezra or Jesus)".

The Arabs said: "I am responding to Your Call (O Allaah), With Whom there is no partner, except only one partner whom You possess along with all that he possesses". The Magians said: "Had it not been for Allaah's allies, He would have been given to humiliation". On that occasion, Allaah revealed this Quraanic Ayaah. [Ibn Jareer]

Soorah Al-Kahf

A narration on the authority of Ibn 'Abbaas [Allaah be pleased with them] that he said: The Quraysh sent An-Nadr Ibn Al-Haarith and 'Uqbah Ibn Abu Mu'ayt to the rabbis of the Yahood in Madeenah, and ordered them saying: "Ask those Yahood about the characteristics and reality of Muhammad, and describe to them his state and what he says: indeed, they are a people of Scripture, and have the knowledge of the Prophets which we have not". They left for Madeenah and when they arrived and asked those Yahood about the Prophet [peace and blessings of Allaah be upon him] and told them about some of his words, and informed them that they had come to them because they were a people of Scripture, and able to tell them the truth of their companion (Muhammad).

They told them: "We advise you to ask him about three things: if he tells you of their reality, then, he should be a Prophet sent (from Allaah), otherwise, he should be an inventor of lies, so, consider how you should deal with him. Ask him about some young men who lived (and were famous) in the early generation: who they were and what had happened to them; and ask him also about a man who went round and reached the Eastern and the Western ends of the earth: who he was and what about the news pertaining to him; moreover ask him about the spirit: what it is. If he tells you about those, he should be a Prophet, and you should follow him; otherwise, he should be an inventor of lies. So, consider what you like to do with him".

They came back to Makkah and said: "O assembly of Quraysh! We have brought to you the decisive criterion between you and Muhammad. The Jewish rabbis told us to ask him about many things: if he tells you of their reality, then, he should be a Prophet sent (from Allaah), otherwise, he should be an inventor of lies, so, consider how you should deal with him".

They went to the Prophet [peace and blessings of Allaah be upon him] and said: "O Muhammad! Tell us about some young men who lived (and were famous) in the early generation: who they were, and what had happened to them; and tell us about a man who went round and reached the Eastern and the Western ends of the earth: who he was and what about the news pertaining to him; and tell us about the spirit: what it is". the Prophet [peace and blessings of Allaah be upon him] said to them: "I shall tell you tomorrow of the (reality of) those about which you've asked". However, he [peace and blessings of Allaah be upon him] made no exception (by saying Allaah willing). They left him.

The Prophet [peace and blessings of Allaah be upon him] spent fifteen days, during which he received no revelation, nor did Jibreel [peace and blessings of Allaah be upon him] come to him, to the extent that the rumors spread among the Makkans, who said: "Muhammad promised to answer us tomorrow; and now fifteen nights have elapsed and he gave us no answer to what we have asked him about". The delay of the Divine revelation aggrieved the Prophet [peace and blessings of Allaah be upon him], and the spreading talks of the Makkans were difficult on him. Then, Jibreel [peace and blessings of Allaah be upon him] came to him from Allaah Almighty (the Most High) with Soorah Al-Kahf (the Cave), in which Allaah blamed him for his grief for the disbelievers (al-Kaafireen), and briefed him on the news of what they asked about, concerning the youths, the wandering man and the spirit. [Ibn Jareer and Ibn Ishaaq]

Verse Number 6

6- Perhaps you (O Muhammad) would kill yourself in grief over their footsteps (for their turning away from you), because they believe not in this narration (the Quraan).

A narration on the authority of Ibn 'Abbaas [Allaah be pleased with them] that he said: Both 'Utbah and Shaybah, sons of Rabee'ah, Abu Jahl Ibn Hishaam, An-Nadr Ibn Al-Haarith, Umayyah Ibn Khalaf, Al-'AAs Ibn Waa'il, Al-Aswad Ibn Al-Muttalib and Abu Al-Bakhtari and some men from the Quraysh gathered together. the Prophet [peace and blessings of Allaah be upon him] had already felt it difficult that his people disobeyed him and rejected the advice he brought to them, thereupon he grieved so much. On that occasion, Allaah Almighty (the Most High) revealed this Quraanic Ayaah. [Ibn Mardawayh]

Verse Number 23

23- And never say about anything: "I shall do such and such thing tomorrow.

A narration on the authority of Ibn 'Abbaas [Allaah be pleased with them] that he said: the Prophet [peace and blessings of Allaah be upon him] took oath to do something and then forty days elapsed (and he did not do it). On that occasion, Allaah revealed to him this Quraanic Ayaah. [Ibn Jareer and Ibn Mardawayh]

Verse Number 25

25- And they stayed in their Cave three hundred (solar) years, and add nine (according to lunar years).

A narration on the authority of Ibn 'Abbaas [Allaah be pleased with them] that when Allaah revealed (what means): {And they stayed in their cave for three hundred}, they asked: "O Messenger of Allaah! Three hundred years or months?" On that occasion, Allaah Almighty (the Most High) revealed in addition (what means): {(solar) years, and add nine (according to lunar years)}. [Ibn Mardawayh]

Verse Number 28

28- And keep yourself (O Muhammad) patiently with those who invoke their Lord (Rabb) in the morning and afternoon, seeking (by their worship) His Countenance (other than the worldly benefits); and let not your eyes overlook them, desiring the pomp and glitter of the life of the world; and obey not him whose heart We have made heedless of Our Remembrance, and who follows his own inclination (to polytheism), and whose affair (deeds) has been lost. See Al-An'aam, no. 51.

A narration on the authority of Ibn 'Abbaas [Allaah be pleased with them], concerning Allaah's saying (what means): {and obey not him whose heart We have made heedless of Our Remembrance, and who follows his own inclination (to polytheism), and whose affair (deeds) has been lost}, he said: It was revealed in Umayyah Ibn Khalaf Al-Jumahi when he invited the Prophet [peace and blessings of Allaah be upon him] to something which Allaah disliked, that is to drive away the poor from him and draw the chiefs of Makkah close to him. [Ibn Mardawayh]

A narration on the authority of Ar-Rabee' that he said: We were informed that the Prophet [peace and blessings of Allaah be upon him] talked to Umayyah Ibn Khalaf while he was heedless of what was being said to him, thereupon this was revealed. [Ibn Abu Haatim]

A narration on the authority of Abu Hurayrah [may Allaah be pleased with him] that he said: 'Uyaynah Ibn Hisn entered upon The Messenger of Allaah [peace and blessings of Allaah be upon him] and Salmaan was with him. He said to him: "If we come to visit you, you should drive this (and his likes) out and receive us". On that occasion, Allaah revealed this Quraanic Ayaah. [Ibn Abu Haatim]

Verse Number 109

109- Say: "If the sea were ink for (writing) the Words of my Lord (Rabb) (indicative of His ruling, wisdom and wonders), surely, the sea would get exhausted (in writing them) before the Words of my Lord (Rabb) would be finished, even if We brought (another sea) like it for its aid."

A narration on the authority of Ibn 'Abbaas [Allaah be pleased with them] that the disbelievers (al-Kaafireen) of Quraysh said to the Yahood: "Tell us something so that we ask this man (Muhammad) about it". They said: "Ask him about the spirit". They asked him about the spirit thereupon Allaah revealed (what means): {And they (the Yahood) ask you (O Muhammad) concerning the Spirit (which gives life to man); Say: "The Spirit is one of the affairs (whose knowledge is only with) my Lord (Rabb). And of knowledge, you (mankind) have been given only a little (in comparison with Allaah's)."} [Al-Israa', verse 85] The Yahood said: "No doubt, we have been given much knowledge". On that occasion, Allaah Almighty (the Most High) revealed this Quraanic Ayaah. [Al-Haakim and others]

Verse Number 110

110- Say: "I am only a man like you. It has been revealed to me that your God is One God (that is Allaah). So whoever hopes for the Meeting with his Lord (Rabb) (by resurrection and reward), let him work righteous deeds and associate no partner in the worship of his Lord (Rabb)."

A narration on the authority of Ibn 'Abbaas [Allaah be pleased with them] that he said: A man said to the Prophet [peace and blessings of Allaah be upon him]: "O Messenger of Allaah! I stand (in prayer) seeking the Countenance of Allaah, and like that Allaah should see me in this position". He [peace and blessings of Allaah be upon him] gave no reply till this Quraanic Ayaah was revealed. [Al-Haakim who renders it authentic according to the conditions stipulated by Al-Bukhaari and Muslim]

A narration on the authority of Mujaahid that he said: One of the Muslims used to fight, and liked that Allaah should see his position. On that occasion, Allaah revealed this Quraanic Ayaah. [Ibn Abu Haatim]

A narration on the authority of Ibn 'Abbaas [Allaah be pleased with them] that he said: Jundub Ibn Zuhayr said: "If a man prays, fasts or gives in charity, and he is mentioned with a good mention among the people, he then will get comforted by that and tend to do more (good deeds)". On that occasion, Allaah Almighty (the Most High) revealed this Quraanic Ayaah. [Abu Na'eem and Ibn 'Asaakir]

Soorah Maryam

Verse Number 64

64- And we (angels) descend not except by the Command of your Lord (Rabb) (O Muhammad). To Him belongs (the knowledge of) what is before us (concerning the hereafter affairs) and what is behind us (concerning the worldly affairs), and what is between those two (that is from this time on to the establishment of the final Hour); and your Lord (Rabb) is never forgetful (to forsake you and delay the divine revelation from you).

A narration on the authority of Ibn 'Abbaas [Allaah be pleased with them] that he said: the Prophet [peace and blessings of Allaah be upon him] asked Jibreel: "What does prevent you from visiting us more than you do?" On that occasion, this Quraanic Ayaah was revealed. [Al-Bukhaari]

A narration on the authority of 'Ikrimah that he said: Once Jibreel [peace and blessings of Allaah be upon him] did not visit the Prophet [peace and blessings of Allaah be upon him] for forty days... and the rest is the same. [Ibn Abu Haatim]

A narration on the authority of Anas [may Allaah be pleased with him] that he said: the Prophet [peace and blessings of Allaah be upon him] asked Jibreel: "Which part of the land is the dearest to Allaah?" He replied: "I do not know. Give me respite till I ask".

When he came to him, and he had not visited him for a long time, the Prophet [peace and blessings of Allaah be upon him] told him: "You have delayed to come to me, O Jibreel, so much that I started to have bad assumptions". He said (what means): {"We (angels) descend not except by the Command of your Lord (Rabb)...} [Ibn Mardawayh]

A narration on the authority of Ibn 'Abbaas [Allaah be pleased with them] that he said: When the disbelievers (al-Kaafireen) of the Quraysh asked the Prophet [peace and blessings of Allaah be upon him] about the men of the cave, he did not receive divine revelation for fifteen days. When Jibreel descended to him he said: "You have delayed to come to me..." and the rest is the same. [Ibn Ishaaq]

Verse Number 77

77- Have you seen him who disbelieved in Our signs and said: "(Then if I be resurrected after death as you claim) I shall certainly be given wealth and children."

A narration on the authority of Khabbaab Ibn Al-Aratt [may Allaah be pleased with him] that he said: I came to Al-'AAs Ibn Waa'il As-Sahmi and demanded something which he owed me. He said: "I will not give you (your money) till you disbelieve in Muhammad." I told him: "No, I shall not disbelieve in Muhammad till you die and then be resurrected." He asked: "Will I die and then be resurrected?" I replied: "Yes". He said': "Then I will have wealth and children there, and I will pay you (there)." On that occasion, this Quraanic Ayaah was revealed. [Al-Bukhaari and Muslim]

Verse Number 96

96- Verily, for those who believe (in Allaah) and work deeds of righteousness, (Allaah) the Most Gracious will bestow affection.

A narration on the authority of 'Abd-Ar-Rahmaan Ibn 'Awf [may Allaah be pleased with him] that when he emigrated to Madeenah, he grieved for leaving such of his companions in Makkah as Shaybah and 'Utbah, sons of Rabi'ah and Umayyah Ibn Khalaf. On that occasion, Allaah revealed (what means): {Verily, for those who believe (in Allaah) and work deeds of righteousness, (Allaah) the Most Gracious will bestow affection}, that is affection and love in the hearts (Qalb) of the believers (al-Mumineen). [Ibn Jareer]

Soorah Taa-Haa

Verse Number 1-3

1- Taa-Haa. 2- We have not sent down the Quraan to you (O Muhammad) so that you would be distressed (because of your long standing in prayer at night). 3- But (We have revealed it) only as a Reminder to those who fear (Allaah).

A narration on the authority of Ibn 'Abbaas [Allaah be pleased with them] that he said: At the beginning, when the Prophet [peace and blessings of Allaah be upon him] received the divine revelation, he would stand on the front parts of his feet while praying. On that occasion, Allaah revealed these Quraanic Aayaat. [Ibn Mardawayh]

A narration on the authority of Ar-Rabee' Ibn Anas that he said: the Prophet [peace and blessings of Allaah be upon him] used to alternate between his feet, and stand on them by turns (during prayer) till this Quraanic Ayaah was revealed. ['Abd Ibn Humayd]

A narration on the authority of Ibn 'Abbaas [Allaah be pleased with them] that he said: This man (Muhammad) troubled himself (while receiving the divine revelation), thereupon Allaah revealed this Quraanic Ayaah. [Ibn Mardawayh]

Verse Number 105

105- And they ask you about the mountains (how they will be on the Day of Resurrection). Say: "My Lord (Rabb) will blast them (by fragmenting them into sand) and scatter them (by the wind). A narration on the authority of Ibn Jurayj that he said: The men of Quraysh asked the Prophet [peace and blessings of Allaah be upon him]: "O Muhammad! What will your Lord (Rabb) do with those mountains on the Day of Resurrection?" On that occasion, this Quraanic Ayaah was revealed. [Ibn Al-Mundhir]

Verse Number 114

114- Then Supremely Exalted be Allaah (above what the polytheists ascribe to Him), the True Sovereign. And be not in haste (O Muhammad) with the Quraan before its revelation is completed to you, and say: "My Lord (Rabb)! Increase knowledge." me in

A narration on the authority of As-Suddi that he said: It was the habit of the Prophet [peace and blessings of Allaah be upon him] that whenever Jibreel descended upon him with divine revelation, he would trouble himself with memorizing it till this was difficult on him; and he did so for fear Jibreel would leave him before memorizing it. On that occasion, Allaah revealed this Quraanic Ayaah. [Ibn Abu Haatim]

Verse Number 131

131- And stretch not your eyes in longing for the things We have given for enjoyment to various groups of them (polytheists and disbelievers (al-Kaafireen)), the splendor of the life of this world, that We may test them thereby (to transgress beyond the due limits). But the provision of your Lord (Rabb) (one will receive in Paradise) is better and more enduring (than what they have been given in this world).

A narration on the authority of Abu Raafi' [may Allaah be pleased with him] that he said: Once, the Prophet [peace and blessings of Allaah be upon him] had a guest and he sent me to one of the Yahood with the message: "Lend me an amount of baking powder till the new moon of Rajab". The Jew said: "No except with a mortgage". I returned to him and made a mention to him of that thereupon he said: "Verily, by Allaah, I am a trustworthy in the heaven and a trustworthy on earth". I did not leave him till this Quraanic Ayaah was revealed. [Ibn Abu Shaybah; Ibn Mardawayh; Al-Bazzaar and Ibn Abu Ya'li]

Soorah Al-Anbiyaa'

Verse Number 6

6- No (population of a) town, of those which We destroyed (for rejecting the signs We sent unto them), believed before them: will they (that is the disbelievers (al-Kaafireen) of Makkah) then believe (if such a sign as they asked for was sent down to them)? (Of course no).

A narration on the authority of Qataadah that he said: The polytheists of the Quraysh said to the Prophet [peace and blessings of Allaah be upon him]: "If that which you have brought is the truth, turn Safa (mount) into gold".

Jibreel [peace and blessings of Allaah be upon him] then came and said to the Prophet [peace and blessings of Allaah be upon him]: "You can give them respite if you so like, or respond to their request if you so like, but in this case, if they disbelieve afterwards, they will be destroyed immediately as those before them were destroyed".

The Prophet [peace and blessings of Allaah be upon him] said: "No, I will give them respite".

On that occasion, Allaah Almighty (the Most High) revealed this Quraanic Ayaah. [Ibn Mardawayh]

Verse Number 34

34- And We granted not to any human being before you (O Muhammad) immortality (a perpetual residence in this world). Then if you die, would they live forever? (Of course no).

A narration on the authority of Ibn Jurayj that he said: the Prophet [peace and blessings of Allaah be upon him] received his death news thereupon he said: "O Lord (Rabb)! Then who after me will instruct my ummah?"

On that occasion, Allaah revealed this Quraanic Ayaah. [Ibn Al-Mundhir]

Verse Number 36

36- And when those who disbelieve (in Allaah) see you (O Muhammad) they take you not except for ridicule (saying): "Is this the one who talks (badly) about your gods?" While they disbelieve in the mention of (Allaah) the Most Gracious (claiming they do not know Him).

A narration on the authority of As-Suddi that once the Prophet [peace and blessings of Allaah be upon him] came upon Abu Jahl and Abu Sufyaan and they were talking. Having seen him, Abu Jahl laughed and said to Abu Sufyaan: "That is the Prophet of Banu 'Abd Manaaf".

Abu Sufyaan grew angry and said: "Do you deny that Banu 'Abd Manaaf should have a Prophet?"

Having heard it, the Prophet [peace and blessings of Allaah be upon him] returned to Abu Jahl and frightened him (of Allaah's punishment), saying: "I do think that you will not desist (from your evil) till you would be befallen by the same (torment) that afflicted those who broke their promise". On that occasion, Allaah revealed this Quraanic Ayaah. [Ibn Abu Haatim]

Verse Number 101

101- Verily, those for whom the good has gone forth before

from Us, they will be removed far therefrom (that is the Hellfire). A narration on the authority of Ibn 'Abbaas [Allaah be pleased with them] that when Allaah revealed (what means): {Indeed, you (disbelievers (al-Kaafireen)) and what you worship other than Allaah are the firewood of Hell}, [Al-Anbiyaa', verse 98] 'Abdullaah Ibn Az-Zaba'ra said: "The objects of worship: the sun, the moon, the angels and Ezra will be in the Fire along with our gods". On that occasion, Allaah revealed (what means): {Indeed, those for whom the good has gone forth before from Us - they will be removed far therefrom (that is the Hellfire)}. [verse 101] Allaah also revealed (what means): {And when the son of Mary was presented as an example, immediately your people laughed aloud. And they said: "Are your gods better, or is he?" They did not present the comparison except for (mere) argument. But, (in fact), they are a people prone to dispute}. [Az-Zukhruf verse 57-58] [Al-Haakim]

Soorah Al-Hajj

Verse Number 3

3- And among mankind is he who disputes concerning Allaah without knowledge, and follows (in his argumentation) every rebellious devil.

A narration on the authority of Abu Maalik that he said: This Quraanic Ayaah was revealed in connection with An-Nadr Ibn Al-Haarith. [Ibn Abu Haatim]

Verse Number 11

11- And among people is he who worships Allaah as it were upon a verge (of mountain, that is in doubt about his worship): if good touches him (in his property, health and offspring), he is content therewith; but if a trial befalls him (that is illness, poverty and adversity), he turns back (prone) on his face (that is reverts to disbelief after belief). He loses this world (by missing what he hopes thereof) and the Hereafter (by his disbelief in Allaah). That is indeed the evident loss.

A narration on the authority of Ibn 'Abbaas [Allaah be pleased with them] that he said: The habit of some men was if they came to Madeenah and embraced Islam, and one wife of anyone of them gave birth to male children from him and his horses produced offspring, he would say: "That (Islam) is a good religion". But if the wife did not give birth to male children, nor did his horses produce offspring, he would say: "That is a bad religion". On that occasion, Allaah revealed this Quraanic Ayaah. [Al-Bukhaari]

A narration on the authority of Ibn Mas'ood [may Allaah be pleased with him] that one of the Yahood embraced Islam and it happened that he lost his eyesight, property and his child died. On that he said: "No doubt, I have got no good from this religion: I have lost my eyesight, property and my child died". On that occasion, Allaah revealed this Quraanic Ayaah. [Ibn Mardawayh]

Verse Number 19

19- These (believers (al-Mumineen) and disbelievers (al-Kaafireen)) are two adversaries who dispute with each other about (the religion of) their Lord (Rabb): then as for those who disbelieved, garments of fire will be cut out for them (to put on), scalding fluid will be poured down over their heads.

A narration on the authority of Abu Dharr [may Allaah be pleased with him] that he said: This Quraanic Ayaah was revealed in connection with Hamzah, 'Ali Ibn Abu Taalib and 'Ubaydah Ibn Al-Haarith on one side, and 'Utbah and Shaybah, sons of Rabee'ah and Al-Waleed Ibn 'Utbah on the other side. [Al-Bukhaari and Muslim]

A narration on the authority of 'Ali [may Allaah be pleased with him] that he said: In connection with us, that is our swordfight with the polytheists, on the day of Badr, those Quraanic Aayaat (up to 22) were revealed. [Al-Haakim]

It is narrated on the same authority that it was revealed in connection with the swordfight that took place between 'Ali, Hamzah and 'Ubaydah on the one hand, and 'Utbah, Shaybah and Al-Waleed Ibn 'Utbah on the other hand. [Al-Haakim]

A narration on the authority of Ibn 'Abbaas [Allaah be pleased with them] that it was revealed in connection with the people of Scripture when they said to the believers (al-Mumineen): "We are closer to Allaah than you, because our Book is older and our Prophet (Moses) was sent before yours". The believers (al-Mumineen) replied: "Nay! We are worthier of Allaah than you because we believe in Muhammad as well as in your Prophet (Moses) and the Scripture which Allaah revealed". [Ibn Jareer]

Verse Number 25

25- Verily, those who disbelieve and avert (men) from the Path of Allaah, and from Al-Masjid Al-Haraam (the Ka'bah) which We have made (open) to (all) people (to perform their rites and worship Allaah), the dweller in it and the visitor from the country are equal there; and (also) whoever intends to deviation (in the religion) therein or injustice, We shall cause him to taste a painful torment.

A narration on the authority of Ibn 'Abbaas [Allaah be pleased with them] that he said: the Prophet [peace

and blessings of Allaah be upon him] sent 'Abdullaah Ibn Unays along with two men: one from the Muhaajiroon and the other from the Ansaar. Both vied in glory with each other concerning their ancestries, thereupon 'Abdullaah Ibn Unays grew angry and killed the Ansaari and renegaded from Islam and fled to Makkah. In connection with him, this Quraanic Ayaah was revealed. [Ibn Abu Haatim]

Verse Number 27

27- And proclaim Hajj (pilgrimage) to people: they will come to you on foot and on every lean camel; and they will come from every deep and far mountain pass (to perform Hajj).

A narration on the authority of Mujaahid that he said: They (the pilgrims) used to come (to perform Hajj) on foot. On that occasion, this Quraanic Ayaah was revealed, in which Allaah commanded them to take provision with them and to ride mounts in their journey. [Ibn Jarir]

Verse Number 37

37- It is neither their meat nor their blood that reaches Allaah, but it is piety from you that reaches Him. Thus have We made them subject to you that you may glorify Allaah because He has Guided you (to the symbols of His religion and the ceremonies of Hajj to Him). And give glad tidings (O Muhammad) to the doers of good (who worship Allaah Alone).

A narration on the authority of Ibn Jurayj that he said: The people of the pre-Islamic days used to stain the House with the meat and blood of their sacrifices. The Companions of the Prophet [peace and blessings of Allaah be upon him] said: "Then, we have more right to do so". On that occasion, Allaah revealed this Quraanic Ayaah. [Ibn Abu Haatim]

Verse Number 39

39- Permission to fight (the disbelievers (al-Kaafireen)) is given to those (believers (al-Mumineen)) who are being fought, because they have been wronged (by the disbelievers (al-Kaafireen) and polytheists); and surely, Allaah is Able to give them (the believers (al-Mumineen)) victory (over their enemies).

A narration on the authority of Ibn 'Abbaas [Allaah be pleased with them] that he said: when the Prophet [peace and blessings of Allaah be upon him] came out of Makkah, Abu Bakr said: "They (the disbelievers (al-Kaafireen)) have driven out their Prophet. They would surely be ruined". On that occasion, Allaah revealed this Quraanic Ayaah. [Ahmad; At-Tirmidhi who renders it Hasan and Al-Haakim who renders it Saheeh]

Verse Number 52

52- Never did We send before you a Messenger or a Prophet but that when he did recite the divine revelation, Satan threw (some falsehood) in it. But

Allaah abrogates that which Satan throws in. Then Allaah establishes His Revelations. And Allaah is All-Knower (of what Satan cast as mentioned above), All-Wise (in doing what He wills).

A narration on the authority of Sa'eed Ibn Jubayr that the Prophet [peace and blessings of Allaah be upon him] recited Soorah An-Najm to Allaah's saying (what means): {So have you considered al-Laat and al-'Uzza? And Manaat, the third - the other one?} [An-Najm, verse 19-20] Then Satan inspired him to say: "Those are the high goddesses whose intercession is expected". The polytheists said: "He (Muhammad) has never mentioned our gods with good before this day". Then he prostrated and they prostrated with him. On that occasion, Allaah revealed this Quraanic Ayaah. [Ibn Abu Haatim; Ibn Jareer and Ibn Al-Mundhir]

The same is narrated on the authority of Ibn 'Abbaas [Allaah be pleased with them]. [Al-Bazzaar and Ibn Mardawayh]

Verse Number 60

60- That is so. And whoever (among the believers (al-Mumineen)) responds (to injustice) with the like of the harm he has received (unjustly from the polytheists), and then has again been inequitably treated (by being expelled from his homeland), Allaah will surely help him. Verily Allaah indeed is Oft-Pardoning (for the believers (al-Mumineen)), Oft-Forgiving (for their engagement in fight in the Sacred month). A narration on the authority of Muqaatil that he said: This

Quraanic Ayaah was revealed in connection with a military expedition dispatched by the Prophet [peace and blessings of Allaah be upon him] who met the polytheists and remained there only two nights to the end of Muharram. The polytheists told one another: "Fight the Companions of Muhammad because they forbid fighting during the sacred month". The Companions besought them not to fight them because they render it unlawful to fight in the sacred month. But the polytheists refused and fought them and transgressed upon them. The Muslims, anyway, fought them and emerged victorious over them. On that occasion, this Quraanic Ayaah was revealed. [Ibn Abu Haatim]

Soorah Al-Mu'minoon

Verse Number 2

2- Those who perform their prayers humbly and submissively. A narration on the authority of Abu Hurayrah [may Allaah be pleased with him] that it was the habit of the Prophet [peace and blessings of Allaah be upon him] to raise his head towards the sky whenever he prayed. Then Allaah revealed this Quraanic Ayaah, thereupon he lowered his head. [Al-Haakim]

The same is narrated except that he used to turn sideways in prayer (rather than to raise his head towards the sky). [Ibn Mardawayh] The same is narrated on the authority of Ibn Seereen. [Sa'eed Ibn Mansoor]

A narration on the authority of Ibn Seereen that he said: The Companions used to raise their heads in prayer thereupon this Quraanic Ayaah was revealed. [Ibn Abu Haatim]

Verse Number 14

14- Then We made the sperm-drop into a leech-like clot (of congealed blood), then We made the clot into a morsel of flesh, then We made out of that morsel of flesh bones, then We clothed the bones with flesh, and then We brought it forth as another creation (by blowing into it of Our Spirit to give life to it). So Blessed is Allaah, the Best of creators.

A narration on the authority of 'Umar [may Allaah be pleased with him] that he said: (The revelation of) my Lord (Rabb) agreed with me in four things.

One of them is that Allaah revealed (what means): {And certainly did We create man from an extract of clay..} [verse 12] Then I said: "So blessed is Allaah, the best of creators".

Then it was revealed as such. [Ibn Abu Haatim]

Verse Number 67

67- Waxing proud (against belief) because of it (that is Al-Bayt Al-Haraam), (with your gathering) talking by night badly about it (that is the Quraan, or him, that is the Prophet [peace and blessings of Allaah be upon him]).

A narration on the authority of Sa'eed Ibn Jubayr that he said: The men of Quraysh used to engage in night talks around the House and perform no Tawaaf; also they used to pride themselves on that. On that occasion, Allaah revealed this Quraanic Ayaah. [Ibn Abu Haatim]

Verse Number 76

76- And indeed We seized them with torment (that is severe hunger), but they humbled not themselves to their Lord (Rabb), nor did they submissively implore (Allaah).

A narration on the authority of Ibn 'Abbaas [Allaah be pleased with them] that Abu Sufyaan went to the Prophet [peace and blessings of Allaah be upon him] and said: "O Muhammad! I beseech you by (the right of) Allaah and the kinship ties (to invoke Allaah for us)! We have indeed (been compelled to) eat wool and blood (because of this severe famine)".

On that occasion, Allaah revealed this Quraanic Ayaah. [An-Nasaa'i and Al-Haakim]

A narration on the authority of Ibn 'Abbaas [Allaah be pleased with them] that when the Prophet [peace and blessings of Allaah be upon him] released Ibn Iyaas Al-Hanafi from his captivity, he embraced Islam and then went to Makkah.

Then he returned and impeded the provision of Yamaamah from coming to Makkah (and the men of Quraysh were exposed to severe hunger) that they were forced to eat the wool and blood. Abu Sufyaan came to the Prophet [peace and blessings of Allaah be upon him] and said: "Do you not pretend that you have been sent as a mercy to the worlds?" He answered in the affirmative.

He said: "Then (you should know that) you have killed the fathers with the sword and the children with hunger".

On that occasion, Allaah revealed this Quraanic Ayaah.
[Al-Bayhaqi in Ad-Dalaa'il]

Soorah An-Noor

Verse Number 3

3- The adulterer marries not but an adulteress or a polytheistic woman, and none marries the adulteress except an adulterer or a polytheistic man. Such a thing is forbidden to the believers (al-Mumineen) (in Allaah).

A narration on the authority of 'Abdullaah Ibn 'Amr [may Allaah be pleased with him] that he said: There was a prostitute called Umm Mahzool and one of the Companions of the Prophet [peace and blessings of Allaah be upon him] liked to marry her. On that occasion, Allaah Almighty (the Most High) revealed this Quraanic Ayaah. [An-Nasaa'i]

A narration on the authority of Marthad Ibn Abu Marthad Al-Ghanawi, who used to carry the captives in Mecca, that there was in Mecca a prostitute called 'Anaaq who was his friend. He said: I came to the Prophet [peace and blessings of Allaah be upon him] and said: "O Messenger of Allaah! Should I marry 'Anaaq?" He kept silent and gave no reply to me till Allaah revealed this Quraanic Ayaah. Then he recited it to me and said to me: "Do not marry her". [Abu Daawood; At-Tirmidhi and Al-Haakim]

A narration on the authority of Mujaahid that he said: When Allaah forbade illegal sexual intercourse, there were some prostitutes who were pretty. Some people said: "Let them go and marry". On that occasion, this Quraanic Ayaah was revealed. [Sa'eed Ibn Mansoor]

Verse Number 6

6- And for those who accuse their wives (of fornication), but have no witnesses (to confirm their allegation) except themselves, let the witness of anyone of them be four testimonies (swearing) by Allaah that he is telling the truth (in his charge against his wife). A narration on the authority of Ibn 'Abbas [Allaah be pleased with

them] that he said: Hilaal Ibn Umayyah accused his wife of committing illegal sexual intercourse with Shareek Ibn Sahmaa' and filed the case before the Prophet [peace and blessings of Allaah be upon him]. The Prophet [peace and blessings of Allaah be upon him] said (to Hilaal): "Either you bring forth a proof (four witnesses) or you will receive the legal punishment (lashes) on your back." Hilaal said: "O Messenger of Allaah! If anyone of us saw a man over his wife, would he go to seek after witnesses?" The Prophet [peace and blessings of Allaah be upon him] kept on saying: "Either you bring forth the witnesses or you will receive the legal punishment (lashes) on your back." Hilaal then said: "By Him Who sent you with the Truth, I am telling the truth and Allaah will reveal to you what will save my back from legal punishment." Then, Jibreel came down and revealed to him this Quraanic Ayaah. [Al-Bukhaari]

A narration on the authority of Ibn 'Abbaas [Allaah be pleased with them] that he said: When Allaah revealed (what means): {And those who accuse chaste women and then do not produce four witnesses - lash them with eighty lashes and do not accept from them testimony ever after. And those are the defiantly disobedient}, [verse 4] and the Prophet [peace and blessings of Allaah be upon him] recited it, Sa'd Ibn 'Ubaadah, the chief of Ansaar, said: "Is that how it has been revealed, O Messenger of Allaah?" The Prophet [peace and blessings of Allaah be upon him] said: "O People of Ansaar! Do you hear what your chief is saying?" They replied: "Do not blame him, O Messenger of Allaah! He is a man with a keen sense of honor. He has never married a woman unless she was a virgin. If he divorced a woman, none of us would dare to marry her because we know how he considers it". Sa'd said: "O Messenger of Allaah! I know that is true and that it comes from Allaah. I only wondered that if I would find a man on top of my wife, I could not disturb him until I have brought four witnesses. By the time I bring them, he would have finished his business".

After a short time, Hilaal ibn Umayyah went to the Prophet [peace and blessings of Allaah be upon him]. He had been on his farm before going home at night. He found a man with his wife. He saw things with his own eyes and he heard things with his ears. He did not fight with the man, but the next morning, he told the Prophet [peace and blessings of Allaah be upon him]: "O Messenger of Allaah! I went home last night and I found my wife with a man. I saw and heard things with my own eyes and ears". The Prophet [peace and blessings of Allaah be upon him] was very displeased when he heard this and found it hard to deal with. The Ansaar said: "What Sa'd ibn 'Ubaadah foretold has come to pass. The Prophet [peace and blessings of Allaah be upon him] must now subject Hilaal ibn Umayyah to punishment by flogging and declare him unacceptable as a witness". Hilaal said to his people: "By Allaah, I certainly hope that He will provide a way out for me". Addressing the Prophet [peace and blessings of Allaah be upon him], he said: "O Messenger of Allaah! I see that my story has been very difficult for you but Allaah knows that I am telling the truth".

The Prophet [peace and blessings of Allaah be upon him] was about to command that punishment should be inflicted on Hilaal when he received the divine revelation. Those who were around him recognized this fact by the change in his face. These verses dealing with the situation were revealed. The Prophet's face regained its color, and he said: "O Hilaal! Rejoice, for Allaah has given you a way out". Hilaal replied: "I certainly hoped that Allaah would grant me that". The Prophet [peace and blessings of Allaah be upon him] commanded that the woman be brought to him. When she came, the Prophet [peace and blessings of Allaah be upon him] recited these Quraanic verses to them both, reminding them both that punishment in the hereafter is far more severe than any punishment in this life. Hilaal said: "O Messenger of Allaah! I have certainly told the truth when I accused her". She said: "He is lying".

The Prophet [peace and blessings of Allaah be upon him] then said: "Let them both take their oaths (of Mulaa'anah)". Hilaal was the first who have been told to swear. He swore by Allaah four times that what he said was the truth. Before saying his fifth oath, people said to him: "O Hilaal! Fear Allaah! This is the one that incurs upon you punishment in the hereafter, while punishment in this world is that much less". He said: "By Allaah! He will not punish me for this, just like He did not let me be flogged for it". He made the fifth oath, invoking Allaah's curse on himself if he were lying. The woman was then offered the chance to refute the charge. She swore by Allaah four times that he was lying. When she was about to make her fifth oath, people said to her: "Fear Allaah and remember that punishment in the hereafter is much more severe. This is the oath that incurs Allaah's punishment upon you". She stopped for a while and thought about confession. She then said: "I will not bring shame on my people". She made her fifth oath, invoking Allaah's curse on herself if her husband was telling the truth.

The Prophet [peace and blessings of Allaah be upon him] ordered that their marriage irrevocably be terminated. He also judged that her child, should she be pregnant, would not be named after a father, and that the child would not be shamed. If anyone was to hurl an accusation at the child, then that person would be punished. His judgment also made it clear that she could not claim shelter in her husband's home, and she could not have any maintenance from him, as the marriage was dissolved without divorce or death. He also said: "If her child, when born, has slightly reddish hair, a thin bottom and small legs, then he is Hilaal's child. If he is born dark, with strong features and curly hair, of large body, with large legs and a fat bottom, then he belongs to the man she has been accused of having sex with". When the child was born, he was of the second description. The Prophet [peace and blessings of Allaah be upon him] said: "Were it not for the oaths, I would have had something to sort out with her". [Ahmad]

A narration on the authority of Sahl Ibn Sa'd [may Allaah be pleased with him] that he said: 'Uwaymir came to 'AAsim Ibn 'Adiyy who was the chief of Banu 'Ajlaan and said: "What do you say about a man who has found another man with his wife? Should he kill him whereupon you would kill him (that is the husband), or what should he do? Please ask the Prophet [peace and blessings of Allaah be upon him] about this matter on my behalf." 'AAsim then went to The Prophet [peace and blessings of Allaah be upon him] and said: "O Messenger of Allaah!" (And he asked him that question) but the Prophet [peace and blessings of Allaah be upon him] disliked the question. When 'Uwaymir asked 'Asim (about The Prophet's answer) 'AAsim replied that the Prophet [peace and blessings of Allaah be upon him] disliked such questions and considered it shameful. 'Uwaymir then said: "By Allaah, I will not give up asking unless I ask the Prophet [peace and blessings of Allaah be upon him] about it."

'Uwaymir came (to The Prophet [peace and blessings of Allaah be upon him]) and said: "O Messenger of Allaah! A man has found another man with his wife! Should he kill him whereupon you would kill him (the husband, in Qisaas) or what should he do?" The Prophet [peace and blessings of Allaah be upon him] said: "Allaah has revealed regarding you and your wife's case in the Quraan," (referring to the Quraanic Ayaah in issue). So the Prophet [peace and blessings of Allaah be upon him] ordered them to perform the measures of Mulaa'anah according to what Allaah had mentioned in His Book. 'Uwaymir did Mulaa'anah with her and said: "O Messenger of Allaah! If I kept her I would oppress her." So 'Uwaymir divorced her and so divorce became a tradition after them for those who happened to be involved in a case of Mulaa anah. The Prophet [peace and blessings of Allaah be upon him] then said: "Look! If she ('Uwaymir's wife) delivers a black child with deep black large eyes, big hips and fat legs, then I will be of the opinion that 'Uwaymir has spoken the truth; but if she delivers a red child looking like a Wahrah then we will consider that 'Uwaymir has told a lie against her." Later on she delivered a child carrying the qualities which the Prophet [peace and blessings of Allaah be upon him] had mentioned as a proof for 'Uwaymir's claim; therefore the child was ascribed to its mother henceforth. [Al-Bukhaari]

Verse Number 11-21

11- Verily! Those who brought forth the slander are a group among you (O believers (al-Mumineen)). Consider it not a bad thing for you. Nay, it is good for you. Unto every man among them will be paid (the evil of) that which he had earned of the sin, and as for the one among them who took upon himself the greater share thereof, his will be a severe torment. 12- Why then did not the believers (al-Mumineen), men and women, when you heard it (the slander) have good assumption of one another and say: "This (charge) is an obvious lie?" 13- Why did they (who faked that slander) not produce four witnesses (to support their allegation)? Since they (the slanderers) have not produced witnesses, then in the Sight of Allaah they are the liars. 14- Had it not been for the Grace of Allaah and His Mercy unto you in this world and in the Hereafter, a great torment would have touched you (O slanderers, in the hereafter) for that whereof you had spoken. 15- When you were propagating it with your tongues (transmitting it from one to another), and uttering with your mouths that whereof you had no knowledge, you considered it insignificant (in sin), while it was, in the Sight of Allaah, very tremendous (in sin). 16- And why did you not, when you heard it, say? "It is not fit for us to speak of this. Exalted be You (O Allaah)! This is a great lie." 17- Allaah forbids you from it and warns you not to repeat the like of it forever, if you are indeed believers (al-Mumineen) (and worthy of instruction). 18- And Allaah clarifies the signs to you (in His command and forbiddance), and Allaah is All-Knowin Full of Wisdom (in all He does). 19- Verily, those (that is the slanderers) who like that immorality should be widespread among those who believe, they will have a painful torment in this world (with the corporal punishment prescribed for launching a false charge against chaste women) and in the Hereafter (with the fire of Hell since that is the right of Allaah). And Allaah knows (that the believers (al-Mumineen) are free from such immorality) and you (O slanderers, by what you have falsely alleged) know not. 20- And had it not been for the Grace of Allaah and His Mercy on you (O slanderers), and that Allaah is full of kindness, Most Merciful (Allaah would have hastened on the punishment for you). 21- O you who believe! Follow not the footsteps of Satan (therewith he makes alluring to you the evil things). And whosoever follows the footsteps of Satan, then, (it should be known to you that) verily he (Satan) enjoins immorality and evildoing. And had it not been for the Grace of Allaah and His Mercy on you (O slanderers), none of you would ever have been purified (from that sin by repentance). But Allaah purifies (from sin and accepts repentance from) whom He wills, and Allaah is All-Hearing (of what you have said), All-Knowing (of your intention).

A narration on the authority of 'AA'ishah [Allaah be pleased with her] that she said: henever the Messenger Allaah [peace and blessings of Allaah be upon him] intended to set out on a journey, he would draw lots amongst his wives and would take with him the one upon whom the lot fell. In the battle of Banu Al-Mustaliq, he drew lots amongst us as was his use and the lot fell upon me, and I set out with the Prophet [peace and blessings of Allaah be upon him] (after Allaah Had Imposed Hijaab on women). At that time, women were light in weight, thin and lean and did not use to eat much.

Whenever my camel was ready I then would sit in my howdah and the people assigned to prepare it would come to carry me and lift the howdah from underneath and then place it on the back of the camel and tie it with the ropes and then take hold of the camel's head and drive it.

She added: When the Prophet [peace and blessings of Allaah be upon him] finished his battle and started his journey back home, when we approached Madeenah, he descended at a particular station and stayed there for a part of the night. the Prophet [peace and blessings of Allaah be upon him] then ordered us to proceed on. When that order was given, I walked until I was past the army to answer the call of nature. I had a necklace made of Azfaar which was surreptitiously lost. After finishing, I returned (to the camp) to depart (with the others) and suddenly realized that my necklace was missing. So, I returned to look for it and delayed because of that. The people who used to carry me on the camel came to my howdah and put it on the back of the camel, thinking that I was in it. They did not feel the difference in the weight of the howdah while lifting it, and they put it over the camel.

At that time I was a young lady. They set the camel moving and proceeded on. I found my necklace after the army had gone, and came to their camp to find nobody. So, I went to the place where I used to stay, thinking that they would discover my absence and come back searching for me. I covered myself with my gown and while in that state, I felt asleep and lay down. Safwaan Ibn Al-Mu'attal As-Sulami Adh-Dhakwaani, who delayed for some of his needs and did not spend the night with the army, came upon me. When he saw a sleeping person, he came to me and he used to see me before wearing Hijaab. So, I got up when I heard him saying: "Indeed we belong to Allaah, and indeed to Him we will return. Ah! The wife of the Prophet [peace and blessings of Allaah be upon him]! What has delayed you may Allaah bestow mercy upon you?" I was covering my face with my gown and gave no reply to him even with a single word. He got down from his camel, and put his leg on the front legs of the camel and then I rode and sat over it. Safwaan set out walking, leading the camel by the nose string as quickly as he could to join the people and by Allaah it was not before morning that we reached the army and none felt I was absent, and the people had been halting to take rest when the man appeared driving the camel with me. Then some people slandered me falsely which spread among the men and I did not know anything about it.

After that we returned to Madeenah, I became ill for one month, while the people were spreading the forged statements of the false accusers and I did not know anything about that, neither the Prophet [peace and blessings of Allaah be upon him] nor my parents made a mention of that to me. I only felt, during my ailment, that I did not receive the usual kindness from the Prophet [peace and blessings of Allaah be upon him] which I used to receive from him. It was his habit, before that, that whenever I felt ill, he would be kind and merciful to me. But in this ailment of mine, he did not do the same, which I did not hold with. whenever he entered upon me and my mother (Umm Roomaan: Zaynab Bint 'Abd Duhmaan) was with me to look after me he would say: "How is that (girl)?" and he would not say anything more.

Having perceived his apathy, I felt it and told him: "O Messenger of Allaah! Would you please give me leave to go to be nursed in the house of my mother?" He replied: "You could go". I then left for the house of my mother and did not know anything about what was going on until I recovered from my ailment after over twenty nights.

We, Arabs, had not yet taken near our houses lavatories taken by the foreigners: on the contrary, we used to dislike them; and we rather used to go to the far open spaces of Madeenah (to answer the call of nature). We, women, used to go out only from night to night to answer the call of nature. I went out with Umm Mistaah Bint Ruhm Ibn Al-Muttalib Ibn 'Abd Manaaf, whose mother was the daughter of Sakhr Ibn 'AAmir, the maternal aunt of Abu Bakr As-Siddeeq. While walking, Umm Mistaah stumbled because of her long dress and on that she said: "Let Mistaah be ruined!" I said: "What a bad thing that you are saying! How could you say that about a man who took part in (the Battle of) Badr?" She said: "O daughter of Abu Bakr, have you not heard what he said?" I answered in the negative, then she told me the rumors that were spread by the slanderers. I asked: "Has this really taken place?" she answered in the affirmative.

She added: By Allaah, I had no sooner heard that than I was hardly able to answer the call of nature. I returned home and went on weeping till I thought this would damage my liver. I asked my mother: "May Allaah forgive for you O mother! How do people say about me these things and you do not tell me about it?" She said: "O my daughter! Do not worry much about this matter. By Allaah, never is there a charming woman loved by her husband who has co-wives, but the women would forge false news about her".

She added: On that day which I did not know anything about it, the Prophet [peace and blessings of Allaah be upon him] ascended the pulpit and addressed the people saying: "O company of the Muslims, what is the matter with some men ('including Abdullaah Ibn Ubayy Ibn Salool) who have hurt me by slandering my family? By Allaah, I know nothing about my family but good, they have also accused a person (Safwaan Ibn Al-Mu'attal) about whom I know nothing but good and he has never entered my house but in my company".

She added: those who took the lead of spreading this untrue speech were 'Abdullaah Ibn Ubayy Ibn Salool, along with men from among the Khazraj, Mistaah and Hamnah Bint Jahsh. Her sister Zaynab Bint Jahsh was one of the wives of the Prophet [peace and blessings of Allaah be upon him], but none among his wives was competing with me in beauty and love of the Prophet [peace and blessings of Allaah be upon him] more than her. Yet Allaah Protected her (from destruction) for she had piety and said nothing except good. Her sister Hamnah Bint Jahsh started to spread such false slanders in order to struggle me on behalf of her sister, by which she was miserable.

Usayd Ibn Hudayr got up and said: "O Messenger of Allaah! By Allaah, I will relieve you of them. If they are from the Aws, then we will suffice you against them; and if they are from our brothers, the Khazraj, then order us, and we will fulfill your order: by Allaah, they are entitled to have their heads chopped off". On that, Sa'd Ibn 'Ubaadah, the chief of the Khazraj who, before this incident, was a pious man, got up, motivated by his bigotry for his tribe, and said: "By Allaah, you have told a lie; you cannot kill them and you will never be able to kill them. By Allaah, you have only said this because you know that they are from the Khazraj; but had they been from your people, you would not have said it". Usayd said: "You have told a lie! But by Allaah, you are a hypocrite and arguing on behalf of the hypocrites (al-Munaafiqeen)". On this, the two tribes of Aws and Khazraj got excited and were about to fight each other while the Prophet [peace and blessings of Allaah be upon him] was standing on the pulpit. He got down and pacified them until they became silent and he kept quiet. Then, the Prophet [peace and blessings of Allaah be upon him] left and entered upon me.

She added: the Prophet [peace and blessings of Allaah be upon him] called 'Ali Ibn Abu Taalib and Usaamah Ibn Zayd [Allaah be pleased with them] to consult them about the matter. Usaamah Ibn Zayd appreciated me and said nothing but good about me, and added: "O Messenger of Allaah! Keep your wife, for what is said is nothing but falsehood, and by Allaah, we know nothing about her but good". 'Ali Ibn Abu Taalib said: "O Messenger of Allaah! Allaah Has not Imposed restrictions on you (concerning marriage), and there are a lot of women and you are able to take wives other than her. Nevertheless, you may ask the female servant who will tell you the truth". On that, the Prophet [peace and blessings of Allaah be upon him] invited Bareerah to ask her. 'Ali Ibn Abu Taalib stood towards her and beat her severely and said: "Tell the Prophet [peace and blessings of Allaah be upon him] the truth". She said: "By Allaah, I know about her nothing but good. I have never seen in 'AA'ishah any fault except that whenever I made the dough and asked her to take care of it, she (being a girl of immature age) would sometimes sleep and leave the dough for the goat to eat".

She added: the Prophet [peace and blessings of Allaah be upon him] came in and sat with me, and my parents along with a woman from the Ansaar were with me while I was still weeping and she was also weeping because of me. He sat down, praised Allaah Almighty (the Most High) and lauded Him and then said: "O 'AA'ishah! Of course the news has reached you about what the people are saying. So, fear Allaah, and if you committed such a sin as about which the people are talking, then repent to Allaah and ask Him to Forgive you, for Allaah Accepts the repentance of those among His servants who repent to Him".

When the Prophet [peace and blessings of Allaah be upon him] finished his speech my tears ceased completely and there remained not even a single drop. I expected my parents to answer the Prophet [peace and blessings of Allaah be upon him] on my behalf, but they said nothing. By Allaah, I never thought that Allaah Would Reveal in my case Quraan to be recited and people pray with in the mosques, as I considered myself too insignificant to be mentioned in the Quraan. I only hoped that the Prophet [peace and blessings of Allaah be upon him] would have a vision in which Allaah Would belie the falsehood he knew about me, and rather Prove my innocence; or that he would receive a news about my innocence. But by Allaah, that a Quraan would be revealed in my connection, I thought myself more insignificant than this.

She added: I told my parents: "Would you not answer the Prophet [peace and blessings of Allaah be upon him] on my behalf?" They replied: "By Allaah, we do not know what to say to the Prophet [peace and blessings of Allaah be upon him]". By Allaah, I did not know a family exposed to a trial more severe than that to which the family of Abu Bakr was exposed at that time. When they gave no reply, I went on weeping. Then I said: "By Allaah, I never repent to Allaah from what you are saying. By Allaah, if I confessed to you falsely what the people are saying, and Allaah Knows that I am innocent, I would then attribute to myself something false but if I denied what they are saying, you would not believe me". I then sought the name of Jacob and did not remember it thereupon I said: "But I will say the same as the father of Joseph had previously said (what means): {So (for me) patience is most fitting against that which you assert and it is Allaah (Alone) whose help can be sought}. [Yoosuf, verse 18]

She added: By Allaah, the Prophet [peace and blessings of Allaah be upon him] had not left his sitting place before the revelation came to him. So, there overtook him the same state which used to overtake him (whenever he received revelation), thereupon he was covered with his garment and a cushion of leather was placed underneath his head. Seeing that, by Allaah, I neither got scared nor gave care, since I knew that I was innocent and that Allaah Almighty (the Most High) would never deal with me unjustly. As for my parents, by Him in Whose Hand is the soul of 'AA'ishah, before the state of the Prophet [peace and blessings of Allaah be upon him] was over, they remained so much terrified that I thought they would die for fear that Allaah Almighty (the Most High) would reveal the confirmation of what the people were saying.

She added: Then, the state of the Prophet [peace and blessings of Allaah be upon him] was over and he sat down and was sweating so much that perspiration was dropping like pearls though it was a (cold) wintry day. He started to wipe the sweat off is forehead and said: "O 'AA'ishah! Rejoice because Allaah Has revealed (what proves) your innocence". I said: "That is only by praise of Allaah".

She added: Then he came out to the people and addressed them, and recited to them what Allaah had revealed of the Quraan in this respect. He ordered that Mistaah Ibn Uthaathah, Hassaan Ibn Thaabit and Hamnah Bint Jahsh, who talked explicitly about the immorality, should receive the legal punishment (prescribed for the crime of launching a false charge of adultery against the innocent). On that occasion, Allaah revealed those Quraanic Aayaat [11-21] [Al-Bukhaari; Muslim and others]

Verse Number 22

22- And let not those among you who are endued with grace and wealth swear not to give (any sort of help) to their poor kinsmen, and those who left their homes for Allaah's Cause. Let them pardon and forgive. Do you not love that Allaah should forgive you? And Allaah is Oft-Forgiving, Most Merciful (towards the believers (al-Mumineen)).

A narration on the authority of 'AA'ishah [Allaah be pleased with her], that she said: When Allaah revealed the declaration of my innocence, Abu Bakr, who used to provide for Mistaah Ibn Uthaathah, a poor relative of his, said: "By Allaah, I will never provide for Mistaah because of what he said about 'AA'ishah". But Allaah later revealed (what means): {And let not those among you who are endued with grace and wealth swear not to give (any sort of help) to their poor kinsmen...} On that Abu Bakr said: "Yes! By Allaah! I like that Allaah should forgive me", and resumed helping Mistaah, whom he used to help before and said: "By Allaah, I will never withhold it from him". [Al-Bukhaari; Muslim and others]

Verse Number 23

23- Verily, as for those who accuse (of illegal sexual intercourse) chaste indiscreet believing women, they are cursed in this life and in the Hereafter, and for them will be a severe torment.

A narration on the authority of Ad-Dahhaak Ibn Muzaahim that he said: This Quraanic Ayaah was revealed in connection with the wives of the Prophet [peace and blessings of Allaah be upon him] in particular. [At-Tabaraani]

A narration on the authority of Ibn 'Abbaas [Allaah be pleased with them] that this Quraanic Ayaah was revealed in connection with 'AA'ishah in particular. [Ibn Abu Haatim]

A narration on the authority of 'AA'ishah [Allaah be pleased with her] that she said: I was accused of this false slander, and I was indiscreet; later on I received the news thereof. While the Prophet [peace and blessings of Allaah be upon him] was in my house he was divinely revealed thereupon he sat upright and wiped the sweat off his face and said: "O 'AA'ishah! Receive the glad tidings (of your innocence)!" I said: "Praise be to Allaah and not to you". Then he recited this Quraanic Ayaah up to Allaah's saying (what means): {such (good people) are declared innocent of (every) bad word which they (the evil men and women) say (about them); for them (the good) is

Forgiveness and generous provision (in Paradise)}. [verse 26] [Ibn Jareer]

Verse Number 26

26- Bad words are fit for bad people (or bad women for bad men) and bad people for bad words (or bad men for bad women). Good words are fit for good people (or good women for good men) and good people for good words (or good men for good women); such (good people) are declared innocent of (every) bad word which they (the evil men and women) say (about them); for them (the good) is Forgiveness and generous provision (in Paradise).

A narration on the authority of 'Abd-Ar-Rahmaan Ibn Zayd Ibn Aslam that he said: Allaah's saying (what means): {Bad words are fit for bad people (or bad women for bad men) and bad people for bad words (or bad men for bad women)...} was revealed in connection with 'AA'ishah [Allaah be pleased with her] when the hypocrites (al-Munaafiqeen) accused her of such fabricated slander. [At-Tabaraani]

A narration on the authority of Al-Hakam Ibn 'Utaybah that he said: When 'AA'ishah [Allaah be pleased with her] was accused of the fabricated invented slander the Prophet [peace and blessings of Allaah be upon him] summoned her and said: "O 'AA'ishah! Tell me about the truth of what the people are saying". She said: "I will give no excuse till my innocence comes from the heaven". Then, Allaah revealed in connection with her fifteen Quraanic

Aayaat [An-Noor 11-26] which the Prophet [peace and blessings of Allaah be upon him] recited. [At-Tabaraani]

Verse Number 27

27- O you who believe! Enter not houses other than your own, until you have asked permission and greeted those in them; that is better for you (than coming in without asking permission), in order that you may remember (and consequently act upon it).

A narration on the authority of 'Adiyy Ibn Thaabit that a woman came to the Prophet [peace and blessings of Allaah be upon him] and said: "O Messenger of Allaah! When I am in my house, I will be in a state in which I do not like that anyone should see me; yet some men of my relatives may enter upon me while I am in such a state. Then, what should I do?" Then, this Quraanic Ayaah was revealed. [Al-Firyaabi and Ibn Jareer]

A narration on the authority of Muqaatil Ibn Hayyaan that when Allaah revealed (what means): {O you who believe! Enter not houses other than your own, until you have asked permission and greeted those in them}, Abu Bakr [may Allaah be pleased with him] said: "O Messenger of Allaah! What about the merchants of Quraysh who always go and return between Makkah, Madeenah and Shaam, and have known houses on the way? Then how should they seek permission and greet since those houses have no dwellers?" On that occasion, Allaah revealed (what means): {There is no sin on you that you enter (even without seeking permission) houses uninhabited (not possessed by anybody) in which you have any interest (like hospices and public places)}. [verse 29] [Ibn Abu Haatim]

Verse Number 31

31- And tell the believing women to lower their gaze (from looking at what is unlawful for them to look at) And protect their private parts (from illegal sexual acts) and not to disclose their adornment except only that which (necessarily) appears thereof and to draw their headcovers all over their chests (in such a way as to screen their heads, necks and breasts) and not to disclose their (hidden) adornment (other than the face and hands) except to their husbands, or their fathers, or their husband's fathers, or their sons, or their husband's sons, or their brothers or their brother's sons, or their sister's sons, or their (Muslim) women (that is their sisters in religion), or the slaves whom their right hands possess, or old male servants who lack vigor, or young children who have no sense of feminine sex. And let them not stamp their feet so as to reveal what they hide of their adornment (like anklets). And repent to Allaah, all of you, O believers (al-Mumineen) (from all sins including such forbidden gazes), that you may be successful.

A narration on the authority of Muqaatil that he said: Jaabir Ibn 'Abdullaah [may Allaah be pleased with him] reported that once Asmaa' Bint Marthad was in a garden of date-palms belonging to her when women visited her and they had no lower garments over their bodies, thereupon their bangles and breasts appeared. She said: "How ugly is this!" On that occasion, Allaah revealed this Quraanic Ayaah. [Ibn Abu Haatim]

A narration on the authority of Hadrami that once a woman put on two bangles of silver and a stem and came upon some people and struck the ground with her feet. Then the bangle fell on the stem and clattered. On that occasion, Allaah revealed this Quraanic Ayaah. [Ibn Jareer]

Verse Number 33

33- And let those who cannot afford for marriage keep themselves chaste, until Allaah enriches them of His Bounty. And such of your slaves (be they male or female) as seek a writing (of emancipation), give them such writing, if you find that there is good in them. And (as masters) give them something yourselves out of the wealth of Allaah which He has bestowed upon you. And force not your maids (female-slaves) to prostitution, if they desire chastity, in order that you may gain a worldly benefit in this life. But if anyone compels them (to prostitution), then after such compulsion, Allaah is Oft-Forgiving, Most Merciful (to those women because they have been forced to such prostitution unwillingly).

A narration on the authority of 'Abdullaah Ibn Subayh from his father that he said: I was a slave belonging to Huwaytib Ibn 'Abdul-'Uzza whom I asked for a written deed of freedom in return for a sum of money, thereupon Allaah Almighty (the Most High) revealed (what means): {And such of your slaves (be they male or female) as seek a writing (of emancipation), give them such writing, if you find that there is good in them}. [Ibn As-Sakan in Ma'rifat As-Sahaabah]

A narration on the authority of Jaabir Ibn 'Abdullaah [Allaah be pleased with them] that 'Abdullaah Ibn Ubayy Ibn Salool told a female slave belonging to him: "Go and seek something for us (from prostitution)". On that occasion, Allaah revealed (what means): {And force not your maids (female-slaves) to prostitution, if they desire chastity, in order that you may gain a worldly benefit in this life}. [Muslim]

It is narrated on the same authority that 'Abdullaah Ibn Ubayy had two female slaves: Musaykah and Umaymah whom he compelled to commit illegal sexual intercourse. They made a complaint of that to the Prophet [peace and blessings of Allaah be upon him], thereupon Allaah revealed (what means): {And force not your maids (female-slaves) to prostitution, if they desire chastity, in order that you may gain a worldly benefit in this life}. [Muslim]

A narration on the authority of Jaabir [may Allaah be pleased with him] that he said: Musaykah belonged to one of the Ansaar and she said: "My master compels me to prostitution". On that occasion, Allaah revealed (what means): {And force not your maids (female-slaves) to prostitution, if they desire chastity, in order that you may gain a worldly benefit in this life}. [Al-Haakim]

A narration on the authority of Ibn 'Abbaas [Allaah be pleased with them] that he said: 'Abdullaah Ibn Ubayy had a female slave who used to commit illegal sexual intercourse in the pre-Islamic days. When Islam forbade adultery she said: "No, by Allaah, I will never commit illegal sexual intercourse". On that occasion, Allaah Almighty (the Most High) revealed (what means): {And force not your maids (female-slaves) to prostitution, if they desire chastity, in order that you may gain a worldly benefit in this life}. [Al-Bazzaar and At-Tabaraani]

A narration on the authority of 'Ikrimah that he said: 'Abdullaah Ibn Ubayy had two female slaves: Musaykah and Mu'aadhah whom he used to compel to prostitution. One of them said: "If it is good, then I have done it so much; but if it is otherwise, then I am not in need of it". On that occasion, Allaah revealed (what means): {And force not your maids (female-slaves) to prostitution, if they desire chastity, in order that you may gain a worldly benefit in this life}. [Sa'eed Ibn Mansoor]

Verse Number 48

48- And when they are called to Allaah and His Messenger to judge between them, behold! A party of them refuse (to come) and turn away.

A narration on the authority of Al-Hasan that he said: The habit was, if there was a dispute between two men and one of them was summoned to the Prophet [peace and blessings of Allaah be upon him] for judgment, and he was right, he would submit because he was sure that the Prophet [peace and blessings of Allaah be upon him] would give a judgment in his favor; and if he had the intention to be unjust to his opponent and he was summoned to the Prophet [peace and blessings of Allaah be upon him], he would not accept and would rather say: "Let us go to so and so". On that occasion, Allaah revealed this Quraanic Ayaah. [Ibn Abu Haatim]

Verse Number 55

55- Allaah has promised those among you who believe and do righteous deeds, that He will certainly make them successors (of the disbelievers (al-Kaafireen)) on earth, as He made those before them, and that He will establish in authority for them their religion (of Islam) which He has approved for them. And He will surely grant them safety in substitute for their fear (of the disbelievers (al-Kaafireen)). (That is because) they worship Me and do not associate partners with Me. But whoever disbelieve after this (favor), they are the rebellious disobedient.

A narration on the authority of Ubayy Ibn Ka'b [may Allaah be pleased with him] that he said: When the Prophet [peace and blessings of Allaah be upon him] and his Companions came to Madeenah and the Ansaar gave them shelter, all the Arabs gathered against them. The Muslims then used to spend the night till morning clad in arms. They said: "Do you see that we will live till the time we spend the night in safety and fear none except for Allaah?" On that occasion, Allaah revealed this Quraanic Ayaah. [Al-Haakim who renders it Saheeh; and At-Tabaraani]

A narration on the authority of Al-Baraa' [may Allaah be pleased with him] that he said: In connection with us this Quraanic Ayaah was revealed while we were in a state of severe fear. [Ibn Abu Haatim]

Verse Number 61

61- There is no difficulty on the blind, nor any difficulty on the lame, nor any difficulty on the sick (to share food with those opposite to them), nor on yourselves, to eat from your houses (that is the houses of your children), or the houses of your fathers, or the houses of your mothers, or the houses of your brothers, or the houses of your sisters, or the houses of your father's brothers, or the houses of your father's sisters, or the houses of your mother's brothers, or the houses of your mother's sisters, or (from that) whereof you hold keys (to keep in store for others), or (from the house) of a friend. There is no sin on you whether you eat together or apart. But when you enter houses, greet yourselves with a greeting from Allaah blessed and good. Thus Allaah makes clear to you the signs (that is the symbols of your religion) perchance you may have reason (to understand).

A narration on the authority of Mujaahid that he said: They used to go with the blind, the lame and the one who had chronic disease to the house of his father, brother, sister, paternal or maternal aunt. But those disabled felt it difficult upon themselves and said:

"They indeed take us to houses other than theirs". On that occasion, this Quraanic Ayaah was revealed as a concession to them. ['Abd-Ar-Razzaaq]

A narration on the authority of Ibn 'Abbaas [Allaah be pleased with them] that he said: When Allaah revealed (what means): {O you who believe, do not consume one another's wealth unjustly but only (in lawful) business by mutual consent}, [An-Nisaa', verse 29] the people felt it difficult and said: "No doubt, the food is among the best and most lawful of the property. So it is unlawful for anyone of us to eat in the house of another". They then refrained from this. On that occasion, Allaah revealed (what means): {There is no difficulty on the blind ... or (from that) whereof you hold keys (to keep in store for others)}. [Ibn Jareer]

A narration on the authority of Ad-Dahhaak that he said: Before the Prophet [peace and blessings of Allaah be upon him] was sent as a Prophet, the men of Madeenah did not have the blind, the lame and the sick share food with them, because the blind did not see the good kinds of food, the sick did not eat his fill like the sound and the lame could not crowd on food like others. Then, this Quraanic Ayaah was revealed as a concession to share food with them. [Ibn Jareer]

A narration on the authority of Muqassam that he said: They avoided sharing food with the blind, the lame and the sick thereupon this Quraanic Ayaah was revealed. [Ibn Jareer]

A narration on the authority of Ibn 'Abbaas [Allaah be pleased with them] that he said: Once, Al-Haarith set out in a military expedition with the Prophet [peace and blessings of Allaah be upon him] and left Khaalid Ibn Zayd to take care of his family on behalf of him. But since he was sick he felt it difficult to eat of his food. On that occasion, Allaah revealed this Quraanic Ayaah. [Ath-Tha'labi in his Tafseer]

A narration on the authority of 'AA'ishah [Allaah be pleased with her] that she said: The Muslims liked to go forth along with the Prophet [peace and blessings of Allaah be upon him] and give the keys of their houses to the sick among them and say to them: "We have made it lawful for you to eat of what you like". But they would say: "That is unlawful for us since they have given us permission against their will". On that occasion, Allaah revealed (what means): {There is no difficulty on the blind ... or (from that) whereof you hold keys (to keep in store for others}. [Al-Bazzaar]

A narration on the authority of Az-Zuhri that he was asked about Allaah's saying (what means): {There is no difficulty on the blind, nor any difficulty on the lame, nor any difficulty on the sick (to share food with those opposite to them)...}: "Why are those only mentioned here?"

He replied: "I was reported by 'Abdullaah Ibn 'Abdullaah that whenever the Companions set out for fighting, they would give the keys of their houses to the sick among them and make lawful for them to eat of what they liked thereof. But those disabled felt difficulty and forbade themselves from entering their houses in their absence. On that occasion, Allaah revealed this Quraanic Ayaah. [Ibn Jareer]

A narration on the authority of Qataadah that he said: Concerning Allaah's saying (what means): {There is no sin on you whether you eat together or apart}, it was the habit of the Arabs that if anyone did not like to eat alone and would rather carry his food with him for even a whole day till he found such as would share food with him. On that occasion, it was revealed. [Ibn Jareer]

A narration on the authority of 'Ikrimah and Abu Saalih that they said: It was the habit of the Ansaar that whenever they received a guest they would not eat till he would share food with them. On that occasion, this was revealed. [Ibn Jareer]

Verse Number 62

62- The true believers (al-Mumineen) are only those, who believe in Allaah and His Messenger, and when they are with him on a matter of common interest (like the Friday Khutbah), they go not away (for a worldly benefit whatsoever) until they have asked his permission. Verily! Those who ask your permission, those are they who (really) believe in Allaah and His Messenger. So if they ask your permission (to go away) for some affairs of theirs, give permission to whom you will of them (to go away), and ask Allaah for their forgiveness. Truly, Allaah is Oft-Forgiving, Most Merciful.

A narration on the authority of 'Urwah, Muhammad Ibn Ka'b Al-Qurathi and others that they said: When the Muslims had completed digging the trench, the Quraysh arrived and camped at a place called al-Asyaal near Rawmah under leadership of Abu Sufyaan. The Ghatfaan and their followers from Najd marched to their camping place of Nu'ma near Uhud. The Prophet [peace and blessings of Allaah be upon him] received the news, thereupon He commanded that a trench be dug round Madeenah, in which he worked along with the Muslims. But some hypocrites (al-Munaafiqeen) were heavy and slow and did only the trivial acts, and then went stealthily to their homes without knowledge or permission of the Prophet [peace and blessings of Allaah be upon him]. Whenever anyone of the Muslims had to leave for a dire need, he would make a mention of that to the Prophet [peace and blessings of Allaah be upon him], and seek his permission to go to fulfill his need. He then would give him permission and once this man fulfilled his need he would return. In connection with those believers (al-Mumineen), Allaah revealed this Quraanic Ayaah. [Ibn Ishaaq and Al-Bayhaqi in Ad-Dalaa'il]

Verse Number 63

63- Make not the calling of the Messenger among you as your calling of one another. Verily, Allaah knows those of you who slip away (from the masjid during the Friday Khutbah) hiding themselves by others (without seeking permission from the Prophet to leave). And let those who violate the command (of Allaah and His Messenger) beware, lest a trial would befall them (in this world) or a painful torment afflict them (in the hereafter).

A narration on the authority of Ibn 'Abbaas [Allaah be pleased with them] that he said: They used to call the Prophet [peace and blessings of Allaah be upon him]: "O Muhammad! O Abu Al-Qaasim!" On that occasion, Allaah revealed this Quraanic Ayaah, thereupon they called him: "O Prophet of Allaah! O Messenger of Allaah!" [Abu Na'eem in Ad-Dalaa'il]

Soorah Al-Furqaan

Verse Number 10

10- Blessed be He Who, if He wills, will give you better than (all) that (they have previously mentioned) - Gardens under which rivers flow, and will grant you palaces (in Paradise).

A narration on the authority of Khaythamah that he said: It was said to the Prophet [peace and blessings of Allaah be upon him]: "If you so like, We shall give you the land's treasures and keys, and this would reduce naught from your reward with Us in the hereafter; and if you so like I shall gather them for you in the hereafter".

He said: "No, I like You to gather them for me in the hereafter". On that occasion, Allaah revealed this Quraanic Ayaah. [Ibn Abu Shaybah in Al-Musannaf; Ibn Jareer and Ibn Abu Haatim]

Verse Number 20

20- And We never sent before you (O Muhammad) any of the Messengers but that they ate food and walked in the markets (like you). And We have made some of you as a trial for others: will you have patience (on what you hear from those by whom you are tried)? And ever is your Lord (Rabb) All-Seer (of those among you who keep patient and those among you who are impatient).

A narration on the authority of Ibn 'Abbaas [Allaah be pleased with them] that he said: The polytheists put shame on the Prophet [peace and blessings of Allaah be upon him] because of his poverty saying (what means): {"What is this messenger that eats food and walks in the markets? Why was there not sent down to him an angel so he would be with him a warner?"} [verse 7] On that occasion, Allaah revealed this Quraanic Ayaah. [Al-Waahidi]

A similar Hadeeth is narrated on the same authority. [Ibn Jareer]

Verse Number 27

27- And (remember) the Day (of Resurrection) when the wrongdoer (polytheist) will bite at his hands (in grief and regret), saying: "Oh! Would that I had taken a path (to guidance) with the Messenger (Muhammad)!"

A narration on the authority of Ibn 'Abbaas [Allaah be pleased with them] that Ubayy Ibn Khalaf used to visit the Prophet [peace and blessings of Allaah be upon him], but 'Uqbah Ibn Abu Mu'ayt would deter him to do so.

On that occasion, Allaah revealed Quraanic Aayaat up to: {And ever is Satan, to man, a deserter."} [verse 27-29] [Ibn Jareer] The same is narrated on the authority of Ash-Sha'bi and Muqassam

A narration on the authority of Ibn 'Abbaas [Allaah be pleased with them] that he said:

The polytheists said: "If Muhammad is a Prophet as he claims, then why does his Lord (Rabb) trouble him as such? Why does he not send him the Book all at once instead of revealing to him little by little?"

On that occasion, Allaah revealed this Quraanic Ayaah. [Ibn Abu Haatim; Al-Haakim who renders it authentic and Ad-Diyaa in Al-Mukhtaarah] Verse Number 68-70

68- And those who invoke not any other god along with Allaah, nor kill the soul which Allaah has forbidden (to be killed) except for just cause, nor commit illegal sexual intercourse - and whoever does (any of) those shall receive penalty. 69- The torment will be doubled to him on the Day of Resurrection, and therein he will abide forever in ignominy; 70- Except those (among them) who repent and believe (in Allaah), and do righteous deeds: for those, Allaah will change their sins (previously mentioned) into good deeds (in the hereafter), and Allaah is Oft-Forgiving, Most Merciful.

A narration on the authority of 'Abdullaah Ibn Mas'ood [may Allaah be pleased with him] that he said: I asked the Prophet [peace and blessings of Allaah be upon him]: "What is the greatest sin in the Sight of Allaah?" He said: "That you set up a rival unto Allaah though He Alone created you."

I said: "That is indeed a great sin."

Then I asked: "What is next?"

He said: "To kill your son lest he should share your food with you."

I asked: "What is next?" He said: "To commit illegal sexual intercourse with the wife of your neighbor." [Al-Bukhaari and Muslim] A narration on the authority of Ibn 'Abbaas [Allaah be pleased with them] that he said: Some polytheists killed so many people illegally and committed adultery so much before they came to the Prophet [peace and blessings of Allaah be upon him], and said: "No doubt, that which you are saying (concerning Islam) is good (and we are ready to believe) if only you tell us that there is expiation for what we have done".

On that occasion, Allaah revealed these Quraanic Aayaat, in addition to Allaah's saying (what means): {Say: "O My servants who have transgressed against themselves (by sinning), do not despair of the mercy of Allaah. Indeed, Allaah forgives all sins. Indeed, it is He who is the Forgiving, the Merciful."} [Az-Zumar, verse 53] [Al-Bukhaari and Muslim]

A narration on the authority of Ibn 'Abbaas [Allaah be pleased with them] that he said: When Allaah revealed (what means): {And those who invoke not any other god along with Allaah, nor kill the soul which Allaah has forbidden (to be killed) except for just cause, nor commit illegal sexual intercourse and whoever does (any of) those shall receive penalty}, [verse 68] the polytheists of Makkah said: "No doubt, we invoked other deities with Allaah, unlawfully killed the soul which Allaah has forbidden and committed illegal sexual intercourse". -

Then Allaah revealed (what means): {Except those (among them) who repent and believe (in Allaah), and do righteous deeds: for those, Allaah will change their sins (previously mentioned) into good deeds (in the hereafter), and Allaah is Oft-Forgiving, Most Merciful}. [verse 70] [Al-Bukhaari and others]

Soorah Ash-Shu'araa'

Verse Number 205-207

205- Tell Me (even) if We do let them enjoy for years, 206- And afterwards comes to them that (punishment) which they had been promised, 207- All that with which they used to enjoy shall not avail them (in the least in removing or even alleviating the punishment from them).

A narration on the authority of Abu Jahdam that he said: Once, the Prophet [peace and blessings of Allaah be upon him] seemed in confusion, when he was asked about that, he said: "Why not since my enemy to come after my death would be from my ummah?" On that occasion, Allaah revealed these Quraanic Aayaat. [Ibn Abu Haatim]

Verse Number 214-215

214- And warn (O Muhammad) your tribe of nearest kindred. 215- And lower your wing (that is be kind and humble) to the believers (al-Mumineen) who closely follow you.

A narration on the authority of Ibn Jurayj that he said: When Allaah revealed (what means): {And warn (O Muhammad) your tribe of nearest kindred}, [214] the Prophet [peace and blessings of Allaah be upon him] began with his relatives and near clansmen, thereupon the Muslims felt it difficult upon themselves. On that

"

occasion, Allaah revealed (what means): {And lower your wing (that is be kind and humble) to the believers (al-Mumineen) who closely follow you}. [verse 215] [Ibn Jarir]

Verse Number 224-227

224- As for the poets, it is the deviators who follow them, 225Do you not see that they wander about distracted in every valley (that is art of poetry)? 226- And that they say what they do not do (that is they lie). 227- Except those (of poets) who believe (in Allaah), and do righteous deeds, and remember Allaah more often, and vindicate themselves (and the Muslims by lampooning the disbelievers (al-Kaafireen) with their poetry) after they have been wronged (by the disbelieving poets' lampooning the Muslims). And those who do wrong (from among the poets and others) will come to know what final place of turning they shall turn back (after death).

A narration on the authority of Ibn 'Abbaas [Allaah be pleased with them] that he said: During the era of the Prophet [peace and blessings of Allaah be upon him], two men lampooned each other, one from the Ansaar and the other from other people; and with each there were deceivers from among his people, and they were the fools. On that occasion, Allaah revealed those Quraanic Aayaat. [Ibn Abu Haatim and Ibn Jareer]

A narration on the authority of 'Urwah that when Allaah revealed (what means): {As for the poets, it is the deviators who follow them... And that they say what they do not do}, [verse 224-226] 'Abdullaah Ibn Rawaahah said: "Allaah knows that I am one of them". On that occasion, Allaah revealed (what means): {except those (of poets) who believe (in Allaah), and do righteous deeds, and remember Allaah more often, and vindicate themselves...} [verse 227] [Ibn Abu Haatim]

A narration on the authority of Abu Hasan Al-Barraad that he said: When Allaah revealed (what means): {As for the poets, it is the deviators who follow them... And that they say what they do not do}, [verse 224-226], 'Abdullaah Ibn Rawaahah, Ka'b Ibn Maalik and Hassaan Ibn Thaabit came to the Prophet [peace and blessings of Allaah be upon him] and said: "O Messenger of Allaah! This revelation was revealed, and Allaah knows that we are poets. We then have been ruined". On that occasion, Allaah revealed (what means): {Except those (of poets) who believe (in Allaah), and do righteous deeds, and remember Allaah more often, and vindicate themselves...} [verse 227], thereupon the Prophet [peace and blessings of Allaah be upon him] summoned them and recited it to them. [Ibn Jareer and Al-Haakim]

Soorah Al-Qasas

Verse Number 51-52

51- And indeed now We have conveyed the Word (this Quraan) to them, perchance they may remember (that is receive admonition and then believe). 52- Those to whom We gave the Scripture (that is the Torah and the Gospel) before it: they believe in it (the Quraan).

A narration on the authority of Rifaa'ah Al-Qurathi that he said: These Quraanic Aayaat were revealed in connection with ten, and I was one of them. [Ibn Jareer and At-Tabaraani]

A narration on the authority of 'Ali Ibn Rifa'ah that he said: Ten from among the people of Scripture including Rifaa'ah, that is his father, came out and went to the Prophet [peace be upon hin and believed thereupon they were harmed severely. In connection with them Allaah Almighty (the Most High) revealed (what means): {Those to whom We gave the Scripture (that is the Torah and the Gospel) before it: they believe in it (the Quraan)}. [verse 52] [Ibn Jareer]

A narration on the authority of Qataadah that he said: We were told that these Quraanic Aayaat were revealed in connection with some belonging to the people of Scripture who were on the truth till the Prophet [peace and blessings of Allaah be upon him] was sent as a Prophet thereupon they believed in him, including 'Uthmaan and 'Abdullaah Ibn Salaam. [Ibn Jareer]

Verse Number 56

56- Verily you (O Muhammad) guide not whom you like (to guide), but Allaah guides whom He wills. And He knows best those who are the (rightly) guided.

A narration on the authority of Abu Hurayrah [may Allaah be pleased with him] that he said: the Prophet [peace and blessings of Allaah be upon him] said to his paternal uncle (Abu Taalib when death approached him): "O uncle! Testify that there is none worthy of worship but Allaah, therewith I shall witness in your favor on the Day of Resurrection".

He said: "O my nephew! Had it not been for the fact that the women of Quraysh would put me to shame, saying that I have said it only for fear of death, I would have said it just to please you". On that occasion, Allaah Almighty (the Most High) revealed this Quraanic Ayaah. [Muslim]

A narration on the authority of Abu Sa'eed Ibn Raafi' that he said: I asked Ibn 'Umar [Allaah be pleased with them] about this Quraanic Ayaah: Was it revealed in connection with Abu Jahl and Abu Taalib (when death approached the later)?" He answered in the affirmative. [An-Nasaa'i and Ibn 'Asaakir in Taareekh Dimashq with a good chain of narrators]

Verse Number 57

57- And they (Muhammad's people) say: "If we follow the guidance with you, we would be snatched away from our land." Have We not established for them a secure sanctuary (Makkah), to which are brought fruits of all kinds, a provision from Ourselves, but most of them know not (that all what We say is the truth).

A narration on the authority of Ibn 'Abbaas [Allaah be pleased with them] that he said: Some people said to the Prophet [peace and blessings of Allaah be upon him]: "If we follow you, the people then would sweep us away (from our land)". On that occasion, this Quraanic Ayaah was revealed. [Ibn Jareer]

A narration on the authority of Ibn 'Abbaas [Allaah be pleased with them] that it was Al-Haarith Ibn 'AAmir Ibn Nawfal who said this statement to the Prophet [peace and blessings of Allaah be upon him]. [An-Nasaa'i]

Verse Number 61

61- Is he (that is the believer) whom We have promised a goodly promise (Paradise), which he will receive (and find true), like him (that is the disbeliever) whom We have made to enjoy (for a while) the (consumable) luxuries of the life of (this) world, then on the Day of Resurrection, he will be among those brought up (to be punished in the Hell-fire)?

A narration on the authority of Mujaahid that he said: This Quraanic Ayaah was revealed in connection with the Prophet [peace and blessings of Allaah be upon him] and Abu Jahl Ibn Hishaam. [Ibn Jareer]

It is narrated on the same authority that it was revealed in connection with Hamzah [may Allaah be pleased with him] and Abu Jahl. [Ibn Jareer]

Verse Number 85

85- Verily, He (that is Allaah) Who has (revealed and) ordained on you (O Muhammad) the Quraan will surely bring you back to the place of return (that is Makkah). Say (O Muhammad to the disbelievers (al-Kaafireen)): "My Lord (Rabb) knows best him who brings guidance, and him who is in manifest error."

A narration on the authority of Ad-Dahhaak that he said: When the Prophet [peace and blessings of Allaah be upon him] left Makkah (for Madeenah) and reached Al-Juhfah, he longed for Makkah, thereupon Allaah Almighty (the Most High) revealed this Quraanic Ayaah. [Ibn Abu Haatim]

Soorah Al-'Ankaboot

Verse Number 1

1- Alif-Laam-Maam.

A narration on the authority of Ash-Sha'bi that he said: Some people in Makkah embraced Islam (and concealed their matter). The Companions of the Prophet [peace and blessings of Allaah be upon him] sent to them that Islam would not be accepted from them till they have emigrated to Madeenah. They then emigrated and on the way were caught and brought back by the polytheists. Then when this Quraanic Ayaah [1-2] was revealed, they sent to them informing them that Allaah had said about them such and such. They said: "Let us come out then and if anyone followed us we would kill him". They came out and were followed by the polytheists with whom they fought and some of them were killed and others saved. In connection with them Allaah Almighty (the Most High) revealed (what means): {Then, indeed your Lord (Rabb), to those who emigrated after they had been compelled (to renounce their religion) and thereafter fought (for the cause of Allaah) and were patient - indeed, your Lord (Rabb), after that, is Forgiving and Merciful}. [An-Nahl, verse 110] [Ibn Abu Haatim]

A narration on the authority of Qataadah that he said: These Quraanic Aayaat [1-2] were revealed in connection with some people in Makkah who came out

"

as emigrants to the Prophet [peace and blessings of Allaah be upon him], thereupon they were caught in the way. When they were revealed, their companions in Madeenah sent to them informing them of what was said about them. Then, they decided to go out and on the way they were caught by the polytheists and there was fighting between them which left some dead and others were saved. Then Allaah Almighty (the Most High) revealed (what means): {And those who strive for Us - We will surely guide them to Our ways. And indeed, Allaah is with the doers of good}. [Al-'Ankaboot, verse 69] [Ibn Abu Haatim]

A narration on the authority of 'Abdullaah Ibn 'Ubayd Ibn 'Umayr that he said: This was revealed in connection with 'Ammaar Ibn Yaasir who was under severe torment. [Ibn Sa'd]

Verse Number 8

8- And We have enjoined on man to be good and dutiful to his parents; but if they strive to make you associate with Me (as partners in worship) anything of which you have no knowledge, then obey them not. Unto Me is your return, and I shall inform you about what you used to do (in order to give you reward according to it).

A narration on the authority of Sa'd Ibn Abu Waqqaas [may Allaah be pleased with him] that he said: The mother of Sa'd told him: "Does not Allaah enjoin dutifulness (to parents)? By Allaah, I will neither eat nor drink till you disbelieve". On that occasion, Allaah

Almighty (the Most High) revealed this Quraanic Ayaah. [Muslim and At-Tirmidhi]

Verse Number 51

51- Is it not sufficient for them (in what they ask for of miracles) that We have sent down to you the Book (the Quraan) which is recited to them? Verily, in this (Book) is mercy and a reminder (or an instruction) for a people who believe.

A narration on the authority of Yahya Ibn Ja'dah that he said: Some Muslims brought books having written things they transmitted from the Yahood to the Prophet [peace and blessings of Allaah be upon him], who said: "It suffices a people for error to turn away from that which their Prophet has brought to them to that which another has brought to others than them". On that occasion, this Quraanic Ayaah was revealed. [Ibn Jareer and Ibn Abu Haatim]

Verse Number 60

60- And how many a moving (living) creature which carries not its own provision (due to its weakness)! Allaah provides for it and for you (O emigrants even when you have no provision nor spending). And He is the All-Hearer (of your words), the All-Knower (of your intentions).

A narration on the authority of Ibn 'Umar [Allaah be pleased with them] that he said: I came out with the Prophet [peace and blessings of Allaah be upon him] till he entered one of the walled gardens in Madeenah and went on picking and eating some dates. He asked me: "O Ibn 'Umar! Why are you not eating?" I replied: "I do not like it". He said: "But I like it and this is the morning of the fourth day I have not tasted nor found food; and had I so liked, I would have supplicated my Lord (Rabb) and He would have given me as much as is equal to the kingdom of Caesar and Khosrau. Then, how would you be O Ibn 'Umar if you meet a people who store the sustenance for a full year because they are weak in certainty (of faith)?" By Allaah, we did not leave before this Quraanic Ayaah was revealed. On that, the Prophet [peace and blessings of Allaah be upon him] said: "Verily, Allaah has not commanded me to hoard the things of this world nor to follow the desires. Behold! I do not keep much money nor do I store sustenance for the day to come". ['Abd Ibn Humayd; Al-Bayhaqi; Ibn Abu Haatim and Ibn 'Asaakir with a weak chain of narrators]

Verse Number 67

67- Have they not seen that We have made (Makkah) a secure sanctuary (for them), while men are being snatched away from all around them (through falling victims of killing and capture)? Then is it that in the false (idols) do they believe and deny (with ungratefulness) the favor of Allaah (by association of partners with Him in worship)?

A narration on the authority of Ibn 'Abbaas [Allaah be pleased with them] that he said: They told the Prophet [peace and blessings of Allaah be upon him]: "O

Muhammad! Nothing prevents us from adopting your religion except that we fear lest we would be snatched away by the Arabs who excel us in number; and once they know we have adopted your religion, we would be snatched away as if it were a single meal". On that occasion, Allaah revealed this Quraanic Ayaah. [Juwaybir]

Soorah Ar-Room

Verse Number 1-5

1- Alif-Laam-Meem. 2- The Byzantines have been defeated. 3- In the nearest land, and they, after their defeat, will be victorious. 4Within three to nine years. The decision of the matter, before and after (these events) is only with Allaah. And on that Day (the Byzantines will be victorious), the believers (al-Mumineen) (that is Muslims) will rejoice, 5- In the victory given by Allaah (to the Byzantines over the Persians). He gives victory to whom He wills, and He is the Exalted in Might, the Most Merciful (towards the believers (al-Mumineen)).

A narration on the authority of Abu Sa'eed [may Allaah be pleased with him] that he said: When it was the day of the battle of Badr, the news reached that the Romans emerged victorious and the Muslims rejoiced. On that occasion, Allaah had already revealed this Quraanic Ayaah. [At-Tirmidhi]

The same is narrated on the authority of Ibn Mas'ood [may Allaah be pleased with him]. [Ibn Jareer]

A narration on the authority of Ibn Shihaab that he said: We were reported that the polytheists argued the Muslims in Makkah before the Prophet [peace and blessings of Allaah be upon him] emigrated to Madinah, saying: "The Romans witness that they are a people of Scripture and now they have been defeated by the Magians. You also claim that you will defeat us with the help of the Book that has been revealed to your Prophet.

Then, how have the Magians defeated the Romans, who are a people of Scripture? We will defeat you in the same way as the Persians have defeated the Romans". On that occasion, Allaah revealed this Quraanic Ayaah. [Ibn Abu Haatim]

The same is narrated on the authority of 'Ikrimah, Yahya Ibn Ya'mur and Qataadah. [Ibn Jareer]

Verse Number 27

27- And He it is Who originates the creation (from nothing), then will repeat it (after it has been perished); and this is easier for Him. His is the highest description in the heavens and on earth. And He is the Exalted in Might (concerning His dominion), Full of Wisdom (in His creation).

A narration on the authority of 'Ikrimah that he said: The disbelievers (al-Kaafireen) wondered how Allaah gives life to the dead. On that occasion, Allaah revealed this Quraanic Ayaah. [Ibn Abu Haatim] Verse Number 28

28- He sets forth for you (O polytheists) a parable from your own selves: Do you have partners among (your slaves) whom your right hands possess to share you as equals in the wealth We have bestowed on you, and whom you fear as you fear each other (of the free people)? Thus do We explain the signs in detail to a people who have reason (to understand).

A narration on the authority of Ibn 'Abbaas [Allaah be pleased with them] that he said: The polytheists used to recite Talbiyah as follows: "I am responding to Your Call (O Allaah! With Whom there is no partner, except only one partner whom You possess along with all that he possesses". On that occasion, Allaah revealed this Quraanic Ayaah. [At-Tabaraani]

The same is narrated on the authority of Muhammad Ibn 'Ali from his father. [Juwaybir]

Soorah Luqmaan

Verse Number 6

6- And of people is he who purchases idle talks to mislead (men) from the Path of Allaah (the religion of Islam) without knowledge, and takes it (the Path of Allaah) for mockery. Such will receive a humiliating torment (in the fire of Hell).

A narration on the authority of Ibn 'Abbaas [Allaah be pleased with them] that he said: This Quraanic Ayaah was revealed in connection with a man from Quraysh who bought a slave-girl who was a songstress. [Ibn Jareer]

A narration on the authority of Ibn 'Abbaas [Allaah be pleased with them] that he said: An-Nadr Ibn Al-Haarith bought a songstress, and whenever he heard about anyone who intended to embrace Islam, he would take him to his songstress and say to her: "Feed him, give him wine to drink and make him listen to your singing: that is better for him than what Muhammad invites you to, of prayer and fighting under his leadership". On that occasion, this Quraanic Ayaah was revealed. [Juwaybir]

Verse Number 27

27- And if all the trees on earth were pens and the sea replenished thereafter with (further) seven seas (were ink wherewith to write), yet the Words of Allaah would not get exhausted. Verily, Allaah is Exalted in Might, Full of Wisdom.

A narration on the authority of 'Ikrimah that the people of Scripture asked the Prophet [peace and blessings of Allaah be upon him] about the spirit thereupon Allaah revealed (what means): {And they ask you, [O Muhammad], about the soul. Say, "The soul is of the affair of my Lord (Rabb). And mankind have not been given of knowledge except a little."} [Al-Israa', verse 85] The Yahood said: "No doubt, we have been given the Torah and it is the wisdom; and whoever is given wisdom has indeed been given much good". On that occasion, Allaah revealed this Quraanic Ayaah. [Ibn Jareer]

A narration on the authority of "Ataa Ibn Yasaar that he said: Allaah revealed in Makkah (what means): {And mankind have not been given of knowledge except a little."} [Al-Israa', verse 85] When the Prophet [peace and blessings of Allaah be upon him] emigrated to Madeenah the Jewish rabbis went to him and said: "We have been informed that you recite (what means): {And mankind have not been given of knowledge except a little."} Do you mean us or your people?" the Prophet [peace and blessings of Allaah be upon him] said: "I mean both (you and my people)". They said: "You recite that we have been given the Torah in which there is a clarification of all things".

The Prophet [peace and blessings of Allaah be upon him] said: "No doubt, it is only a little compared with the knowledge of Allaah". On that occasion, Allaah revealed this Quraanic Ayaah. [Ibn Ishaaq]

The same is narrated on the authority of Ibn 'Abbaas [Allaah be pleased with them]. [Ibn Abu Haatim]

A narration on the authority of Qataadah that he said: The polytheists said: "This speech (of the Quraan) is about to be used up". On that occasion, Allaah revealed this Quraanic Ayaah. [Abu Ash-Shaykh in Al-'Athamah and Ibn Jareer]

Verse Number 34

34- Verily, with Allaah (Alone) is the knowledge of the Hour, He sends down the rain, and knows that which is in the wombs. No person knows what (good or evil) he will earn tomorrow, and no person knows in what land he will die. Verily, Allaah is All-Knowing (of all things), Well-Acquainted (with the inwards just like the outwards).

A narration on the authority of Mujaahid that a man came from the desert to the Prophet [peace and blessings of Allaah be upon him], and said: "My wife is pregnant: tell me what she will give birth to (a male or a female). Furthermore, our land is arid: tell me when it will rain. I know when I was born: then tell me when I will die". On that occasion, Allaah revealed this Quraanic Ayaah. [Ibn Jareer and Ibn Abu Haatim]

Soorah As-Sajdah

Verse Number 16

16- Their sides forsake their beds, to invoke their Lord (Rabb) in fear (of His punishment) and hope (of His mercy), and out of what We have bestowed on them they spend (in charity in Allaah's Cause).

A narration on the authority of Anas [may Allaah be pleased with him] that this Quraanic Ayaah was revealed in connection with those who sit in the masjid waiting the 'Ishaa' prayer. [At-Tirmidhi who renders it Saheeh]

Verse Number 18

18- Is then he who is a believer like him who is defiantly disobedient? Not equal are they.

A narration on the authority of Ibn 'Abbaas [Allaah be pleased with them] that Al-Waleed Ibn 'Uqbah ibn Abu Mu'ayt told 'Ali: "I am stronger than you in using weapons, sharper than you in speech and more ready to fill the eyes of the people than you". Ali replied him: "Keep silent since you are wicked". On that occasion, this Quraanic Ayaah was revealed. [Al-Waahidi; Ibn 'Asaakir; Ibn 'Adiyy and Al-Khateeb in his Taareekh]

The same is narrated on the authority of 'Ataa' Ibn Yasaar. [Ibn Jareer]

Verse Number 28

28- They say (to the believers (al-Mumineen)): "When will this decision (of cases between you and us) be, if you are telling the truth?" A narration on the authority of Qataadah that the Companions said: "One day we shall get comforted and take pleasure". The polytheists said: "When will this day be if you are truthful?" On that occasion, this Quraanic Ayaah was revealed. [Ibn Jareer]

Soorah Al-Ahzaab

Verse Number 1

1- O Prophet! Fear Allaah (by Keeping your duty to Him), and obey not the disbelievers (al-Kaafireen) and hypocrites (al-Munaafiqeen) (in what violates your Sharia and religion). Verily, Ever is Allaah All-Knower (of everything before creating it), All-Wise (in what He creates and does).

A narration on the authority of Ibn 'Abbaas [Allaah be pleased with them] that he said: The chiefs of Quraysh, Al-Waleed Ibn Al-Mugheerah, 'Utbah and Shaybah, sons of Rabee'ah, and others suggested to the Prophet [peace and blessings of Allaah be upon him] to retract from his invitation (to Allaah) and they would give him half of their property. The Yahood and hypocrites (al-Munaafiqeen) in Madeenah frightened him that unless he retracted they would kill him. On that occasion, Allaah revealed this Quraanic Ayaah. [Juwaybir]

Verse Number 4

4- Allaah has not made for any man two hearts (Qalb) inside his body. Neither has He made your wives whom you declare as (unlawful for you) as the backs of your mothers your real mothers (in their being prohibited to you), nor has He made your adopted sons your real sons. That is only your saying with your mouths. But Allaah tells the truth (in this respect) and He guides to the (Right and straight) Way.

A narration on the authority of Ibn 'Abbaas [Allaah be pleased with them] that once the Prophet [peace and blessings of Allaah be upon him] was leading the Muslims in prayer when he engaged in some thought, thereupon the hypocrites (al-Munaafiqeen) who were praying behind him said: "Do you not see that he has two hearts (Qalb): one with you and the other with Him?" On that occasion, Allaah revealed this Quraanic Ayaah. [At-Tirmidhi]

A narration on the authority of Mujaahid and 'Ikrimah that he said: There was a man called Dhul-Qalbayn (the two-Hearted). In connection with him this Quraanic Ayaah was revealed. [Ibn Abu Haatim] Al-Hasan added: He used to say: I have two souls: one to command me and the other to forbid me. [Ibn Jareer] A narration on the authority of Mujaahid that he said: It was revealed in conncction with a man from Banu Fahm who used to say: "I have two hearts (Qalb) with each of which I understand better than Muhammad. [Ibn Jareer]

Verse Number 5

5- Call them (adopted sons) by (the names of) their fathers: that is more just (and more equitable) in the sight of Allaah. But if you know not (the names of) their fathers, call them) your brothers in religion and your cousins. And there is no sin on you concerning that in which you made a mistake, except in regard to what your hearts (Qalb) deliberately intend (after that forbiddance). And Ever is Allaah Oft-Forgiving (of your faults in this issue), Most Merciful.

A narration on the authority of Ibn 'Umar [Allaah be pleased with them] that he said: We used to call Zayd Ibn Haarithah Zayd Ibn Muhammad till this Quraanic Ayaah was revealed. [Al-Bukhaari] Verse Number 9

9- O you who believe! Remember Allaah's Favor to you, when there came against you hosts (of disbelievers (al-Kaafireen) in companies in the battle of Al-Ahzaab), and We sent against them a wind and forces that you saw not (that is angels) And Allaah Sees well what you/they do.

A narration on the authority of Hudhayfah [may Allaah be pleased with him] that he said: On the night of Al-Ahzaab, I saw ourselves (Muslims) sitting in lines and Abu Sufyaan with the Confederates over us and Quraythah below us of whom we felt afraid lest they would attack our children and women. No night darker and stormier has ever come upon us than this night. The hypocrites (al-Munaafiqeen) went on seeking the permission of the Prophet [peace and blessings of Allaah be upon him], saying: "Our houses are exposed (to the enemies)", but they indeed were not so. None of them has taken permission but that he was given leave and they slipped away from the camp. Then, the Prophet [peace and blessings of Allaah be upon him] received us man by man till he came upon me. He said: "Detect for me the news of the people (disbelievers (al-Kaafireen))". I went to find that the wind was blowing on their camp and did not go beyond it even for a span.

By Allaah, while I was hearing the voice of stones in their tents and luggage with which the wind was striking them, and they were saying: "Let us go! Let us go!" I came back and informed him about the news of the people. On that occasion, Allaah revealed this Quraanic Ayaah. [Al-Bayhaqi in Ad-Dalaa'il]

Verse Number 12

12- And when the hypocrites (al-Munaafiqeen) and those in whose hearts (Qalb) is a disease (suspicion and weak faith) said: "Allaah and His Messenger (Muhammad) did not promise us (victory) but only to delude (us with falsehood)."

A narration on the authority of 'Amr Al-Muzni that he said: the Prophet [peace and blessings of Allaah be upon him] dug the trench in the year of Al-Ahzaab and Allaah brought out of the heart of the trench a rounded white rock. the Prophet [peace and blessings of Allaah be upon him] took the mattock and struck and crushed it. A spark flashed out of it which enlightened the area between the two mountains of Madeenah. He glorified Allaah and the Muslims glorified Allaah after him. Then, he struck it once again and crushed it and a spark flashed out of it which enlightened the area between Madeenah's mountains. He glorified Allaah and the Muslims did so after him. Then, he struck it for the third time and crushed it and a spark flashed out of it which enlightened the area between Madeenah's mountains. He glorified Allaah and the Muslims did so after him. When he was asked about that he said: "I have given the first strike thereupon the palaces of Heerah and Al-Madaa'in of Khosrau and Jibreel told me that my ummah would emerge victorious over them. Then, with the second strike the red palaces of the Byzantine territories enlightened to me; Jibreel told me that my ummah would emerge victorious over them. With the third strike the palaces of San'aa' enlightened to me; and Jibreel told me that my ummah would emerge victorious over them". The hypocrites (al-Munaafiqeen) said: "Do you not wonder at this? He talks and gives you hope and promises you of what is impossible. He tells you that he sees the palaces of Heerah and Madaa'in of Khosrau, and that they would be conquered by you. Yet, you are digging the trench out of fear (of your enemies) and cannot go out". On that occasion, this Quraanic Ayaah was revealed. [Ibn Abu Haatim and Al-Bayhaqi in Ad-Dalaa'il]

A narration on the authority of Ibn 'Abbaas [Allaah be pleased with them] that he said: It was revealed in connection with Mu'tib Ibn Qushayr (the hypocrite) who said this sentence (mentioned above). [Juwaybir]

A narration on the authority of 'Urwah and Muhammad Ibn Ka'b Al-Qurathi that this Mu'tib said: "Muhammad used to promise us that we would devour the treasures of the Persian and Byzantine Emperors, while today we feel unsafe to go to the toilet". Another, Aws Ibn Qaythi, told the Prophet [peace and blessings of Allaah be upon him] in front of a number of his clansmen: "O Messenger of Allaah! Our homes are exposed. So permit us to leave and go home, as our homes are outside Madinah". [Ibn Ishaaq and Al-Bayhaqi]

Verse Number 23

23- Among the believers (al-Mumineen) are men who have been true to their covenant with Allaah; of them some have fulfilled their obligations (that is fell martyrs or were killed in the Cause of Allaah); and some of them are still waiting (martyrdom), and they have never changed (their covenant with Allaah) even in the least (unlike the hypocrites (al-Munaafiqeen)).

A narration on the authority of Anas Ibn Maalik that he said: My uncle, Anas Ibn An-Nadr was absent from the battle of Badr and he felt it difficult. He said: "I have remained behind from the first battle fought by the Prophet [peace and blessings of Allaah be upon him]. If Allaah willed me to attend another battle with the Prophet [peace and blessings of Allaah be upon him], I will see Allaah what I am going to do". Then he attended the day of Uhud (battle), in which he fought till he was killed. His body had more than seventy wounds of sword strikes, lance stabs and arrow shots. In connection with him this Quraanic Ayaah was revealed. [Muslim; At-Tirmidhi and others]

Verse Number 28

28- O Prophet! Say to your wives: If you desire the life of this world, and its glitter, Then come! I vill provide for you and release you graciously (by divorce in which there is neither harm nor malice).

A narration on the authority of Jabir Ibn Abdullah "Allaah be pleased with both" that: Abu Bakr came to ask the permission to enter upon the Prophet [peace and blessings of Allaah be upon him], but he found the people sitting beside his door, and none of them was admitted. Then, Abu Bakr was admitted. Then, Umar came, and he was admitted. He found The Prophet [peace and blessings of Allaah be upon him] sitting as frowned and silent, with his wives around him. He (Umar) said: "I'm going to say something as a result of which the Prophet [peace and blessings of Allaah be upon him] would smile". Then he said: "O Messenger of Allaah! If I told you about ye daughter of Khaarijah (Umar's wife, you would smile). She asked me for more expense. So, I stood up towards her and slapped her on the neck". Upon this the Prophet [peace and blessings of Allaah be upon him] smiled and said: "They (my wives) are around me as you see, asking me for more expense". Then, Abu Bakr stood up towards AA'ishah in order to slap her on the neck, and Umar also stood up towards Hafsah in order to slap her on the neck, and both of them were saying: "Do you ask the Prophet [peace and blessings of Allaah be upon him] for what he doesn't have?" They said: "By Allaah! We never ask the Prophet [peace and blessings of Allaah be upon him] for anything he doesn't have". Then, he kept away from them for a month, or for twenty-nine (nights), after which the following Ayaah was revealed: "O Prophet say to thy Consorts: if it be that ye desire the life of this world, and its glitter, then come I will provide for your enjoyment and set free in a handsome manner. But if ye seek Allaah and His

Messenger, and the Home of the Hereafter, verily Allaah has prepared for the well-doers amongst you a great reward". Then, he (The Prophet) started with AA'ishah. He said: "O AA'ishah! I want to offer something to you, and I like that you should not give a hasty reply to it until you consult your parents". She asked: "What is it, O Messenger of Allaah?" He recited the Ayaah to her. Then she said: "Would I consult my parents (whether to choose) you, O Messenger of Allaah? Surely, I choose Allaah, His Messenger and the hereafter. Moreover, I request you not to tell anyone of your wives of that which you said (to me)". He said: "No woman of them asks me (about that) but that I would tell her (the same). Indeed, Allaah has sent me neither as one who gives (the people) hard instructions (concerning religion), nor as one who asks others to do what is difficult for them to do. But, He has sent me as a tauter who facilitates (things to the people)". [Muslim; Ahmad; An-Nasaa'i]

Verse Number 35

35- Verily, the Muslim men and the Muslim women (who surrender to Allaah in Islam), the believing men and the believing women, the obedient men and the obedient women (who comply with Allaah's command), the truthful men and the truthful women (in their faith), the patient men and the patient women (who persevere on doing the acts of worship and abstaining from what is forbidden by Allaah), the humble men and the humble women, the almsgiving men and the almsgiving women, the fasting men and the fasting women, the men who guard their chastity (from illegal sexual relations) and the women who do so, and the men who remember Allaah often and the women who do so: for them Allaah has prepared forgiveness (of all their sins) and a great reward (for performing all acts of worship enjoined upon them).

A narration on the authority of Umm 'Umaarah Al-Ansaari that she came to the Prophet [peace and blessings of Allaah be upon him], and said: "I see that all things are mentioned for men and women have no share of mention (in the Quraan)". On that occasion, this Quraanic Ayaah was revealed. [At-Tirmidhi who renders it Hasan]

A narration on the authority of Ibn 'Abbaas [Allaah be pleased with them] that he said: The women said to the Prophet [peace and blessings of Allaah be upon him]: "O Messenger of Allaah! What is the matter with Allaah that He mentions the believing men (and not the believing women)?" On that occasion, Allaah revealed this Quraanic Ayaah. [At-Tabaraani]

A narration on the authority of Qataadah that when a mention was made of the wives of the Prophet [peace and blessings of Allaah be upon him], the women said: "Had there been good in us, we would have been mentioned (in the Quraan)". On that occasion, this Quraanic Ayaah was revealed. [Ibn Sa'd]

Verse Number 36

36- It is not for a believing man or a believing woman, when Allaah and His Messenger have decreed a matter, that they should have (thereafter) any choice in their affair. And whoever disobeys

Allaah and His Messenger, he has indeed strayed into a clear error. A narration on the authority of Qataadah that he said: the Prophet [peace and blessings of Allaah be upon him], demanded to marry Zaynab Bint Jahsh [Allaah be pleased with her] to Zayd Ibn Haarithah and she thought he had betrothed her for himself. But when she knew that he betrothed her for Zayd she rejected. On that occasion, Allaah revealed this Quraanic Ayaah, as a result of which she approved and submitted (to the command of Allaah and His Messenger). [At-Tabaraani with an authentic chain of narrators]

A narration on the authority of Ibn 'Abbaas [Allaah be pleased with them] that he said: the Prophet [peace and blessings of Allaah be upon him], demanded to marry Zaynab Bint Jahsh to Zayd Ibn Haarithah and she disdained him and said: "I am better than him in ancestry and family status". On that occasion, Allaah revealed this Quraanic Ayaah. [Ibn Jareer]

Verse Number 37

37- And (remember) when you said to him (Zayd Ibn Haarithah) whom Allaah has conferred favor upon (by guiding him to Islam) and you (O Muhammad) have done favor to (by manumission): "Keep your wife with yourself, and fear Allaah (as regards divorcing her)." But you did conceal in yourself that which Allaah is going to disclose, you did fear people whereas Allaah had more right that you should fear Him (in all things). So when Zayd had no longer any need from her (and consequently divorced her), We gave her to you in marriage, so that (in future) there may be no difficulty for the believers (al-Mumineen) in respect of (marrying) the wives of their adopted sons when the latter have no longer any need from them (and divorce them). And ever is Allaah's Command accomplished.

A narration on the authority of Anas [may Allaah be pleased with him] that he said: This Quraanic Ayaah was revealed in connection with Zaynab Bint Jahsh and Zayd Ibn Haarithah. [Al-Bukhaari]

A narration on the authority of Anas [may Allaah be pleased with him] that he said: When the period of 'Iddah of Zaynab (Bint Jahsh) had finished, the Prophet [peace and blessings of Allaah be upon him] told Zayd (Ibn Haarithah): "Demand her hand for me". Zayd went to her, while she was fermenting her dough. When I saw her, I respected her so much that I could no longer be able to look at her, because the Prophet [peace and blessings of Allaah be upon him] mentioned her (offering the proposal of marrying her). I turned my back towards her, and then turned on my heels. I said: "O Zaynab! the Prophet [peace and blessings of Allaah be upon him] sent (me) to demand your hand for him". She said: "I'm not to do anything until I ask my Lord (Rabb) for the better guidance". Then, she got up and went to her praying place. But, The Quraan was revealed (in connection with this matter). the Prophet [peace and blessings of Allaah be upon him] came and entered upon her without asking for her permission.

He (Anas) added: I saw ourselves and the Prophet [peace and blessings of Allaah be upon him] served us with bread and meat when the day rose. Then, all the people went out (of the house) except a few men, who stayed talking after the meal. the Prophet [peace and blessings of Allaah be upon him] went out and I followed him. He started visiting the chambers of his wives, greeting them, and they would ask him: "O Messenger of Allaah! How did you find your wife?"

He (Anas) added: indeed, I do not know whether I told him or he told me that the people (who were still in the house after the meal) had gone out. He (Anas) said: He went until he entered the house. I went to enter along with him, but, he threw the curtain between him and me. Then, the (Ayaah of) screening The Prophet's wives was revealed, and the people were instructed with that with which they were instructed (what means): {O you who Believe! enter not the Prophet's houses- until leave is given you...} [Al-Ahzaab, verse 53] [Muslim; Ahmad and An-Nasaa'i]

Verse Number 40

40- Muhammad is not the father of any of your men, but he is the Prophet and the last of the Prophets. And ever is Allaah, of all things, Knowing.

A narration on the authority of 'AA'ishah [Allaah be pleased with her], that she said: When the Prophet [peace and blessings of Allaah be upon him] married Zaynab they said: "He has married the wife of his son". On that occasion, Allaah revealed this Quraanic Ayaah. [At-Tirmidhi]

Verse Number 43

43- He it is Who confers blessing upon you, and so do His angels (invoke Allaah's blessing and forgiveness upon you), that He may bring you out from darkness (of disbelief) into light (of Belief). And towards the believers (al-Mumineen) He is Most Merciful.

A narration on the authority of Mujaahid that he said: When Allaah revealed (what means): {Indeed, Allaah confers blessing upon the Prophet, and His angels [ask Him to do so]. O you who have believed, ask [Allaah to confer] blessing upon him and ask [Allaah to grant him] peace}, [verse 56] Abu Bakr said: "O Messenger of Allaah! Allaah has never given anything good to you but that He made us share in it". On that occasion, Allaah revealed this Quraanic Ayaah. ['Abd Ibn Humayd]

Verse Number 47

47- And inform the believers (al-Mumineen) (in Allaah) that they will have from Allaah a Great Bounty (that is Paradise).

A narration on the authority of 'Ikrimah and Al-Hasan Al-Basri that they said: When Allaah revealed (what means): {That Allaah may forgive for you what preceded of your sin and what will follow and complete His favor upon you and guide you to a straight path}, [Al-Fath, verse 2] some believers (al-Mumineen) said: "Blessed be you O Messenger of Allaah! We have known what is going to be done with you. Then, what is going to be done with us?" On that occasion, Allaah revealed (what means): {[And] that He may admit the believing men and the believing women to gardens beneath which rivers flow to abide therein eternally and remove from them their misdeeds and ever is that, in the sight of Allaah, a great attainment}. [Al-Fath, verse 5] He also revealed this Quraanic Ayaah of Soorah Al-Ahzaab. [Ibn Jareer]

A narration on the authority of Ar-Rabee' Ibn Anas that he said: When Allaah revealed (what means): {nor do I know what will be done with me or with you. I only follow that which is revealed to me}, [Al-Ahqaaf, verse 9] then Allaah revealed (what means): {That Allaah may forgive for you what preceded of your sin and what will follow and complete His favor upon you and guide you to a straight path}, [Al-Fath, verse 2] They said: "Blessed be you O Messenger of Allaah! We have known what is going to be done with you. Then, what is going to be done with us?" On that occasion, Allaah revealed this Quraanic Ayaah. The great bounty stands for Paradise. [Al-Bayhaqi in Dalaa'il An-Nubuwwah]

Verse Number 50

50- O Prophet! Verily, We have made lawful for you your wives whom you have paid their dowry, and those (slave-women) whom your right hand possesses -

whom Allaah has given to you (of non-Muslim captives), and the daughters of your paternal uncles and the daughters of your paternal aunts and the daughters of your maternal uncles and the daughters of your maternal aunts who emigrated (from Makkah to Madeenah) with you, and a believing woman if she gives herself to the Prophet (for marriage), and the Prophet wishes to marry her (without a dowry) privilege for you only, not for the (rest of) the believers (al-Mumineen). Indeed We know what We have enjoined upon them about their wives and those (slave women) whom their right hands possess. (That is so for you) in order that there should be no difficulty on you (concerning marriage). And ever is Allaah Oft-Forgiving (of what - is done which is too difficult to avoid), Most Merciful (in respect of making this matter extensive).

A narration on the authority of Umm Haani' Bint Abu Taalib [Allaah be pleased with her] that she said: the Prophet [peace and blessings of Allaah be upon him] demanded my hand and I apologized and he accepted my apology. Then Allaah revealed (what means): {and the daughters of your paternal uncles and the daughters of your paternal aunts and the daughters of your maternal uncles and the daughters of your maternal aunts who emigrated with you...} Indeed, I was not lawful for him since I did not emigrate with him. [At-Tirmidhi who renders it Hasan and Al-Haakim who renders it Saheeh]

A narration on the authority of Umm Haani' that she said: In connection with me, the following statement was revealed (what means): {and the daughters of your paternal uncles and the daughters of your paternal aunts and the daughters of your maternal uncles and the daughters of your maternal aunts who emigrated with you}. the Prophet [peace and blessings of Allaah be upon him], wanted to marry me and he was forbidden to do so because I did not emigrate with him. [Ibn Abu Haatim]

A narration on the authority of 'Ikrimah that he said: Allaah's saying (what means): {and a believing woman if she gives herself to the Prophet [and] if the Prophet wishes to marry her...} was revealed in connection with a woman called Umm Shurayk Ad-Dawsiyyah. [Ibn Sa'd]

A narration on the authority of Muneer Ibn 'Abdullaah Ad-Du'ali that Umm Shurayk Ad-Dawsiyyah offered herself to the Prophet [peace and blessings of Allaah be upon him] (to marry) and she was beautiful, and he accepted her. 'AA'ishah [Allaah be pleased with her] said: "No good lies in a woman when she offers herself to a man (to marry)". Umm Shurayk said: "Then I am this woman". Allaah named her a believing woman saying: {and a believing woman if she gives herself to the Prophet [and] if the Prophet wishes to marry her...} When this Quraanic Ayaah was revealed, 'AA'ishah said: "No doubt, Allaah hastens to fulfill for you (O Prophet) your desire". [Ibn Sa'd]

Verse Number 51

51- You (O Muhammad) can postpone (the turn of) whom you will of them (your wives), and you may take to yourself whom you will. And whomever you desire of those whom you have set aside (temporarily), it is no sin on you (to take her to yourself again): that is better that they may be content and grieve not, and may all be pleased with what you give them. Allaah knows what is in your hearts (Qalb) (concerning women and the possible inclination to any of them more than others). And Ever is Allaah All-Knowing (of His creation), Most Forbearing (on punishing people in spite of their mistakes).

A narration on the authority of 'AA'ishah [Allaah be pleased with her] that she said: "Does not a woman feel shy of giving herself to a man (to marry)?" On that occasion, Allaah revealed this Quraanic Ayaah. Then 'AA'ishah said: "No doubt, Allaah hastens to fulfill for you your desire". [Al-Bukhaari and Muslim]

A narration on the authority of Abu Razeen that he said: the Prophet [peace and blessings of Allaah be upon him] intended to divorce some of his wives but they made him free from the obligatory day-and-night turns to be assigned to them and made him free to choose to visit and give preference to whomever he liked of them (provided that he should not divorce them). On that occasion, Allaah revealed this Quraanic Ayaah. [Ibn Sa'd]

Verse Number 52

52- It is not lawful for you (to marry other) women after this, nor to change them for other wives even though their beauty attracts you, except those (slave women) whom your right hand possesses. And Ever is Allaah, over all things, a Watcher.

A narration on the authority of 'Ikrimah that he said: the Prophet [peace and blessings of Allaah be upon him] gave his wives the freedom to choose, and they chose Allaah and His Messenger [peace and blessings of Allaah be upon him]. On that, Allaah revealed this Quraanic Ayaah. [Ibn Sa'd] Verse Number 53

53- O you who believe! Enter not the Prophet's houses, unless permission is given to you for a meal, (and ente not (so arly as) to wait for its preparation. But when you are invited, enter, and when you have taken your meal, disperse without seeking to remain for conversation. Verily, such (behavior) annoys the Prophet, and he is shy of (asking) you (to go); but Allaah is not shy of (telling you) the truth. And when you ask (his wives) for anything you want, ask them from behind a screen: that is purer for your hearts (Qalb) and for their hearts (Qalb) (from the evil self-talks). And it is not (lawful) for you that you should annoy Allaah's Messenger, nor that you should ever marry his wives after him (his death). Verily, in the sight of Allaah, that would be a grievous (sin).

A narration on the authority of Anas Ibn Maalik [may Allaah be pleased with him] that he said: when he married Zaynab bint Jahsh, he invited the people to a meal. They took the meal and remained sitting and talking. Then The Prophet [peace and blessings of Allaah be upon him] (showed them) as if he is ready to get up, yet they did not get up. When he noticed that (there was no response to his movement), he got up, and the others too, got up except three persons who kept on sitting. The Prophet [peace and blessings of Allaah be upon him] came back in order to enter his house, but he went away again. Then they left, whereupon I set out and went to The Prophet [peace and blessings of Allaah be upon him] to tell him that they had departed, so he came and entered his house. I wanted to enter along with him, but he put a screen between me and him. Then Allaah revealed this Quraanic Ayaah. [Al-Bukhaari]

A narration on the authority of Anas [may Allaah be pleased with him] that he said: I was with the Prophet [peace and blessings of Allaah be upon him], when he knocked the door of a woman (his wife) with whom he was to consummate marriage. But there were some people in the house. He came out and then returned once again and the people had left. Then he entered and put a screen between them and me. I made a mention of that to Abu Talhah, thereupon he said: "If what you have said is true, then divine revelation will come on that occasion". Then the Quraanic Ayaah of Hijaab was revealed. [At-Tirmidhi who renders it Hasan]

A narration on the authority of 'AA'ishah [Allaah be pleased with her] that she said: I was eating with the Prophet [peace and blessings of Allaah be upon him] in a bowl when 'Umar came whom he invited and he entered and shared food with us. Then his finger touched mine. On that he said: "Oh! Had he (the Prophet) obeyed me concerning you (his wives), your eye would have not seen you". On that occasion, Allaah revealed this Quraanic Ayaah. [At-Tabaraani]

A narration on the authority of Ibn 'Abbaas [Allaah be pleased with them] that he said: A man entered upon the Prophet [peace and blessings of Allaah be upon him], and sat for a long time. the Prophet [peace and blessings of Allaah be upon him] came out thrice in order for this man to leave, but he did not do. Then 'Umar entered and having seen the (signs of) aversion in his (the Prophet's) face, said to the man: "Perhaps you have done harm to the Prophet [peace and blessings of Allaah be upon him]". the Prophet [peace and blessings of Allaah be upon him], said: "I have come out thrice in the hope that he would follow me and he did not do". "Umar said: "O Messenger of Allaah! Would that you made a partition for your wives since your wives are not like the other women: no doubt that will be purer for their hearts (Qalb)". On that occasion, this Quraanic Ayaah was revealed. [Ibn Mardawayh] According to Al-Haafith, perhaps this event took place a short time before the story of Zaynab Bint Jahsh [Allaah be pleased with her]. A narration on the authority of Muhammad Ibn Ka'b that he said: It was the habit of the Prophet [peace and blessings of Allaah be upon him] that if he stood to leave for his house, they would hasten to take their sitting places; and the signs of aversion would be seen on the face of the Prophet [peace and blessings of Allaah be upon him], and he would not stretch his hand to the food out of shyness of them. They were blamed for that. On that occasion, Allaah revealed (what means): {O you who have believed, do not enter the houses of the Prophet except when you are permitted for a meal...} [Ibn Sa'd]

A narration on the authority of Ibn Zayd that he said: The news reached the Prophet [peace and blessings of Allaah be upon him], about somebody's saying: "If the Prophet [peace and blessings of Allaah be upon him] die I will marry so and so of his wives after him". On that occasion, Allaah revealed (what means): {And it is not [conceivable or lawful] for you to harm the Prophet or to marry his wives after him...} [Ibn Abu Haatim]

A narration on the authority of Ibn 'Abbaas [Allaah be pleased with them] that he said: It was revealed in connection with a man who intended to marry one of the Prophet's wives after his death. [Ibn Abu

Verse Number 57

57- Verily, as for those (that is the disbelievers (al-Kaafireen)) who annoy Allaah and His Messenger, Allaah has cursed them in this world and in the Hereafter (by drive them back from His mercy), and has prepared for them a humiliating torment (in the fire of Hell).

A narration on the authority of Ibn 'Abbaas [Allaah be pleased with them] that he said: This Quraanic Ayaah was revealed in connection with those who criticized the Prophet [peace and blessings of Allaah be upon him] when he took Safiyyah Bint Huyayy (as his wife). [Ibn Abu Haatim]

According to Sufyaan, they mentioned that she was 'AA'ishah [Allaah be pleased with her]. According to As-Suddi that he said: We were informed that Talhah Ibn 'Ubaydullaah [may Allaah be pleased with him] that he said: "Does Muhammad veil us from the daughters of our uncles at the time he himself marries our women? If he dies, we will marry his wives after his death". On that occasion, this Quraanic Ayaah was revealed. A narration on the authority of Abu Bakr Ibn 'Amr Ibn Hazm that he said: It was revealed in connection with Abu Talhah Ibn 'Ubaydullaah because he said: "If the Prophet [peace and blessings of Allaah be upon him] dies, I will marry 'AA'ishah (after his death)". [Ibn Sa'd]

A narration on the authority of Ibn 'Abbaas [Allaah be pleased with them] that a man went to one of the wives of the Prophet [peace and blessings of Allaah be upon him], and talked to her, who was her paternal cousin. the Prophet [peace and blessings of Allaah be upon him] said: "Do not stand in this position after this day of yours". He said: "O Messenger of Allaah! She is my paternal female cousin. By Allaah, I have not said to her anything evil nor has she done". the Prophet [peace and blessings of Allaah be upon him] said: "I have known this. None has a sense of Gheerah stronger than Allaah; and none has a sense of Gheerah stronger than me". He then left and said: "He forbids me to talk to my paternal female cousin. I will marry her after his death". On that occasion, Allaah revealed this Quraanic Ayaah. Ibn 'Abbaas [Allaah be pleased with them] said: "This man emancipated a slave and paid the cost of transportation on ten camels in Allaah's cause, and performed Hajj on foot to repent from his word". [Juwaybir]

A narration on the authority of Ibn 'Abbaas [Allaah be pleased with them] that he said: It was revealed in connection with 'Abdullaah Ibn Ubayy Ibn Salool when he slandered 'AA'ishah [Allaah be pleased with her]. On that, the Prophet [peace and blessings of Allaah be upon him] addressed the people saying: "Who among you could support me against a man who harms me (concerning my wife) and gathers in his house those who harm me?" [Juwaybir]

Verse Number 59

59- O Prophet! Tell your wives and your daughters and the women of the believers (al-Mumineen) (whenever they come out) to draw (part of) their outer garments all over themselves. That is more convenient that they should be recognized (as free women) so as not to be abused. And Ever is Allaah Oft-Forgiving (of what was otherwise done before that revelation), Most Merciful (towards them by enjoining upon them to get screened).

A narration on the authority of 'AA'ishah [Allaah be pleased with her] that she said: Sawdah (Bint Zam'ah, the wife of The Prophet) went out to answer the call of nature after Hijaab was made obligatory (upon all Muslim women). She was a fat huge lady, and everybody who knew her before could recognize her. So 'Umar Ibn Al-Khattaab saw her and said: "O Sawdah! By Allaah, you cannot hide yourself from us, so think of a way by which you should not be recognized on going out. Sawdah returned while the Prophet [peace and blessings of Allaah be upon him] was in my house taking his supper and a bone covered with meat was in his hand. She entered and said: "O Messenger of Allaah! I went out to answer the call of nature and 'Umar said to me such and such." Then Allaah inspired him (The Prophet [peace and blessings of Allaah be upon him]) and when the state of inspiration was over and the bone was still in his hand as he had not put in down, he said (to Sawdah), "You (women) have been allowed to go out for your needs." [Al-Bukhaari]

A narration on the authority of Abu Maalik that he said: The wives of the Prophet [peace and blessings of Allaah be upon him] used to go out at night to fulfill their needs and on the way the hypocrites (al-Munaafiqeen) would do harm to them. They made a complaint of that to the Prophet [peace and blessings of Allaah be upon him] and when the hypocrites (al-Munaafiqeen) were talked about that they said: "We do so only with the slave-girls". On that occasion, Allaah revealed this Quraanic Ayaah. [Ibn Sa'd]

The same is narrated on the authority of Al-Hasan and Muhammad Ibn Ka'b Al-Qurathi. [Ibn Sa'd in At-Tabaqaat]

Soorah Saba'

Verse Number 15

15- Indeed there was for Saba' (Sheba) in their dwelling place a sign (which indicates to Allaah's omnipotence) - two gardens on the right and on the left (side of their valley); (and it was said to them:) "Eat of the provision of your Lord (Rabb), and be grateful to Him (for His favor)." A fair land and an Oft-Forgiving Lord (Rabb) (that is Allaah Almighty).

A narration on the authority of 'Ali Ibn Rabaah that he said: I was told that Farwah Ibn Nusayk entered upon the Prophet [peace and blessings of Allaah be upon him] and said: "O Messenger of Allaah! It is known that in the pre-Islamic days, the people of Saba' (Sheba in Yemen) were endued with honor and power, and I feel afraid lest they would renegade from Islam: shall I fight them?" the Prophet [peace and blessings of Allaah be upon him] said: "I have received no commands concerning them". On that occasion, Allaah revealed this Quraanic Ayaah. [Ibn Abu Haatim]

Verse Number 34

34- And We did not send a warner to a township, but those (that is its chiefs) blessed in comfort and luxuries among them said: "We disbelieve in the (Message) with which you have been sent."

A narration on the authority of Ibn Razeen that he said: Before Islam there were two partners one of whom left for Shaam and the other remained. When the Prophet [peace and blessings of Allaah be upon him] was sent as a Prophet, the one in Shaam sent to his partners asking him about his (Muhammad's) news. His partner sent to him a message telling him that none among the men of Quraysh followed him but the lowly and poor". The one in Shaam left his trade and went back and asked his companion to guide him to the Prophet [peace and blessings of Allaah be upon him]. He used to read some Scriptures. He came to the Prophet [peace and blessings of Allaah be upon him] and said: "To which things do you invite?" the Prophet [peace and blessings of Allaah be upon him] said: "To such and such (good things)".

He said: "I testify that you are really the Messenger of Allaah". He [peace and blessings of Allaah be upon him] asked him: "Then, what has led you to know that (I am really Allaah's Messenger)?". He said: "No Prophet has ever been sent but that he was followed by the lowly and poor among the people". On that occasion, Allaah revealed this Quraanic Ayaah. the Prophet [peace and blessings of Allaah be upon him] sent to him, telling him that Allaah had revealed the confirmation of his statement. [Ibn Abu Haatim and Ibn Al-Mundhir]

Soorah Faatir

Verse Number 8

8- Is he to whom the evil of his deed is made alluring, so that he considers it as good (equal to one who is rightly guided)? Verily, Allaah leaves to stray whom He wills, and guides whom He wills. So fret not yourself (O Muhammad) in sorrow over them (that is those whose evil deed is made fair-seeming to them because they do not believe). Surely, Allaah knows well what they do (for which He will reward them).

A narration on the authority of Ibn 'Abbaas [Allaah be pleased with them] that he said: the Prophet [peace and blessings of Allaah be upon him] said: "O Allaah! Empower Your religion with either 'Umar Ibn Al-Khattaab or Abu Jahl: 'Amr Ibn Hishaam!" Allaah then guided 'Umar Ibn Al-Khattaab (and he embraced Islam), and led astray Abu Jahl. It is in connection with them that Allaah revealed this Quraanic Ayaah. [Juwaybir]

Verse Number 29

29- Verily, those who recite the Book of Allaah (this Quraan), and establish regular prayer, and spend (in charity) out of what We have provided for them, secretly and openly, hope for a (sure) profit that will never perish.

A narration on the authority of Ibn 'Abbaas [Allaah be pleased with them] that he said: This Quraanic Ayaah was revealed in connection with Husayn Ibn Al-Haarith Ibn 'Abd-Al-Muttalib Ibn 'Abd Manaaf. [*Abd-Al-Ghani Ibn Sa'eed Ath-Thaqafi in his Tafseer]

Verse Number 35

35- Who, out of His bounty, has lodged us in a home that will last forever, where neither toil nor weariness will touch us."

A narration on the authority of 'Abdullaah Ibn Abu Awfa that he said: A man asked the Prophet [peace and blessings of Allaah be upon him]: "O Messenger of Allaah! Sleep is one of the things which comforts men in this world: will there be sleep in Paradise?" the Prophet [peace and blessings of Allaah be upon him] said: "No doubt, sleep is like death; and there will be no death in Paradise". He asked: "Then, how will they take rest?" the Prophet [peace and blessings of Allaah be upon him] felt it difficult and said: "In Paradise, men will have no fatigue because they will live in rest (and satisfaction) forever". On that occasion, this Quraanic Ayaah was revealed. [Al-Bayhaqi in Al-Ba'th and Ibn Abu Haatim]

Verse Number 42

42- And they (the disbelievers (al-Kaafireen)) swore by Allaah their strongest oaths that if a warner (Messenger) came to them, they would be more guided than any of the nations (before them); yet when a warner (Prophet Muhammad peace be upon him) came to them, this (his coming) did not increase them save in aversion (for, and flight from guidance)

A narration on the authority of Ibn Abu Hilaal that he said: We were reported that the men of Quraysh used to say: "Were there to be a Prophet sent from among us, we would be the most submissive to Allaah, the most obedient to His Messenger, and the most sticking to His Book". On that occasion, Allaah revealed (what means): {And indeed, the disbelievers (al-Kaafireen) used to say, "If we had a message from [those of the former peoples, We would have been the chosen servants of Allaah"}. [As-Saffaat, verse 167-169] and: {"If only the Scripture had been revealed to us, we would have been better guided than they."} [Al-An'aam, verse 157] He also revealed this Quraanic Ayaah in issue. On the other side, the Yahood used to pray for victory over the Yahood saying: "We find (in the Scripture) that a Prophet will appear". [Ibn Abu Haatim]

Soorah Yaa-Seen

Verse Number 1-10

1- Yaa-Seen. 2- By the Quraan, full of wisdom, 3- Verily, you (O Muhammad) are one of the Messengers, 4- On the Straight Path. 5- (This Quraan is) the revelation sent down by (Allaah) the Exalted in Might (concerning His dominion), the Most Merciful (to His servants), 6- In order that you (O Muhammad) may warn a people whose forefathers had not been warned (at the time of break in the series of Messengers), so they are heedless (of the truth and guidance). 7- Indeed the Word (of punishment) has come into effect upon most of them for they do not believe. 8Verily, We have put shackles on their necks reaching to their chins, so that they, with their heads, are kept aloft. 9- And We have put a barrier before them, and a barrier behind them, and We have covered them up, so that they cannot see. 10- It is the same to them whether you warn them or you warn them not, they will not believe.

A narration on the authority of Ibn 'Abbaas [Allaah be pleased with them] that he said: the Prophet [peace and blessings of Allaah be upon him] used to recite aloud in his prayer and this disturbed some people of Quraysh who decided to stand up towards him to do harm to him. But behold! their hands were tied to their necks and they were blind, not seeing anything. They went to the Prophet [peace and blessings of Allaah be upon him] and said: "We beseech you by Allaah and the kinship ties, O Muhammad (to remove this from us)!" He invoked Allaah till they recovered. On that occasion, those Quraanic Aayaat were revealed. Indeed, none of those group believed. [Abu Na'eem in Ad-Dalaa'il]

A narration on the authority of 'Ikrimah that he said: Abu Jahl said: "If I see Muhammad I will do such and such (harm to him". On that occasion, Allaah revealed Quraanic Aayaat no. 8-9. Consequently, whenever he saw the Prophet [peace and blessings of Allaah be upon him], he would not see him and would rather ask: "Where is he? Where is he?" [Ibn Jarir]

Verse Number 12

12- Verily, it is We Who give life to the dead (on the Day of Resurrection), and We record (in the Preserved Tablet all good and evil deeds) which they put forth (in this world to be rewarded for them), and (the deeds) which they leave behind (and survive after them and the people act upon) and all things We have enumerated in a Clear Book (that is the Preserved Tablet).

A narration on the authority of Abu Sa'eed Al-Khudri [may Allaah be pleased with him] that he said: The dwelling places of (the tribe of) Banu Salamah were in a far side of Madeenah, so they liked to move to be close to the masjid. But when Allaah revealed this Quraanic Ayaah, the Prophet [peace and blessings of Allaah be upon him] told them: "No doubt, your steps (you take towards the masjid) are written (as good deeds) for you: so do not leave your dwellings". [At-

Tirmidhi who renders it authentic and At-Tabaraani on the authority of Ibn 'Abbaas]

Verse Number 77-83

77- Does not man see that We have created him from a sperm-drop (mixed with a female reproductive discharge, till he grew strong and mature)? Yet behold he (stands forth) as an open opponent (to Us in denial of resurrection). 78- And he sets forth for Us a parable, and forgets his own creation (from semen). He says: "Who will give life to these (dry) bones after they have rotten away and decomposed?" 79- Say: "He will give life to them Who created them for the first time! And He is the All-Knower of every creation!" 80- He, Who produces for you fire out of the green tree, when behold you kindle therewith. 81- Is not He Who created the heavens and the earth (in their grandeur), Able to create the like of them (living and non-living beings who are more insignificant compared with the heavens and the earth)? Yes (that is so), indeed! He is the Superb Creator (of all things) Who has full knowledge of everything. 82- Verily, His Command, when He intends (to create or do) a thing, is only that He says to it, "Be!" - and it is! 83- So Exalted be He in Whose Hands is the dominion of all things: and to Him you shall be returned (in the hereafter).

A narration on the authority of Ibn 'Abbaas [Allaah be pleased with them] that he said: Al-'AAs Ibn Waa'il came to the Prophet [peace and blessings of Allaah be upon him] with a decayed bone in his hand and said, while crumbling it: "O Muhammad! Will Allaah resurrect this (bone) after it had been rotten (and decomposed)?" the Prophet [peace and blessings of Allaah be upon him] said to him: "Y Allaah will resurrect it; and He will also send you to death and then bring you to life once again and then admit you to Hell". On that occasion, these Quraanic Aayaat were revealed. [Al-Haakim who renders it authentic]

The same is narrated on the authority of Mujaahid, 'Ikrimah and others. According to this narration, the man is Ubayy Ibn Khalaf (instead of Al-'AAs Ibn Waa'il). [Ibn Abu Haatim]

Soorah As-Saffaat

Verse Number 64

64- Verily, it is a tree that springs out of the bottom of Hellfire (and its branches rise up to cover its grades),

A narration on the authority of Qataadah that he said: Abu Jahl said: "This, that is your companion (Muhammad) pretends that there is a tree in the fire (of Hell); and it is known that the fire consumes the trees. Furthermore, we do not know except that the Zaqqoom is nothing other than dates mixed with butter". In reply to their wonder how there will be a tree in the fire (of Hell), Allaah revealed this Quraanic Ayaah. [Ibn Jareer]

Verse Number 158

158- And they have invented a blood-relationship between Him (Allaah) and the angels (claiming their being His daughters), but the angels know well that they (who have invented such a claim) will indeed (have to) be brought forth (to punishment in the fire of Hell).

A narration on the authority of Ibn 'Abbaas [Allaah be pleased with them] that he said: This Quraanic Ayaah was revealed in connection with three tribes: Sulaym, Khuzaa'ah and Juhaynah. [Juwaybir]

A narration on the authority of Mujaahid that he said: The chiefs of Quraysh claimed that the angels were the daughters of Allaah. Abu Bakr As-Siddeeq [may Allaah be pleased with him] asked them: "Then, who are their mothers?" They replied: "The female-slaves taken from the jinn". On that occasion, Allaah Almighty (the Most High) revealed this Quraanic Ayaah. [Al-Bayhaqi in Shu'ab Al-EEmaan] Verse Number 165

165- And verily, we (angels) indeed are those who stand in rows (for prayer);

A narration on the authority of Yazeed Ibn Abu Maalik that the people used to pray as dispersed (and nor in rows). Then, when this Quraanic Ayaah was revealed, they were commanded to pray in rows. [Ibn Abu Haatim and Ibn Al-Mundhir on the authority of Ibn Jurayj]

Verse Number 176

176- Do they seek to hasten on Our Torment?

A narration on the authority of Ibn 'Abbaas [Allaah be pleased with them] that he said: The disbelievers (al-Kaafireen) said: "O Muhammad! Show us the torment (of Allaah) which you frighten us with! Hasten on it for us". On that occasion, Allaah revealed this Quraanic Ayaah. [Juwaybir: authentic according to the conditions stipulated by Al-Bukhaari and Muslim]

Soorah Saad

Verse Number 1-8

1- Saad, by the Quraan full of reminder (it is not so as the disbelievers (al-Kaafireen) allege that there are several gods). 2- Nay, those (of Makkah) who disbelieve are in false pride (self-glory and zeal for disbelief) and schism (hostility towards Prophet Muhammad). 3How many a generation have We destroyed before them! And they cried out when (the torment befell them and) it was not a time for escape. 4- And they (Arab pagans) wonder that a warner (Messenger) has come to them from among themselves. And the disbelievers (al-Kaafireen) say: "This is a sorcerer, a liar. 5- (By asking them to say 'there is none worthy of worship except Allaah) Has he made the gods (all) into One God (that is Allaah)? Verily, this is a curious thing!" 6- And the leaders among them went about (saying to one another): "Go on, and remain constant to (the worship of) your gods! Verily, This (monotheism we were asked to observe) is a thing designed (against us)! 7- We have not heard (the like) of this in the religion of these later days (that is Christianity of Jesus). This is nothing but an invented lie! 8- Has the Reminder (that is the Quraan) been sent down to him (Muhammad alone) from among us?" Nay, but they are in doubt about My Reminder (this Quraan since they belied the one who brought it)! Nay, but they have not tasted (My) Torment!

A narration on the authority of Ibn 'Abbaas [Allaah be pleased with them] that he said: When Abu Taalib became fatally ill the men of Quraysh and The Prophet [peace and blessings of Allaah be upon him] visited him. They complained of him to Abu Talib who told him: "O my nephew! What do you like from your people?" He replied: "I like from them only one word by which they will gain supremacy over the Arabs, and the non-Arabs would pay Jizyah. It is only one word". He asked: "What is it?" He said: "There is none worthy of worship but Allaah". They said: "Do you like to make the gods only one god? That is indeed an amazing thing!" In connection with them these Quraanic Aayaat were revealed. [Ahmad; At-Tirmidhi; An-Nasaa'i; Al-Haakim who renders it authentic]

Soorah Az-Zumar

Verse Number 3

3- Surely the religion (that is faith) is for Allaah only. And those (that is disbelievers (al-Kaafireen) and polytheists) who take (idols and false deities as) allies besides Him (say): "We worship them only that they may bring us near to Allaah." Verily Allaah will judge between them (Muslims and disbelievers (al-Kaafireen)) concerning that wherein they differ. Truly, Allaah guides not him who is a liar, and a disbeliever.

A narration on the authority of Ibn 'Abbaas [Allaah be pleased with them] that he said: It was revealed in connection with three tribes: 'AAmir, Kinaanah and Banu Salamah: they worshipped idols and say that the angels were Allaah's daughters. They said: "We worship them only to bring us close to Allaah". [Juwaybir]

Verse Number 9

9- Is one who is obedient to Allaah, prostrating himself or standing (in prayer) during the hours of the night, fearing the (punishment of the) Hereafter and hoping for the Mercy (that is Paradise) of his Lord (Rabb) (like one who is disobedient to his Lord (Rabb) with disbelief)? Say: "Are those who know equal to those who know not?" It is only men endued with reason who will remember (that is get a lesson from Allaah's Signs).

A narration on the authority of Ibn 'Umar [Allaah be pleased with them] that he said: This Quraanic Ayaah was revealed in connection with 'Uthmaan Ibn 'Affaan [may Allaah be pleased with him]. [Ibn Abu Haatim]

A narration on the authority of Ibn 'Abbaas [Allaah be pleased with them] that he said: It was revealed in connection with 'Ammaar Ibn Yaasir [may Allaah be pleased with him]. [Ibn Sa'd]

A narration on the authority of Ibn 'Abbaas [Allaah be pleased with them] that he said: It was revealed in connection with Ibn Mas'ood,

'Ammaar Ibn Yaasir and Saalim, the freed slave of Abu Hudhayfah [Allaah be pleased with them]. [Juwaybir]

A narration on the authority of 'Ikrimah that he said: It was revealed in connection with 'Ammaar Ibn Yaasir. [Juwaybir] Verse Number 17

17- Those who avoid the worship of Taaghoot (false deities and idols) and turn to Allaah (in repentance), for them are glad tidings (of Paradise); so give good news to My slaves -

A narration on the authority of Jaabir Ibn 'Abdullaah [Allaah be pleased with them] that he said: When the following was revealed (what means): {It has seven gates; for every gate is of them a portion designated}, [Al-Hijr, verse 44] a man from the Ansaar came to the Prophet [peace and blessings of Allaah be upon him] and said: "O Messenger of Allaah! I have seven slaves, and I have emancipated one for each gate of those (seven)". In connection with him Allaah revealed (what means): {So give good news to My slaves, Who listen to speech and follow the best of it. Those are the ones Allaah has guided, and those are people of understanding}. [Az-Zumar, verse 17-18]

A narration on the authority of Zayd Ibn Aslam that in connection with three men who used to say in the pre-Islamic days, "There is none worthy of worship but Allaah': Zayd Ibn 'Amr Ibn Nufayl, Abu Dharr Al-Ghifaari, and Salmaan Al-Faarisi, the following was revealed (what means): {Those who avoid the worship of Taaghoot (false deities and idols) and turn to Allaah (in repentance), for them are glad tidings (of Paradise); so give good news to My slaves}. [verse 17] [Ibn Abu Haatim]

Verse Number 23

23- Allaah has sent down (from time to time) the Best Statement, a consistent Book (this Quraan wherein promises of reward are) paired (with threats of punishment), therefrom the skins of those who fear their Lord (Rabb) shiver (when remembering Allaah's threats), and then their skin and their hearts (Qalb) soften to the celebration of Allaah (when remembering His promises). That (Book) is the guidance of Allaah therewith He Guides whomever He wills; and whomever Allaah sends astray, for him there is no guide. See Yoosuf Verse Number 3.

Verse Number 36

36- Is not Allaah Sufficient for His slave (that is Muhammad)? Yet they try to frighten you with the (idols which they worship) besides Him! And whomever Allaah sends astray, for him there is no guide.

A narration on the authority of Ma'mar that he said: A man told me: They said to the Prophet [peace and blessings of Allaah be upon him]: "You should either hold back from insulting our gods or we would command them to befog you". On that occasion, this Quraanic Ayaah was revealed. ['Abd-Ar-Razzaaq]

Verse Number 45

45- And when Allaah Alone is mentioned, the hearts (Qalb) of those who believe not in the Hereafter are filled with disgust (from the Oneness of Allaah); and when those (idols and false deities they worship) besides Him are mentioned, behold, they rejoice!

A narration on the authority of Mujaahid that it was revealed in connection with the recitation of Soorah An-Najm by the Prophet [peace and blessings of Allaah be upon him] near the Ka'bah, and the joy of the disbelievers (al-Kaafireen) when their gods were mentioned. [Ibn Al-Mundhir]

Verse Number 53

53- Say: "O My slaves who have transgressed against themselves (by committing evil deeds and sins)! Despair not of the Mercy of Allaah: verily, Allaah forgives all sins (for him who repents from polytheism). Verily, He is Oft-Forgiving, Most Merciful.

A narration on the authority of Ibn 'Abbaas [Allaah be pleased with them] that he said: This Quraanic Ayaah was revealed in connection with the polytheists of Makkah. [Ibn Abu Haatim with an authentic chain of narrators]

A narration on the authority of Ibn 'Umar [Allaah be pleased with them] that he said: We used to say: "No repentance will be accepted from him who has been turned (by force) from his religion, in case he left his religion after his reversion to Islam". When the Prophet [peace and blessings of Allaah be upon him] arrived in Madeenah, this Quraanic Ayaah was revealed in connection with them. [Al-Haakim and At-Tabaraani]

A narration on the authority of Ibn 'Abbaas [Allaah be pleased with them] that he said: the Prophet [peace and blessings of Allaah be upon him] sent to Wahshiyy, the murderer of Hamzah [may Allaah be pleased with him] inviting him to Islam. He sent to him saying: "How do you invite me given that you claim that he who kills, commits illegal sexual intercourse or steals will receive penalty, and the torment will be doubled to him on the Day of Resurrection, and therein he will abide forever in ignominy? I have done all this: so, do you find any concession for me?" On that occasion, Allaah revealed (what means): {Except such as repents (from his sins) and does righteous deeds; then verily, he turns to Allaah with true repentance (for which he deserves forgiveness from Allaah)}. [Al-Furqaan, verse 70] Wahshiyy said: "That is indeed a very hard condition: {Except such as repents (from his sins) and does righteous deeds}. Perhaps I could not do so". On that occasion, Allaah revealed (what means): {Verily, Allaah forgives not association (of partners with Him in worship), but He forgives what is less than that (of sins) to whom He wills; and whoever associates partners with Allaah (in worship), he has indeed invented a tremendous sin}. [An-Nisaa', verse 48] Wahshiyy said: "But this is suspended on Allaah's will, and I do not know then whether or not my sins will be forgiven by Him. Is there anything other than this?" On that occasion, Allaah revealed this Quraanic Ayaah in issue [53] Wahshiyy said: "That is acceptable". Then he embraced Islam. [At-Tabaraani with a weak chain of narrators]

Verse Number 64-66

64- Say: "Do you order me to worship other than Allaah O ignorant ones?" 65- And indeed it has been revealed to you (O Muhammad) as it was to those (Allaah's Messengers) before you: "If you associate partners in worship with Allaah, surely (all) your deeds will be fruitless, and you will certainly be among the losers." 66- Nay! But worship Allaah (Alone), and be among the grateful (to Him for His favors upon you).

A narration on the authority of Al-Hasan Al-Basri that he said: The polytheists told the Prophet [peace and blessings of Allaah be upon him]: "Do you render in error your forefathers O Muhammad?" On that occasion, Allaah revealed those Quraanic Aayaat. [Al-Bayhaqi in Ad-Dalaa'il]

Verse Number 67

67- (When they associated partners with Allaah in worship) they made no just estimate of Allaah such as is due to Him. And on the Day of Resurrection the whole earth will be (within) His Grasp and the heavens will be rolled up in His Right Hand. Exalted be He and High be He above all that they associate as partners with Him!

A narration on the authority of Ibn 'Abbaas [Allaah be pleased with them] that he said: A Jew passed by the Prophet [peace and blessings of Allaah be upon him] and said: "What do you say O Abu Al-Qaasim, when Allaah will put the heavens on this (finger), the earths on that (finger), the water on that (finger) and the mountains on that (finger)?" On that occasion, Allaah revealed this Quraanic Ayaah. [At-Tirmidhi who renders it authentic]

A narration on the authority of Al-Hasan that he said: The Yahood went on considering the creation of the heavens and the earth and when they finished they went on estimating that. On that occasion, Allaah revealed this Quraanic Ayaah. [Ibn Abu Haatim]

A narration on the authority of Sa'eed Ibn Jubayr that he said: The Yahood talked about the attributes of the Lord (Rabb) Almighty, with what they did not know or see. On that occasion, Allaah revealed this Quraanic Ayaah. [Ibn Abu Haatim]

A narration on the authority of Ar-Rabee' Ibn Anas that he said: When the following was revealed (what means): {His Kursiyy extends over the heavens and the earth}, [Al-Baqarah, verse 255] they said: "O Messenger of Allaah! That is the Kursiyy: then what about the Throne (of Majesty)?" On that occasion, Allaah revealed this Quraanic Ayaah. [Ibn Al-Mundhir]

Soorah Ghaafir

Verse Number 4

4- None disputes in the revelations of Allaah (that is this Quraan) but those who disbelieve (from among the people of Makkah). So let not their moving about through the land (safely to earn their living) delude you (O Muhammad, for their ultimate end will be the fire of Hell)!

A narration on the authority of Abu Maalik that he said: This Quraanic Ayaah was revealed in connection with Al-Haarith Ibn Qays As-Sahmi. [Ibn Abu Haatim]

Verse Number 56

56- Verily, those who dispute about the revelations of Allaah (that is the Quraan), without any (proof of) authority having come to them, they have nothing in their breasts except arrogance (to accept your invitation). They will never attain it (that is Prophethood). So seek refuge with Allaah (from their evil). Verily, it is He Who is the All-Hearer (of their words), the All-Seer (of their states).

A narration on the authority of Abu Al-'AAliyah that he said: The Yahood came to the Prophet [peace and blessings of Allaah be upon him] and made a mention of the antichrist, saying: "Towards the end of time, there will be from among us such and such..." and they exalted his affair. They said: "He will make such and such things". On that occasion, Allaah revealed this Quraanic Ayaah. By it He Almighty commanded His Prophet [peace and blessings of Allaah be upon him] to seek refuge with Him from the Fitnah of the antichrist. [Ibn Abu Haatim]

A narration on the authority of Ka'b Al-Ahbaar that he said: As for those who dispute about the signs of Allaah with no authority they receive, they are the Yahood. This Quraanic Ayaah was revealed in connection with them and what they expect concerning the antichrist. [Ibn Abu Haatim]

Verse Number 66

66- Say (O Muhammad): "I have been forbidden to worship those whom you invoke (worship) besides Allaah, since there have come to me (clear) evidences (signs of Allaah's Oneness) from my Lord (Rabb); and I am commanded to submit (in Islam) to the Lord (Rabb) of the worlds.

A narration on the authority of Ibn 'Abbaas [Allaah be pleased with them] that Al-Waleed Ibn Al-Mugheerah and Shaybah Ibn Rabee'ah said: "O Muhammad! Retract from what you are saying and abide by the religion of your forefathers". On that occasion, Allaah revealed this Quraanic Ayaah. [Juwaybir]

Soorah Fussilat

Verse Number 22

22- And in no way did you hide yourselves (while committing the immoralities and shameful deeds), so that neither your ears, nor your eyes, nor your skins should testify against you (because you were not certain of resurrection in the hereafter); but you thought that Allaah knew not much of what you used to do.

A narration on the authority of Ibn Mas'ood [may Allaah be pleased with him] that he said: Three men engaged in argument near the House: Two from Quraysh and one from Thaqeef or two from Thaqeef and one from Quraysh. One of them said: "Do you see that Allaah hears what we are saying?" The other replied: "He hears what we pronounce and does not hear what we conceal". The third said: "If he hears what we pronounce, then He should, inevitably, hear what we conceal". On that occasion, Allaah revealed this Quraanic Ayaah. [Al-Bukhaari; Muslim; At-Tirmidhi; Ahmad and others]

Verse Number 40

40- Verily, those who deviate from Our revelations (that is this Quraan by denying them) are not hidden from Us (for which We shall requite them). Is he who is cast into the Fire better or he who comes secure on the Day of Resurrection? Do what you will. Verily He is All-Seer of what you do.

A narration on the authority of Basheer Ibn Fath that he said: This Quraanic Ayaah was revealed in connection with Abu Jahl and 'Ammaar Ibn Yaasir [may Allaah be pleased with him]. [Ibn Al-Mundhir]

Verse Number 44

44- And had We made it (the Message) a Quraan in a nonArabic language, they would have said: "Why are not its Aayaat explained in detail (in our language so that we would be able to understand them)?" What! (can it be a non- Arabic Book and an Arab (Messenger)?" Say: "It is for those who believe a guide (from error) and a healing (from ignorance). And as for those who disbelieve, there is deafness in their ears (so that they hear not), and it (the Quraan) is (a source of) blindness for them (so that they understand not). They are (like) those called from a place far away (so that they neither listen nor understand).

A narration on the authority of Sa'eed Ibn Jubayr that he said: The men of Quraysh said: "What! (can it be a non- Arabic Book and an Arab (Messenger)?" On that occasion, Allaah revealed this Quraanic Ayaah. After it, Allaah revealed in it from all languages. [Ibn Jareer]

Soorah Ash-Shoora

Verse Number 16

16- And those (that is the Yahood) who dispute (with Allaah's Prophet) concerning (the religion of) Allaah after it has been accepted (by the people who believed in it when its clear signs and evidences seemed clear), useless is their dispute before their Lord (Rabb), and on them is wrath, and for them will be a severe torment.

A narration on the authority of 'Ikrimah that he said: When Allaah revealed (what means): {When there comes the Help of Allaah (to you, O Muhammad (peace be upon him) against your enemies) and the conquest (of Makkah), and you see that the people enter Allaah's religion (Islam) in crowds, so glorify the Praises of your Lord (Rabb), and ask for His Forgiveness. Verily, He is the One Who accepts the repentance and forgives}, the polytheists in Makkah said, addressing these of the believers (al-Mumineen) among them: "The people have entered in the religion of Allaah in groups: so, leave us. Why do you still live among us?" On that occasion, Allaah revealed this Quraanic Ayaah. [Ibn Al-Mundhir]

A narration on the authority of Qataadah that he said, concerning Allaah's saying (what means): {And those who dispute (with Allaah's Prophet) concerning (the religion of) Allah...}: They are the Yahood and Nasaara. They said: "Since our Book was revealed before yours, and Our Messenger was sent before yours, then we are better than you". ['Abd-Ar-Razzaaq]

Verse Number 23-26

23- That is (the Paradise) of which Allaah gives glad tidings to His slaves who believe (in Him) and do righteous deeds. Say (O Muhammad): "I ask you no reward for this (that is conveying Allaah's Message to you) except to be affectionate for (my) kinship." And whoever earns a good deed, We shall give him an increase of good in respect thereof. Verily, Allaah is Oft-Forgiving (of sins), Most Ready to appreciate (the few number of deeds by multiplying them many times). 24- Or do they say: "He has invented a lie against Allaah (by attributing the Quraan to Him)?" If Allaah willed, He would bind fast your heart (with patience over what they say; and He did accordingly). And Allaah wipes out falsehood (which they claim) and establishes the truth with His speech (this Quraan sent down on His Prophet). Verily, He knows well what (secrets) are in the (people's) breasts. 25- And He it is Who accepts repentance from His slaves, and forgives sins (from which they repent), and He knows what you do. 26- And He answers (the requests of) those who believe (in Allaah) and do righteous deeds, and gives them increase of His Bounty. And as for the disbelievers (al-Kaafireen), theirs will be a severe torment.

A narration on the authority of Ibn 'Abbaas [Allaah be pleased with them] that he said: The Ansaar said:

"Would that we gather wealth for the Prophet [peace and blessings of Allaah be upon him]!" On that occasion, Allaah revealed this Quraanic Ayaah. One of them said: "He said so in order that we should fight on behalf of and support his household". In this connection, Allaah revealed (what means): {Or do they say: "He has invented a lie against Allaah (by attributing the Quraan to Him)?" ...} up to: {And He it is Who accepts repentance from His slaves...} Thus He offered repentance to them to His saying (what means): {and gives them increase of His Bounty}. [At-Tabaraani with a weak chain of narrators]

Verse Number 27

27- And were Allaah to extend sustenance for (all) His slaves, they would surely transgress in the earth, but He sends down (provision) by measure as He wills. Verily! He is, of His slaves, Well-Acquainted, All-Seeing.

A narration on the authority of 'Ali [may Allaah be pleased with him] that he said: This Quraanic Ayaah was revealed in connection with the men of Suffah. They said: "Would that we have such and such (good things)", hoping for the worldly benefits. [Al-Haakim who renders it authentic]

The same is narrated on the authority of 'Amr Ibn Hurayth. [At-Tabaraani]

Soorah Az-Zukhruf

Verse Number 19

19- And they make the angels who themselves are slaves of (Allaah) the Most Gracious as females. Did they witness their creation? Their testimony (that they are females) will be recorded, and (about which) they will be questioned (in the hereafter to be punished for it)!

A narration on the authority of Qataadah that he said: Some hypocrites (al-Munaafiqeen) said: "Verily, Allaah had married jinn and therefrom the angels were produced". In connection with them, Allaah revealed this Quraanic Ayaah. [Ibn Al-Mundhir]

Verse Number 31

31- And they say: "Why is this Quraan not sent down to any of the great men of the two towns (Makkah and Taa'if)?" See Yoonus Verse Number 2.

Verse Number 36

36- And whoever turns away blindly from the remembrance of (Allaah) the Most Gracious (that is this Quraan), We assign to him Satan to be a companion (that never leaves him).

A narration on the authority of Qataadah that he said: Al-Waleed Ibn Al-Mugheerah said: "Had what

Muhammad is saying been true, it would then have been revealed to me or to Abu Mas'ood Ath-Thaqafi". On that occasion, Allaah revealed this Quraanic Ayaah. [Ibn Al-Mundhir]

A narration on the authority of Muhammad Ibn 'Uthmaan Al-Makhzoomi that the men of Quraysh said: "Assign to each one of Muhammad's companions a man to seize him". They assigned to Abu Bakr Talhah. He came to him while he was sitting among the people thereupon Abu Bakr said: "To what do you invite me?" He said: "I invite you to worship Laat and 'Uzza". Abu Bakr said: "What is Al-Laat?" He said: "He is our lord". He said: "Then, what is Al-'Uzza?" He said: "The daughter of Allaah". He asked: "Then who is her mother?" Talhah then kept silent and gave no reply. Talhah said to his companions: "Answer the man". They all kept silent. Talhah said: "Stand up O Abu Bakr! I testify that there is none worthy of worship except for Allaah, and that Muhammad is the Messenger of Allaah". On that occasion, Allaah Almighty (the Most High) revealed this Quraanic Ayaah. [Ibn Abu Haatim]

Verse Number 57

57- And when (Jesus) son of Mary is put forward as an example, behold, your people laugh out (at it rejoicing in what they hear).

A narration on the authority of Ibn 'Abbaas [Allaah be pleased with them] that the Prophet [peace and blessings of Allaah be upon him] said to the men of

Quraysh: "No good lies in anyone that is worshipped other than Allaah". They said: "Do you not claim that Jesus was a Prophet and a righteous slave? Yet he was worshipped other than Allaah". On that occasion, Allaah revealed this Quraanic Ayaah. [Ahmad with an authentic chain of narrators; and At-Tabaraani]

Verse Number 80

80- Or do they think that We hear not their secrets and their private talks? (Yes We do) and Our Messengers (appointed angels in charge of people) are with them to record (all what they say).

A narration on the authority of Muhammad Ibn Ka'b Al-Qurathi that he said: While three men were in between the Ka'bah and its curtains: Two from Quraysh and one from Thaqeef or two from Thaqif and one from Quraysh, one of them said: "Do you see that Allaah hears what we are saying?" The other replied: "He hears what you pronounce and does not hear what you conceal". On that occasion, Allaah revealed this Quraanic Ayaah. [Ibn Jareer]

Soorat Ad-Dukhaan

Verse Number 10

10- Then wait you for the Day when the sky will bring forth a visible smoke

A narration on the authority of Ibn Mas'ood [may Allaah be pleased with him] that he said: when the Prophet [peace and blessings of Allaah be upon him] saw the refusal of the people to accept Islam he said: "O Allaah! Send (famine) years on them for (seven years) like the seven years (of famine during the time) of (Prophet) Joseph." So famine overtook them for one year and destroyed every kind of life to such an extent that the people started eating hides, carcasses and rotten dead animals. Whenever one of them looked towards the sky, he would (imagine himself to) see smoke because of hunger. So Abu Sufyaan went to The Prophet [peace and blessings of Allaah be upon him] and said: "O Muhammad! You order people to obey Allaah and to keep good relations with kith and kin. No doubt the people of your tribe are dying, so please pray to Allaah for them." So Allaah Almighty (the Most High) revealed this Quraanic Ayaah. [Al-Bukhaari]

Verse Number 15-16

15- Verily, We are going to remove the torment (from you) for a while. Verily you will return (to disbelief). 16- On the Day when We shall seize you with the greatest seizure (punishment). Verily, We will exact retribution.

A narration on the authority of Ibn Mas'ood [may Allaah be pleased with him] that he said: When the famine was taken off, the people renegaded once again to disbelief. On that occasion, Allaah revealed those Quraanic Aayaat. Ibn Mas'ood commented: "And that was what happened on the day of the battle of Badr." the Prophet [peace and blessings of Allaah be upon him] prayed for them and it rained heavily for seven days. So the people complained of the excessive rain. The Prophet [peace and blessings of Allaah be upon him] said: "O Allaah! (Let it rain) around us and not on us". So the clouds dispersed over his head and it rained over the surroundings." [Al-Bukhaari]

Verse Number 43-44

43- Verily, the tree of Zaqqoom 44- Will be the food of the sinners.

A narration on the authority of Abu Maalik that he said: Abu Jahl used to bring dates and butter and say: "Eat the Zaqqoom: that is the Zaqqoom therewith Muhammad threatens you". On that occasion, Allaah revealed those Quraanic Aayaat. [Sa'eed Ibn Mansoor]

Verse Number 49

49- (It will be said to the sinner) "Taste you (of this torment)!

Verily, you were (pretending to be) the mighty, the generous! A narration on the authority of 'Ikrimah that he said: the Prophet [peace and blessings of Allaah be upon him] met Abu Jahl and told him: "Verily, Allaah commanded me to say to you (what means): {Woe to you (O disbeliever)! And then (again) woe! Again, woe to you (O disbeliever)! And then (again) woe!} [Al-Qiyaamah, verse 34-35] He then took his garment off his hand and said: "Neither you nor your companion can do anything harmful to me. You know that I protect the inhabitants of Al-Bathaa' and I am the exalted in might, the generous". On the day of Badr battle, Allaah killed him and put him to shame because of his statement. In connection with him, Allaah Almighty (the Most High) revealed this Quraanic Ayaah in issue. [Al-Umawi in his Maghaazi]

The Same is narrated on the authority of Qataadah. [Ibn Jareer]

Soorah Al-Jathiyah

Verse Number 23

23- Do you see him who takes his own desire as his god, and Allaah, having known (him as such before his creation), sent him astray, and sealed up his hearing and his heart (so that he would not listen to nor understand guidance), and put a cover on his sight (so that he would not see the truth)? Who then will guide him after Allaah (left him astray)? Will you not then receive admonition?

A narration on the authority of Sa'eed Ibn Jubayr that he said: The men of Quraysh worshipped the stone for a while; and if they found something better, they would leave the former and worship the latter.

On that occasion, Allaah Almighty (the Most High) revealed this Quraanic Ayaah. [Ibn Al-Mundhir and Ibn Jareer]

Verse Number 24

24- And they (who deny the resurrection) say: "There is nothing but our life (which we live in) this world, we die and we live and nothing destroys us except the (passage of) time". And they have no knowledge of it: they only conjecture.

A narration on the authority of Abu Hurayrah [may Allaah be pleased with him] that he said: The people of the pre-Islamic days used to say: "Nothing ruins us but day and night". On that occasion, Allaah revealed this Quraanic Ayaah. [Ibn Jareer]

Soorah Al-Ahqaaf

Verse Number 10

10- Say: "Tell me! If this (Quraan) is from Allaah, and you reject it, and a witness from among the Children of Israel testifies that this Quraan is from Allaah (like the previous Books: Torah and Gospel) so he believed (in Islam) while you are too arrogant (to believe: will you not be wrongdoers because of your disbelief?)" Verily! Allaah guides not the wrongful people.

A narration on the authority of 'Awf ibn Maalik Al-'Ashja'i [may Allaah be pleased with him] that he said: "The Prophet [peace and blessings of Allaah be upon him] and I went out until we entered the temple of the Yahood in Madeenah on their feast. They disliked that we entered upon them. The Prophet [peace and blessings of Allaah be upon him] said: "O Yahood! Show me twelve men who testify that there is no deity worthy of worship but Allaah, so that Allaah will remove from every Jew under heavens the wrath He Brought on them". They all kept silent and none of them gave any reply. Then he went away and behold! A man appeared from behind his back and said: "Remain in your place O Muhammad!" He then approached him and said: "Which type of man do you know me O assembly of Yahood?" They said: ""By Allaah, we do not know that there is anyone among us who has better knowledge of the Book of Allaah and better religious comprehension than you and your father and your grandfather before your father".

He said: "Then, I testify that he (Muhammad) is the same Prophet you find in the Torah". They said: "You have told a lie". They then went on defaming him and talking badly about him. On that occasion, Allaah revealed this Quraanic Ayaah. [At-Tabaraani with an authentic chain of narrator]

A narration on the authority of Sa'd Ibn Abu Waqqaas [may Allaah be pleased with him] that he said: In connection with 'Abdullaah Ibn Salaam this Quraanic Ayaah was revealed, esp. Allaah's saying (what means): {... and a witness from among the children of Israel testifies to it...} [Al-Bukhaari and Muslim]

A narration on the authority of 'Abdullaah Ibn Salaam [may Allaah be pleased with him] that he said: In connection with me, this Quraanic Ayaah was revealed. [Ibn Jareer]

Verse Number 11

11- And those (rich) who disbelieve say of those (poor) who believe: "Had it (Islam) been good, they (the poor) would not have preceded us thereto!" And since they have not been guided by it (this Quraan), they say: "This (Quraan) is an ancient lie!"

A narration on the authority of Qataadah that he said: Some polytheists said: "We are more powerful and better in honor; we are better in such and such (good things)... had it (what Muhammad has brought) been good, none like so and so, and so and so, would have preceded us to it". On that occasion, Allaah revealed this Quraanic Ayaah. [Ibn Jareer]

A narration on the authority of 'Awn Ibn Abu Shaddaad that he said: 'Umar Ibn Al-Khattaab [may Allaah be pleased with him] had a slave-girl who embraced Islam before him, called Zaneen. 'Umar used to beat her for her reversion to Islam till he wearied.

The disbelievers (al-Kaafireen) of Quraysh then said: "Had it (what Muhammad has brought) been good, no doubt, Zaneen would not have preceded us to it". In connection with her, Allaah revealed this Quraanic Ayaah. [Ibn Al-Mundhir]

The same is narrated on the authority of Ad-Dahhaak and Al-Hasan. [Ibn Sa'd]

Verse Number 17-19

17- But he who says to his parents: "Fie upon you both! Do you promise me that I shall be raised up (again from the grave after my death) when generations before me have passed away (and were not raised up)?" While they (his parents) invoke Allaah for help (addressing their son): "(Unless you return from your disbelief) Woe to you! Believe (in the resurrection)! Verily, the Promise of Allaah is true." But he says: "This (promise of resurrection) is nothing but the tales of the ancient." 18- They are those against whom the Word (of torment) has been justified among the previous generations of jinn and men that have passed away. Verily, ever are they losers. 19- And for all (believers (al-Mumineen) and disbelievers (al-Kaafireen)), there will be degrees according to what they did, that He (Allaah) may recompense them in full for their deeds. And they will not be dealt unjustly (even in the least).

A narration on the authority of As-Suddi that he said: This Quraanic Ayaah was revealed in connection with 'Abd-Ar-Rahmaan Ibn Abu Bakr: he said "Fie upon you both" to his parents who embraced Islam and he rejected to do. Whenever they ordered him to embrace Islam he would reply to them harshly and belie them and say: "Where is so and so, and so and so", referring to the old men of Quraysh who died?

Later on, tie embraced Islam and was good in faith. His repentance then was revealed in Allaah's saying (what means): {And for all (believers (al-Mumineen) and disbelievers (al-Kaafireen)), there will be degrees according to what they did, that He (Allaah) may recompense them in full for their deeds. And they will not be dealt unjustly (even in the least)}. [verse 19] [Ibn Abu Haatim]

The same is narrated on the authority of Ibn 'Abbaas [Allaah be pleased with them]. [Ibn Jareer]

A narration on the authority of Yoosuf Ibn Maahaan that he said: Marwaan said: In connection with 'Abd-Ar-Rahmaan Ibn Abu Bakr this Quraanic Ayaah was revealed (what means): {But he who says to his parents: "Fie upon you both!} [verse 17] On that,

'AA'ishah [Allaah be pleased with her] said from behind the partition: "Allaah Almighty (the Most High) has revealed in connection with us (the family of Abu Bakr) nothing of the Quraan save my innocence". [Al-Bukhaari]

A narration on the authority of Makki that he heard 'AA'ishah [Allaah be pleased with her] having denied that this Quraanic Ayaah was revealed in connection with 'Abd-Ar-Rahmaan Ibn Abu Bakr. She said: "It was rather revealed in connection with so and so", and named him. ['Abd-Ar-Razzaaq] According to Al-Haafith Ibn Hajar, the denial given by 'AA'ishah [Allaah be pleased with her] is more authentic with regard to the chain of narrators, and more reliable.

Verse Number 29-32

29- And (remember) when We sent towards you (O Muhammad) a group of jinn, listening to the Quraan. When they stood in the presence thereof, they said: "Listen in silence!" And when it was finished, they returned to their people, as warners (of torment if they did not believe). 30- They said: "O our people! Verily, we have listened to a Book (this Quraan) sent down after Moses, confirming what came before it (that is the Torah and Gospel): it guides to the truth (that is Islam) and to a Straight Path. 31- O our people! Respond (with obedience) to Allaah's Caller (that is Muhammad [peace and blessings of Allaah be upon him]) and believe in him. He (Allaah) will forgive you some of your sins, and will save you from a painful torment". 32- And whoever does not respond to

(Muhammad) Allaah's Caller, he cannot escape on earth (from Allaah's torment): and such will have no allies besides Allaah (to protect him from Allaah's Punishment). Those (who do not respond to Allaah's caller) are in manifest error.

A narration on the authority of Ibn Mas'ood [may Allaah be pleased with him] that he said: The jinn descended upon the Prophet [peace and blessings of Allaah be upon him] while he was reciting the Quraan in the valley of Nakhlah. Having heard him, they ordered each other to be silent. They were nine one of whom was Zawba'ah. On that occasion, Allaah revealed those Quraanic Aayaat. [Ibn Abu Shaybah]

Soorah Muhammad

Verse Number 1-2

1- Those who disbelieve (in Allaah, from among the Makkans and others) and avert (people) from the Path of Allaah (Islam), He will render fruitless their deeds. 2- But those who believe (in Allaah from among the Ansaar and others) and do righteous deeds, and believe in that (Quraan) which has been sent down to Muhammad (peace be upon him) - as it is the truth from their Lord (Rabb) - He will remove from them their sins and will make good their state.

A narration on the authority of Ibn 'Abbaas [Allaah be pleased with them] that concerning Allaah's saying (what means): {Those who disbelieve (in Allaah, from among the Makkans and others) and avert (people) from the Path of Allaah (Islam), He will render fruitless their deeds}, he said: Those are the disbelievers (al-Kaafireen) of Makkah, in connection with whom it was revealed. As for His saying (what means): {But those who believe (in Allaah from among the Ansaar and others) and do righteous deeds, and believe in that (Quraan) which has been sent down to Muhammad (peace be upon him) - as it is the truth from their Lord (Rabb) - He will remove from them their sins and will make good their state}, he said: Those are the Ansaar. [Ibn Abu Haatim]

Verse Number 4

4- So, when you meet (in fight) those who disbelieve, strike (their) necks till when you have killed and wounded many of them, then (stop from killing them and take the rest as captives and) bind a bond firmly (on them). Thereafter either free them without ransom (out of generosity) or with ransom, until the war lays down its burden. Thus (you are ordered by Allaah), but had it been Allaah's Will, He Himself could certainly have vindicated them (without fighting). But (He commands you to fight them) in order to test some of you with others. But those who are killed in the way of Allaah, never will He cause their deeds to be lost.

A narration on the authority of Qataadah that he said: This Quraanic Ayaah was revealed on the day of Uhud (battle) while the Prophet [peace and blessings of Allaah be upon him] was in the defile and the Muslims were suffering from severe injuries and many victims. Then the polytheists cried out: "Be superior O Hubal!" The Muslims replied: "Allaah is more superior and more glorious!" The polytheists said: "We have Al-'Uzza and you have no 'Uzza". the Prophet [peace and blessings of Allaah be upon him] said: "say: 'Allaah is our guardian and you have no guardian." [Ibn Abu Haatim]

Verse Number 13

13- And how many a (population of a) town We have destroyed, stronger than (the population of) your town (Makkah O Muhammad) which has driven you out. And there was none to help them (against Our destruction of them).

A narration on the authority of Ibn 'Abbaas [Allaah be pleased with them] that he said: When the Prophet [peace and blessings of Allaah be upon him] went out to the cave, he looked at Makkah and said: "Verily, you are the dearest of Allaah's cities to me; and had it not been for the fact that your inhabitants expelled me from you, I would have not left you". On that occasion, Allaah revealed this Quraanic Ayaah. [Abu Ya'li]

Verse Number 16

16- And among them (that is the hypocrites (al-Munaafiqeen)) are some who listen to you (O Muhammad in Khutbah of Jumu'ah prayer) till when they go out from you, they say to those who have received knowledge (from amongst the Companions): "What has he said just now? Such are men whose hearts (Qalb) Allaah has sealed up (with disbelief), and they follow their desires (that is for hypocrisy).

A narration on the authority of Ibn Jurayj that he said: The believers (al-Mumineen) and hypocrites (al-Munaafiqeen) used to gather with the Messenger of Allaah [peace and blessings of Allaah be upon him] and he believers (al-Mumineen) would listen and understand what he said, whereas the hypocrites (al-Munaafiqeen) would hear but understand not. If they came out they would ask the believers (al-Mumineen): "What has he just said?" On that occasion, this Quraanic Ayaah was revealed. [Ibn Al-Mundhir]

Verse Number 33

33- O you who believe! Obey Allaah, and obey the Messenger (Muhammad) and render not vain your deeds (with sins and misdeeds).

A narration on the authority of Abu Al-'AAliyah that he said: The Companions of the Prophet [peace and blessings of Allaah be upon him] saw that no sin would harm with (the testification that) 'There is none worthy of worship except for Allaah' as well as no deed would avail with polytheism. On that occasion, Allaah revealed this Quraanic Ayaah. They feared lest the sin would make fruitless the deed. [Ibn Abu Haatim]

Soorah Al-Fath

Verse Number 1

1- Verily, We have decreed for you (O Muhammad) a manifest victory.

A narration on the authority of Al-Miswar Ibn Makhramah and Marwaan Ibn Al-Hakam that they said: Soorah Al-Fath was revealed in the way between Makkah and Madeenah and it entirely addressed the Hudaybiyah, from the beginning to the end. [Al-Haakim and others] Verse Number 2-5

2- That (with your striving) Allaah may forgive you your earlier and later sins, and (by that conquest) complete His Favor on you, and guide you to a Straight Path (that is the way of Islam), 3- And that Allaah may help you with a mighty help. 4- He it is Who sent down tranquility into the hearts (Qalb) of the believers (al-Mumineen), that they may increase in Faith along with their (present) Faith (in Allaah). And to Allaah belong the hosts of the heavens and the earth, and Ever is Allaah All-Knower (of the states and affairs of His creation), All-Wise (in what He makes and does). 5- (He enjoined Jihaad upon you so) that He may admit the believing men and women to Gardens beneath which rivers flow (in Paradise), to abide therein forever, and He may remove from them their sins; and that is, in the sight of Allaah, a great attainment.

A narration on the authority of Anas [may Allaah be pleased with him] that he said: Allaah revealed to the Prophet [peace and blessings of Allaah be upon him] (what means): {That (with your striving) Allaah may forgive you your earlier and later sins, and (by that conquest) complete His Favor on you, and guide you to a Straight Path (that is the way of Islam)}, [verse 2] in his way of return from Hudaybiyah. On that, the Prophet [peace and blessings of Allaah be upon him] said: "A Quraanic Ayaah has been revealed to me and it is dearer to me than whatever is on the earth". He recited it to them thereupon they said: "Blessed be you O Messenger of Allaah! Allaah has showed to you what He is going to do with you. Then, what shall He do with us?" On that occasion, Allaah revealed (what means): {that He may admit the believing men and women to Gardens beneath which rivers flow (in Paradise), to abide therein forever, and He may remove from them their sins; and that is, in the sight of Allaah, a great attainment}. [verse 5] [Al-Bukhaari; Muslim; At-Tirmidhi and Al-Haakim]

Verse Number 18

18- Indeed, Allaah was pleased with the believers (al-Mumineen) when they gave you the pledge of allegiance under the tree: He knew what was in their hearts (Qalb) (of truthfulness and faithfulness), and He sent down tranquility upon them, and He rewarded them with a near victory,

A narration on the authority of Salamah Ibn Al-Akwa' [may Allaah be pleased with him] that he said: While we were sleeping, a caller of the Prophet [peace and blessings of Allaah be upon him] cried out: "O people! come to give the pledge of allegiance! Come to give the pledge of allegiance! The Noble Spirit (Jibreel) has descended". We went to the Prophet [peace and blessings of Allaah be upon him] and he was underneath a huge Samurah and gave him the pledge of allegiance. On that occasion, Allaah revealed this Quraanic Ayaah. [Ibn Abu Haatim]

Verse Number 24

24- And He it is Who has withheld their hands from you and your hands from them in the midst of Makkah, after He had given you victory over them. And ever is Allaah, of what you do, All-Seer. A narration on the authority of Anas Ibn Malik "may Allaah be pleased with him" that eighty Persons from the people of Mecca came down upon the Prophet [peace and blessings of Allaah be upon him] from the mountain of Tan'eem. They were armed and they wanted to attack the Prophet [peace and blessings of Allaah be upon him] and his Companions who were not ready. He (The Prophet) captured them but spared their lives. On that occasion, Allaah revealed this Quraanic Ayaah. [Muslim; At-Tirmidhi and An-Nasaa'i]

The same is narrated on the authority of Salamah Ibn Al-Akwa' [may Allaah be pleased with him]. [Muslim]

The same is narrated on the authority of 'Abdullaah Ibn Mughaffal Al-Muzni [may Allaah be pleased with him]. [At-Tirmidhi and Ahmad]

A narration on the authority of Ibn 'Abbaas [Allaah be pleased with them]. [Ibn Ishaaq]

Verse Number 25

25- They are these who disbelieved (in Allaah) and averted you from Al-Masjid Al-Haraam (at Makkah) and detained the Had'y from reaching their place of sacrifice (at Muzdalifah). Had there not been believing men and believing women (living at Makkah along with the disbelievers (al-Kaafireen)) whom you did not know (by name), that you may kill them (along with the disbelievers (al-Kaafireen) without learning that they were believers (al-Mumineen) if you were given permission to conquer Makkah) and on whose account a sin would have been incurred upon you without (your) knowledge (you would have been allowed to conquer it; yet you were given no permission to do so) that Allaah might bring into His Mercy whom He wills, (and) had they (the believers (al-Mumineen)) been apart (from the disbelievers (al-Kaafireen)), We would had punished those of them who disbelieved with painful torment (by allowing you to conquer Makkah).

A narration on the authority of Abu Jumu'ah: Junayd Ibn Sabu that he said:

I fought with the Prophet [peace and blessings of Allaah be upon him] at the beginning of the day as a disbeliever and then I fought in his side at the end of the day as a Muslim. We were three men and seven women. In connection with us, this Quraanic Ayaah was revealed. [At-Tabaraani and Abu Ya'li]

Verse Number 27

27- Indeed Allaah has fulfilled the vision for His Messenger in very truth. Certainly, you shall enter Al-Masjid Al-Haraam, if Allaah wills, secure, having your heads shaved, and having your hair cut short, and with no fear. He knew what you knew not (of goodness in the peace treaty), and He granted besides that a near victory.

A narration on the authority of Mujaahid that he said: the Prophet [peace and blessings of Allaah be upon him] was shown in a dream, while being at Hudaybiyah, that he would enter Makkah along with his Companions in safety with their heads shaved and their hair cut short. When the sacrificial animals were sacrificed in Hudaybiyah his Companions said: "Where is your vision O Messenger of Allaah?" On that occasion, Allaah Almighty (the Most High) revealed this Quraanic Ayaah. [Al-Firyaabi; 'Abd Ibn Humayd and Al-Bayhaqi in Ad-Dalaa'il]

Soorah Al-Hujuraat

Verse Number 1

1- O you who believe! Put forward not (any word or deed) before Allaah and His Messenger (without their permission), and fear Allaah. Verily! Allaah is All-Hearing (of your words), All-Knowing (of your states).

A narration on the authority of Ibn Abu Mulaykah that 'Abdullaah Ibn Az-Zubayr [may Allaah be pleased with him] told him that a group of riders belonging to Banu Tameem came to The Prophet [peace and blessings of Allaah be upon him] and Abu Bakr said (to The Prophet): "Appoint Al-Qa'qaa' Ibn Ma'bad Ibn Zuraarah as (their) ruler." 'Umar said (to The Prophet): "No! But appoint Al-Aqra' Ibn Haabis." On that Abu Bakr said (to 'Umar): "You just wanted to oppose me." 'Umar replied: "I did not want to oppose you." Both of them argued so much that their voices became louder. On that occasion, Allaah revealed those Quraanic Aayaat up to Allaah's saying (what means): {And if they had patience till you could come out to them, it would have been better for them}. [verse 5] [Al-Bukhaari and others]

A narration on the authority of Al-Hasan that some people slaughtered their sacrifices on the day of Nahr before the Prophet [peace and blessings of Allaah be upon him] did, thereupon he ordered them to repeat it. On that occasion, Allaah revealed this Quraanic Ayaah. [Ibn Al-Mundhir]

A narration on the authority of 'AA'ishah [Allaah be pleased with her] that some people used to fast the first days of months before the Prophet [peace and blessings of Allaah be upon him], thereupon this Quraanic Ayaah was revealed. [At-Tabaraani in Al-Awsat]

A narration on the authority of Qataadah that he said: It was mentioned to us that some people said: "Would that such and such (revelation) has been revealed concerning me! Would that such and such (revelation) has been revealed in connection with me!" On that occasion, this Quraanic Ayaah was revealed. [Ibn Jareer]

Verse Number 2

2- O you who believe! Raise not your voices above the voice of the Prophet (Muhammad), nor speak aloud to him in talk as you speak aloud to one another, lest your deeds should be rendered fruitless while you perceive not.

A narration on the authority of Qataadah that he said: They used to talk to the Prophet [peace and blessings of Allaah be upon him], with high voices and raise their voices in his presence. On that occasion, Allaah revealed this Quraanic Ayaah. [Ibn Jareer]

Verse Number 3

3- Verily! those who lower their voices in the presence of Allaah's Messenger, they are the ones whose hearts (Qalb) Allaah has tested (in order) for righteousness (to be made evident). For them is forgiveness and a great reward (that is Paradise).

A narration on the authority of Muhammad Ibn Thaabit Ibn Qays Ibn Shamaas that he said: When Allaah Almighty (the Most High) revealed (what means): {O you who believe! Raise not your voices above the voice of the Prophet (Muhammad), nor speak aloud to him in talk as you speak aloud to one another, lest your deeds should be rendered fruitless while you perceive not}, [verse 2] Thaabit Ibn Qays sat on the way weeping. 'AAsim Ibn 'Adiyy Ibn Al-'Ajlaan passed by him and then asked him: "What causes you to weep?" He replied: "This Quraanic Ayaah: I fear lest it has been revealed in connection with me and I am of loud voice in talking". 'AAsim raised the matter to the Prophet [peace and blessings of Allaah be upon him], who summoned him and said: "Are you not be pleased to live praiseworthy die as a martyr and enter Paradise?" He said: "I am pleased, and I will never raise my voice over the voice of the Prophet [peace and blessings of Allaah be upon him]". On that occasion, Allaah revealed this Quraanic Ayaah [3]. [Ibn Jareer]

Verse Number 4-5

4- Verily those who call you from behind the dwellings, most of them have no sense (to their evil deed which contradicted the high estimate that is due to you). 5- And if they had patience till you could come out to

them, it would have been better for them. And Allaah
is Oft-Forgiving (for those among them who repent),
Most Merciful.

A narration on the authority of Zayd Ibn Arqam [may
Allaah be pleased with him] that he said: Some
Bedouins came to the chambers of the Prophet [peace
and blessings of Allaah be upon him], and went on
calling out: "O Muhammad! O Muhammad!" On that
occasion, Allaah revealed those Quraanic Aayaat. [At-
Tabaraani and Abu Ya'li with a good chain of
narrators]

A narration on the authority of Qataadah that he said:
A man came to the Prophet [peace and blessings of
Allaah be upon him] and said: "O Muhammad! No
doubt, praising me is good and abusing me is bad". the
Prophet [peace and blessings of Allaah be upon him]
said: "That is Allaah (to Whom only this applies)".

On that occasion, this Quraanic Ayaah was revealed.
['Abd-Ar-Razzaaq: Mursal but it has witnesses in
Sunan At-Tirmidhi on the authority of Al-Baraa' [may
Allaah be pleased with him] with no mention of the
revelation of this Quraanic Ayaah.

The same is narrated on the authority of Al-Hasan.
[Ibn Jareer]

A narration on the authority of Al-Aqra' Ibn Haabis
that he called out the Prophet [peace and blessings of
Allaah be upon him] from behind the chambers but he
gave no reply. He said: "O Muhammad! No doubt,

praising me is good and abusing me is bad". the Prophet [peace and blessings of Allaah be upon him] said: "That is Allaah (to Whom only this applies)". [Ahmad with an authentic chain of narrators]

A narration on the authority of Al-Aqra' that he came to the Prophet [peace and blessings of Allaah be upon him] and said: "O Muhammad! Come out to us!" On that occasion, those Quraanic Aayaat were revealed. [Ibn Jareer and others]

Verse Number 6-8

6- O you who believe! If a wicked comes to you with any news, verify it, lest you should harm people in ignorance, and afterwards you become regretful for what you have done. 7- And know that among you there is the Messenger of Allaah. Were he to obey you in much of the matter (which you tell in opposition to the reality), you would surely be in trouble. But Allaah has endeared the Faith to you and has made it pleasing in your hearts (Qalb), and has made hateful to you disbelief, wickedness and disobedience (to Allaah and His Messenger). Those are the rightly guided. 8- (This is) as a bounty and favor from Allaah. And Allaah is All-Knowing (of His creation), Full of Wisdom (in what He does).

A narration on the authority of Al-Haarith Ibn Zuraar Al-Khuzaa'i that he said: I came to the Prophet [peace and blessings of Allaah be upon him] and he invited me to Islam so I accepted it and embraced Islam. He invited me to give Zakaah so I also accepted it and said:

"O Messenger of Allaah! Let me return to my people to invite them to Islam, and give Zakaah; and then I will gather the objects of Zakaah of him who responds to my invitation. Then when it is time for it you can send to me the Zakaah collector to bring you what I would gather thereof".

When Al-Haarith gathered the items of Zakaah and it was time for the Zakaah collector to take it, he did not come to take it from him. Having thought the Zakaah collector might have grown angry for something, Al-Haarith invited the almsgivers of his people and said to them: "the Prophet [peace and blessings of Allaah be upon him] had appointed a time to send to me his courier to take what I have of Zakaah items; and the Prophet [peace and blessings of Allaah be upon him] never fails in his appointments. I think that nothing has prevented his courier from coming except that he might be angry. So, let us go to the Prophet [peace and blessings of Allaah be upon him]."

At the same time, the Prophet [peace and blessings of Allaah be upon him] sent Al-Waleed ibn 'Uqbah to take what he had. While he was on the way, Al-Waleed, having been scared by the multitude of the people, returned to the Prophet [peace and blessings of Allaah be upon him] and said: "Al-Haarith has withheld Zakaah items from me and intended to kill me". the Prophet [peace and blessings of Allaah be upon him] prepared a military expedition to attack Al-Haarith, who came along with his companions to face the military expedition to whom he said: "To where have you been dispatched?" They said: "To you". He asked:

"Why?" They replied: "the Prophet [peace and blessings of Allaah be upon him] has sent to you Al-Waleed Ibn 'Uqbah (to take your Zakaah items) and Al-Waleed pretended you had withheld it from him and intended to kill him". He said: "No, by Him Who sent Muhammad [peace and blessings of Allaah be upon him] with the truth. I have neither seen him, nor has he come to me". When he entered upon the Prophet [peace and blessings of Allaah be upon him], he said: "You have withheld Zakaah and intended to kill my courier". He said: "No, by Him Who sent you with the truth". On that occasion, Allaah revealed those Quraanic Aayaat. [Ahmad and others with a good chain of narrators; and its men of narration are reliable]

A narration on the authority of Jaabir Ibn 'Abdullaah [Allaah be pleased with them] and 'Alqamah ibn Naajiyah and Umm Salamah [Allaah be pleased with her]. [At-Tabaraani]

A narration on the authority of Ibn 'Abbaas [Allaah be pleased with them]. [Ibn Jareer]

Verse Number 9

9- And if two parties among the believers (al-Mumineen) engage in fighting, then make peace between them both. But if one of them does wrong to the other, then fight you (all) against the one which does wrong till it complies with the Command of Allaah (which is the truth). Then if it complies, then make peace between them with justice, and be equitable. Verily! Allaah loves those who are equitable.

A narration on the authority of Anas [may Allaah be pleased with him] that he said: it was said to the Prophet [peace and blessings of Allaah be upon him]: "Would that you see Abdullah Ibn Ubayy." So, The Prophet [peace and blessings of Allaah be upon him] went to him, riding a donkey and the Muslims accompanied him, walking on salty barren land. When The Prophet [peace and blessings of Allaah be upon him] reached Abdullah Ibn Ubayy, the latter said: "Keep away from me! By Allaah, the bad smell of your donkey has harmed me." On that, an Ansari man said (to Abdullah), "By Allaah! The smell of the donkey of the Prophet [peace and blessings of Allaah be upon him] is better than your smell." On that, a man from Abdullah's tribe got angry for Abdullah's sake, and the two men abused each other which caused the friends of the two men to get angry so the two groups started fighting with sticks, shoes and hands. We were informed that on that occasion, this Quraanic Ayaah was revealed. [Al-Bukhaari and Muslim]

A narration on the authority of Abu Maalik that he said: Two Muslim persons quarreled and the people of each grew angry for his sake therefore, they fought with hands and sandals. On that occasion, Allaah revealed this Quraanic Ayaah. [Sa'eed Ibn Mansoor and Ibn Jareer]

A narration on the authority of As-Suddi that he said: An Ansaari man called 'Imran had a woman (his wife) called Umm Zayd. The woman liked to visit her family but was detained by her husband in an upper room of attic belonging to him.

The woman then sent a letter to her family who came and got her down to go with her. At the same time, the man had gone to seek the aid of his family who also came to prevent the woman from going with her family. They fought with sandals and in connection with them this Quraanic Ayaah was revealed. the Prophet [peace and blessings of Allaah be upon him] sent a letter to them and settled the dispute between them thereupon they returned to the command of Allaah. [Ibn Jareer and Ibn Abu Haatim]

A narration on the authority of Al-Hasan that he said: Once, there was a dispute between two tribes and they would be invited to somebody to judge between them; yet they would reject. On that occasion, Allaah revealed this Quraanic Ayaah. [Ibn Jareer]

A narration on the authority of Qataadah that he said: It was mentioned to us that this Quraanic Ayaah was revealed in connection with two Ansaari men between whom there was a dispute over a right. One of them told the other: "I will take it by force", depending on the great number of his clansmen.

The other invited him to litigate him before the Prophet [peace and blessings of Allaah be upon him], but he rejected. The dispute between them rose up to fighting with hands and sandals rather than with swords. [Ibn Jareer]

Verse Number 11

11- O you who believe! Let not a group scoff at another group, it may be that the latter are (in the sight of Allaah) better than the former. Nor let (some) women scoff at other women, it may be that the latter are better than the former. Nor defame one another, nor insult one another by (offensive) nicknames. How wretched is the name of wickedness after having Faith (in Allaah). And whoever does not repent (from that sin), then such are indeed the wrongdoers.

A narration on the authority of Abu Jubayr Ibn Ad-Dahhaak that he said: It was the habit that anyone of us might have two or three nicknames and he would be called by one of them which he disliked. On that occasion, Allaah revealed this Quraanic Ayaah. [Abu Daawood; Ibn Maajah, An-Nasaa'i and At-Tirmidhi who renders it Hasan]

A narration on the authority of Abu Jubayr Ibn Ad-Dahhaak that he said: During the pre-Islamic days, anyone had more than a nickname. Once, the Prophet [peace and blessings of Allaah be upon him] called somebody by one of those nicknames he had and it was said to him: "O Messenger of Allaah! He dislikes that nickname". On that occasion, Allaah revealed this Quraanic Ayaah. [Al-Haakim and others]

A narration on the authority of Abu Jubayr Ibn Ad-Dahhaak that he said: It was in connection with us, Banu Salamah, that this Quraanic Ayaah was revealed.

The Prophet [peace and blessings of Allaah be upon him] arrived in Madeenah and there was none of us but that he had two or three nicknames. Whenever anyone of them was called by any of those nicknames, they said: "O Messenger of Allaah! He angers because of that (nickname)". On that occasion, this Quraanic Ayaah was revealed. [Ahmad]

Verse Number 12

12- O you who believe! Avoid much suspicions; indeed some suspicions are sins. And neither spy, nor backbite one another. Would one of you like to eat the flesh of his dead brother? You would hate it (so hate backbiting). And safeguard yourselves against (the punishment of) Allaah (for backbiting, by repenting from it). Verily, Allaah is the One Who accepts the repentance (of those who repent), Most Merciful.

A narration on the authority of Ibn Jurayj that he said: It was pretended that this Quraanic Ayaah was revealed in connection with Salmaan Al-Faarisi [may Allaah be pleased with him]. Once, he ate and slept and then snored (during his sleep) so a man made a mention of his eating, sleeping and snoring, thereupon it was revealed. [Ibn Al-Mundhir]

Verse Number 13

13- O mankind! We have created you from a male and a female, and made you into peoples and tribes, that you may recognize one another. Verily, the most honorable of you with Allaah is the most righteous. Verily, Allaah is All-Knowing (of all your states and affairs), Well-Acquainted (with your innermosts).

A narration on the authority of Ibn Abu Mulaykah that he said: When it was the day of the conquest (of Makkah), Bilaal [may Allaah be pleased with him] climbed to the back of the Ka'bah and pronounced Adhaan.

Some people said: "Is it fit for this black slave to pronounce Adhaan on the back of the Ka'bah?" Others replied: "If Allaah disliked this, He then will change it". On that occasion, Allaah revealed this Quraanic Ayaah. [Ibn Abu Haatim]

A narration on the authority of Ibn Bashkawaal from Abu Bakr Ibn Daawood in his commentaries that it was revealed in connection with Abu Hind: the Prophet [peace and blessings of Allaah be upon him] commanded Banu Bayaadah to give him in marriage a woman belonging to them. They said: "O Messenger of Allaah! Should we give in marriage our women to our freed slaves?" On that occasion, this Quraanic Ayaah was revealed. [Ibn 'Asaakir in Al-Mubhamaat]

Verse Number 17

17- They regard it a favor to you (O Muhammad) that they have embraced Islam. Say: "Consider not your Islam as a favor upon me. Nay, but Allaah has conferred a favor upon you that He has guided you to

Faith if you indeed are true (to your claim that you believe).

A narration on the authority of 'Abdullaah Ibn Abu Awfa [may Allaah be pleased with him] that some Bedouins said: "O Messenger of Allaah! We have embraced Islam and have not fought with you, whereas sons of so and so have fought with you". On that occasion, Allaah revealed this Quraanic Ayaah. [At-Tabaraani with a good chain of narrators]

The same is narrated on the authority of Ibn 'Abbaas [Allaah be pleased with them]. [Al-Bazzaar]

A similar one is narrated on the authority of Al-Hasan in which it is mentioned that this took place when Makkah was conquered. [Ibn Abu Haatim]

A narration on the authority of Muhammad Ibn Ka'b Al-Qurathi that he said: Ten men from Banu Asad came to the Prophet [peace and blessings of Allaah be upon him], in 9 A.H., including Talhah Ibn Khuwaylid. the Prophet [peace and blessings of Allaah be upon him] was sitting in the masjid along with his Companions. They greeted and one of them stood and said: "O Messenger of Allaah! We have testified that there is none worthy of worship but Allaah with Whom there is no partner, and that you are His slave and Messenger. We have come to you O Prophet even though you have not sent to us any military expedition. That means that we intend peace". On that occasion, Allaah revealed this Quraanic Ayaah. [Ibn Sa'd]

A narration on the authority of Sa'eed Ibn Jubayr that he said: Some Bedouins from Banu Asad came to the Prophet [peace and blessings of Allaah be upon him] and said: "We have come to you and we have not fought with you". On that occasion, Allaah revealed this Quraanic Ayaah. [Sa'eed Ibn Mansoor in his Sunan]

Soorah Qaaf

38- And indeed We created the heavens and the earth and what is between them in six Days and no fatigue touched Us.

A narration on the authority of Ibn 'Abbaas [Allaah be pleased with them] that he said: The Yahood came to the Prophet [peace and blessings of Allaah be upon him] and asked him about the creation of the heavens and the earth, he said: "Allaah created the earth on Sunday and Monday, the mountains and what they have of benefits on Tuesday; and on Wednesday, He created trees, water, cities, valleys and deserts; and on Thursday He created the heaven; and on Friday He created the stars, the moon and the angels till only three hours remained out of it. In the first hour, He created the death terms till those who die would die. In the second, He cast evil on everything of benefit to the people. In the third hour He created AAdam and made him to dwell in Paradise and commanded Iblees to fall in prostration to him and then drove him out of Paradise in the last hour". The Yahood said: "Then, what is next O Muhammad?" He said: "Then, Allaah established Himself on the Throne (of authority in a way fit for His Majesty)".

They said: "You have told the truth if you complete it". They added: "Then, He took rest". the Prophet [peace and blessings of Allaah be upon him] grew angry so much thereupon Allaah revealed this Quraanic Ayaah. [Al-Haakim who renders it Saheeh]

A narration on the authority of Ibn 'Abbaas [Allaah be pleased with them] that he said: They said: "O Messenger of Allaah! Would that you warn us!" then the following was revealed (what means): {But warn with the Quraan such as fears My Threat (that is the believers (al-Mumineen))}. [verse 45] [Ibn Jareer]

Soorah Adh-Dhaariyaat

Verse Number 19

19- And in their properties (and possessions) the beggar (who asks) and the deprived (who refrains from begging) had their due right.

A narration on the authority of Muhammad Ibn Al-Hasan Ibn al-Hanafiyyah that the Prophet [peace and blessings of Allaah be upon him] sent a military expedition which fought and defeated the enemies and gained booty. Then, after they had finished (from distributing it), other people came. On that, Allaah revealed this Quraanic Ayaah. [Ibn Jareer and Ibn Abu Haatim]

Verse Number 54-55

54- So turn away (O Muhammad) from them: in naught are you blamable (because you have conveyed Allaah's Message). 55And remind (people with the Quraan) for verily, the reminder benefits the believers (al-Mumineen).

A narration on the authority of 'Ali [may Allaah be pleased with him] that he said: When Allaah revealed (what means): {So turn away (O Muhammad) from them: in naught are you blamable (because you have conveyed Allaah's Message)}, [verse 54] there was none of us but that he was sure of destruction, since the Prophet [peace and blessings of Allaah be upon him] was commanded to turn away from us. Then Allaah revealed (what means): {And remind (people with the Quraan) for verily, the reminder benefits the believers (al-Mumineen)}. [verse 55] In this way, we grew happy. [Ibn Manee'; Ibn Rahawayh; Al-Haytham Ibn Kulayb in their Musnads]

A narration on the authority of Qataadah that he said: It was mentioned to us that when Allaah revealed (what means): {So turn away (O Muhammad) from them...} it was difficult upon the Companions of the Prophet [peace and blessings of Allaah be upon him], seeing that the divine revelation ceased and the torment came. On that occasion, Allaah revealed (what means): {And remind (people with the Quraan) for verily, the reminder benefits the believers (al-Mumineen)}. [Ibn Jareer]

Soorah At-Toor

30- Or do they say: "(He is) a poet! We await for him a misfortune of time (a calamity of death, a fate like that of other poets)!"

A narration on the authority of Ibn 'Abbaas [Allaah be pleased with them] that when the men of Quraysh gathered in Daar An-Nadwah to discuss the affair of the Prophet [peace and blessings of Allaah be upon him], one of them said: "Detain him in fetters and then, await for him the misfortune of time (that is death) till he would be destroyed like the destruction of those of poets before him, Zuhayr and An-Naabighah. He is but like anyone of them". In this connection, Allaah revealed this Quraanic Ayaah. [Ibn Jareer]

Soorah An-Najm

Verse Number 32

32- (The doers of good are) those who avoid major sins and immoralities except the minor faults, - verily, your Lord (Rabb) is All-Embracing in (His) Forgiveness (and acceptance of repentance). He knows you best when He created you from the earth, and when you are embryos in your mothers' wombs. So justify not yourselves. He knows best him who wards off (evil and fears Allaah).

A narration on the authority of Thaabit Ibn Al-Haarith Al-Ansaari that he said: The habit of Yahood was, whenever a child of theirs died, they say: "He is a sincere affirmer of truth". Having been informed about that, the Prophet [peace and blessings of Allaah be upon him] said: "The Yahood have told a lie. There is no human being created by Allaah in the womb of its mother but that He knows whether he is wretched or happy". On that occasion, Allaah revealed this Quraanic Ayaah. [Al-Waahidi; At-Tabaraani; Ibn Al-Mundhir and Ibn Abu Haatim]

Verse Number 33-41

33- Have you seen him who turned his back (from faith), 34- And gave a little (of the specified money) and withheld (the rest)? 35- Does he have the knowledge of the Unseen so that he sees (that others may, possibly, avert from him the hereafter punishment)? 36- Or is he not informed of what is in the Books of Moses (the Torah), 37- And (the Books) of Abraham who fulfilled all that Allaah ordered him to do, 38- That no bearer of burdens (sins) shall bear the burden of another. 39- And that man has nothing but (the fruits of) what he does (be it good or bad).

40- And that his deeds will be seen (in the hereafter). 41- Then he will be recompensed (for it) with the fullest recompense.

A narration on the authority of 'Ikrimah that the Prophet [peace and blessings of Allaah be upon him] set out for a battle and a man came to him and liked to be provided with a riding mount (to transport him) but found no mount to set out with the people. He met a friend of him to whom he said: "Give me something". He said: "I shall give you this camel of mine provided that you should bear my sins (on behalf of me)". He replied: "Well I will do". On that occasion, Allaah revealed those Quraanic Aayaat. [Ibn Abu Haatim]

A narration on the authority of Daraaj Ibn As-Samh that he said: A military expedition was dispatched and a man asked the Prophet [peace and blessings of Allaah be upon him] to give him a riding mount. the Prophet [peace and blessings of Allaah be upon him] said: "I have nothing to make you ride". He turned away sad and came upon a man whose camel was kneeling down in front of him. He made a complaint to him and he said: "Do you like to give you this riding mount and you join the army with your good deeds?" He acceplted. He then rode (and set out with them).

On that occasion, Allaah revealed those Quraanic Aayaat. [Ibn Abu Haatim]

A narration on the authority of Ibn Zayd that he said: A man embraced Islam and was met by somebody who put shame on him saying: "Have you given up the religion of the old men and rendered them in error, pretending they are in the Fire?" He replied: "I have felt afraid of Allaah's torment". He said: "Give me something and I will bear all torments due on you". Then he gave him something. He asked him for increase till they became mutually insolvent. Then he gave him something and wrote a deed and took witnesses to it. In connection with him, those Quraanic Aayaat were revealed. [Ibn Jareer]

Verse Number 61

61- While you are amusing yourselves (heedless of what you are commanded and required to do)?

A narration on the authority of Ibn 'Abbaas [Allaah be pleased with them] that he said: They came upon the Prophet [peace and blessings of Allaah be upon him] with their heads raised up. In connection with them, Allaah revealed this Quraanic Ayaah. [Ibn Abu Haatim]

Soorah Al-Qamar

Verse Number 1-2

1- The (final) Hour (of Judgment) has drawn near, and the moon has been cleft asunder. 2- And if they (the disbelievers (al-Kaafireen) of the Quraysh) see a sign (miracle for Prophet Muhammad), they turn away, and say: "This is (but) a strong continuous magic."

A narration on the authority of Ibn Mas'ood [may Allaah be pleased with him] that he said: I saw the moon having been split into two in Makkah before the Prophet [peace and blessings of Allaah be upon him] left it (for Madinah); and the people said (commenting on that): "The moon has been bewitched". On that occasion, this Quraanic Ayaah was revealed. [Al-Bukhaari; Muslim and Al-Haakim]

A narration on the authority of Anas [may Allaah be pleased with him] that he said: the Makkans asked the Prophet [peace and blessings of Allaah be upon him] for a sign (miracle), thereupon the moon was cleft asunder twice in Makkah. On that occasion, Allaah revealed those Quraanic Aayaat. [At-Tirmidhi]

Verse Number 45

45- Soon their multitude will be put to flight, and they will turn their backs (in retreat).

A narration on the authority of Ibn 'Abbaas [Allaah be pleased with them] that he said: On the day of Badr (battle), they (the disbelievers (al-Kaafireen)) said: "We all will emerge victorious". On that occasion, Allaah revealed this Quraanic Ayaah. [Ibn Jareer]

Verse Number 47-49

47- Verily, the criminals are in error (being given to destruction in this world) and will (be burnt) in the blazing Fire (in the hereafter). 48- The Day they will be dragged in the Fire on their faces (it will be said to them): "Taste you the touch of Hell!"

49- Verily, We have created all things in due proportion, by due measure (and with divine predestination).

A narration on the authority of Abu Hurayrah [may Allaah be pleased with him] that he said: The polytheists of Quraysh came to the Prophet [peace and blessings of Allaah be upon him] to dispute him over the divine decree. On that occasion, Allaah revealed those Quraanic Aayaat. [Muslim and At-Tirmidhi]

Soorah Ar-Rahmaan

Verse Number 46

46- But for him who fears the standing before his Lord (Rabb) (for reckoning, by keeping his duties to Him, there will be two Gardens (in Paradise).

A narration on the authority of 'Ataa' that one day Abu Bakr As-Siddiq [may Allaah be pleased with him] made a mention of the Day of Resurrection, scales (of deeds), Paradise and Fire, and said: "Would that I had been one of those green herbs to be eaten by an animal rather than my being a human being". On that occasion, Allaah revealed this Quraanic Ayaah. [Ibn Abu Haatim and Ibn Abu Ash-Shaykh in Kitaab Al-'Athamah]

A narration on the authority of Ibn Shawdhab that he said: This Quraanic Ayaah was revealed in connection with Abu Bakr As-Siddeeq [may Allaah be pleased with him]. [Ibn Abu Haatim]

Soorah Al-Waqi'ah

13- (Those foremost will consist of) a multitude from the former peoples, 14- And a few number from the later peoples. Verse Number 39-40

39- (The companions of the Right Hand will consist of) a multitude from the former peoples, 40- And a multitude from the later peoples.

A narration on the authority of Abu Hurayrah [may Allaah be pleased with him] that he said: When Allaah revealed (what means): {(Those foremost will consist of) a multitude from the former peoples, and a few number from the later peoples}, [verse 13-14] this was difficult on Muslims. On that, Allaah revealed (what means): {(The companions of the Right Hand will consist of) a multitude from the former peoples, and a multitude from the later peoples}. [verse 39-40] [Ahmad; Ibn Al-Mundhir and Ibn Abu Haatim with a chain of narrators having unidentified men]

A narration on the authority of Jaabir Ibn 'Abdullaah [Allaah be pleased with them] that he said: When Allaah revealed Soorah Al-Waaqi'ah in which He said (what means): {(Those foremost will consist of) a multitude from the former peoples, and a few number from the later peoples}, 'Umar [may Allaah be pleased with him] said: "O Messenger of Allaah! How should it be from the foremost and a few from among us?"

It was not before a year elapsed that Allaah revealed (what means): {(The companions of the Right Hand will consist of) a multitude from the former peoples, and a multitude from the later peoples}. [verse 39-40] [Ibn 'Asaakir in Taareekh Dimashq with a suspicious chain of narrators]

The same is narrated on the authority of 'Urwah ibn Ruwaym. [Ibn Abu Haatim: Mursal]

Verse Number 27-28

27- And the companions of the Right Hand - how (prosperous) will be the companions of the Right Hand? 28- (They will be) among thornless lote-trees,

A narration on the authority of 'Ataa' and Mujaahid that they said: When the men of Taa'if asked that the valley of honey be made a protected zone for them, he [peace and blessings of Allaah be upon him] did accordingly. It was an amazing valley. Having heard the people saying that in Paradise there will be such and such (good things), they said: "Would that in Paradise we will have the like of this valley!" On that occasion, Allaah revealed (what means): {And the companions of the Right Hand - how (prosperous) will be the companions of the Right Hand? (They will be) among thornless_lote-trees}. [verse 27-28] [Sa'eed Ibn Mansoor in his Sunan; and Al-Bayhaqi in Al-Ba'th]

v. no. 29

29- And among banana-trees layered (with fruits one above another),

A narration on the authority of Mujaahid that he said: They wondered at Wajj, a valley in Taa'if, and its shadows, trees and lotes. On that, Allaah revealed (what means): {And the companions of the Right Hand how (prosperous) will be the companions of the Right Hand? (They will be) among thornless lote-trees, And among banana-trees layered (with fruits one above another), In shade long-extended}. [verse 27-30] [Al-Bayhaqi]

Verse Number 75-82

75- So I swear by the sites of the stars (where they fall and set). 76- And verily that is indeed a great oath, if you but know. 77- That (this which is recited to you) is indeed a noble Quraan, 78- In a Book well-guarded (with Allaah in the heaven), 79- Which none touches but these who are purified (from impurities). 80- (It is) a Revelation from the Lord (Rabb) of the worlds. 81- Is it such a talk (this Quraan) that you (disbelievers (al-Kaafireen)) hold in contempt (and deny)? 82- And make (your gratitude for) the provision (He gives you from rain) that you reject (the Provider)!

A narration on the authority of Ibn 'Abbaas [Allaah be pleased with them] that he said: During the lifetime of the Prophet [peace and blessings of Allaah be upon him] it rained, thereupon the Prophet [peace and blessings of Allaah be upon him] said: "Some people have become grateful and others disbelievers (al-

Kaafireen). Some said: 'That is a mercy placed by Allaah.' Others said: 'It rained by virtue of such and such a star. .'" On that occasion, Allaah revealed those Quraanic Aayaat. [Muslim]

A narration on the authority of Abu Hazrah that he said: Those Quraanic Aayaat were revealed in connection with an Ansaari in the battle of Tabook. When they descended at Al-Hijr the Prophet [peace and blessings of Allaah be upon him] ordered them not to carry anything of its water. Then they left and descended at another place and had no water with them. They made a complaint of that to the Prophet [peace and blessings of Allaah be upon him]. He stood and performed a two-rak'ah prayer after which Allaah sent a cloud which rained upon them till they got their need of water. A man from the Ansaar said to another of his people accused of hypocrisy: "Woe to you! Do you not see how the Prophet [peace and blessings of Allaah be upon him] invoked Allaah thereupon it rained upon us?" He said: "It has rained by virtue of such and such a star". [Ibn Abu Haatim]

Soorah Al-Hadeed

Verse Number 16

16- Is it not due time for those who believe (in Allaah) that their hearts (Qalb) should be humbly submissive to the remembrance of Allaah, and that which has been revealed of the truth (this Quraan), lest they should become as those (Yahood and Nasaara) who were given the Scripture (Torah and Gospel) before, and a long period passed over them (while contending against their Prophets) and so their hearts (Qalb) became hardened (and did not soften to Allaah's reminder)? Verily, many of them were wicked transgressors.

A narration on the authority of 'Abd-Al-'Azeez Ibn Abu Rawaad that the Companions of the Prophet [peace and blessings of Allaah be upon him] were given to joking and laughter. In this connection, this Quraanic Ayaah was revealed. [Ibn Abu Shaybah in Al-Musannaf]

A narration on the authority of Muqaatil Ibn Hayyaan that he said: The Companions of the Prophet [peace and blessings of Allaah be upon him] were given to joking to some extent. In this respect, Allaah revealed this Quraanic Ayaah. [Ibn Abu Haatim]

A narration on the authority of Al-Qaasim that he said: The Companions of the Prophet [peace and blessings of Allaah be upon him] felt exhausted, thereupon they said: "Talk to us O Messenger Allaah!" On that occasion, Allaah revealed Allaah's saying (what means): {We relate unto you (O Muhammad) the best of stories in what We have revealed to you, of this Quraan. And before this (revelation), you were among the heedless (of the Quraan)}. [Yoosuf, verse 3] Then they got exhausted once again after which they said: "Talk to us O Messenger of Allaah!" In this connection, Allaah revealed this Quraanic Ayaah in issue. [Ibn Abu Haatim]

A narration on the authority of Al-A'mash that he said: When the Companions of the Prophet [peace and blessings of Allaah be upon him] came to Madinah, and enjoyed of good livelihood after the hardship which they had already suffered. It seemed as though they wearied to do what they used to do. On that occasion, Allaah revealed this Quraanic Ayaah. [Ibn Al-Mubaarak in Az-Zuhd]

Verse Number 28

28- O you who believe (in Jesus)! Fear Allaah, and believe in His Messenger (Muhammad as you believe in Jesus) that He will give you a double portion of His Mercy (for your belief in both Messengers), and He will give you light by which you shall walk (on the Siraat in the hereafter), and He will forgive you. And Allaah is Oft-Forgiving, Most Merciful.

A narration on the authority of Ibn 'Abbaas [Allaah be pleased with them] that forty men belonging to the Negus came to the Prophet [peace and blessings of

Allaah be upon him] and attended (the battle of) Uhud with him and many of them were injured but none of them were killed. Having seen the dire need of the believers (al-Mumineen), they said: "O Messenger of Allaah! We are wealthy: so give us leave to bring our property therewith to support the Muslims. In connection with them, Allaah revealed (what means): {Those to whom We gave the Scripture (that is the Torah and the Gospel) before it: they believe in it (the Quraan)}. [Al-Qasas, verse 52] When it was revealed they said: "O community of Muslims! He among us who believed in your Book (the Quraan) will have a double reward; and he who did not believe in your Book will have only a single reward like yours". On that occasion, Allaah revealed this Quraanic Ayaah in issue. [At-Tabaraani in Al-Awsat with a chain of narrators containing unidentified men]

A narration on the authority of Muqaatil that he said: When Allaah revealed (what means): {These will be given their reward twice (for their belief in the two Books: the Torah and the Quraan), because they are patient (on acting upon their teachings), and repel evil with good, and spend (in charity) out of what We have provided them}, [Al-Qasas, verse 54] the believers (al-Mumineen) among the men of Scripture boasted over the Companions of the Prophet [peace and blessings of Allaah be upon him] saying: "We will have a double reward and you will have only a single reward". This was difficult on the Companions thereupon Allaah revealed this Quraanic Ayaah in issue. In this way a double reward was assigned to them like the believers (al-Mumineen) among the men of Scripture. [Ibn Abu Haatim]

Verse Number 29

29- So that the people of the Scripture (that is the Torah who believed in Muhammad) may know that they have no power whatsoever over the bounty of Allaah, and that the bounty is in His Hand which He bestows upon whomever He wills. And Allaah is the Owner of Great Bounty.

A narration on the authority of Qataadah that he said: We were informed that when Allaah revealed (what means): {O you who believe! Fear Allaah, and believe in His Messenger (Muhammad) that He will give you a double portion of His Mercy ...} [verse 28] the men of Scripture envied the Muslims because of it. On that occasion, Allaah revealed this Quraanic Ayaah. [Ibn Jareer]

A narration on the authority of Mujaahid that he said: The Yahood said: "A Prophet is about to appear from among us and he will cut off the hands and feet". When the Prophet (Muhammad [peace and blessings of Allaah be upon him]) appeared from among the Arabs they (the Yahood) disbelieved in him. On that occasion, Allaah revealed this Quraanic Ayaah. The bounty here stands for Prophethood. [Ibn Al-Mundhir]

Soorah Al-Mujaadilah

Verse Number 1-4

1- Verily, Allaah has heard the statement of the woman that disputes with you (O Muhammad) concerning her husband, and complains to Allaah. And Allaah hears the argument between you both. Verily, Allaah is Ever-Hearing, Ever-Seeing (of all things). 2As for those among you who make their wives unlawful for them by Thihaar, in naught will they be their mothers. Their mothers are only those who give them birth. And verily, (by doing such Thihaar) they utter an iniquitous word and falsehood. And indeed, Allaah is Oft-Pardoning (to such as do so), Oft-Forgiving (of sins). 3- And those who make unlawful to them their wives by Thihaar and wish to retract from what they uttered, (the expiation) in that case is to free a slave before they both touch each other. That is an admonition to you (so that you may not return to such a sin). And Allaah, with what you do, is Well-Acquainted. 4- And he who cannot find (nor afford for freeing a slave) must fast two months consecutively before they both touch each other. And due on him, who is unable to do so, is the feeding of sixty needy persons. That (reduction of expiation) is in order that you may have perfect Faith in Allaah and His Messenger. These (rulings mentioned above) are the limits set by Allaah. And for the disbelievers (al-Kaafireen) (in them), there is a painful torment.

A narration on the authority of 'AA'ishah [Allaah be pleased with her] that she said: Blessed be He Whose hearing extends over all things. While I was hearing the speech of Khawlah Bint Tha'labah some of which was hidden from me, and she was complaining of her husband to the Prophet [peace and blessings of Allaah be upon him], saying: "O Messenger of Allaah! He devoured my youth, and I gave birth many children for him till when I grew old and unable to give birth, he made me as unlawful for him as is the back of his mother. O Allaah! I am complaining to You". She did not leave before Jibreel descended with those Quraanic Aayaat. Her husband is Aws Ibn As-Saamit. [Al-Haakim who renders it authentic]

Verse Number 8

8- Do you not see those who were forbidden to hold private conferences, and afterwards returned to that which they had been forbidden, and conspired together for sin and aggression, and disobedience to the Messenger (Muhammad)? And when they come to you, they greet you with a greeting wherewith Allaah greets you not, and say within themselves: "Why should Allaah punish us not for what we say?" Hell will be sufficient for them therein they will burn. And worst indeed is that destination!

A narration on the authority of Muqaatil Ibn Hayyaan that he said: There was a peace treaty between the Prophet [peace and blessings of Allaah be upon him] and the Yahood.

Whenever one of the Companions passed by them they would sit talking privately among themselves, till the passer-by of the believer would think they would conspire to kill him or at least do harm to him.

the Prophet [peace and blessings of Allaah be upon him] forbade them from the private talk but they did not desist. On that occasion, Allaah revealed this Quraanic Ayaah. [Ibn Abu Haatim]

A narration on the authority of 'Abdullaah Ibn 'Amr [Allaah be pleased with them] that the Yahood used to say to the Prophet [peace and blessings of Allaah be upon him]: "As-Saam (death) be upon you!" Then they would say in themselves: "Would Allaah punish us for what we say?"

On that occasion, Allaah revealed this Quraanic Ayaah. [Ahmad; Al-Bazzaar and At-Tabaraani with a good chain of narrators]

Verse Number 10

10- Verily, private conversation (about sin and wrongdoing) is only from Satan in order that he (with his vanity) may aggrieve the believers (al-Mumineen) but in naught can he harm them, except by permission of Allaah, and on Allaah let the believers (al-Mumineen) rely.

A narration on the authority of Qataadah that he said: The hypocrites (al-Munaafiqeen) used to talk privately among themselves, and this enraged the believers (al-

Mumineen) and was difficult on them. On that occasion, Allaah revealed this Quraanic Ayaah. [Ibn Jareer]

Verse Number 11

11- O you who believe! When you are told to make room in the assemblies (where Allaah is remembered), (spread out and) make room (for such as comes to sit). Allaah will give you (ample) room (in Paradise). And when you are told to rise up (for prayers or any other good deeds), rise up. Allaah will exalt in degree (in Paradise) those of you who believe (and comply with Allaah's command), and those who are granted knowledge. And Allaah, with what you do, is Well-Acquainted.

A narration on the authority of Qataadah that he said: Whenever they saw anyone coming to them in the gathering of the Prophet [peace and blessings of Allaah be upon him] they would not allow him to sit with them. On that occasion, Allaah revealed this Quraanic Ayaah. [Ibn Jareer]

A narration on the authority of Muqaatil that this Quraanic Ayaah was revealed on Friday when some of Badr warriors came and found no place to sit and no space was made for them to sit. They then kept standing on their feet. the Prophet [peace and blessings of Allaah be upon him] made some to stand for the men of Badr to sit in their places. But those (whom the Prophet made to stand) disliked that. On that occasion, Allaah revealed this Quraanic Ayaah. [Ibn Abu Haatim]

Verse Number 12-13

12- O you who believe! When you (intend to) talk to the Messenger (Muhammad) in private, spend something in charity before your private conversation. That will be better for you and purer (for your sins). But if you cannot afford (for it), then verily, Allaah is Oft-Forgiving (of your private conversation with the Messenger even without giving in charity first), Most Merciful (towards you in this respect). 13- Do you fear that you will not (be able to) present a charity before your private conversation (with the Messenger)? If then you do it not, and Allaah forgives you (for not doing it), then (at least) establish prayer and give Zakaah and obey Allaah (regularly and persistently). And Allaah is Well-Acquainted with what you do.

A narration on the authority of Ibn 'Abbaas [Allaah be pleased with them] that he said: The Muslims asked the Prophet [peace and blessings of Allaah be upon him] so many questions till they troubled him. Having intended to lighten the burden from His Prophet, Allaah revealed (what means): {O you who believe! When you (intend to) talk to the Messenger (Muhammad) in private, spend something in charity before your private conversation}. When it was revealed, many people kept silent and refrained from asking him importunately. In response Allaah revealed (what means): {Do you fear that you will not (be able to) present a charity before your private conversation (with the Messenger)?} [Ibn Abu Haatim]

A narration on the authority of 'Ali [may Allaah be pleased with him] that he said: When Allaah revealed (what means): {O you who believe! When you (intend to) talk to the Messenger (Muhammad) in private, spend something in charity before your private conversation}, the Prophet [peace and blessings of Allaah be upon him] told me: "What do you think? A Dinar?" I said: "They cannot bear it". He said: "Then, half a Dinar?" I replied: "They cannot bear it". He asked: "Then, how much?" I said: "A single (spike of) barley". He said: "No doubt, your suggestion is quite trivial". On that occasion, Allaah revealed (what means): {Do you fear that you will not (be able to) present a charity before your private conversation (with the Messenger)?} By virtue of me ('Ali), Allaah alleviated the burden from this ummah. [At-Tirmidhi who renders it Hasan]

Verse Number 14

14- Do you not see those (hypocrites (al-Munaafiqeen)) who take as allies a people with whom Allaah is angry (that is Yahood)? They are neither of you (believers (al-Mumineen)) nor of them (Yahood), and they swear to falsehood (that they are believers (al-Mumineen)) while they know (that they are liars).

A narration on the authority of As-Suddi that he said: We were informed that this Quraanic Ayaah was revealed in connection with 'Abdullaah Ibn Nabtal. [Ibn Abu Haatim]

Verse Number 18

18- (Remember) the Day when Allaah will resurrect them all together (for reckoning); then they will swear to Him as they swear to you (in this world that they are really believers (al-Mumineen)). And they think that they have something (to stand upon). No indeed, they are but liars!

A narration on the authority of Ibn 'Abbaas [Allaah be pleased with them] that he said: "the Prophet [peace and blessings of Allaah be upon him] was sitting in the shade of his chambers when the shadows was about to shrink. Then he said: "A man will come to you and look at you with the eye of a devil. So, if he comes to you, do not talk to him". A short time later, a blue-complexioned man appeared to them whom the Prophet [peace and blessings of Allaah be upon him] invited. Having seen him, he said to him: "For which reason do you and your companions abuse me?" He replied: "Let me bring them to you". He went and invited them and they swore that they did not do so. In connection with them, Allaah revealed this Quraanic Ayaah. [Ahmad; Al-Haakim who renders it Saheeh]

Verse Number 22

22- In naught will you find a people who believe in Allaah and the Last Day, having affection for those who contravene Allaah and His Messenger

(Muhammad) even though they (the contraveners) were their (the befrienders') fathers, or their sons, or their brothers, or their clansmen. For such (who do not befriend the opponents of Allaah and His Messenger), He (Allaah) has written down Faith in their hearts (Qalb), and supported them with a spirit (light) from Himself. And He will admit them to Gardens beneath which rivers flow (in Paradise) therein they will abide forever. Allaah is well-pleased with them (because of their obedience to Him), and they with Him (because of His reward to them). They are the Party of Allaah (who comply with His command and refrain from what He forbids). Verily, it is the Party of Allaah that will be the successful.

A narration on the authority of Ibn Shawdhab that he said: This Quraanic Ayaah was revealed in connection with Abu 'Ubaydah Ibn Al-Jarraah [may Allaah be pleased with him] when he killed his father on the day of Badr (battle). [Ibn Abu Haatim]

The same is narrated At-Tabaraani and Al-Haakim in which they said: The father of Abu 'Ubaydah Ibn Al-Jarraah sought to face Abu 'Ubaydah on the day of Badr (battle), and Abu 'Ubaydah did his best to avoid him. But when the former insisted, Abu 'Ubaydah killed him. On that occasion, this Quraanic Ayaah was revealed.

A narration on the authority of Ibn Jurayj that he said: I was told that Abu Quhaafah abused the Prophet [peace and blessings of Allaah be upon him] thereupon Abu Bakr [may Allaah be pleased with him] slapped him on the face and he fell down on the ground. When a mention of that was made to the Prophet [peace and blessings of Allaah be upon him] he said: "Have you done it O Abu Bakr?" He replied: "By Allaah, had the sword been at hand, I would have struck him with it". On that occasion, Allaah revealed this Quraanic Ayaah. [Ibn Al-Mundhir]

Soorah Al-Hashr

1- Whatever is in the heavens and whatever is on earth exalts Allaah - and He is the Exalted in Might (concerning His dominion), Full of Wisdom (in all what He does and makes).

A narration on the authority of Ibn 'Abbaas [Allaah be pleased with them] that he said: Soorah Al-Anfaal was revealed in connection with the battle of Badr and Soorah Al-Hashr was revealed in connection with Banu An-Nadeer. [Al-Bukhaari]

A narration on the authority of 'AA'ishah [Allaah be pleased with her] that she said: The battle of Banu An-Nadeer, a sect of Yahood, took place about six months after the battle of Badr. Their dwelling places and palm-trees were in one side of Madeenah. the Prophet [peace and blessings of Allaah be upon him] besieged them till they agreed to leave Madinah, provided that they should with them such of their luggage and property as their camels were able to carry, except weapons. In connection with them Allaah revealed (what means): {Whatever is in the heavens and whatever is on earth exalts Allaah - and He is the Exalted in Might (concerning His dominion), Full of Wisdom (in all what He does and makes)...} [Al-Haakim who renders it Saheeh] Verse Number 5

5- Whatever palm-trees (of theirs) you (O Muslims) cut down or left standing on their roots, it was by Leave of Allaah, and (He gave you leave to cut down) in order that He might disgrace the defiantly disobedient.

A narration on the authority of Ibn 'Umar [Allaah be pleased with them] that the Prophet [peace and blessings of Allaah be upon him] burnt and cut down the palm-trees of Banu An-Nadeer. On that occasion, Allaah revealed this Quraanic Ayaah. [Al-Bukhaari and others]

A narration on the authority of Jaabir [may Allaah be pleased with him] that he said: They were given concession to cut down the palm-trees and then hard terms were put on them in this respect. They came to the Prophet [peace and blessings of Allaah be upon him] and said: "O Messenger of Allaah! Is there a sin on us in what we have cut down or left standing?" On that occasion, Allaah revealed this Quraanic Ayaah. [Abu Ya'li with a weak chain of narrators]

A narration on the authority of Yazeed Ibn Roomaan that he said: When the Prophet [peace and blessings of Allaah be upon him] camped near (the dwelling places of) Banu An-Nadeer, they were in their fortresses, thereupon he ordered that their palm-trees be cut down and burnt. They called out: "O Muhammad! You used to forbid and criticize corruption! What is the matter that you cut down and burn the palm-trees?" On that occasion, this Quraanic Ayaah was revealed. [Ibn Ishaaq]

The same is narrated on the authority of Qataadah and Mujaahid. [Ibn Jareer]

Verse Number 9

9- And (the same is for) those who, before them, had homes (in Madeenah) and adopted the Faith: they love those who emigrate to them, and have no jealousy in their breasts for that which they (the Messenger and the emigrants) have been given (from this booty of Banu An-Nadeer), and give them (emigrants) preference over themselves even though they were in need of that. And whoever is saved from his own greediness (for wealth), such are they who will be the successful.

A narration on the authority of Yazeed Al-Asamm that the Ansaar said: "O Messenger of Allaah! Divide the land between us and our brothers of Muhaajiroon". He said: "No. But you may look after the land on their behalf and make them share you in the fruits; and the land remains yours". They said: "We have accepted". On that occasion, Allaah revealed this Quraanic Ayaah. [Ibn Al-Mundhir]

A narration on the authority of Abu Hurayrah, may may Allaah be pleased with him, who said: "O Messenger of Allaah! I am suffering from fatigue and hunger." The Prophet [peace and blessings of Allaah be upon him] sent (somebody) to his wives (to get something), but the messenger found nothing with them. Then the Prophet [peace and blessings of Allaah be upon him] said (to his Companions, may Allaah be pleased with them): "Isn't there anybody who can entertain this man tonight so that Allaah May Be Merciful to him?" An Ansaari man got up and said: "I (will, entertain him), O Messenger of Allaah!" So he went to his wife and said to her: "This is the guest of the Prophet [peace and blessings of Allaah be upon him] so do not keep anything away from him." She said: "By Allaah, I have nothing but the children's food." He said: "When the children ask for their dinner, put them to bed and put out the light; we shall not take our meals tonight." So she did. In the morning the Ansaari man went to the Prophet [peace and blessings of Allaah be upon him] who said: "Allaah Wondered at so-and-so and his wife (because of their good deed)." Then Allaah Revealed this Quraanic Ayaah. [Al-Bukhaari]

According to the narration of Muslim, this man is Abu Talhah [may Allaah be pleased with him]. [Muslim]

A narration on the authority of Abu Al-Mutawakkil An-Naaji that a man from the Muslims... and the rest is the same as previous according to the which the host was Thaabit Ibn Qays Ibn Shamaas [may Allaah be pleased with him] in connection with him, this Quraanic Ayaah was revealed. [Musaddad in his Musnad; and Ibn Al-Mundhir]

A narration on the authority of Ibn 'Umar [Allaah be pleased with them] that he said: A sheep's head was given as a gift to one of the Companions of the Prophet [peace and blessings of Allaah be upon him] thereupon he said: "My brother so and so and his children are needier of this than us". Then he sent it to him. They continued to send it one to another till it was circulated between seven families, and in the end returned to the first one. In connection with them, this Quraanic Ayaah was revealed. [Al-Waahidi]

Verse Number 11

11- Do you not pay attention to the hypocrites (al-Munaafiqeen)? They say to their friends among the people of the Scripture who disbelieve: "(By Allaah) If you are expelled, we (too) indeed will go out with you, and we shall never obey any one against you; and if you are attacked (in fight), we shall indeed help you." But Allaah is Witness that they indeed are liars.

A narration on the authority of As-Suddi that he said: Some from Quraythah embraced Islam and there were hypocrites (al-Munaafiqeen) among them.

They used to say to those of Nadeer: "If you are driven out we will come out with you". In connection with them, this Quraanic Ayaah was revealed. [Ibn Abu Haatim]

Soorah Al-Mumtahanah

Verse Number 1

1- O you who believe! Take not as allies My enemies and your enemies (that is disbelievers (al-Kaafireen) of Makkah to disclose to them the secrets of the Prophet), showing affection for them, while they have disbelieved in what has come to you of the truth (that is Islam and the Quraan) and have driven out the Messenger (Muhammad) and yourselves (from your homeland by making life intolerable for you) because you believe in Allaah your Lord (Rabb)! If you have set out to strive in My Cause and to seek My Good Pleasure (then take not these disbelievers (al-Kaafireen) and polytheists as allies). You show affection for them in secret, while I know best what you conceal and what you reveal. And whoever of you (Muslims) does that, then indeed he has gone (far) astray from the Straight Path (that is the way of guidance).

A narration on the authority of 'Ali [may Allaah be pleased with him] that he said: the Prophet [peace and blessings of Allaah be upon him] sent me, Az-Zubayr Ibn Al-'Awwaam and Abu Marthad Al-Ghanawi, and all of us were horsemen, saying: "Proceed till you reach Rawdat Khaakh, where there is a woman from the pagans carrying a letter sent by Haatib Ibn Abu Balta'ah to the disbelievers (al-Kaafireen) (of Makkah)." We overtook her while she was proceeding on her camel at the same place fixed by the Prophet [peace and blessings of Allaah be upon him]. We said (to her): "Where is the letter you have with you?" She said: "I have no letter with me." So we made her camel kneel down and searched her mount (luggage) but could find nothing. My two companions said: "We do not see any letter." I said: "I know that the Prophet [peace and blessings of Allaah be upon him] did not tell a lie. By Allaah, if you (woman) do not bring out the letter, I will strip you of your clothes". When she noticed that I was serious, she put her hand into the knot of her waist sheet, for she was tying a sheet round herself, and brought out the letter. So we proceeded to the Prophet [peace and blessings of Allaah be upon him] with the letter. The Prophet [peace and blessings of Allaah be upon him] said (to Habeeb): "What made you do what you have done, O Haatib?" Haatib replied: "I have done nothing except that I believe in Allaah and His Apostle, and I have not changed or altered (my religion). But I wanted to do a favor to the people (of Mecca) through which Allaah might protect my family and my property. Indeed, there is none among your companions but has someone in Mecca through whom Allaah protects his property". The Prophet [peace and blessings of Allaah be upon him] said: "Haatib is true in what he said. Do not say to him but good." 'Umar Ibn Al-Khattaab said: "Verily he has betrayed Allaah, His Apostle, and the believers (al-Mumineen)! Allow me to chop his neck off!" The Prophet [peace and blessings of Allaah be upon him] said: "O 'Umar! How do you come to know? Perhaps Allaah looked upon the Badr warriors and said: "Do whatever you want, for I have decreed that you will enter into Paradise". 'Umar wept and said: "Allaah and His Apostle know best." In connection with him, Allaah revealed this Quraanic Ayaah. [Al-Bukhaari and Muslim]

Verse Number 8

8- Allaah does not forbid you to deal justly and kindly with those (of the disbelievers (al-Kaafireen)) who fought not against you on account of religion nor drove you out of your homes. Verily, Allaah loves those who act justly.

A narration on the authority of Asmaa' Bint Abu Bakr [Allaah be pleased with them] that she said: My mother came to me desiring (that I should give her something). I asked the Prophet [peace and blessings of Allaah be upon him] whether I could give her by way of maintaining kinship ties, so he accepted. In connection with her, Allaah revealed this Quraanic Ayaah. [Al-Bukhaari]

A narration on the authority of 'Abdullaah Ibn Az-Zubayr [Allaah be pleased with them] that he said: Qutaylah came upon her daughter Asmaa' Bint Abu Bakr and Abu Bakr had already divorced her in the pre-Islamic days. She came upon her daughters with gifts and Asmaa' did not accept them or even get her into her (Asmaa's) house. She sent to 'AA'ishah (a message) to ask the Prophet [peace and blessings of Allaah be upon him] about that. She told him so he ordered her to accept her gifts and get her into her house. On that occasion, Allaah revealed this Quraanic Ayaah. [Ahmad; Al-Bazzaar and Al-Haakim who renders it Saheeh]

10- O you who believe! When believing women come to you as emigrants, examine them; Allaah knows best as to their Faith, then if you ascertain (from such oath as they take) that they are true believers (al-Mumineen), send them not back to the disbelievers (al-Kaafireen). They are not lawful (wives) for the disbelievers (al-Kaafireen) nor are the disbelievers (al-Kaafireen) lawful (husbands) for them. But give (their husbands of) the disbelievers (al-Kaafireen) whatever (dowries) they have spent on them. And there will be no sin on you to marry them if you have paid their dowries to them. Likewise hold not to the marriage bonds with the disbelieving women, and ask (those of the disbelievers (al-Kaafireen) who marry them) for (the return of) whatever (dowries) you have spent, and let them (the disbelievers (al-Kaafireen)) ask back for that which they have spent. That is the ruling of Allaah. He judges between you. And Allaah is All-Knowing, All-Wise.

A narration on the authority of Al-Miswar Ibn Makhramah and Marwaan Ibn Al-Hakam that when the Prophet [peace and blessings of Allaah be upon him] made the peace treaty with Quraysh on the day of Hudaybiyah, some believing women came him. On that occasion, Allaah revealed (what means): {O you who believe! When believing women come to you as emigrants, examine them... and hold not to the marriage bonds with the disbelieving women}. [Al-Bukhaari and Muslim]

A narration on the authority of 'Abdullaah Ibn Abu Ahmad that he said: Umm Kulthoom, daughter of 'Uqbah Ibn Abu Mu'ayt emigrated during the truce (between the Muslims and disbelievers (al-Kaafireen) after Hudaybiyah treaty), thereupon her brothers, 'Umaarah and Al-Waleed, sons of 'Uqbah, came out and went to the Prophet [peace and blessings of Allaah be upon him] and talked to him to return Umm Kulthoom to them. But Allaah rescinded the covenant between him and the polytheists especially concerning women, and forbade that they should be brought back to the polytheists. In this connection, Allaah revealed the Quraanic Ayaah of examination [10] [At-Tabaraani with a weak chain of narrators].

A narration on the authority of Yazeed Ibn Abu Habeeb that he was informed that this Quraanic Ayaah was revealed in connection with Umaymah Bint Bishr, the wife of Abu Hassaan Ad-Dahdaahah. [Ibn Abu Haatim]

A narration on the authority of Muqaatil that a woman called Sa'eedah, the wife of Sayfi Ibn Ar-Raahib, who was a polytheist, came to the Muslims during the time of armistice. Her family asked the Prophet [peace and blessings of Allaah be upon him] to return her to them. On that occasion, this Quraanic Ayaah was revealed. [Ibn Abu Haatim]

A narration on the authority of Az-Zuhri that it was revealed to the Prophet [peace and blessings of Allaah be upon him] while he was in the lower part of

Hudaybiyah. He had made a peace treaty with the polytheists to return to them such as came to him. But when the women came to him this Quraanic Ayaah was revealed. [Ibn Jareer]

A narration on the authority of Ibn 'Abbaas [Allaah be pleased with them] that he said: 'Umar Ibn Al-Khattaab embraced Islam but his wife remained behind among the polytheists. In this connection, Allaah revealed (what means): {Likewise hold not to the marriage bonds with the disbelieving women}. [Ibn Manee']

Verse Number 11

11- And if you have lost any (of your dowries) from your wives (when they have gone) to the disbelievers (al-Kaafireen) (as apostates), and then you set out for a battle (against them and) gained booty, then pay from that booty to those whose wives have gone the equivalent of (the dowries) that they had spent. And fear Allaah in Whom you believe.

A narration on the authority of Al-Hasan that he said: This Quraanic Ayaah was revealed in connection with Umm Al-Hakam Bint Abu Sufyaan: she renegaded from Islam and got married to a man from Thaqeef. No women other than her from the Quraysh renegaded. [Ibn Abu Haatim]

Verse Number 13

13- O you who believe! Take not as allies the people with whom Allaah grew angry (that is the Yahood). Surely, they have despaired of (the good of) the Hereafter, just as the disbelievers (al-Kaafireen) (buried) in graves have despaired (of receiving any good in the hereafter).

A narration on the authority of Ibn 'Abbaas [Allaah be pleased with them] that he said: 'Abdullaah Ibn 'Umar and Zayd Ibn Al-Haarith showed affection for some men of the Yahood. In connection with them Allaah revealed this Quraanic Ayaah. [Ibn Al-Mundhir]

Soorah As-Saff

Verse Number 1-2

1- Whatever is in the heavens and whatever is on earth exalts Allaah. And He is the Exalted in Might (concerning His dominion), Full of Wisdom (in what He does and makes). 2- O you who believe! Why do you say that which you do not do (with respect to asking for Jihaad in Allaah's cause)?

A narration on the authority of 'Abdullaah Ibn Salaam [may Allaah be pleased with him] that he said: We, a group of the Companions of the Prophet [peace and blessings of Allaah be upon him], sat and had some discussion. We said: "If we know which deed is the dearest to Allaah, we would do it". On that occasion, Allaah revealed those Quraanic Aayaat. the Prophet [peace and blessings of Allaah be upon him] recited it to the end. [At-Tirmidhi and Al-Haakim who renders it authentic]

The same is narrated on the authority of Ibn 'Abbaas [Allaah be pleased with them]. [Ibn Jareer]

A narration on the authority of Abu Saalih that he said: They said: "If we know which deed is the dearest to Allaah, and the best (in His sight) we would do it". On that occasion, Allaah revealed (what means): {O You who believe! Shall I guide you to a trade that will save you from a painful torment? (That is) you believe in Allaah and His Messenger (Muhammad) and strive hard in the Cause of Allaah with your wealth and your lives: that is better for you, if you but know!} [verse 10-11] They disliked Jihaad (striving in Allaah's cause), thereupon Allaah revealed (what means): {O you who believe! Why do you say that which you do not do (with respect to asking for Jihaad in Allaah's cause)?} [verse 2] [Ibn Jareer]

The same is narrated on the authority of Ibn 'Abbaas [Allaah be pleased with them]. [Ibn Abu Haatim]

A narration on the authority of Ibn 'Abbaas [Allaah be pleased with them] that he said: Allaah revealed this Quraanic Ayaah [2] in connection with a man who says in fighting what he does not do, concerning striking and stabbing. [Ibn Abu Haatim]

The same is narrated on the authority of Ad-Dahhaak. [Ibn Jareer]

A narration on the authority of Muqaatil that this Quraanic Ayaah [2] was revealed in connection with their flight on the day of (the battle of Uhud). [Ibn Abu Haatim]

Verse Number 10-11

10- O You who believe! Shall I guide you to a trade that will save you from a painful torment? 11- (That is) you believe in Allaah and His Messenger (Muhammad) and strive hard in the Cause of Allaah with your wealth and your lives: that is better for you, if you but know!

A narration on the authority of Sa'eed Ibn Jubayr that he said: When Allaah revealed (what means): {O You who believe! Shall I guide you to a trade that will save you from a painful torment?} [verse 11] They said: "If we know this trade, we would sacrifice for its sake our property and families". Then Allaah revealed (what means): {(That is) you believe in Allaah and His Messenger (Muhammad) and strive hard in the Cause of Allaah...} [verse 11]. [Ibn Abu Haatim]

Soorah Al-Jumu'ah

11- And when they see transaction or amusement they rush to it, and leave you (Muhammad) standing (while delivering Jumu'ah's Khutbah) Say: "That which Allaah has (of good reward) is better (for those who believe) than any amusement or transaction! And Allaah is the Best of providers."

A narration on the authority of Jaabir [may Allaah be pleased with him] that he said: the Prophet [peace and blessings of Allaah be upon him] was delivering his Khutbah on Friday when a caravan came thereupon, they left to receive it and only twelve men remained with him. On that occasion, Allaah revealed this Quraanic Ayaah. [Al-Bukhaari and Muslim]

A narration on the authority of Jaabir [may Allaah be pleased with him] that he said: Whenever girls were taken in marriage, people would pass by tambourines and musical wind instruments and leave the Prophet [peace and blessings of Allaah be upon him] standing on the pulpit since they would rush towards it. On that occasion, Allaah revealed this Quraanic Ayaah. [Ibn Jareer]

It seemed as though it was revealed on both occasions, as shown clearly in the narration of Ibn Al-Mundhir on the authority of Jaabir [may Allaah be pleased with him] that it was revealed in connection with both the marriage and the arrival of the caravan: all perfect praise be to Allaah.

Soorah Al-Munafiqoon

Verse Number 5

5- And when it is said to them: "Come (to present your apology), so that the Prophet may ask Allaah's forgiveness for you", they turn aside their heads, and you would see them evading in pride.

A narration on the authority of Qataadah that he said: It was said to 'Abdullaah Ibn Ubayy: "Would that you go to the Prophet [peace and blessings of Allaah be upon him] to seek forgiveness for you!" He went on twisting his head. In connection with him this Quraanic Ayaah was revealed. [Ibn Jareer]

The same is narrated on the authority of 'Ikrimah. [Ibn Al-Mundhir]

Verse Number 6

6- It is the same to them whether you (Muhammad) ask forgiveness or ask not forgiveness for them (Allaah will not forgive for them). Verily, Allaah guides not the defiantly disobedient people.

It is rrated on the authority of 'Urwah that he said: Allaah revealed (what means): {Whether or not you (O Muhammad) ask forgiveness for them (hypocrites (al-Munaafiqeen), their sin will not be forgiven for them) (and even) if you ask seventy times for their forgiveness Allaah will not forgive them because they have disbelieved in Allaah and His Messenger. And Allaah guides not the defiantly disobedient people}. [At-Tawbah, verse 80] the Prophet [peace and blessings of Allaah be upon him] said: "I will ask for forgiveness for them more than seventy times". On that occasion, Allaah revealed this Quraanic Ayaah. [Ibn Al-Mundhir]

The same is narrated on the authority of Mujaahid and Qataadah. [Ibn Al-Mundhir]

A narration on the authority of Ibn 'Abbaas [Allaah be pleased with them] that he said: When Allaah revealed the Quraanic Ayaah of At-Tawbah [80] the Prophet [peace and blessings of Allaah be upon him] said and I was listening: "I have been given concession with regard to them. By Allaah, I will seek Allaah's forgiveness for them more than seventy times, perchance Allaah would forgive for them. On that occasion, Allaah revealed this Quraanic Ayaah in issue. [Ibn Al-Mundhir]

Verse Number 7-8

7- They are the ones who say (to their friends from among the Ansaar): "Spend not on those who are with Allaah's Messenger, they disband (and leave) him." And to Allaah belong the treasures of the heavens and the earth (and it is He Who provides for all creatures), but the hypocrites (al-Munaafiqeen) understand not. 8- They (hypocrites (al-Munaafiqeen)) say: "If we return to Madeenah, indeed the more honorable (meaning themselves) will expel therefrom the meaner (meaning the believers (al-Mumineen))." Therefore, honor and might belong to Allaah, His Messenger and to the believers (al-Mumineen), but the hypocrites (al-Munaafiqeen) know not (this fact).

A narration on the authority of Zayd Ibn Arqam "may Allaah be pleased with him" the following: I was with my uncle when I heard Abdullah Ibn Ubayy Ibn Salool saying: "Don't spend on those who are with Allaah's Apostle, so that they may disperse and go away from him". He further said: "If we return (to Madinah), surely, the more honorable will expel the meaner amongst them." I reported that to my uncle who, in his turn, informed The Prophet "Allaah's blessing and peace be upon him" of it. Then, Allaah's Apostle "Allaah's blessing and peace be upon him" sent for Abdullah Ibn Ubayy and his companions, so they took an oath that they did not say that. So Allaah's Apostle "Allaah's blessing and peace be upon him" disbelieved my saying and believed his. I was distressed as I never was before. I stayed at home, my uncle told me: "You just wanted Allaah's Apostle "Allaah's blessing and peace be upon him" to disbelieve your statement and hate you." So Allaah revealed Soorah Al-Munaafiqoon. The Prophet "Allaah's blessing and peace be upon him" then sent for me and recited it and said: "O Zayd! Allaah confirmed your statement." [Al-Bukhaari]

According to many narrations on the same authority, this took place during the battle of Tabook and the Soorah was revealed at night.

Soorah At-Taghaabun

Verse Number 14

14- O you who believe! Verily, from among your wives and your children there are enemies for you, therefore beware of them! But if you pardon (them) and overlook, and forgive (their faults), then verily, Allaah is Oft-Forgiving, Most Merciful.

A narration on the authority of Ibn 'Abbaas [Allaah be pleased with them] that he said: Allaah's saying (what means): {O you who believe! Verily, from among your wives and your children there are enemies for you, therefore beware of them!} was revealed in connection with a people of Makkans who embraced Islam and their wives and children rejected to let them go to Madeenah. When they went to the Prophet [peace and blessings of Allaah be upon him], they saw the people having understood the religion. They intended to punish them, thereupon Allaah revealed (what means): {But if you pardon (them) and overlook, and forgive (their faults), then verily, Allaah is Oft-Forgiving, Most Merciful}. [At-Tirmidhi and Al-Haakim and they both render it Saheeh]

A narration on the authority of 'Ataa' Ibn Yasaar that he said: Soorah At-Taghabun was revealed in Makkah except those Quraanic Aayaat [14-16] which were revealed in connection with 'Awf Ibn Maalik Al-Ashja'i. He was endowed with a wife and children, and whenever he intended to take part in fighting (in

Allaah's cause), they would go on weeping in order that he would not go forth, and say to him: "To which of men will you leave us?" Then he would sympathize for them and remain behind. Thus all those Quraanic Aayaat up to the end of the Soorah were revealed in Madeenah. [Ibn Jareer]

Verse Number 16

16- So fear Allaah (and keep to your duty to Him) as much as lies within your capacity; listen (and accept what has been enjoined upon you) and obey; and spend in charity, that is better for yourselves. And whoever is saved from his own greediness, it is those who will be the successful.

A narration on the authority of Sa'eed Ibn Jubayr that he said: When Allaah revealed (what means): {So, fear Allaah as He should be feared}, [AAl 'Imraan, verse 102], doing deeds became hard on people, they kept standing (the whole night in prayer) till their feet got swollen and their foreheads were sore. Allaah then revealed, by way of alleviating the burden from the Muslims (what means): {So fear Allaah (and keep to your duty to Him) as much as lies within your capacity}. [Ibn Abu Haatim]

Soorah At-Talaaq

Verse Number 1

1- O Prophet! When you divorce women, divorce them at (the beginning of) their 'Iddah (post-marriage waiting term), and count (accurately) their 'Iddah. And fear Allaah your Lord (Rabb) (and keep to His command and forbiddance). And turn them not out of their (husband's) homes nor shall they (themselves) leave, except in case they commit an open illegal sexual relation. And those are the limits set by Allaah. And whoever transgresses the limits set by Allaah, then indeed he has wronged himself. You (the one who divorces his wife) know not: it may be that Allaah will afterward bring some new thing to pass.

A narration on the authority of Anas [may Allaah be pleased with him] that he said:

The Prophet [peace and blessings of Allaah be upon him] divorced Hafsah [Allaah be pleased with her] and then she went to her family. On that occasion, Allaah revealed this Quraanic Ayaah. It was said to him: "Take her back since she is in the habit of observing fasts and standing (the night in prayer)". [Ibn Abu Haatim]

A similar one is narrated on the authority of Qataadah [Ibn Jareer: Mursal]

The same is narrated on the authority of Ibn Seereen. [Ibn al-Mundhir: Mursal]

A narration on the authority of Muqaatil that he said: We were informed that this Quraanic Ayaah was revealed in connection with 'Abdullaah Ibn 'Amr Ibn Al-'AAs, Tufayl Ibn Al-Haarith, and 'Amr Ibn Sa'eed Ibn Al-'AAs. [Ibn Abu Haatim] Verse Number 2

2- Then when they are about to attain their appointed term, either take them back in a good manner (causing no harm to them) or leave them in a good manner (till their 'Iddah is over). And take as witness (to taking them back or leaving them) two upright trustworthy men from among you (Muslims). And establish the witness for Allaah (rather than for the object of witness). That is an admonition for him who believes in Allaah and the Last Day. And whoever fears Allaah, He will make a way for him to get out (from the discomforts of this world and the hereafter).

A narration on the authority of Saalim Ibn Abu Al-Ja'd that he said: This Quraanic Ayaah, that is {And whoever fears Allaah, He will make a way for him to get out (from the discomforts of this world and the hereafter)}, was revealed in connection with a man from Ashja' who had many dependents and was poor and needy. He went to the Prophet [peace and blessings of Allaah be upon him] and begged him. He told him: "Fear Allaah and keep patient". After a while, one of his sons brought him some sheep, but he had previously been taken by the enemy. He went to the Prophet [peace and blessings of Allaah be upon him] once again and told him the story. On that, the Prophet [peace and blessings of Allaah be upon him] told him: "Then, take it (as it is lawful for you)". On that occasion, this Quraanic Ayaah was revealed. [Ibn Jareer]

The same is narrated on the authority of Ibn Mas'ood [may Allaah be pleased with him], according to which the man was named 'Awf Al-Ashja'i. [Al-Haakim]

A narration on the authority of Ibn 'Abbaas [Allaah be pleased with them] that he said: 'Awf Ibn Maalik Al-Ashja'i went to the Prophet [peace and blessings of Allaah be upon him], and told him: "O Messenger of Allaah! My son has been taken a captive by the enemy and his mother got scared because of that. What do you order me to do?" He said: "I order you and her to say, more often: 'There is no might and no power save in Allaah.'" The woman said: "How excellent is his command!" They said it so much. A short time later, while the enemy was heedless of this son, he drove the sheep of this enemy and brought it to his father. On that occasion, Allaah revealed (what means): {And whoever fears Allaah, He will make a way for him to get out (from the discomforts of this world and the hereafter)}. [Ibn Mardawayh]

The same is narrated on the authority of Ibn 'Abbaas [Allaah be pleased with them]. [Al-Khateeb in his Taareekh]

Verse Number 4

4- And such of your women as have passed the age of menstruation, for them the 'Iddah, if you have doubt (about their periods), is three months; and for those who have not (attained the age of) menses (their 'Iddah is three months likewise). And for those who are pregnant (whether they are divorced or left behind by their deceased husbands), their 'Iddah is till they give birth; and whoever fears Allaah, He will make his matter easy for him (in this world and in the hereafter).

A narration on the authority of Ubayy Ibn Ka'b [may Allaah be pleased with him] that he said: When Allaah revealed in Soorah Al-Baqarah the Quraanic Aayaat about the 'Iddah (post-marriage waiting period) of the different kinds of divorced women, they said: "There remains only the women who do not menstruate because of their youngness, oldness or pregnancy". On that occasion, Allaah revealed this Quraanic Ayaah. [Ibn Jareer; Ishaaq Ibn Rahawayh; Al-Haakim and others: its chain of narrators is authentic]

A narration on the authority of Muqaatil that Khallaad Ibn 'Amr Ibn Al-Jamooh asked the Prophet [peace and blessings of Allaah be upon him] about the 'Iddah of the women who does not menstruate. On that occasion, Allaah revealed this Quraanic Ayaah. [Muqaatil in his Tafseer]

Soorah At-Tahreem

Verse Number 1

1- O Prophet! Why do you prohibit (for yourself) that which Allaah has made lawful for you, seeking (by such prohibition) to please your wives? And Allaah is Oft-Forgiving (of that prohibition), Most Merciful.

A narration on the authority of Anas [may Allaah be pleased with him] that the Prophet [peace and blessings of Allaah be upon him] had a slave-girl with whom he had sexual intercourse. Hafsah [Allaah be pleased with her] kept asking him importunately to leave her till he made her unlawful for himself. On that occasion, Allaah revealed this Quraanic Ayaah. [Al-Haakim and An-Nasaa'i with an authentic chain of narrators]

A narration on the authority of Abu Hurayrah [may Allaah be pleased with him] that he said: the Prophet [peace and blessings of Allaah be upon him] had sexual intercourse with Maariyyah, his slave-girl, in the house of Hafsah. When she came, she found her with him. She said: "O Messenger of Allaah! Do you do so in my house from among all your wives?" He replied: "She then is unlawful for me to approach O Hafsah; and conceal this story for me". She came out and went to 'AA'ishah and told her. On that occasion, Allaah revealed those Quraanic Aayaat [1-4]. [At-Tabaraani with a weak chain of narrators]

A narration on the authority of Ibn 'Abbaas [Allaah be pleased with them] that he said: the Prophet [peace and blessings of Allaah be upon him] used to drink honey in the house of Sawdah. Once he entered upon 'AA'ishah who told him: "I detect from you a (bad) smell". Then he entered upon Hafsah who said the same to him. He said: "I see that it is from a drink which I have drunk in the house of Sawdah. By Allaah, I will not get it once again". On that occasion, Allaah revealed this Quraanic Ayaah. [At-Tabaraani with an authentic chain of narrators]

It has a witness in both Saheehs.

According to Al-Haafith Ibn Hajar, this Quraanic Ayaah might, probably, have been revealed on both occasions.

A narration on the authority of 'Abdullaah Ibn Raafi' that he said: Umm Salamah [Allaah be pleased with her] was asked about this Quraanic Ayaah, and she said: "I had a container of honey and the Prophet [peace and blessings of Allaah be upon him] used to drink therefrom as much as he liked. 'AA'ishah told him: "It seems that its bees gets from the 'Urfut". On that, he forbade it to himself. In this connection, this Quraanic Ayaah was revealed. [Ibn Sa'd]

Verse Number 2

2- Allaah has already ordained for you (O believers (al-Mumineen)) the (lawful) absolution of your oaths.

And Allaah is your Guardian-Protector, and He is the All-Knowing, the All-Wise.

A narration on the authority of Ibn 'Umar from 'Umar [may Allaah be pleased with him] that he said: the Prophet [peace and blessings of Allaah be upon him] said to Hafsah: "Do not tell anyone that the mother of Ibraaheem had become unlawful for me". He did not approach her till Hafsah told 'AA'ishah. On that occasion, Allaah revealed this Quraanic Ayaah. [Ad-Diyaa' in Al-Mukhtaarah]

A narration on the authority of Ibn 'Abbaas [Allaah be pleased with them] that he said: This Quraanic Ayaah [1] was revealed in connection with his slave-girl. [Al-Bazzaar with an authentic chain of narrators]

Verse Number 5

5- It may be if he (the Prophet) divorced you (all) that his Lord (Rabb) will give him, in exchange, wives better than you - Muslims (who submit to Allaah), faithfully believers (al-Mumineen), devoutly obedient (to Allaah), turning to Allaah in repentance, worshipping Allaah sincerely, given to fasting or emigrants (for Allaah's sake), previously married and virgins.

See Al-Baqarah 125.

Soorah Al-Qalam

Verse Number 2

2- You (O Muhammad) are not, for the favor of (Allaah) your Lord (Rabb) (upon you, that is Prophethood), a madman.

A narration on the authority of Ibn Jurayj that he said: They used to describe the Prophet [peace and blessings of Allaah be upon him] as a madman and then a devil. On that occasion, this Quraanic Ayaah was revealed. {Ibn Al-Mundhir]

Verse Number 4

4- And verily, you (O Muhammad) are of a great moral character.

A narration on the authority of 'AA'ishah [Allaah be pleased with her] that she said: None was better in manners than the Prophet [peace and blessings of Allaah be upon him]. No one of his Companions or family invited him but that he responded to the invitation. For this reason, Allaah revealed this Quraanic Ayaah. [Abu Na'eem in Ad-Dalaa'il; and Al-Waahidi]

Verse Number 10-13

10- And (O Muhammad) obey not every worthless despicable habitual swearer (to falsehood), 11- A slanderer (backbiter), going about with calumnies, 12-Withholder of good, transgressor, sinful, 13- Cruel, and, after all that, baseborn.

A narration on the authority of As-Suddi that he said: Allaah's saying (what means): {And (O Muhammad) obey not every worthless despicable habitual swearer (to falsehood)}, [verse 10] was revealed in connection with Al-Akhnas Ibn Shurayq. [Ibn Abu Haatim]

The same is narrated on the authority of Al-Kalbi. [Ibn Al-Mundhir]

A narration on the authority of Mujaahid that he said: It was revealed in connection with Al-Aswad Ibn 'Abd Yaghooth. [Ibn Abu Haatim]

A narration on the authority of Ibn 'Abbaas [Allaah be pleased with them] that he said: Allaah revealed unto the Prophet [peace and blessings of Allaah be upon him] (what means): {And (O Muhammad) obey not every worthless despicable habitual swearer (to falsehood), A slanderer (backbiter), going about with calumnies}. [verse 10-11] We did not recognize him till afterwards Allaah revealed (what means): {Cruel, and, after all that, baseborn}. [verse 13] In this way, we came to know him, having a tail like that of the ewe. [Ibn Jareer]

Verse Number 17

17- Verily, We have tried them (disbelievers (al-Kaafireen) with famine and drought) as We tried the people of the garden, when they swore to pluck its fruits in the (early) morning.

A narration on the authority of Ibn Jurayj that Abu Jahl said on the day of (the battle of) Badr: "Take them, then tie them in ropes and kill none of them". On that occasion, this Quraanic Ayaah was revealed. that is they had power over them as the owners of the gardens had power over it. [Ibn Abu Haatim]

Soorah Al-Haaqqah

Verse Number 12

12- That We might make it (saving the believers (al-Mumineen) and drowning the disbelievers (al-Kaafireen)) an admonition for you and that it might be retained by conscious (retaining) ears.

A narration on the authority of Buraydah that he said: the Prophet [peace and blessings of Allaah be upon him] told 'Ali Ibn Abu Taalib: "I have been commanded to bring you near to me rather than to keep you far from me; to teach so that you would understand and you are entitled to understand". On that occasion, this Quraanic Ayaah was revealed. [Ibn Jareer; Ibn Abu Haatim and Al-Waahidi: inauthentic]

Soorah Al-Ma'aarij

Verse Number 1

1- A supplicant asked for a torment about to happen. A narration on the authority of Ibn 'Abbaas [Allaah be pleased with them], concerning Allaah's saying (what means): {A supplicant asked for a torment about to happen}, that he said: That was An-Nadr Ibn Al-Haarith, who said: "O Allaah! If this (Quraan) is indeed the truth (revealed) from You, then rain down stones on us from the sky or bring on us a painful torment.} [Al-Anfaal, verse 32] [An-Nasaa'i and Ibn Abu Haatim]

A narration on the authority of As-Suddi that he said concerning this Quraanic Ayaah: It was revealed in Makkah in connection with An-Nadr Ibn Al-Haarith, when he said: "O Allaah! If this (Quraan) is indeed the truth (revealed) from You, then rain down stones on us from the sky or bring on us a painful torment." [Al-Anfaal 32] He received this torment on the day of (the battle of) Badr. [Ibn Abu Haatim]

Verse Number 2

2- To the disbelievers (al-Kaafireen), which none can avert.

A narration on the authority of Al-Hasan that he said: Allaah's saying (what means): {A supplicant asked for a torment about to happen}, [verse 1] was revealed thereupon the people asked: "Upon whom will the torment nflicted?" On that occasion, Allaah revealed (what means): {To the disbelievers (al-Kaafireen), which none can avert}. [verse 2] [Ibn Al-Mundhir]

Soorah Al-Jinn

Verse Number 1

1- Say (O Muhammad to the people): "It has been revealed to me (by Allaah) that a group of jinn listened (to my recitation of this Quraan). They said (to their people when they returned to them): 'Verily, we have heard an amazing Quraan!

A narration on the authority of Ibn 'Abbaas [Allaah be pleased with them] that he said: the Prophet [peace and blessings of Allaah be upon him] never recited to the jinn, nor did he see them. But he set out with the intention of going to the market of Ukaath along with some of his companions. At the same time, a barrier was put between the devils and the news of heaven. Fire commenced to be thrown at them. The Devils went to their people, who asked them, "What is wrong with you?" They said: "A barrier has been placed between us and the news of heaven. And fire has been thrown at us." They said: "The thing which has put a barrier between you and the news of heaven must be something which has happened recently. Go eastward and westward and see what has put a barrier between you and the news of heaven." Those who went towards Tihaamah came across The Prophet [peace and blessings of Allaah be upon him] at a place called Nakhlah and it was on the way to Sooq 'Ukaath and The Prophet [peace and blessings of Allaah be upon him] was offering the Fajr prayer with his companions. When they heard the Quraan they listened to it and said: "By Allaah, this is the thing which has put a barrier between us and the news of heaven." They went to their people and said: "O our people; verily we have heard a wonderful recital (Quraan) which shows the true path; we believed in it and would not ascribe partners to our Lord (Rabb)." Allaah revealed the following verses to his Prophet (Soorah Jinn') (72): "Say: "It has been revealed to me." And what was revealed to him was the conversation of the Jinns. [Al-Bukhaari; At-Tirmidhi and others]

A narration on the authority of Kurdum Ibn Abu As-Saa'ib Al-Ansaari that he said: I came out in the company of my father to Madeenah for some need, during the early days a mention was made of the Prophet [peace and blessings of Allaah be upon him]. We then took shelter to a shepherd of sheep. When it was midnight, a wolf came and took a ram from the sheep, thereupon the shepherd jumped and said: "O 'AAmir! The valley is under your protection!" Then, an invisible caller called out: "O Sarhaan!" Then the ram came running till it entered among the sheep. On that occasion, Allaah revealed to His Messenger [peace and blessings of Allaah be upon him] this Quraanic Ayaah in Makkah. [Ibn Al-Mundhir; Ibn Abu Haatim and Abu Ash-Shaykh in Al-'Athamah]

A narration on the authority of Abu Rajaa' Al-'Utaaridi from Banu Tameem that he said: the Prophet [peace and blessings of Allaah be upon him] was sent as a Prophet and I was grazing sheep like my family did and got my earnings therefrom. When the Prophet [peace and blessings of Allaah be upon him] was sent as a

Prophet, we set out in flight till we came upon a piece of desert. Whenever evening entered upon us in this land our Shaykh would say: "We seek refuge with the strong one in this valley from among the jinn for this night", and we would repeat it after him. It was said to us: "The way to this man (Muhammad) is to testify that there is none worthy of worship but Allaah, and that Muhammad is the Messenger of Allaah: whoever professes it will be safe for his life and property". We returned and embraced Islam. Abu Rajaa' said: "I think that this Quraanic Ayaah was revealed in connection with me and my companions. [Ibn Sa'd]

A narration on the authority of Sa'eed Ibn Jubayr that a man from Tameem called Raafi' Ibn 'Umayr talked about how he embraced Islam, saying: "I was walking on a hill of sand one night, when I was overtaken by slumber. I dismounted and made my she-camel kneel and then slept. Before my sleep, I sought refuge saying: "I seek refuge with the great one in this valley from among the jinn". In a dream I saw a man having in his hand a spear which he liked to place in my she-camel. I then got up scared and looked rightward and leftward and saw nothing. I said: "That is a dream". Then, I returned to sleep once again and saw the same. I woke up to find my she-camel moving. I turned my face and behold! There was a young man like the one I had seen having a spear in his hand and an old one taking hold of his hand to avert him from it. While they were fighting, three male wild animals appeared, thereupon, the old one said to the young: "Get up and take whichever of those you like, as a ransom for the she-camel of this man who is under my protection".

The young man stood and took one of those wild animals and then left. Then the old one turned to me and said: "O man! If you descend one of those valleys and fear its terrors, then say: "I seek refuge with the Lord (Rabb) of Muhammad from the terror of this valley". Do not seek refuge with anyone of the jinn since their affair has become null". I said to him: "Who is this Muhammad?" He said: "An Arab Prophet, neither from the East nor from the West. He was sent as a Prophet on Monday". I asked: "Where is his residence?" He replied: "Yathrib of palm-trees". I then rode my mount when it was morning, and went proceeded on till I reached Madinah.

the Prophet [peace and blessings of Allaah be upon him] saw me and told me about my story before I mentioned anything thereof to him, and invited me to Islam and I embraced Islam". Sa'eed Ibn Jubayr said: We think that it was him in connection with whom Allaah revealed this Quraanic Ayaah. [Al-Kharaa'iti in Kitaab Hawaatif Al-Jaan]

Verse Number 16

16- And (Allaah revealed that) had they (the disbelievers (al-Kaafireen) of the Quraysh) believed in Allaah, and followed the Right course, We would surely have bestowed on them water (rain) in abundance. A narration on the authority of Muqaatil that he said: This Quraanic Ayaah was revealed in connection with the disbelievers (al-Kaafireen) of Quraysh when rain stopped for seven years. [Al-Kharaa'iti]

Verse Number 18

18- And the masjids are for Allaah (to be worshipped Alone); so invoke not anyone along with Allaah.

A narration on the authority of Ibn 'Abbaas [Allaah be pleased with them] that he said: The jinn said: "O Messenger of Allaah! Give us permission to attend the congregational prayers with you in your mosque". On that occasion, Allaah revealed this Quraanic Ayaah. [Ibn Abu Haatim]

A narration on the authority of Sa'eed Ibn Jubayr that he said: The jinn told the Prophet [peace and blessings of Allaah be upon him]: "How could we go to the masjid and we are far from you?" or: "How could we attend the (congregational) prayer and we are far from you?" On that occasion, this Quraanic Ayaah was revealed. [Ibn Jareer]

Verse 22

22- Say: "None can protect me from (the punishment of) Allaah (if I should disobey Him), nor shall I find refuge except in Him.

A narration on the authority of Hadrami that it was reported to him that a jinni of their nobles who had followers said: "Muhammad likes only that Allaah should grant him protection; and I grant him protection". On that occasion, Allaah revealed this Quraanic Ayaah. [Ibn Jareer]

Soorah Al-Muzzammil

1- O you (Prophet) wrapped in garments!

A narration on the authority of Jaabir [may Allaah be pleased with him] that he said: The men of Quraysh gathered in Daar An-Nadwah and said: "Give this man a name by which people may keep off him". They said: "Let him be a soothsayer". They replied: "No, he is not a soothsayer". They said: "Then, let him be a madman". They replied: "No, he is not a madman". They said: "Then, let him be a sorcerer". They then replied: "No, he is not a sorcerer". The news reached the Prophet [peace and blessings of Allaah be upon him] thereupon, he wrapped himself in his garment. Jibreel [peace and blessings of Allaah be upon him] came to him and said: "O you (Prophet) wrapped up in garments!" "O you (Prophet) enveloped (in garments)!" [Al-Bazzaar and At-Tabaraani with a feeble chain of narrators]

A narration on the authority of Ibraaheem An-Nakh'i that he said: This Quraanic Ayaah was revealed while the Prophet [peace and blessings of Allaah be upon him] was wrapped up in a piece of amaranth. [Ibn Abu Haatim]

Verse Number 20

20- Verily, (Allaah) your Lord (Rabb) knows that you stand (in prayer at night) a little less than two-thirds of the night, or half the night, or a third of the night, and also a party of those with you. And Allaah measures the night and the day. He knows that you are unable to keep count thereof, so He has turned to you (in mercy, and lightened the burden from you). So, recite you what is easy for you of the Quraan. He knows that there will be some among you sick, others traveling through the land seeking of Allaah's Bounty, yet others fighting in Allaah's Cause. So recite of the Quraan what is easy (for you), and establish prayer and give Zakaah, and lend to Allaah a goodly loan. And whatever good you put forward for yourselves, you will certainly find it with Allaah better (than you have left behind) and greater in reward. And seek Forgiveness of Allaah. Verily, Allaah is Oft-Forgiving, Most Merciful (towards the believers (al-Mumineen)).

A narration on the authority of 'AA'ishah [Allaah be pleased with her] that she said: When the following verses were revealed (what means): {O you (Prophet) wrapped in garments! Stand (in prayer) all night, except a little}, [verse 1-2] they kept standing the whole night in prayer till their feet got swollen. Then Allaah revealed (what means): {So, recite you what is easy for you of the Quraan}. [Al-Haakim]

The same is narrated on the authority of Ibn 'Abbaas [Allaah be pleased with them]. [Ibn Jareer]

Soorah Al-Muddaththir

Verse Number 1-2

1- O you (Prophet) enveloped (in garments)! 2- Arise and warn (people of the fire of Hell if they do not believe)!

A narration on the authority of Jaabir [may Allaah be pleased with him] that he said: the Prophet [peace and blessings of Allaah be upon him] said: "I lived in seclusion in Hiraa; for a month, and when the time was over, I came down to the valley. I was called by a particular voice and I looked but saw nothing. I raised up my head and behold! I saw the same angel who came to me in Hiraa'. I returned home and said: "Wrap me in garments! On that occasion, Allaah revealed (what means): {O you (Prophet) enveloped (in garments)! 2- Arise and warn (people of the fire of Hell if they do not believe)!} [verse 1-2] [Al-Bukhaari and Muslim]

Verse Number 1-7

1- O you (Prophet) enveloped (in garments)! 2- Arise and warn (people of the fire of Hell if they do not believe)! 3- And glorify (Allaah) your Lord (Rabb)! 4- And purify your garments! 5- And shun the idols! 6- And do not give a thing expecting to receive more. 7- And be patient for (the sake of) your Lord (Rabb) (on complying with Allaah's commands and avoiding His forbiddances)!

A narration on the authority of Ibn 'Abbaas [Allaah be pleased with them] that Al-Waleed Ibn Al-Mugheerah prepared food for the men of Quraysh and when they ate he said: "Give this man a name by which people may keep off him". They said: "Let him be a soothsayer". They replied: "No, he is not a soothsayer". They said: "Then, let him be a madman". They replied: "No, he is not a madman". They said: "Then, let him be a sorcerer". They replied: "No, he is not a sorcerer". Some of them said: "His (speech) is but magic handed down (from those of old)". The news reached the Prophet [peace and blessings of Allaah be upon him] thereupon he grieved and covered his head, and wrapped himself in his garment. On that occasion, Allaah Almighty (the Most High) revealed those Quraanic Aayaat. [At-Tabaraani with a weak chain of narrators]

Verse Number 11

11- Leave Me (to deal) with the one whom I created alone! It is narrated by Ibn Jareer on the authority of Ikrimah that Al-Waleed Ibn Al-Mugheerah came to the Prophet [peace and blessings of Allaah be upon him], and heard the Quraan from him, he seemed to have been inclined to it. When this news reached Abu Jahl, he came to him and said: "O uncle! Your people intended to gather money for you". He asked: "Why?" He said: "In order to give it to you, since you came to Muhammad to ask him of what he has". He said: "Quraysh has known that I'm the wealthiest of them all". He said: "Then, say in him something, therewith your people would know you reject what he says". He said: "What should I say in him? By Allaah: there is none of you, having better knowledge than me of the Arabic poetry: its compositions, Rajaz, and further of the poetry of the jinns. By Allah: what he says is not like anything of that. By Allaah, that which he says has such a sweetness, brilliance, whose high part is shining and low part rising (as the human speech has never had), and it prevails over anything, and nothing prevails over it, and it surely it excels anything beneath it". He told him: "By Allaah: your people would not be pleased unless you say in it (something showing your dislike for it)". He said: "Then, leave me think it over". When he thought of the matter deeply, he came to say: "It is no but magic, which he learns from others". On that occasion, Allaah revealed this up to 26. [Al-Haakim; and its chain of narrators is authentic according to the conditions stipulated by Al-Bukhaari]

Verse Number 30

30- Over it are nineteen (angels as its guardians and keepers). A narration on the authority of Al-Baraa' [may Allaah be pleased with him] that a group of Yahood asked one from among the Companions of the Prophet [peace and blessings of Allaah be upon him] about the keepers of the Hellfire. He came to the Prophet [peace and blessings of Allaah be upon him] and told him about that thereupon Allaah revealed (what means): {Over it there are nineteen (strong angels)} [verse 30]. [Ibn Abu Haatim and Al-Bayhaqi]

Verse Number 31

31- And We have set none but angels as guardians of the Fire. And We have fixed their number only as a trial for the disbelievers (al-Kaafireen), in order that the people of the Scripture (Yahood) may be convinced and the believers (al-Mumineen) (among them) may increase in Faith and that no doubt may be left for the people of the Scripture and the believers (al-Mumineen), and that those in whose hearts (Qalb) is a disease (that is doubt in Madeenah) and the disbelievers (al-Kaafireen) (in Makkah) may say: "What Allaah intends by this (number as) example?" Thus (as Allaah leads astray the rejecters of this number) Allaah leads astray whom He wills and guides whom He wills. And none can know the hosts of your Lord (Rabb) but He. And this (Saqar) is but a (warning) reminder to human beings.

A narration on the authority of Ibn Ishaaq that he said: One day, Abu Jahl told his people: "O assembly of Quraysh! Muhammad pretends that Allaah's soldiers who will punish you in the Fire are nineteen; and you are the greatest in number among the people. Will one hundred men among them fail to overpower one of them?" On that occasion, Allaah revealed this Quraanic Ayaah. [Ibn Abu Haatim]

A narration on the authority of Qataadah that he said: It was mentioned to us... and the rest is the same. [Ibn Abu Haatim]

A narration on the authority of As-Suddi that he said: When Allaah revealed (what means): {Over it there are nineteen (strong angels)}, [verse 30] a man from Quraysh called Abu Al-Ashadd said: "O assembly of Quraysh! Let not the nineteen terrify you. I can avert from you ten with my right arm and nine with my left arm". On that occasion, Allaah revealed this Quraanic Ayaah [31]. [Ibn Abu Haatim]

Verse Number 52

52- Nay, every one of them desires that he should be given pages spread out (from Allaah confirming the truth of Prophet Muhammad in order that they would follow him).

A narration on the authority of As-Suddi that he said: They said: "If Muhammad is truthful, let there be underneath the head of anyone of us a book containing declaration of his guiltlessness and immunity from the Fire". This this Quraanic Ayaah was revealed. [Ibn Al-Mundhir]

Soorah Al-Qiyaamah

Verse Number 16

16- Move not your tongue (O Muhammad) with (the recitation of the Quraan) to make haste therewith (before Jibreel finishes from it for fear it may escape you).

A narration on the authority of Ibn 'Abbaas [Allaah be pleased with them] that he said: It was the habit of the Prophet [peace and blessings of Allaah be upon him] that whenever the revelation came down to him, he would move his tongue with it intending to memorize it. On that occasion, Allaah revealed this Quraanic Ayaah. [Al-Bukhaari]

Verse Number 34-35

34- Woe to you (O disbeliever)! And then (again) woe! 35Again, woe to you (O disbeliever)! And then (again) woe!

A narration on the authority of Ibn 'Abbaas [Allaah be pleased with them] that he said: When Allaah revealed (what means): {Over it there are nineteen (strong angels)}, [verse 30] Abu Jahl said to the men of Quraysh: "May your mothers be bereaved of you! Ibn Abu Kabshah (Muhammad) tells you that the keepers of Hell are nineteen, and you are numerous. Should each ten of you fail to overpower one of the keepers of Hell?" Allaah then inspired to His Messenger [peace

and blessings of Allaah be upon him] to go to Abu Jahl
and say to him (what means): {Woe to you (O
disbeliever)! And then (again) woe! Again, woe to you
(O disbeliever)! And then (again) woe!} [verse 34-35]
[Ibn Jareer]

A narration on the authority of Sa'eed Ibn Jubayr that
he asked Ibn 'Abbaas [Allaah be pleased with them]
about the saying: "Woe to you (O disbeliever)! And
then (again) woe": Is it something which the Prophet
[peace and blessings of Allaah be upon him] said from
himself or Allaah ordered him to say it? He said: "He
said it from his own self and then Allaah revealed it".
[An-Nasaa'i]

Soorah Al-Insaan

Verse Number 8

8- And they give food, in spite of their love (and appetite) for it, to the poor, the orphan, and the captive,

A narration on the authority of Ibn Jareer that he said: the Prophet [peace and blessings of Allaah be upon him] did not take as captives the Muslims.

But it was revealed in connection with the captives of polytheists whom they captured and put under torment. In connection with them it was revealed. the Prophet [peace and blessings of Allaah be upon him] then came to order them to do good to them. [Ibn Al-Mundhir]

Verse Number 20

20- And when you look there (in Paradise), you will see an (indescribable) bliss and a great (infinite) dominion.

A narration on the authority of 'Ikrimah that he said: 'Umar Ibn Al-Khattaab [may Allaah be pleased with him] entered upon the Prophet [peace and blessings of Allaah be upon him] and he was lying on a straw mat, which left marks on his side.

On that 'Umar wept. the Prophet [peace and blessings of Allaah be upon him] said: "What causes you to weep?" "Umar said: "I have remembered Khosrau and his kingdom, Hurmuz and his kingdom and the Negus and his kingdom, while you, the Prophet [peace and blessings of Allaah be upon him] are lying on a straw mat!" the Prophet [peace and blessings of Allaah be upon him] said: "Are you not pleased that they will have the world and we (Muslims) the hereafter?" On that occasion, Allaah Almighty (the Most High) revealed this Quraanic Ayaah. [Ibn Al-Mundhir]

Verse Number 24

24- Therefore be patient for the Command of (Allaah) your Lord (Rabb) (by conveying His Message to people), and obey neither a sinner nor a disbeliever among them.

A narration on the authority of Qataadah that he was informed that Abu Jahl said: "If I see Muhammad praying, I will tread on his neck". On that occasion, Allaah Almighty (the Most High) revealed this Quraanic Ayaah. ['Abd-Ar-Razzaaq; Ibn Jareer and Ibn Al-Mundhir]

Soorah Al-Mursalaat

Verse Number 48

48- And when it is said to them: "Bow down yourself (in prayer)," they do not bow down (because they do not establish prayer).

A narration on the authority of Mujaahid that he said: This Quraanic Ayaah was revealed in connection with Thaqeef. [Ibn Al-Mundhir]

Soorah An-Naba'

Verse Number 1-2

1- About what do they (the men of Quraysh) ask (one another)? 2- About the great news.

A narration on the authority of Al-Hasan that he said: When the Prophet [peace and blessings of Allaah be upon him] was sent as a Prophet, they wondered one another, thereupon Allaah revealed those Quraanic Aayaat. [Ibn Jareer and Ibn Abu Haatim]

Soorah An-Naazi'aat

Verse Number 10-12

10- They (the owners of such hearts (Qalb) and eyes) say (in ridicule): "Shall we indeed be returned to (our) former state of life (after death)? 11- (Shall we be returned to life) even after we become decayed bones?" 12- They say: "It (our return to life) would, in case (it is to happen), be a losing return!"

A narration on the authority of Muhammad Ibn Ka'b that he said: When Allaah revealed (what means): {They (the owners of such hearts (Qalb) and eyes) say (in ridicule): "Shall we indeed be returned to (our) former state of life (after death)?} [verse 10] the disbelievers (al-Kaafireen) of Quraysh said: "If we live after death, we shall be in loss". On that occasion, Allaah revealed (what means): {They say: "It (our return to life) would, in case (it is to happen), be a losing return!"} [verse 12] [Sa'eed Ibn Mansoor]

Verse Number 42-44

42- They (the disbelievers (al-Kaafireen)) ask you (O Muhammad) about the (final) Hour: when will it come? 43- You have no knowledge to say anything about it. 44- To your Lord (Rabb) is (the ultimate knowledge of) its (appointed) time.

A narration on the authority of 'AA'ishah [Allaah be pleased with her] that she said:

the Prophet [peace and blessings of Allaah be upon him] was often asked about the (final) Hour, till Allaah revealed to him those Quraanic Aayaat, thereupon they desisted. [Al-Haakim and Ibn Jareer]

A narration on the authority of Ibn 'Abbaas [Allaah be pleased with them] that the polytheists of Makkah asked the Prophet [peace and blessings of Allaah be upon him]: "Where the (final) Hour be established?" They did so in ridicule. On that occasion, Allaah revealed those Quraanic Aayaat up to 46. [Ibn Abu Haatim]

A narration on the authority of Taariq Ibn Shihaab that he said: the Prophet [peace and blessings of Allaah be upon him] often made a mention of the (final) Hour till Allaah revealed to him those Quraanic Aayaat 43-44. [At-Tabaraani and Ibn Jareer]

Soorah 'Abasa

Verse Number 1-2

1- He (Prophet Muhammad) frowned and turned away. 2 Because there came to him the blind man. A narration on the authority of 'AA'ishah [Allaah be pleased with her] that she said: Those Quraanic Aayaat was revealed in connection with Ibn Umm Maktoom, the blind. He came to the Prophet [peace and blessings of Allaah be upon him] and went on saying: "O Messenger of Allaah! Guide me!" In the meantime, one of the great men of Quraysh was with the Prophet [peace and blessings of Allaah be upon him]. the Prophet [peace and blessings of Allaah be upon him] turned away from this blind and approach the other (great man), saying to him: "Do you see any harm in what I am saying?" He replied: "No". In this connection, those Quraanic Aayaat were revealed. [At-Tirmidhi and Al-Haakim] The same is narrated on the authority of Anas [may Allaah be pleased with him]. [Abu Ya'li]

Verse Number 17

17- Cursed be (the disbelieving) man! What has made him disbelieve (in Allaah)?

A narration on the authority of 'Ikrimah that he said: This Quraanic Ayaah was revealed in 'Utbah Ibn Abu Lahab when he said: "I have disbelieved in the lord of the star". [Ibn Al-Mundhir]

Soorah At-Takweer

Verse Number 29

29- And you cannot will (to stand straight on the truth) unless Allaah so wills, the Lord (Rabb) of the worlds.

A narration on the authority of Sulaymaan Ibn Moosa that he said: When Allaah revealed (what means): {To whoever wills among you to take a right course (by following the truth)}, [28] Abu Jahl said: "That is up to us: if we so like, we will take a right course; and if we so like, we will not follow a right course". On that occasion, Allaah revealed (what means): {And you cannot will (to stand straight on the truth) unless Allaah so wills, the Lord (Rabb) of the worlds}. [verse 29] [Ibn Jareer and Ibn Abu Haatim]

The same is narrated on the authority of Abu Hurayrah [may Allaah be pleased with him]. [Ibn Abu Haatim]

The same is narrated on the authority of Al-Qaasim Ibn Mukhaymirah. [Ibn Al-Mundhir]

Soorah Al-Infitaar

Verse Number 6

6- O (disbelieving) man! What has deluded you about your Lord (Rabb), the Most Generous (that you disobeyed Him),

A narration on the authority of 'Ikrimah that he said: This Quraanic Ayaah was revealed in connection with Ubayy Ibn Khalaf. [Ibn Abu Haatim]

Soorah Al-Mutaffifeen

Verse Number 1

1- Woe to the defrauders.

A narration on the authority of Ibn 'Abbaas [Allaah be pleased with them] that he said: When the Prophet [peace and blessings of Allaah be upon him] arrived in Madeenah, its inhabitants used to give less than what is due in measure most from among the people. In connection with them, Allaah revealed this Quraanic Ayaah. Then they made good their measure afterwards. [An-Nasaa'i and Ibn Maajah with an authentic chain of narrators]

Soorah At-Taariq

Verse Number 5

5- So let man consider from what he is created!

A narration on the authority of 'Ikrimah that he said: This Quraanic Ayaah was revealed in connection with Abu Al-Ashadd who used to stand on earth and say: "O assembly of Quraysh! Whoever removes me from it, will have such and such (reward)". He also would say: "Muhammad pretends that the keepers of Hell are nineteen. I alone will suffice you against ten and you all suffice me against the remaining nine". [Ibn Abu Haatim]

Soorah Al-A'La

Verse Number 6

6- We shall make you (O Muhammad) to recite (the Quraan), so that you would not forget (what you recite thereof).

A narration on the authority of Ibn 'Abbaas [Allaah be pleased with them] that he said: Whenever Jibreel came to the Prophet [peace and blessings of Allaah be upon him] with the revelation, Jibreel would not finish from it till the Prophet [peace and blessings of Allaah be upon him] has spoken with its beginning for fear he would forget it. On that occasion, Allaah revealed this Quraanic Ayaah. [At-Tabaraani and its Isnaad has Juwaybir who is very weak]

Soorah Al-Ghaashiyah

Verse Number 17

17- Do they (the disbelievers (al-Kaafireen) of Makkah) not consider the camels, how they are created?

A narration on the authority of Qataadah that he said: When Allaah described what Paradise has, the men of error wondered at that. On that occasion, Allaah Almighty (the Most High) revealed this Quraanic Ayaah. [Ibn Jareer and Ibn Abu Haatim]

Soorah Al-Fajr

Verse Number 27

27- (To the righteous it will be said at death): "O reassured (secure) soul (of the faithful believer)!

A narration on the authority of Buraydah [may Allaah be pleased with him] that he said: This Quraanic Ayaah was revealed in connection with Hamzah [may Allaah be pleased with him]. [Ibn Abu Haatim]

A narration on the authority of Ibn 'Abbaas that the Prophet [peace and blessings of Allaah be upon him] said: "Whoever buys the well of Roomah for the Muslims, Allaah will forgive for him". Uthmaan (Ibn 'Affaan) [may Allaah be pleased with him] bought it. On that he said: "Would you make it a source of water for the people?" He then accepted. In connection with 'Uthmaan, Allaah revealed this Quraanic Ayaah. [Ibn Abu Haatim]

Soorah Al-Layl

Verse Number 15

15- Which none shall enter (and be made to taste its burning) except the most wretched.

A narration on the authority of 'Abdullaah Ibn Az-Zubayr [Allaah be pleased with them] that he said: Abu Quhaafah told Abu Bakr [may Allaah be pleased with him]: "I see that you emancipate weak slaves. Would that you emancipate strong men to protect and defend you O my son!" He said: "O my father! I only want what is with Allaah". On that occasion, Allaah revealed this up to the end of the Soorah. [Al-Haakim]

Verse Number 17

17- And far removed from it will be the righteous.

A narration on the authority of 'Urwah that Abu Bakr As-Siddeeq [may Allaah be pleased with him] emancipated seven slaves all of whom were being tortured in (the religion of) Allaah. In connection with him Allaah revealed this Quraanic Ayaah up to the end of the Soorah. [Ibn Abu Haatim]

Verse Number 19

19- And not for anyone who has done him a favor to be rewarded.

A narration on the authority of Ibn Az-Zubayr [may Allaah be pleased with him] that he said: This Quraanic Ayaah up to the end of the Soorah was revealed in connection with Abu Bakr As-Siddeeq [may Allaah be pleased with him]. [Al-Bazzaar]

Soorah Ad-Duha

Verse Number 1-3

1- By the forenoon (the early hours of the day). 2- And by the night when it covers (everything with its darkness and stands still). 3- Your Lord (Rabb) has neither forsaken you (O Muhammad), nor does He hate you.

A narration on the authority of Jundub [may Allaah be pleased with him] that he said: the Prophet [peace and blessings of Allaah be upon him] was ill and did not stand in prayer for one or two nights. A woman then came to him and said: "O Muhammad! I do not think except that your devil has abandoned you". On that occasion, Allaah revealed those Quraanic Aayaat. [Al-Bukhaari; Muslim and others]

A narration on the authority of Jundub [may Allaah be pleased with him] that he said: Jibreel [peace and blessings of Allaah be upon him] did not descend upon the Prophet [peace and blessings of Allaah be upon him] for some time thereupon the polytheists said: "He has forsaken Muhammad". On that occasion, those Quraanic Aayaat were revealed. [Sa'eed Ibn Mansoor and Al-Firyaabi]

A narration on the authority of Zayd Ibn Arqam [may Allaah be pleased with him] that he said: the Prophet [peace and blessings of Allaah be upon him] spent days during which Jibreel [peace and blessings of Allaah be upon him] did not come to him. Umm Jameel, the wife of Abu Lahab said: "I do not think except that your companion has abandoned and forsaken you". On that occasion, Allaah revealed those Quraanic Aayaat. [Al-Haakim]

A narration on the authority of 'Abdullaah Ibn Shaddaad [may Allaah be pleased with him] that Khadeejah [Allaah be pleased with her] said to the Prophet [peace and blessings of Allaah be upon him]: "I do not think except that your Lord (Rabb) has forsaken you". On that occasion, those Quraanic Aayaat were revealed. [Ibn Jareer: Mursal and its narrators are reliable]

A narration on the authority of 'Urwah that he said: Jibreel [peace and blessings of Allaah be upon him] did not come to the Prophet [peace and blessings of Allaah be upon him] for some time thereupon he got scared. Khadijah [Allaah be pleased with her] said: "I think that your Lord (Rabb) has forsaken you as shown from your panic". On that occasion, Allaah revealed those Quraanic Aayaat. [Ibn Jareer: Mursal and its narrators are reliable]

Commenting on that Al-Haafith Ibn Hajar said: "What seems that both Khadijah and Umm Jameel said the same, except that the former said it out of grief, whereas the latter by way of gloating over his misfortune.

Verse Number 4

4- And indeed, the Hereafter (with its enduring never-ending blessings) is better for you than the first (life of this world). A narration on the authority of Ibn 'Abbaas [Allaah be pleased with them] that he said: the Prophet [peace and blessings of Allaah be upon him] said: "I have been shown what will be opened to my ummah after me (of this world), with which I was pleased". On that occasion, Allaah revealed this Quraanic Ayaah. [At-Tabaraani in Al-Awsat: its chain of narrators is good]

Verse Number 5

5- And verily, your Lord (Rabb) will give you (of good things therewith) you will be satisfied.

A narration on the authority of Ibn 'Abbaas [Allaah be pleased with them] that he said: the Prophet [peace and blessings of Allaah be upon him] was shown what would be opened to his ummah (of this world) city by city, with which he was glad. On that occasion, Allaah revealed this Quraanic Ayaah. [Al-Haakim; Al-Bayhaqi in Ad-Dalaa'il; At-Tabaraani and others]

Soorah Ash-Sharh

Verse Number 6

6- Indeed, with every hardship, there is ease.

A narration on the authority of Al-Hasan that he said: When this Quraanic Ayaah was revealed, the Prophet [peace and blessings of Allaah be upon him] said: "Rejoice: the ease has come to you. In no way could a single hardship overcome a double of ease". [Ibn Jareer]

Soorah At-Teen

Verse Number 5

5- Then We reduced him to the lowest of the low.

A narration on the authority of Ibn 'Abbaas [Allaah be pleased with them] that he said concerning this Quraanic Ayaah: It describes people who were sent back to the old geriatric age during the lifetime of the Prophet [peace and blessings of Allaah be upon him]. He was asked about them when they became weak-minded, thereupon Allaah revealed (the declaration of) their excuse that they will have their reward according to what they used to do before they became weak-minded. [Ibn Jareer]

Soorah Al-'Alaq

Verse Number 6-8

6- Nay! Verily, man does transgress (in disbelief and evil deed). 7- Because he considers himself self-sufficient. 8- Surely, unto your Lord (Rabb) is the return.

A narration on the authority of Abu Hurayrah [may Allaah be pleased with him] that he said: Abu Jahl said: "Does Muhammad put his face in the dust among you?" They answered in the affirmative. He said: "By Laat and 'Uzza! If I see him doing so, I will tread on his neck and cover his face in the dust". On that occasion, Allaah Almighty (the Most High) revealed those Quraanic Aayaat. [Ibn Al-Mundhir]

Verse Number 9-16

9- Have you (O Muhammad (peace be upon him)) seen him (that is Abu Jahl) who prevents 10- A slave (Muhammad (peace be upon him)) when he prays? 11- Tell me if he (Muhammad) is on the guidance (of Allaah)? 12- Or enjoins piety? 13- Tell me if he (Abu Jahl) denies (the truth, that is this Quraan), and turns away! 14Knows he not that Allaah does see (what he does)? 15- Nay! If he (Abu Jahl) ceases not, We will catch him by the forelock - 16- A lying, sinful forelock!

A narration on the authority of Ibn 'Abbaas [Allaah be pleased with them] that he said: the Prophet [peace

and blessings of Allaah be upon him] was performing prayer when Abu Jahl came and forbade him. On that occasion, Allaah revealed those Quraanic Aayaat. [Ibn Jareer]

Verse Number 17-18

17- Then, let him call upon his council (of helpers). 18- We will call out the guards of Hell (to deal with him)!

A narration on the authority of Ibn 'Abbaas [Allaah be pleased with them] that he said: the Prophet [peace and blessings of Allaah be upon him] was praying when Abu Jahl came to him and said: "Have I not forbidden you to do so?" the Prophet [peace and blessings of Allaah be upon him] then deterred him thereupon Abu Jahl said: "Verily, you know there is no gathering (in Makkah) more than mine". On that occasion, Allaah revealed those Quraanic Aayaat. [At-Tirmidhi who renders it Hasan and Saheeh]

Soorah Al-Qadr

Verse Number 1-3

1- Verily! We have sent it (this Quraan) down in the night of Power. 2- And what will make you know what the night of Power is? 3- The night of Power is better than a thousand months.

A narration on the authority of Al-Hasan Ibn 'Ali [Allaah be pleased with them] that he said: the Prophet [peace and blessings of Allaah be upon him] saw Banu Umayyah on his pulpit and this aggrieved him.

On that occasion, Allaah revealed (what means): {Verily, We have given you Al-Kawthar (the river of abundance)}. [Al-Kawthar 1] He also revealed those Quraanic Aayaat of Al-Qadr. That is, it is Banu Umayyah who will get sovereignty after you. [At-Tirmidhi; Al-Haakim and Ibn Jareer]

is narrated on he authority of Mujaahid that the Prophet [peace and blessings of Allaah be upon him] made a mention of a man from the children of Israel who put on arms in the cause of Allaah for one thousand months.

The Muslims wondered of that, thereupon, Allaah revealed those Quraanic Aayaat. That is, the one thousand months in which such a man put on arms in the cause of Allaah. [Ibn Abu Haatim and Al-Waahidi]

A narration on the authority of Mujaahid that he said: Among the children of Israel there was a man who used to spend the whole night in prayer till morning and by day he would fight the enemy in the cause of Allaah till evening. He did this for one thousand months. Allaah revealed this Quraanic Ayaah about the one thousand months which this man worked. [Ibn Jareer]

Soorah Az-Zalzalah

Verse Number 7-8

7- So whoever does good equal to the weight of an atom (or a small ant), shall see it. 8- And whoever does evil equal to the weight of an atom (or a small ant), shall see it.

A narration on the authority of Sa'eed Ibn Jubayr that he said: Allaah said (what means): {And they give food, in spite of their love (and appetite) for it, to the poor, the orphan, and the captive}. [Al-Insaan, verse 8] The Muslims saw that they would receive no reward for the little thing if they gave it. Others saw that they would not be taken to account for such an insignificant sin as the lie, the glance, the backbiting, etc., under claim that Allaah promised Fire only for the major sins. On that occasion, Allaah revealed those Quraanic Aayaat. [Ibn Abu Haatim]

Soorah Al-'AAdiyaat

Verse Number 1

1- By the (steeds) that run, with panting.

A narration on the authority of Ibn 'Abbaas [Allaah be pleased with them] that he said: the Prophet [peace and blessings of Allaah be upon him] sent horsemen and received no news about them for a month. On that occasion, this Quraanic Ayaah was revealed. [Al-Bazzaar; Ibn Abu Haatim and Al-Haakim]

Soorah At-Takaathur

Verse Number 1-2

1- The mutual rivalry (for piling up of worldly things) diverts you, 2- Until you visit the graves (that is till you die).

A narration on the authority of Ibn Buraydah that he said: This Quraanic Ayaah was revealed in connection with two tribes of the Ansaar: Banu Haarithah and Banu Al-Haarith who vied each other in glory and mutually rivaled each other (in piling up the worldly things). One of them said: "Do you have among you the like of so and so, and so and so?" The others said the same. They vied each other in glory because of living and then said: "Let us go to the graves". One of them said: "Do you have among you the like of so and so, and so and so", beckoning to the grave? The others said the same. In connection with them, Allaah revealed those Quraanic Aayaat. [Ibn Abu Haatim]

A narration on the authority of 'Ali [may Allaah be pleased with him] that he said: We doubted the torment of the grave till Allaah revealed those Quraanic Aayaat up to 4 concerning the torment of the grave. [Ibn Jareer]

Soorah Al-Humazah

Verse Number 1

1- Woe to every slanderer and backbiter. A narration on the authority of 'Uthmaan and Ibn 'Umar [Allaah be pleased with them] that they said: We heard that this Soorah was revealed in connection with Ubayy Ibn Khalaf. [Ibn Abu Haatim] A narration on the authority of As-Suddi that he said: It was revealed in connection with Al-Akhnas Ibn Shurayq. [Ibn Abu Haatim] A narration on the authority of a man from Riqqah that he said: It was revealed in connection with Jameel Ibn 'AAmir Al-Jumahi. [Ibn Jareer]

A narration on the authority of Ibn Ishaaq that he said: Whenever Umayyah Ibn Khalaf saw the Prophet [peace and blessings of Allaah be upon him], he would slander and backbite him. In connection with him, Allaah revealed this Soorah. [Ibn Al-Mundhir]

Soorah Quraysh

Verse Number 1

1- (It is a great Grace and Protection from Allaah) for the taming of the Quraysh.

A narration on the authority of Umm Haani' Bint Abu Taalib that she said: the Prophet [peace and blessings of Allaah be upon him] said: Allaah has favored Quraysh with seven characteristics..." in which he said: "in connection with them a Soorah was revealed in which none other than them has been mentioned". [Al-Haakim and others]

Soorah Al-Maa'oon

Verse Number 4

4- So woe to those (hypocrites (al-Munaafiqeen)) who perform prayers (to be seen of men).

A narration on the authority of Ibn 'Abbaas [Allaah be pleased with them] concerning this Quraanic Ayaah: It was revealed in connection with the hypocrites (al-Munaafiqeen) who used to make show with their prayer whenever the believers (al-Mumineen) were present, and abandon it whenever they were absent. They also used not to lend them the neighborly needs. [Ibn Al-Mundhir]

Soorah Al-Kawthar

Verse Number 1-3

1- Verily, We have granted you (O Muhammad) Al-Kawthar. 2- Therefore turn in prayer to your Lord (Rabb) and sacrifice (to Him only). 3- For he who hates you (O Muhammad) will be cut off (from all good things in this world and in the Hereafter).

A narration on the authority of Ibn 'Abbaas [Allaah be pleased with them] that he said: Ka'b Ibn Al-Ashraf came to Makkah and the men of Quraysh told him: "You are the chief of Yahood. Do you not see this man who is cut off his people? He claims that he is better than us and we are the men of pilgrims, Siqaayah, Sadaanah". He said: "No doubt, you are better than him". On that occasion, Allaah revealed (what means): {For he who hates you (O Muhammad) will be cut off (from all good things in this world and in the Hereafter)}. [verse 3]. [Al-Bazzaar and others with an authentic chain of narrators]

A narration on the authority of 'Ikrimah that he said: When it was revealed to the Prophet [peace and blessings of Allaah be upon him], Quraysh said: "Muhammad has been cut off us". On that occasion, Allaah revealed (what means): {For he who hates you (O Muhammad) will be cut off (from all good things in this world and in the Hereafter)}. [verse 3] [Ibn Abu Shaybah in Al-Musannaf; and Ibn Al-Mundhir]

A narration on the authority of As-Suddi that he said:
The men of Quraysh used to say if the male child of
anyone died: "So and so has been cut off. When the
child of the Prophet [peace and blessings of Allaah be
upon him], Al-'AAs Ibn Waa'il said: "Muhammad has
been cut off". On that occasion, Allaah revealed (what
means): {For he who hates you (O Muhammad) will be
cut off (from all good things in this world and in the
Hereafter)}. [verse 3] [Ibn Abu Haatim]

The same is narrated on the authority of Muhammad
Ibn 'Ali, in

which the child was named Al-Qaasim. [Al-Bayhaqi in
Ad-Dalaa'il] A narration on the authority of Mujaahid
that he said: This Quraanic Ayaah was revealed in
connection with Al-'AAs Ibn Waa'il when he said: "I
hate Muhammad". [Al-Bayhaqi in Ad-Dalaa'il] A
narration on the authority of Abu Ayyoob [may Allaah
be pleased with him] that he said: When Ibraaheem,
the son of the Messenger of Allaah [peace and
blessings of Allaah be upon him] died, the polytheists
met one another and said: "This inventor of the new
religion has been cut off tonight". On that occasion,
Allaah revealed the entire Soorah. [At-Tabaraani with
a weak chain of narrators]

A narration on the authority of Shamr Ibn 'Atiyyah
that he said: 'Uqbah Ibn Abu Mu'ayt said that no child
would survive for the Prophet [peace and blessings of
Allaah be upon him] since he was cut off. In
connection with him, Allaah revealed (what means):
{For he who hates you (O Muhammad) will be cut off

(from all good things in this world and in the Hereafter)}. [verse 3] [Ibn Jareer]

A narration on the authority of Ibn Jurayj that he said: I was informed that when Ibraaheem, the child of the Prophet [peace and blessings of Allaah be upon him] died, the men of Quraysh said: "Muhammad has been cut off". the Prophet [peace and blessings of Allaah be upon him] then was enraged by that thereupon, this Soorah was revealed to console him. [Ibn Al-Mundhir]

Soorah Al-Kaafiroon

1- Say (O Muhammad to the disbelievers (al-Kaafireen)): "O disbelievers (al-Kaafireen) (who reject faith in Allaah)! 2- (At present) I worship not (the idols) that you worship, 3- Nor do you worship (Allaah) that I worship. 4And (in the future) I will not worship that which you are worshipping. 5- Nor will you worship that which I worship. 6- To you be your religion (polytheism), and to me my religion (Islamic Monotheism)."

A narration on the authority of Ibn 'Abbaas [Allaah be pleased with them] that the men of Quraysh invited the Prophet [peace and blessings of Allaah be upon him] to give him wealth till he would be the richest man in Makkah, and give him in marriage whomever he liked of women. They said: "All this is for you O Muhammad, provided that you should refrain from insulting our gods and mentioning them with bad words. If you do not do, then worship our deities one year". He said: "No till I consider what is to come to me from my Lord (Rabb)". On that occasion, Allaah revealed this Soorah. He also revealed (what means): {Say: "Do you order me to worship other than Allaah O ignorant ones?"} [Az-Zumar, verse 64] [At-Tabaraani and Ibn Abu Haatim] A narration on the authority of Wahb that he said: The disbelievers (al-Kaafireen) of Quraysh said to the Prophet [peace and blessings of Allaah be upon him]: "If you are glad, then worship our deities one year and we shall revert to your religion one year". On that occasion, Allaah revealed this Soorah. ['Abd-Ar-Razzaaq]

The same is narrated on the authority of Ibn Jurayj. [Ibn Al-Mundhir] A narration on the authority of Sa'eed Ibn Meenaa' that he said: Al-Waleed Ibn Al-Mugheerah, Al-'AAs Ibn Waa'il, Al-Aswad Ibn Al-Muttalib and Umayyah Ibn Khalaf met the Prophet [peace and blessings of Allaah be upon him] and said: "O Muhammad! Let us worship what you worship and you worship what we worship, and share, both you and we, in the matter of worship". On that occasion, Allaah revealed this Soorah. [Ibn Abu Haatim]

Soorah An-Nasr

Verse Number 1-3

1- When there comes the Help of Allaah (to you, O Muhammad against your enemies) and the conquest (of Makkah). 2- And you see that the people enter Allaah's religion (Islam) in crowds. 3- So exalt the Praises of your Lord (Rabb), and ask for His Forgiveness. Verily, He is the One Who accepts the repentance and forgives.

A narration on the authority of Az-Zuhri that he said: When the Prophet [peace and blessings of Allaah be upon him] entered Makkah in the year of conquest, he sent Khaalid Ibn Al-Waleed to fight the rows of Quraysh in the lower part of Makkah till Allaah defeated them. Then, he enjoined peace thereupon, Khaalid refrained from fighting them and they entered the religion. On that occasion, Allaah revealed this Soorah. ['Abd-Ar-Razzaaq in his Musannaf]

Soorah Al-Masad

Verse Number 1-5

1- Let the two hands of Abu Lahab perish, and let him perish 2- His wealth and his children will not benefit him! 3- He will be burnt in a Fire of blazing flames! 4- And his wife, too, who carries firewood. 5- In her neck is a twisted rope of Masad (palm fiber).

A narration on the authority of Ibn 'Abbaas [Allaah be pleased with them] that he said: the Prophet [peace and blessings of Allaah be upon him] went out, and when he had ascended As-Safa mountain, he shouted, "O Sabaahaah!" The people said: "Who is that?" "Then they gathered around him, whereupon he said: "Do you see? If I inform you that cavalrymen are proceeding up the side of this mountain, will you believe me?" They said: "We have never heard you telling a lie." Then he said: "I am a plain warner to you of a coming severe punishment." Abu Lahab said: "May you perish! Is it that you gathered us only for this reason?" Then Abu Lahab went away. On that occasion, Allaah revealed this Soorah. [Al-Bukhaari and others]

A narration on the authority of Yazeed Ibn Zayd that the wife of Abu Lahab used to throw the thorns in the way of the Prophet [peace and blessings of Allaah be upon him]. On that occasion, Allaah revealed this Soorah. [Ibn Jareer]

The same is narrated on the authority of 'Ikrimah. [Ibn Al-Mundhir]

Soorah Al-Ikhlaas

Verse Number 1-4

1- Say: "He is Allaah, (the) One. 2- Allaah, the Self-Subsisting (Who neither eats nor drinks, and Whom all creatures need). 3He begets not, nor was He begotten. 4- And there is none equal unto Him."

A narration on the authority of Ubayy Ibn Ka'b [may Allaah be pleased with him] that the polytheists said to the Prophet [peace and blessings of Allaah be upon him]: "Mention to us the ancestry of your Lord (Rabb)". On that occasion, Allaah revealed this Soorah. [At-Tirmidhi; Al-Haakim and Ibn Khuzaymah]

The same is narrated on the authority of Jaabir Ibn 'Abdullaah [Allaah be pleased with them]. [At-Tabaraani and Ibn Jareer] This confirms that this Soorah was revealed in Makkah.

A narration on the authority of Ibn 'Abbaas [Allaah be pleased with them] that some Yahood including Ka'b Ibn Al-Ashraf and Huyayy Ibn Akhtab came to the Prophet [peace and blessings of Allaah be upon him] and said: "O Muhammad! Describe to us your Lord (Rabb) Who has sent you (as a Prophet)". On that occasion, Allaah revealed this Soorah. [Ibn Abu Haatim]

The same is narrated on the authority of Sa'eed Ibn Jubayr. [Ibn Al-Mundhir]

The same is narrated on the authority of Qataadah. [Ibn Jareer] A narration on the authority of Abu Al-'AAliyah that he said: Qataadah said: The Confederates said: "Mention to us the ancestry of your Lord (Rabb)". Then Jibreel [peace and blessings of Allaah be upon him] came to him with this Soorah. [Ibn Jareer] Those are the polytheists referred to in the narration of Ubayy Ibn Ka'b. This means that this Soorah was revealed in Madinah as seems from the narration of Ibn 'Abbaas. However, there is no opposition between both narrations.

A narration on the authority of Anas [may Allaah be pleased with him] that he said: The Yahood of Khaybar came to The Prophet [peace and blessings of Allaah be upon him], and said: "O Abu Al-Qaasim! Verily, Allaah created the angels from the light of veil; AAdam from dried (sounding black) clay of altered mud, Iblees from the flame of fire, the heaven from smoke and the earth from the scum of water. Then, tell us about your Lord (Rabb)". He gave no reply thereupon Jibreel brought him this Soorah. [Abu Ash-Shaykh in Al-'Athamah]

Soorah Al-Falaq

1- Say: "I seek refuge with (Allaah), the Lord (Rabb) of the daybreak, 2- From the evil of what He has created, 3- And from the evil of the darkening (night) as it comes with its darkness; (or the moon as it sets or goes away), 4- And from the evil of those who practice witchcraft when they blow in the knots, 5- And from the evil of the envier when he envies."

Soorah An-Naas

Verse Number 1-6

1- Say: "I seek refuge with (Allaah) the Lord (Rabb) of mankind, 2The King of mankind - 3- The God of mankind, 4- From the evil of the whisperer, the withdrawer. 5- Who whispers in the breasts of men (once they are heedless of Allaah's remembrance). 6- Of jinn and men."

A narration on the authority of Ibn 'Abbaas [Allaah be pleased with them] that he said: the Prophet [peace and blessings of Allaah be upon him] fell ill and was visited by two angels, one of whom sat by his head and the other by his feet. The one by his feet asked the one by his head: "what do you see?"

He replied: "He is ill". He asked: "What is the nature of his illness?" He answered: "Magic". He asked: "Then, who has bewitched him?" He said: "Labeed Ibn Al-A'sam, the Jewish". He asked: "Where is this magic?"

He answered: "In the well of the family of so and so, in a small ball underneath a rock. Then go to the well, remove its water and lift the rock and then take out the small ball and burn it". In the morning, the Prophet [peace and blessings of Allaah be upon him] sent 'Ammaar Ibn Yaasir along with some men to the well and behold! Its water was like the fusion of henna leaves.

They removed the water and lifted the rock, and took out the small ball and burnt it. had a thread containing eleven knots. On that occasion, both Soorahs were revealed to him.

Then, every time he recited a Quraanic Ayaah thereof, one knot was undone. [Al-Bayhaqi in Dalaa'il An-Nubuwwwah] It has a witness in the books of Saheeh Hadeeth without the revelation of those Soorahs; as well as a witness with their revelation.

A narration on the authority of Anas Ibn Maalik [may Allaah be pleased with him] that he said: The Yahood made something to the Prophet [peace and blessings of Allaah be upon him] because of which he was strongly ached.

His Companions visited him and thought he was possessed by a jinni. Then, Jibreel [peace and blessings of Allaah be upon him] brought him those two Soorahs therewith he sought refuge with Allaah to protect him. He then came out to his Companions sound and healthy. [Abu Na'eem in Ad-Dalaa'il]

Reference:

Reasons and Occasions of Revelation of the Holy Quran: Lubaab An-Nuqool Fee Asbab An-Nuzool

www.ingramcontent.com/pod-product-compliance
Lightning Source LLC
Chambersburg PA
CBHW061417150726
47987CB00001B/4